FOUR
STREETS
AND A
SQUARE

FOUR STREETS
AND A
SQUARE

A HISTORY OF MANHATTAN
AND THE NEW YORK IDEA

MARC ARONSON

CANDLEWICK PRESS

First edition 2021

Library of Congress Catalog Card Number pending
ISBN 978-0-7636-5137-4

21 22 23 24 25 26 XXX 10 9 8 7 6 5 4 3 2 1

Printed in City, State, USA

This book was typeset in Minion.

Candlewick Press
99 Dover Street
Somerville, Massachusetts 02144

www.candlewick.com

To New York City's great historians, some of whom I have had the good fortune to know as mentors and friends, others whom I have met through their books. It is your research, dedication, insight, and generosity that made my work possible. May this book serve as an invitation to the next generation of historians to join in our passionate quest to understand and explain this maddening, magical city. And to Sherry Fatla, who turned a project into a passion and handcrafted every page of this beautiful book

CONTENTS

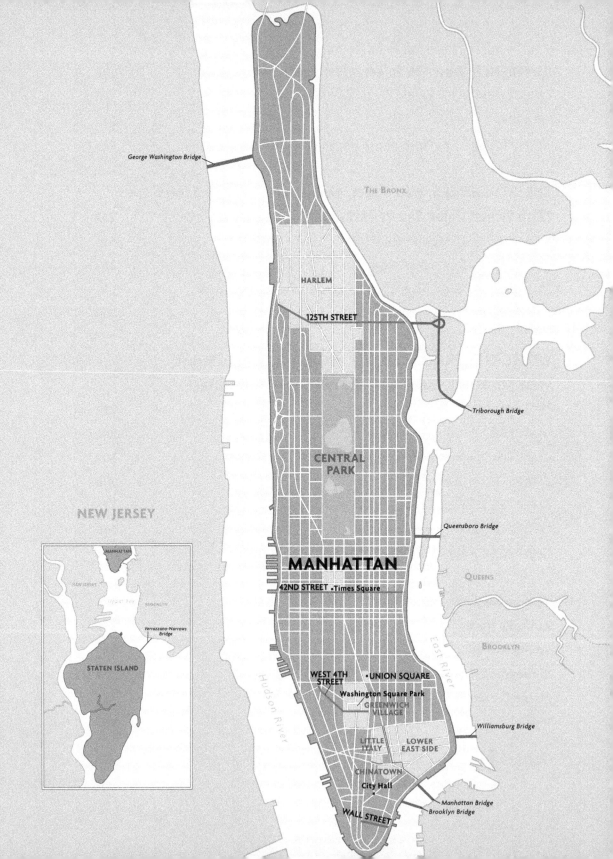

HOW THIS BOOK IS ORGANIZED

This book is a kind of biography, a biography of an island and an idea, not a person, and it is organized around places—four streets, a square, and the vast golden door.

The first two sections of the book explore three hundred years, from roughly 1600 to 1898, through two places that each became the center of Manhattan: Wall Street and then Union Square. As we enter the twentieth century, we reach Forty-Second Street. Other parts of New York City served as tributaries that fed, and helped to create, each center. By the 1910s, two more satellite centers, 125th Street and West Fourth Street, intersected with the older, and still important, locations as Manhattan faced the challenges, disasters, and revivals of its mature life. I use these five nodes and their nearby neighborhoods to capture where clash and combination fostered ideas, art, political organizations, and music that spread across the country and the world. Important events happened all over the island and the broader city, but I am using my streets and a square to capture the essence of what might be called the New York idea, the New York experience. As the book moves forward in time, it uses its locations to highlight the themes of conflict, evolution, and creation. You might see each node in this book as a window into times and places where the intense forces of city life gave birth to thrilling new expressions of human creativity. (Note: the eight neighborhood maps include locations mentioned throughout the book and do not represent a single point in time.)

Once I decided to make this book limited and thematic, rather than comprehensive and encyclopedic, I had to make choices and leave out a great deal. I used illustrations to tell more: periodic "photo essays" treat a location or theme as a kind of character that develops over time. In addition, I have included a set of fact boxes as "Snapshots" outlining the city's changing population and aspects of its economy. I hope readers use those, and the sources I present in the back of the book, to begin their own explorations of the multitude of other stories the city offers.

TWO BOOKS IN ONE

As I was researching Manhattan's history, I repeatedly had the immense pleasure of discovering multimedia experiences of three distinct types that perfectly complemented what I was writing in the text. First, a great deal of this book is about Manhattan's artistic innovations—and I wanted them to be part of the book. I wanted to share those discoveries with readers—not gathered in the back in a list but right here in the text so that you can "experience" the pulsing rhythms, soaring melodies, and vibrant images of historical New York. Nonfiction is the real "transmedia" because it can now be explored in sound and sight as well as images and words.

I decided to marry words and links this way: for multimedia I list each site in the running text with an icon of a screen where it fits with the words. Just open your browser to marcaronson.com and click on resources for Four Streets and a Square. You'll see all of the links there listed by the page number in this book, along with a matching icon (there are two other icons I'll mention in a moment). If you see an icon in the book, glance at the site and click on the appropriate link. Since I am using others' sites, which may change or disappear, I often list how I searched as well as what I found. I hope you have as much fun diving into these links as I did in finding them. Here's an example to get you started. From third grade through twelfth grade, I went to the New Lincoln School, which was on 110th Street between Fifth and Lenox Avenues. What a treat, then, to find Noro Morales's composition "110th Street and 5th Avenue" and Tito Puente's up-tempo version. See if they don't inspire you to follow the other links.

I can't resist giving you a few more examples so you know what to expect: I mention in chapter 24 that Fiorello LaGuardia, the city's ninety-ninth mayor, looked a bit like the comedian Lou Costello of the team that is best known for the immortal "Who's on First" routine. My editor reasonably asked if readers would know Lou. Link 30 gives you a clip of LaGuardia speaking and then Abbott and Costello performing the skit just where I mention them and it. The text is a narrative that carries you along; the media links give you curated experiences to explore and enjoy.

If you try nothing else, you must view and listen to link 23 when you read chapter 23. I leave that one to be a surprise.

The second type of multimedia are sites created by prior historians and fans of city history—from professional scholars and curators to amateur explorers. The sites often contain features such as films or interactive maps, and I include them to give readers access to the wealth of information about Manhattan's history that has been curated by others. History sites are identified with this building symbol in the margin, and on my site by page number. The first of these links takes you to the Welikia site, where you can explore the city as it was before the Dutch arrived—based on the most thorough recent research.

The third type of multimedia are complete texts of historical books or magazines, in the public domain, that you can browse online. Want to see how a succession of photo guides presented the city in the early 1900s? Links that are identified with this open book icon in the margin, and again by page number on my site, will take you to those digital collections. See if you don't get as lost in those pages as I did.

One important caution: some of the images and the links related to blackface minstrelsy are historically important but include performances that were extremely demeaning to African Americans. I have decided to make the links available because minstrelsy was so central in New York (and American) history. We can only make sense of minstrelsy's deep and enduring legacy if we examine it. We cannot ignore or avoid the past; we can be alert and aware as we approach it.

The Bridge

I love walking in New York City—which is where I grew up and have lived most of my adult life. To begin this book about the city, its streets, and the stories they tell, I want to show you why my father—who moved here after living in the great capitals of Europe—called it "this magic city."

New York is alive. I mean alive like a forest, an ecosystem: it grows, flourishes, fades, and nearly dies, only to have the decaying relics of its lost past provide the fertile soil for its next flowering. The city's unquenchable life force is a result of its greatest challenge: the diversity of its population. The city presses unlikely combinations of people against one another so tightly that they explode or blend. Either way, they release new energy—in the form of ideas, art, inventions, ways of living and thinking. Those innovations feed, and challenge, the rest of the world—which, in turn, sends its people to New York to join the great swirl of confrontation and combination that is the city's life.

New York is doubly alive, since for much of its history the city has been the media capital of the nation. The dramas and lifestyles from its streets become the songs, plays, paintings, books, and fashions that shape how Americans see themselves and present their pageant to the world. Within New York, Manhattan was the engine of change, fed by people from throughout the city, the country, the world. That is what this book is about: New York City as a place of mixing—which brings both tragedy and transformation—and media, which makes art out of both.

Here, I can show you.

Let's say it is about 6:30 or 7 p.m. on a beautiful spring day. We cross Tillery Street in Brooklyn and enter the walkway to the Brooklyn Bridge. When the bridge was completed in 1883, Brooklyn and Manhattan were still separate cities. The bridge linked them. Before there was a bridge there was—as there is again now—a ferry. And the great poet of America in the 1800s, Walt Whitman, wrote about what he saw as he took it in "Crossing Brooklyn Ferry." He knew we would follow him:

> Others will enter the gates of the ferry and cross from shore to shore,
> Others will watch the run of the flood-tide,
> Others will see the shipping of Manhattan north and west, and the
>   heights of Brooklyn to the south and east,
> Others will see the islands large and small;
> Fifty years hence, others will see them as they cross, the sun half an
>   hour high,
> A hundred years hence, or ever so many hundred years hence, others
>   will see them,
> Will enjoy the sunset, the pouring-in of the flood-tide, the falling-back
>   to the sea of the ebb-tide.

The overlap of past and present that Whitman described is part of the joy of walking in New York: you see traces of the past even as you feel the swell and crush, the "flood-tide," of the present. There's one sign of the past off to your left as you begin to cross the bridge: New York Harbor. For much of the city's history, hundreds of ships filled those waters, bringing people, ideas, and wealth to the city. When the novelist Henry James returned from England to his native New York in 1905, he looked at the harbor and described the "power of the most extravagant of cities, rejoicing, as with the voice of the morning, in its might, its fortune." The harbor swelled with ships and welcomed the world. Indeed, we see, right there, the symbol of that welcome, the Statue of Liberty lifting, as the poet Emma Lazarus described, her "lamp beside the golden door"—the entry point to America for millions upon millions of immigrants, the ancestors on so many family trees. New York is the city of immigrants, far more than any other place on the planet.

That is the sight we keep seeing to our left as we walk across the bridge: the wide sky, the expanse of the harbor, the passage of ferries and boats, the flights of seagulls, and the steady green goddess standing guard, making sure we always let the world come, come to join us. At the halfway point, the bridge begins to slope down toward Manhattan. It is dusk now. White, golden, and ruby jewels of light blaze amid the grid of skyscrapers. As the poet, lyricist, and diplomat James Weldon Johnson explained, we are beginning to sense Manhattan's "throbbing force, the thrill that comes / From being of her a part." The magical city is luring us, calling us, sparkling, blaring, rising in the highest skyscrapers and the most glittering lights.

Within that warren of buildings, New York is a city of neighborhoods, by turns Native, Dutch, African, English, French, Irish, German, Eastern European, Italian, Chinese, Spanish, Greek, Arab, Puerto Rican, Korean, Mexican, Dominican, South Asian, Guyanese, and on and on. Each group makes a home, and works, and starts businesses. But then the next wave of people washes through, displacing, disrupting, almost but not quite erasing the last. Wash in, wash over, wash out—New York is a heartbeat and heartbreak.

New York must be open to the world: that is its essence. Yet for that reason it is always temporary, always transitional, always contested; someone is always winning and someone is always losing. As the novelist Thomas Wolfe wrote, in New York, "the one permanent thing is change itself." The pulsing heart of New York lets new people, new ideas, new innovations into the country—which can result in the most brutal riots and abuses and the most beautiful combinations and creations. As New York breathes, bleeds, and soars, the rest of America sometimes celebrates and sometimes resents this doorway to the world. But New York seduces the nation—using its songs, and plays, and broadcasts, the end-less talents that fill its streets—to tell its story. In New York, people are crushed together—leading to violence and bitter conflict, and yet also to the opportunity to fall in love, to yearn, to give birth to something utterly new.

This photo from 1911 shows a view of Manhattan from the Brooklyn Bridge.

On one side as we approach the island, there is the welcoming harbor. On the other, we see what those who arrived, and those they met, and those who came in chains built: Manhattan. That is why it makes sense to focus on the island and not the entire city of the Bronx, Brooklyn, Manhattan, Queens, and Staten Island: no matter where people lived, everyone came to Manhattan, used Manhattan, to make money, to create art, to express ideas—to shape and change America and the world. Seen in this way, Manhattan is a natural wonder but conjured up by human minds and built through the muscle power of generations of laborers: magical.

Creating the City
Wall Street
1600 — 1800

~

In which an embattled Dutch port becomes a British city,

a seedbed of revolution, an American capital,

and a center of finance, while elites and working people,

displaced original Americans, colonizing Europeans,

and enslaved Africans press uneasily and unequally against

one another — and sometimes, almost out of sight,

support, tolerate, and mix with one another.

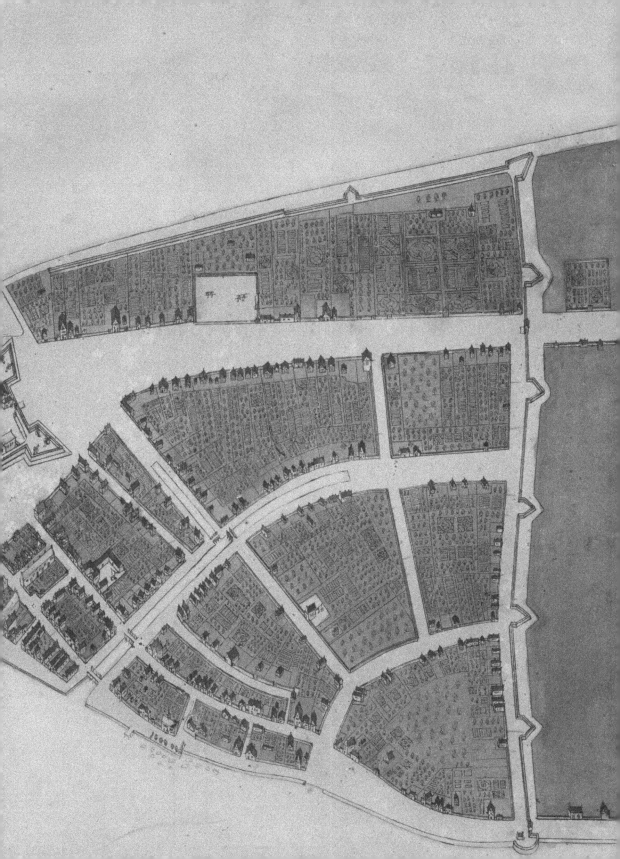

SNAPSHOT

Munsee and Dutch New Amsterdam

10,000 BCE Paleo-Indians live on the island, hunting woolly mammoths and other large game.

9000 BCE In a changing climate, the original Indians move away from the island.

1000 CE People speaking Algonkian languages and living in longhouses are established on the island of Manhattan and in nearby areas.

1524 Giovanni da Verrazzano, sailing for France, explores what will be New York Harbor.

1609 Henry Hudson explores near Manhattan, and Robert Juet records what is probably the Munsee name of the island.

1624 Dutch begin settling in what they call the New Netherland region.

1626 Peter Minuit makes a deal for some access to or use of Manhattan in exchange for sixty guilders' worth of trade goods; enslaved Africans, perhaps captured from Portuguese or Spanish slave ships, are brought to New Amsterdam.

1628 New Amsterdam population: approximately 270 people.

1637 Dutch grant of land in New Harlem.

1641–45 Conflicts with Lenape, including a massacre ordered by Governor Willem Kieft; first wall built.

1647 Peter Stuyvesant becomes governor of New Amsterdam and Curaçao.

1653 Stronger wooden wall constructed.

1654 Jews fleeing Brazil arrive and form the first Jewish community in North America.

1656 Manhattan population estimated at 1,000 people in 120 homes.

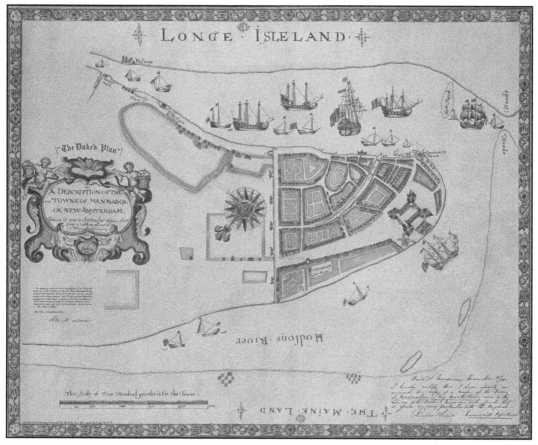

This map is a version of a 1660 map of New Amsterdam created a year or so later in London. It shows boats clustered on the east side of the island facing Long Island (now Brooklyn). This map is called the Duke's Plan.

CHAPTER 1

Manna-hata

The story of Manhattan begins with a mystery and a wondrous product of memory, scholarship, and care. The mystery is what the island was called by the people who lived there before the Europeans arrived. No one knows what name to use, because the Native world as it was experienced on the island was scattered or destroyed and the choices we have come from incomplete European documents. But maybe that is just right—the story of a legendary place should begin with questions we can't quite answer. And yet—name aside—there is so much that has been preserved by the descendants of those who lived on the island, and discovered by generations of scholars, that we can very fully describe the land when it was the home to its original inhabitants: people who called themselves the Munsee, or perhaps the Lenape.

Before the arrival of the Europeans, people living along the coast from what is now Canada to the Carolinas spoke similar languages. But that is like saying a lot of people in the world speak languages linked to Latin—everything from Italian and French to Catalan and Romanian. That tells you something, but not enough to separate one group from another. The people who lived on what is now Manhattan spoke a version of this shared language family that came to be called Munsee. That means "people from Minisink"—a small island on what is now the Delaware River. *Minisink* itself, like *Munsee*—and probably (no one knows for sure) *Manhattan*—seemed to refer to islands. The people who lived on, near, or between certain islands, had close family relations, and spoke a common language saw themselves as a distinct group. They may have used the word *nenapa*—"man"—to define their men as special, distinctive. Related groups who lived in what are now parts of New Jersey and Pennsylvania used a similar term for themselves: *Lenape*.

Island people, real men—that is as much as we know. Before we talk about the Munsee and how they knew and used the island, let's explore on our own to get a sense of the island's many environments.

If we start from where the Brooklyn Bridge now lands in Manhattan and go back in time before the Europeans arrived, we would be on relatively flat land with pine and tall oak trees to shade us. Pause a moment and a couple of squirrels race ahead up one trunk; chipmunks scamper about. If we lean down and watch carefully, we'd soon see mice, voles, and shrews. If we are lucky—and quiet— we'd catch sight of a brown rabbit with a white patch on its behind standing stock-still and eyeing us. Shadows would keep dancing across us, for in the sky are so many birds: red-winged blackbirds and red-tailed hawks, black crows, gray passenger pigeons. An eagle might swoop by overhead.

As we turn south, the land rises slightly into low hills. There are fewer pines and large chestnut trees. We are close enough to the shore that turtles and salamanders keep us company. Not only are the skies filled with birds, their songs are everywhere: sparrows, blue jays, and robins calling to one another.

Nearer to the tip of the island, we leave the forest and come to the edge of a salt marsh. We are in flat, muddy land where grasses grow right up to the edge of the water. Crossing the marsh, we are back in the pines, until we reach the very end of the island. Now we have our pick of eel, fish, and shellfish—we might even sight a whale or porpoise.

MUNSEE

Historians and anthropologists reading documents and speaking with descendants of people who lived in the region when the Europeans arrived have learned enough to allow us to picture how one of the Munsee might have experienced the island. Of course, each specific individual would have had his or her own way of seeing the world. What follows is only the most general portrait.

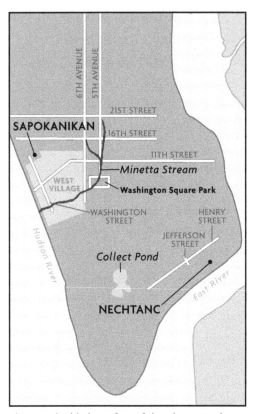

This map highlights a few of the places on the island where the Munsee built longhouses and farmed crops.

He would know where he was walking through his own memories of walking there, through stories he had heard of that spot or similar ones. Seeing a bush, he would know which bird would likely perch there, what the rustle of leaves meant about which animal was just behind it; he could tell whether a leaf was tasty, tangy, minty, dangerous, or not worth tasting. Feeling a breeze, he would know that kind of wind by name.

He would walk the land as a home that he and his people shaped to serve them and that—carefully watched and managed—provided for them. He would know the rivers as places to fish or, if wide enough, to traverse in canoes—passageways to similar landfalls nearby. The land, the animals, the crops, and the water were not merely a physical home that provided food and shelter for the Munsee. They were a spiritual home in which this culture belonged, and to which they belonged.

Where the east side of the island bulges out today (near Jefferson, Henry, Clinton, and Madison Streets), the Munsee had a seasonal settlement, which seems to have been called Nechtanc. The Munsee built longhouses out of wood and burned the trees and underbrush to create fields to grow tobacco and corn. These were not year-round villages. Instead, the Munsee moved with the seasons to where fish and game were plentiful, then returned when it was time to plant or harvest their crops.

The burning took place in the fall when the grass, leaves, and branches were dry. Fire would consume dead limbs but only scorch the bark of young ones—unless so many dead trees lay at angles across the forest that fire could climb up to the highest leaves. "Then," a Dutch visitor later reported, "we can see a great distance by the light of the blazing trees, the flames being driven by the wind, and fed by the tops of trees. But the dead and dying trees remain burning in their standing positions, which appear sublime and beautiful when seen at a distance." Planned burning created clearings to plant, enriched the soil, and opened spaces in the forest that made it easier to spot and hunt game.

A trail led from Nechtanc west, toward what was later called the Collect Pond, which would play several key roles in the city's history. Today the drained and filled pond is a park at Foley Square near the State Court House between Centre and Lafayette Streets. The pond fed streams that worked their way to the rivers on both sides of the island. The flowing waters ran through a large marsh on the western side of the island and a smaller one on the east. It is said that when the waters were high, the Munsee could row along the streams through the marshes, then paddle over the pond, down the next marsh, and across to the other side. Waterways nearly split off the tip of the island.

To the north of the large marsh on the west side of the island was yet another Munsee site, which seems to have been called Sapokanikan. This clearing is now part of the neighborhood called Greenwich Village. The Munsee built trails to traverse the island and planned meeting places where they traded with other peoples. They managed and improved their island home.

The arrival of sailors on a Dutch ship would bring this way of living on the island to an end. Most of the Munsee themselves moved to other locations, merged with other nations, and live today in places such as Canada, Wisconsin, Ohio, and even Oklahoma. The people live; their Manhattan world does not.

TREACHERY

In 1609, Henry Hudson's ship the *Half Moon*, sailing along what is now the Hudson River, made a stop near Manhattan. A sailor named Robert Juet was keeping a diary of the trip, and his pages are filled with what he saw as treachery. Every time Native Americans arrived in canoes offering to trade tobacco, corn, grapes, and beaver and otter pelts, he both reveled in his ability to buy the goods for "trifles" and suspected that there was a plot behind each visit. He was

This is the 1626 letter in which Peter Schagen reports that the Dutch "have purchased the Island Manhattes from the Indians for the value of 60 guilders." Saying "the value" could suggest that the payment was in trade goods, not coins. It has no information about the terms of the agreement, nor even with whom the Dutch had negotiated.

convinced that either the Dutch were fooling the Native Americans by getting them drunk and paying them too little, or the Native people were calculating to steal from or even murder the Dutch. On October 2, the crew reached a cliff "that looked of the colour of a white greene, as though it were either Copper, or Silver Myne [mine]. . . . It is on that side of the River that is Manna-hata. There we saw no people to trouble us: and rode quietly all night; but had much wind and raine." This is how the word *Manhattan* entered written history.

Juet was looking for mines, for people to fool into advantageous trades or to fend off with gunpowder. His focus on treachery, though, was not just a matter of European greed and prejudice. He would later mutiny and send his own captain, Henry Hudson, and Hudson's son to their death. There were layers of plot and calculation on the boat. Any interactions with Native people along the river were pawns' moves in a much larger global chess match.

Juet was perched on the most advanced technology of his time—an oceangoing ship. To him, the island

No images of the Munsee or other local people have survived from the period of the Dutch arrival. In general, historians suspect that later images like this one underestimated how many Indigenous people would have been present and emphasize the size and heft of the European ship.

with white-green cliffs was a tip of land pointed directly to a deep and welcoming harbor. He could see that landing spot as one star in a constellation whose other points were ports he could name in the Caribbean, in Brazil, in Africa, in the islands of Indonesia, in Japan, India, China, and Europe. The European on the ship saw water near a convenient landing. A Munsee person on shore would have seen land girdled by water. One man brought the ideas, guns, and germs of distant lands; another carried deep knowledge of where he lived. You could describe the entire story of Manhattan as the meeting of water, linking the city to the globe, and land, the communities and lives people built on the island over the centuries.

CHAPTER 2

Wall

Washington Irving is best known today for his tales of Rip Van Winkle and the Headless Horseman of Sleepy Hollow, but in his lifetime and for more than a century after, he was best known for his history of Dutch New York. Indeed, the character he created as the supposed author of the book is still mentioned daily: he wrote in the guise of an old Dutchman named Diedrich Knickerbocker—whose last name is memorialized in the moniker of one of New York City's professional basketball teams, the New York Knickerbockers, or the Knicks. Irving's story of how the Dutch tricked the Munsee and bought Manhattan for twenty-four dollars is a fable. It is not historically accurate, but it is historically important.

Here is Irving's story, matched with what we actually do know, and can know, today. The Dutch, he claims, bargained to exchange sixty Dutch coins, or guilders, for as much of the island as could be covered by Mynheer Ten Broeck's underpants. The gullible natives agreed, only to discover that beneath his pants the wide-bottomed Ten Broeck was wearing endless layers of garments, one over the other, and when the underpants were all laid out, they covered the island. Sixty guilders was once calculated as twenty-four dollars, hence the story that the Native people made one of the worst real estate transactions in history.

Irving's story of the underpants was a humorous version of earlier tales about the sale, and it came with a message: the Dutch were cheap, smart, and hard bargainers. The Indians were simple, primitive, and easily fooled. This matches the tone of Juet's diary, but that is seeing the events entirely from a seventeenth-century Dutch point of view. The Dutch did attempt to purchase land from the Native people rather than merely take it by force. We have a record of their negotiations for Staten Island, where they offered not Dutch money but trade goods such as axes, hoes, kettles, and cloth. An early letter does state that it was sixty guilders' worth of goods, though in current buying power that is closer to one thousand dollars than twenty-four. But as no treaty survived, we do not know with whom the Dutch negotiated, or what the agreement said. We do know that the image of clever Dutch and foolish natives is wrong.

The first edition of Irving's book came out in 1808, and for a good century and a half after, many readers were happy to smile at his story and to both smirk at the thrifty Dutch and picture the Indians as simple innocents. Today, historians and anthropologists devote themselves to understanding as much as possible about how each side actually saw the world. Scholars have learned that, in fact, the Munsee were accustomed to making deals and to working out who could use which piece of land. They were neither inexperienced at making trades nor dazzled by the Dutch. As Russell Shorto, who is an expert on this period, puts it, "The Indians were as skilled, as duplicitous . . . as smart and as pig-headed, and as curious and as cruel as the Europeans who met them." The difference was not in skill or craft but power. The biggest unanswerable question is what they meant in the sale—that the Dutch could live on some of the island? Could use it? Could share it with the Munsee who came and left every year? Finally, as one modern scholar notes, the very fact that the Munsee felt a spiritual connection to the land may have influenced the deal. Since newcomers from far away had been landing, and even living, on the island, it may have seemed spoiled. It was no longer the special place of the island people, the real men. As one of their leaders said in a later deal, the land was now just dirt—it was no longer a home-land given to the Munsee by ancestors and spirits they honored and could sense. It was ruined, polluted. Agreeing to let strangers have access to the no-longer-special island in exchange for rare, attractive items may have made good sense. But making a deal to sell—or share—an island is no guarantee that new neighbors will get along.

By 1656, the Dutch settlement of New Amsterdam was a tiny cluster

NIEUW AMSTERDAM
op 't Eylant Manhattans.

This close view of New Amsterdam was created after the British took over but was based on an earlier sketch that gave a good sense of how small and scattered a settlement it was. The windmill, flag, and church tower over the typical Dutch homes.

of buildings on the tip of the island, and the Dutch West India Company had built a fort there to guard the windmill, the houses, and the docks. At first, New Amsterdam was a commercial outpost run by a company, not a colony supervised by the government. Each Dutch family built a house and dug a well wherever they chose. The wood and brick homes scattered hither and thither. The low brick buildings were just like their models in the Netherlands: a first-floor rectangle topped by a triangular gable. Buildings were meant to be solid, efficient, and modest—no attention-getting display. In back were gardens where imported red and white roses, tulips of all colors, white lilies, and purple violets bloomed next to native yellow sunflowers. The trim homes and gardens bursting with color contrasted with the muddy unpaved walkways. A city law of this period mentioned the "rubbish, filth, ashes, oyster-shells, dead animals" that people were forbidden to toss out—which historians take as an indication of the litter that was found in front of many homes.

This perch with a port at the tip of the island was a place to gather and ship the valuable furs purchased from the original Americans near Fort Orange (now Albany). Ships sailed from its docks to harass the Spanish carrying treasure home from their conquests in Mexico and Peru, or sugar from their islands in the Caribbean, or enslaved people from Africa. At first, only a trickle of ambitious Dutch people were interested in coming to this pinprick of a settlement. In order to grow, New Amsterdam could not be choosy about who it welcomed. By

1638, so many different sorts of people had arrived that a visitor reported some eighteen languages were being spoken on the edge of Manhattan.

French, Swedish, Danish, and English speakers lived there, as well as at least one Muslim of mixed Dutch and Moroccan background. The first enslaved Africans had arrived by 1626. We know some of their names—which hint of their origin: Paulo d'Angola, Simon Congo, Anthony Portuguese. Enslaved people could marry, and some could even achieve a kind of "half-freedom," where if they fulfilled a set of specific obligations, they could achieve their own personal liberty but their children were born enslaved. In time, the Dutch West India Company needed more workers than it could supply, so it sent enslaved people to its colony. Fourteen years after the first Africans arrived, there were about one hundred in New Amsterdam—the largest group of enslaved Africans anywhere in North America at the time.

While New Amsterdam was becoming a landing spot for those who did not fit in anywhere else, or had no choice in where they were placed, Dutch traders ranged up and down the Hudson River to Fort Orange to buy beaver pelts. Dutch farmers spread across Munsee territory—areas including what are now Brooklyn, Queens, the Bronx, Staten Island, and New Jersey. An uneasy mood took hold on both sides. Whenever they could, the Dutch traded or purchased Munsee land, set up farms, settled down. This scattering left outposts far from the fort at the tip of Manhattan. The Munsee were in a difficult time of change: diseases brought by Europeans were spreading, lands that were once both familiar and sacred were now filled with strangers. Other Native groups, such as the Mahicans, were also under pressure from the newcomers, and they were pushing into Munsee lands. From a Munsee point of view, managing relations with longstanding Native rivals and friends was crucial, and the newcomers were potential allies or enemies in those familiar struggles.

Looking back from a twenty-first-century viewpoint, the challenges faced by the original Americans could have been an opportunity. If the Dutch had seen their neighbors as potential allies, a lively mixed culture might have arisen. But just the opposite took place. In February 1643, the Mahicans attacked the Lenape in what is now New Jersey. Perhaps as many as a thousand Lenape rushed to the Dutch, hoping for protection. Instead, the leader of the Dutch, Willem Kieft, seized the chance to terrify and destroy. On the night of February 25, Kieft sent his men to massacre the Lenape. Another Dutch group sped to Nechtanc, which was still used as a base by the Munsee. The men, women, and children there were slaughtered. This was Manhattan, the meeting place of peoples, at its bloody worst. And now the only relationship between the original Manhattanites and the current residents was enmity, suspicion, and even open war.

Kieft's massacre ensured that every Munsee or Lenape would see the Dutch as enemies. Fearing reprisal, Kieft ordered his men to build a wooden barrier to protect the colony. But that was hardly reassuring and he was replaced. And in 1653, the new leader of the Dutch colony, Peter Stuyvesant, decided that the barrier needed to be replaced by a full-fledged wall.

Stuyvesant came to New Amsterdam from serving as governor of the Caribbean island of Curaçao, where he'd fought against the Spanish and lost part of one leg. Even while governing New Amsterdam, he was still in charge of Curaçao, indicating that the Dutch West India Company believed one person could manage the two outposts, which they viewed as relatively similar. He bought wood to construct a wall straight across the island. A pathway, Wall Street, ran beside the barrier.

No one has left us a full description of the wall. We do know it featured oak posts with sharpened peaks, stood 12 feet tall, and ran some 2,340 feet from where Pearl Street met the East River to a hill on the opposite side of the island near what is now called the Hudson River.

Some of the Africans who managed to buy their freedom were permitted to purchase land to farm—just on the other side of the wall. Living on what were called "the Negroes's Farms" they served as a buffer, and first warning, should anyone attack. Some moved from the wall to the Collect Pond. Others went even farther north. Domingo Anthony owned a farm that is now part of Washington Square Park. Africans could achieve freedom, could even take the first steps toward a better life by owning land. But the line between African and non-African remained.

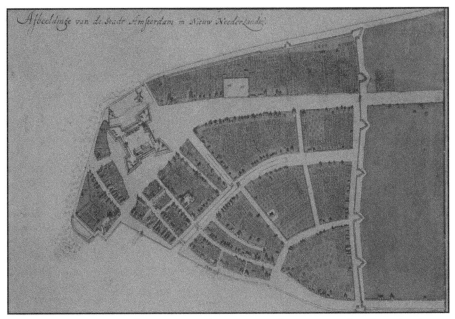

Based on an original map drawn in 1660, this is a view of New Amsterdam featuring the fort and the wall. The map, known as the Castello Plan, featured here was created by the Dutch in the city to plan out its future expansion. The city was growing but early arrivals had grabbed large tracts for themselves, leaving little room behind the wall for newcomers.

Inside the wall sat a town of traders, with many languages, religions, skin tones. New Amsterdam was a port—a place of constant exchange. Not just for goods, but for lives. A sailor might jump ship; generations of pirates—or the legal pirates called privateers—could find anchor. By 1654, twenty-three Jewish people—who had originally fled Spain for Brazil and now sought a new safe haven—arrived in New Amsterdam. Stuyvesant did not like the idea of having Jews, especially poor ones, in his colony and wanted to keep them out. But back in Holland, wealthy Jews were influential in the Dutch West India Company, and he was told to open the city to the new immigrants. At first, Jews had only limited rights and could not even own land. Still, this settlement beside the water was an opening to the world.

Protestants escaping from Catholic France added their history and language to the mix. Quakers, who were considered criminals in New England, came to the city. When Stuyvesant tried to ban the Quakers, residents in what is now Flushing, Queens, objected. They wrote a "remonstrance" asserting that everyone, even "Jews, Turks, and Egyptians," should be allowed to live, and pray, as they pleased. Stuyvesant rejected the plea but was once again overruled by the company back in Holland. If Kieft's massacre was a forecast of New York's history of bloody conflict, the Flushing resolution pointed to the city's future of harboring refugees from throughout the planet.

New Amsterdam offered exchange and separation at the same time. Jews could come, but not as equals; Africans could buy freedom, but their children remained enslaved. The Munsee had been murdered and driven off. Catholic services were banned. The colony did not aim to be perfect—unlike the New England towns that strove to live "godly" lives. New Amsterdam was the site of constant battles between new and old, rich and poor, owner and enslaved; Protestant, Jew, and atheist all pressed against one another in the port town. But original Americans were not the only—or even the most ominous—threat to New Amsterdam. The colony faced a looming enemy in the English.

Spreading south from their New England colonies, English-speaking settlers kept pressing on territory the Dutch saw as theirs. The newcomers were not shy about showing that they would prefer to be ruled by England, and Stuyvesant was just as eager to push back. These local territorial skirmishes, though, are but markers in a global struggle for supremacy at sea, in trade, in other far-flung colonies. The very links to global trade that made New Amsterdam matter also meant that it was an asset to be won, lost, or exchanged in global trade wars.

Which seafaring European nation would control the lucrative trade in black pepper, nutmeg, and the other treasures of the Spice Islands? Which could dominate the slave ports of West Africa, the sugar plantations of Brazil and the Caribbean? The Dutch drove the Portuguese out of many of their holdings in Asia, Africa, and Brazil, but in 1663, the English returned the favor. They took control of the slave ports in West Africa. Now they needed a place in the Americas to which the enslaved people could be sent. They needed a large port, a welcoming harbor, to receive human cargo and to act as a hub for the sugar the Africans would grow and harvest in the Caribbean. New Amsterdam seemed just right. In late August 1664, four ships carrying two thousand English soldiers arrived near New Amsterdam. The English assured the Dutch in the port that they would be safe and could keep what they owned—if they surrendered. On September 8, faced with a generous peace and no chance of winning a war, Stuyvesant gave in. The Dutch port of New Amsterdam was now the property of the brother of King Charles II—James, the Duke of York. Hence: New York.

But that was not the end of the conflict. In the next decade, the city would twice more change names and three times shuttle between the Dutch and the English. "Rule" was not a mere matter of who controlled the port: the majority of citizens were Dutch and used a "new" calendar that the English minority rejected. Dutch weights, measures, and coins did not match the English. Students in Dutch schools learned different lessons in different languages from those in English schools. The Dutch prayed in churches not favored by the English. Every time the port changed hands, one entire system won and the other lost.

Finally, in 1674, the Dutch suggested a deal—they would give up their port on the edge of Manhattan in exchange for one of the English sugar colonies, what is now Suriname on the coast of South America. The English agreed. The trade made clear what had been true all along: New Amsterdam, New York, mattered as a landing spot in the movement of people and goods around the world. It was a city that would stand or fall on commerce—not walls.

SNAPSHOT

British New York

1664   New York's population: 1,500 people. English take over New York.

1678   First tally of vessels registered to owners in Manhattan numbers seventeen.

1685–88   James II makes New York part of an expanded Dominion of New England with the city as its center.

1688–89   William and Mary replace James II; New York is once again its own colony.

1689–91   Jacob Leisler takes control of New York, until deposed and executed on word from London.

1694   At the port of New York, 162 vessels are listed; pirates such as William Kidd sail to the Caribbean and as far as the Red Sea out of East River docks.

1698–1700   First census: New York City's (Manhattan) population is 4,937, including 700 people of African descent. This makes New York the same size as Philadelphia and smaller than Boston by 1,500. By contrast, the most populous cities of Europe—London and Paris—have populations of more than 500,000, and Constantinople, capital of the Ottoman Empire, 700,000. Kings County's (Brooklyn) population is 2,017, including 296 of African descent; Queens County's (Queens) population is 3,565; Richmond's (Staten Island) population is 727.

1704   City hall on Wall Street completed.

1710   Germans immigrate to New York.

1712   Slave revolt, nine whites killed, twenty-four enslaved people executed.

1717–20   More than two hundred boats enter and leave New York's port each year, exporting American goods to England, bringing supplies to the Caribbean, and returning with sugar, rum, molasses, and enslaved people.

1723   Manhattan's population: 7,248, 19 percent of African descent. King's County population: 2,218, 20 percent of African descent.

1732 First theater in New York opens.

1735 Zenger trial.

1737 Manhattan's population: 10,664, 16 percent of African descent and living almost entirely below Wall Street. Kings County's population: 2,348, 24 percent of African descent.

1741 Five hundred thirty ships enter and leave New York's port.

1741–42 Possible slave plot; thirty-two Africans and three whites executed. First outbreak of yellow fever in the city.

1750 Importation of enslaved people directly from Africa to New York increases.

1756 Manhattan's population: 13,046, 17.5 percent of African descent. Kings County's population: 2,207, 38 percent of African descent.

1756–63 Seven Years' War creates economic opportunities for New York, supplying British forces, and for privateers; 128 privateers bring eighty ships worth 1 million British pounds to port.

1765–66 Stamp Act Congress meets in New York; Sons of Liberty protest.

1770 Clash between New Yorkers and British troops at the Battle of Golden Hill, considered by some the first physical violence on the path to the revolution.

1771 Manhattan's population: 21,863, of whom 3,137 are of African descent. Kings County's population: 3,623, of whom 1,162 are of African descent.

1772 More than seven hundred vessels—boats of varying types—are registered to owners in the city.

CHAPTER 3

British New York

THE GRANDEES AND THE SENSELESS PEOPLE
1689

Suddenly there was no New York—or New Amsterdam or New Orange. Between 1664 and 1689, the name of the town's fort had gone from Fort James (English) to Fort Willem Hendrik (back to Dutch) to Fort James (back to English under King James) to Fort William (when James II fled and William became king of England). But in 1689, no one was in charge; indeed, no one could say whether the city was part of the colony of New York or the "dominion of New England," into which New York had been folded when King James II was in power (but which itself was dissolving as King William's views were not known), or if it was part of something new—or whether it was about be taken over by the French Catholics sweeping down from Montreal. Worse yet, who could decide? No one in New York knew who was ruling England, so there was no way to know who was in charge in the town.

Into this chaos stepped Jacob Leisler—a self-made New Yorker if there ever was one. Modern historians still argue over whether he was an anti-Catholic Protestant extremist, a callous manipulator out for power, or a hero of the people bringing democracy a century before the American Revolution. While Leisler rose and fell quickly, the divisions he exposed remained important for centuries.

Leisler arrived in New York from Germany in 1660 as a poor soldier serving the Dutch West India Company. He married well and turned his wife's inheritance into an ever-expanding empire. By 1689, he was one of the richest men in New York. That year, Leisler, a devout Protestant, led a group to take over New York's fort and protect the city from "Popish dogs and devils," meaning Catholics. In 1688, England replaced James II, who was Catholic, with William and Mary, assuring that the country would remain Protestant. Leisler and his men despised the city's "grandees": the English elite who had been cozy with the pro-Catholic allies of the now-deposed King James II. In turn, those powerful men saw the Leislerians as "poor ignorant and senseless people." He gave more New Yorkers

a voice in government and tried to organize the colonies into a collective army to invade French Canada. If you admired these actions, he seemed a fresh, strong, and idealistic leader. To the forces of order, Leisler was a madman, a demagogue, whipping up poor people only so he could rule.

Jacob Leisler's home was said to be the first house made of brick in New Amsterdam. It was located on what is now Whitehall Street, near the very edge of the island.

Who should lead the city? Educated, wealthy, thoughtful men who would work with any government—even one friendly to Catholics—to keep the city stable and prosperous? Or the city's white male working people, bound together in angry protests and efficient voting blocs by skillful organizers? To the Leislerians, the elites seemed corrupt and dangerously close to the Catholic enemy. To the elites, the Leislerians seemed irrational and out of touch with the realities of power. The wealthy understood private deals, written law, and ideas spelled out in books. The organized workers understood the power of the streets, ideas and ideals expressed in collective action. Leisler against the old families, devout Protestants against accommodations with Catholics, senseless people versus grandees—a conflict between cozy insiders and street power would rumble across the history of the city to the present day.

Amid the clashes, and uncertainty, of Leisler's New York, a man named James Graham coined a motto for the town. In 1692, he wrote, "You must be your own friend and everybody will oblidge [*sic*] you, for it is money makes the man." In

New York, as elites and workers battled, the one sure path was to make money yourself. The city would be less warm, less neighborly, perhaps, than others, but also more open. For if "money makes the man," any man with enough money could "make" it—be recognized and admired. It was not family or religion that gave you status; it was wealth—so long as you were not female or enslaved. The New York scramble for wealth was also the New York openness to the world.

Finally, by the spring of 1691, word from London reached New York: the new king William and queen Mary sided with New York's wealthy and against Leisler—who was condemned and executed (though later, after his death, he was pardoned). This was just the beginning of the battles between elites comfortably in their positions of power and political outsiders finding common cause with angry crowds, and the center of the action was all along Wall Street.

ONE STREET, MANY STORIES
Church

In 1699, New York's decaying wooden wall was torn down. The street that ran alongside it, however, retains its name to this day. During New York's British century, Wall Street was the heart of the English city of commerce and conflict.

At the western end of Wall Street near the Hudson River (as it was then; landfill has since extended the width of the island) stood one clear sign of English rule: Trinity Church. At Broadway and Wall Street, Trinity was Church of England—the official faith in the home country. Back in 1687, the English governor had listed the many ways New Yorkers worshipped. You can still hear the cross between puzzlement and annoyance in his list of what struck him as oddball beliefs and lack of faith altogether: "Here bee not many of the Church of England; few Roman Catholicks; abundance of Quakers preachers men and women especially; Singing Quakers, Ranting Quakers, Sabbatarians, Antisabbatarians; some Anabaptists some Independents; some Jews; in short of all sorts of opinions there are some, and the most part none at all."

After William and Mary replaced James II, New Yorkers continued to choose their own forms of religion. Yet as the city became more heavily populated by the English, the Church of England occupied a larger role in the life of the city. When

The view along Wall Street from Trinity Church via city hall, Bayard's sugar refinery, and the slave market perfectly captures the complexities of British New York. This image first appeared in Frederick Hill's 1908 history of Wall Street.

Trinity Church was built in 1698, the stone-and-wood building with the highest steeple in New York was meant to be an anchor for the social and religious life of all wealthy and ambitious New Yorkers. A British visitor in the 1750s wrote that the church was "a very large plain brick building, but within as spacious commodious & handsome a place of worship as I ever saw." By 1764, Trinity had imported

Drawn in 1717 by William Burgis, perhaps to celebrate King George's birthday on May 28, this view of New York from what is now Brooklyn was meant to highlight the bustling

a magnificent, expensive pipe organ. Passing by, you could hear the church's power in the thundering instrument. To belong to Trinity, and to be buried in its graveyard, was to be an elite New Yorker. Of course, that meant those who could not find their final rest there—other denominations of Protestants, Catholics, Jews, Africans, the poor—were almost by definition not part of that inner circle.

Not far from Trinity on and around Wall Street stood churches for other Protestant congregations: most notably the Presbyterian Scots and the remaining Dutch, neither of whom liked the Church of England. Toleration by separation was the rule in New York, at least on Sundays.

In a port city, there are many ways to get rich and join the fashionable upper crust. One of the main sponsors of the new church building was an ambitious captain named William Kidd. Kidd made his reputation capturing pirates and

New York in America

activity of the port city. The tallest building at dead center is Trinity Church, and Wall Street leads directly from it to the slave market.

bringing their plunder back to divide up among his well-connected sponsors. Yet between the prizes he saw glittering before him on the high seas and shifts in power in both London and New York, he decided to become a pirate himself. He was half hero and half villain, representing both the city's shady side and its ambition to rise along with the wealth and power of Great Britain. His fatal mistake was trying to capture ships from the East India Company in the Red Sea. The company enjoyed more sway in London than he or his New York friends did, and in 1701, he was executed for piracy.

Having someone like Captain Kidd serve as one sponsor of Trinity Church is New York at work. If, as James Graham said, "Money makes the man," a person could be a valiant sailor one day, a pirate the next, and all the while remain one of the patrons of the city's leading church.

City Hall

In Dutch times, the most substantial brick building in town was the city tavern, which had started out in 1642 as an inn and lodge for sailors. Eleven years later, the solid three-story structure on Coenties Slip became the town's Stadt Huys, or city hall. By 1697, the Lovelace Tavern, next door to the Stadt Huys, replaced it as the center of city government.

The English were not content to govern the city from a tavern. After four years of construction, in 1703 a brand-new city hall opened, on Wall and Broad Streets. As the story goes, stones that had helped support the old wooden wall were now used to build the new city hall. What had once been a barrier to guard a small city was now the foundation of a civic centerpiece declaring the growing wealth, standing, and stability of the new New York.

The two-story building looked very different from the Dutch tavern turned meeting house of thick brown brick. Clean lines framed a spacious, modern structure that was the center for all law and governance in the city. At the front, two pillars anchored three elegant archways. The center of the roof was highlighted by an open bell tower, which was a kind of information center with its bell to warn the whole city in case of alarm, weathervane to show wind direction, and clock to tell the time. City hall housed a place for city officials to meet, a courtroom, a library of more than sixteen hundred books, and a prison for those who could not pay their debts. Decisions made in the court could be quickly carried out, for directly across the street were many forms of public punishment for criminals: a whipping post, a pillory—where a seated person had hands and feet locked in place so everyone could see and insult them—even a cage to both house and display prisoners.

The solid, modest buildings of the Dutch era presented a blank face to the street, with lively family life taking place inside private rooms. The new British city hall was a public display of refinement, intelligence, and style that linked the city to fashions and taste in London. To walk along the paved Wall Street with its churches and proud new city center was to advertise belonging to the grand British world.

As people increasingly gathered on Wall Street, they needed places to relax and converse. In 1701, Gabriel Thompson purchased a lot on the northwest corner of Wall and William Streets, and it is likely that he kept a tavern there. In a time when all communication needed to be face-to-face or in writing, taverns and, increasingly, coffeehouses created a space for free conversation. Thompson's tavern right near city hall made sense. As the city's official business went on in one building, the key players could retire to the next one to socialize and hash things out.

From the clock tower on the top of the building down to the stocks in the foreground, City hall was built to be the center of power—information, law, and punishment—in British New York.

Today there are coffee shops in every city, town, and mall. That was not always so. The very first store that sold hot coffee in London opened in 1652. Coffee shops soon became the social networking sites of their day for men (respectable women would not go out alone). A man would go to the shop where people who shared his political views gathered. Men would sit for hours reading newspapers, exchanging opinions, debating the issues of the day. Coffee shops especially appealed to those with strict religious views who did not want to be near liquor.

Farther east along Wall Street stood a very large stone building set back from the road. In its own way, it explains as much about New York as all of the other sites along the street. This imposing structure was the sugarhouse of Nicholas Bayard. Bayard opened the building in 1730 as a place to house, process, and sell "all sorts of sugar and sugar candy." He was especially proud to have brought an expert from Europe who could manage the "mystery" of refining sugar. This was not a giant sweetshop; it was a key storehouse for the city's most important business, the international trade in "white gold": sugar.

Sugar sweetened the three new drinks that were all the rage in Europe and its North American colonies—coffee, tea, and hot chocolate. The more sugarcane that was planted in the West Indies, the more the price dropped, and the more people could afford to satisfy their craving for the taste. By the early 1700s, sugar use had doubled in England and sugar imports had risen a hundredfold. Sugar became so profitable that planters in the Caribbean decided to use every possible acre of land for cane and none for food. That meant they would have to import whatever they and their enslaved workers ate. Since New York was a week or more closer to the Caribbean than Boston, ships waited in its harbor to gather everything planters in the Caribbean needed. Once the merchants landed on the sugar islands, they loaded up sugar, rum, molasses, and anything else the islands could produce.

Sugar suited New York, the city of transformation and change; there was always another deal, another trade, to be made—and not just in goods. Each leg of the sugar trade might involve different currency—Spanish, French, English coins, debts written out on paper that could be cashed like checks. New York merchants became the experts at handling all these forms of money. They were the bankers and lenders that made the American sugar trade flow.

Sugar made these New York merchants rich and anxious. New York was wide open. If a businessman arrived on a ship and claimed to have good credit in Jamaica, could anyone trust that piece of paper he showed around? And who was he anyway? Did anyone know him? Concerns about bills and strangers rested on top of the compelling anxiety whose source was most visible at the end of Wall Street.

The Meal Market

All along the East River, markets stood at the ends of the city's five main streets. Each market featured a different sort of product, and at first, Wall Street's was flour, or, as it was termed, "meal." In 1711, though, the Meal Market took on a new function: it became the place where human beings were bought, sold, and hired out. The official ordinance announced that "all negro and Indian slaves that are let out to hire within the city do take up their standing in order to be hired at the market-house at the Wall Street Slip." The end of the street that declared the wealth and power of English New York was a slave market. The more New York made its money in the sugar trade, the more enslaved Africans mattered to the

Know all Men by these Presents, That I *John Livingston of the City of New York Merch.t*

For and in Consideration of of the Sum of *Eighty Pounds* Current Money of the Province of *New York* to me in Hand paid at and before the Ensealing and Delivery of these Presents, by *The Rev.d Mr. Aaron Burr President of the College of New Jersey* the Receipt whereof I do hereby acknowledge, and myself to be therewith fully satisfied, contented and paid: HAVE Granted, Bargained, Sold, Released, and by these Presents do fully, clearly and absolutely grant, bargain, sell and release unto the said *Mr. Aaron Burr his heirs & assigns a certain Negro Man named Caesar*

To HAVE and to HOLD the said *Negro Man Caesar* unto the said *Mr. Aaron Burr his* Executors, Administrators and Assigns for ever. And I the said *John Livingston* for my Self, my Heirs, Executors and Administrators, do covenant and agree to and with the above-named *Aaron Burr His* Executors, Administrators and Assigns, to warrant and defend the Sale of the above-named *Negro Man Caesar* against all Persons whatsoever. In Witness whereof I have hereunto set my Hand and Seal this *Second* Day of *September* Annoq; Dom. One Thousand Seven Hundred and Fifty *Six*

Sealed and Delivered in
the Presence of

Jos Forman

John G Lansing

Jn. Livingston

Left: The Aaron Burr in this bill of sale was the father of Aaron Burr the later vice president, who was born in 1756, the same year that this transaction took place. The enslaved man is called Caesar, and it was typical to use Roman names—both as a nod to slavery in ancient times and as a kind of mocking insult—contrasting the enslaved person's captivity and classical, high-sounding name.

Below: A more detailed view of the Meal Market from the Burgis Prospect

city. Not only did enslaved Africans labor, suffer, and die to harvest cane in the Caribbean; they were treated as a commodity as more and more New Yorkers made use of their labor as servants and workers. By 1721, 20 percent of the people in New York were described as owned, and enslaved men and women lived in four out of every ten New York homes.

The wealth that Trinity Church represented on one end of Wall Street showed how New York was a place where people, money, and goods could change and transform—from buccaneer into civic leader and back again. The Meal Market on the other end of the street was just the opposite. To be an enslaved African was to be trapped. Even the old Dutch versions of half freedom were no longer allowed. African sailors on Spanish ships who were captured in battle and brought to New York had to endure endless court trials to prove that they were free Spaniards, not enslaved Africans. White New York deprived people of their humanity and then lived, uneasily, beside them. Slavery infected the city.

Every boat that sailed down to the sugar islands came back with reports of restless and rebellious slaves. Slave revolts kept breaking out on British islands such as Barbados and Antigua, while on Jamaica runaway slaves were fighting off the British and carving out a territory of their own. In the hope of diminishing the threat of an uprising in their own city, some New Yorkers decided to make sure their enslaved people came directly from Africa—not from the angry islands. But in 1712, that plan backfired.

Most of New York was hammered together out of wood. With so many wooden structures, arson loomed as a terrifying threat. A group of New Yorkers claimed that some twenty-four recently arrived Africans made a blood pact: they would set fire to a building, then kill the white people who came to put it out. Apparently the plan worked—nine white New Yorkers who rushed to the burning building were killed—but then the city took revenge. Some seventy enslaved Africans were rounded up, twenty were hanged, three were burned alive, and, in the most gruesome torture, one had his bones crushed one by one until he died. The more the sugar-slave trade meant to New York, and the more that homes were filled with enslaved people, the more fearful the white city became, and the more brutal its punishments.

CHAPTER 4

Two City Hall Trials

Two Wall Street trials take us past the elite churches and elegant city hall into the deeper conflicts and surprising connections of British New York.

TRUTH

There were no local newspapers at all in New York until November 1725, when William Bradford began publishing the *New York Gazette*. The paper made good money printing official notices and served as a mouthpiece for the colony's administration. In 1732, William Cosby arrived in New York from England to take office as governor. From the first, he announced that he expected large pay-offs and surrounded himself with allies from the city's grandees, who were happy to keep silent about his graft in exchange for access to power. Those shut out from Cosby and his inner circle were furious. The next year, some who opposed Cosby gave enough money to John Peter Zenger, Bradford's former apprentice, to create a competing paper, the *Weekly Journal*. A battle over power was about to be fought in the press—and it wouldn't be nice.

Zenger's paper published advertisements for lost animals—but notices about "a monkey of the larger sort" or a "spaniel of about five feet five inches" were not actually about unusually large missing pets. They were satires of the governor's lapdog allies. Cosby himself was accused of committing a thousand crimes for which a less influential thief would be put in jail. The *Weekly Journal* insisted that its insults had a purpose: the press needed to stand up to power. "If such

This is a reproduction of an actual page from the newspaper in which Zenger's articles appeared. Cato was a Roman critic of Julius Caesar and in a famous set of letters two British authors used his name to frame their critique of the king. Zenger's publication of the Cato letters spread those ideas in New York.

an overgrown criminal, or an impudent monster in inequity, cannot immediately be come at by ordinary justice, let him yet receive the lash of satire, let the glaring truths of his ill administration . . . sting him with shame, and render his actions odious to all honest minds." Alongside its campaign against Cosby, the paper reprinted essays from England that were suspicious of power concentrating in a corrupt Parliament. New York's local clash between insiders and outsiders seemed to be part of a larger conflict throughout the English-speaking world about power, speech, and rights.

The governor fought back, and he had a powerful weapon. According to English law at the time, printing a statement that was damaging to authority—for example, claiming that the governor was taking bribes left and right—was sufficient to send someone to jail. It did not matter at all whether or not what you said was true, just whether it caused harm to those in power. Indeed, if the accusation were true, it would be more likely to be believed and more harmful to the reputation of the regime: more of a crime.

From the point of view of the law, social harmony in which those in power are owed respect was paramount. Undermining the respect owed to the king, his ministers, and his appointees by exposing their crimes was not good journalism; it was criminal. Even today, when presidents and other powerful politicians attack critical journalists as purveyors of "fake news," they are making a similar argument: "I am in power; the press owes me allegiance. To question me is to cross me." At times, President Trump treated criticism of him as something close to treason. Honesty does not matter, only loyalty. A similar view is why umpires can toss players or managers out of a baseball game if they question ball and strike calls. Respect for the umpire's authority matters more than whether the call was correct. An issue that arises daily in the twenty-first century was fought out in New York in the 1730s.

James De Lancey, the chief justice of New York, was a perfect example of the "in" group. A member of one of the city's most powerful French Protestant (Huguenot) families that was linked by marriage to even more established Dutch and English clans, he owed his job to Cosby. One hand washed the other. De Lancey decreed that four editions of the *Weekly Journal*, containing offensive songs, should be burned by the city's hangman, as if the newspaper itself were a criminal. Zenger was arrested for "seditious libel"—that is, harming the governor in print—and jailed in city hall.

For eight months, Zenger sat in his prison cell. Finally, the trial date arrived—a trial in which he would surely be convicted: not only did his case perfectly match the existing libel laws, but De Lancey removed Zenger's lawyers (who were, truth to tell, the original backers of his newspaper) and appointed a lawyer who was on Cosby's side.

Law, lawyer, and judge were perfectly aligned—Zenger had no chance. But Zenger's team had hired an advocate of their own, Alexander Hamilton of Philadelphia (no relation to the subject of a later Broadway musical), the best lawyer in America. While the trial seemed to have been decided before it began, Hamilton realized that there was a flaw in the administration's plan. This was a jury trial: he could speak to twelve New Yorkers, not the laws of distant England. In court, Hamilton offered a bet: prove that Zenger's accusations of Cosby were false, and the lawyer would admit they were libelous. Then he upped the ante: he'd save the government that chore—just let him prove that Zenger's words were true. The issue, Hamilton was arguing, was not what the law called "libel" but truth itself.

Following the law as written, Justice De Lancey ruled that truth could not

This drawing re-creates Hamilton's defense of Zenger.

be considered in the trial. Once again Zenger seemed to have no hope. But Hamilton had been playing a different game all along. A jury, he now explicitly reminded the twelve men, is called because they are assumed to have local knowledge—to be aware of what is likely or unlikely where they live. So, he asked, "you . . . citizens of New York . . . honest and lawful men": Was the paper Zenger published "false, scandalous and seditious"? If libel was anything that could be seen to harm a public person, "how must a man speak or write, or what must he hear, read, or sing? Or when must he laugh, so as to be secure from being taken up as a libeler?"

The trial was drawing to a close, and Hamilton now linked it to the kinds of essays about law and rights that were being published in journals and discussed in coffeehouses. He argued that as "wise men (who value freedom)," they must use "utmost care to support liberty, the only bulwark against lawless power." He did not expressly say that a free press is a necessary form of liberty—as the First Amendment to the United States Constitution would later insist. But he was raising a similar argument.

De Lancey dismissed everything Hamilton said and returned to the basic case: Zenger printed material that fit the definition of libel. He then turned the case to the jury. As Zenger's printed version of the court record accounts, the jury did not take long to give their verdict: "The jury . . . answered by Thomas Hunt, their foreman, *Not Guilty*, upon which there were three huzzas in the hall which was crowded with people." Every time De Lancey had overruled Hamilton on matters of law, Hamilton had been winning the case. He'd been speaking to the jury, not the judge. And they'd listened.

To be fair, Zenger and his supporters were merely the "out" party in local political strife—not necessarily any more interested in a truth-telling press than their opponents. Hamilton did not change the law; he just won a case. The First Amendment to the Constitution was still sixty years and a revolution away, and English libel law did not change to allow truth as a defense until the 1800s. But in Hamilton's victory you can see hints of the issues leading America toward independence: a fear of great power concentrated in hands that were above criticism, a trust in local knowledge, a dawning sense that there were rights that went beyond current law or custom. In the dirty fights for power in moneymaking New York, there was a glint of the right to speak the truth—if you were white.

SLAVERY

How many fires does it take to signal a plot? Or is it not just how many, but where? The first fire in March 1741 came on a Wednesday night in New York's fort while most of the soldiers were sleeping off the previous day's celebration of St. Patrick. The governor's house and those near it went up in flames. The second came exactly one week later—at the home of the brother-in-law of Chief Justice De Lancey, who had run the Zenger trial seven years earlier—though the fire was contained. Right on cue, on April 1 (the third consecutive Wednesday), a warehouse near the East River was consumed by flames. Two more fires in different parts of the city started later that week, hot coals were found under a haystack on April 5, and four more fires broke out on April 6. What was going on? What was behind this rash of burning buildings?

A slave was seen running away from one of the fires on the sixth—and white New Yorkers were convinced he'd set it. Could he have been involved in the others? Was this the start of a slave rebellion? Or even part of a larger plot? Damaging the city's fort could be the first step in letting the French in Canada or the Spanish down in the Caribbean sail in and take over. Daniel Horsmanden, a lawyer and ally of the now-deceased Governor Cosby, was given the charge to run the grand jury called to identify the culprits. This was a perfect assignment for Horsmanden, a lawyer from England hustling for work in New York— if he could not find a rich widow to marry. The bigger the conspiracy, the more important he would be.

Cuffee, the enslaved man who had been caught near the fire, was already in prison, as were a larger group of enslaved people who had been rounded up on general suspicion. One had been heard shouting, "Fire, Fire, Scorch, Scorch," as if he were enjoying the destruction and urging on the flames. The investigation, though, began in a different and revealing fashion. The grand jury set out to find white people who sold alcohol to the enslaved. The implication—which continued throughout the trials—was that if there was a rebellion afoot, it must have been led by white people; it could not have come solely from angry slaves. But there was also a reverse truth hidden in that assumption: everyone knew that white people and Black people were in contact, were not merely defined by status and color but were, at the very edges of New York, coming together.

That is exactly what the jury heard about the white tavern keeper John Hughson. He not only served Black people, but rented a room to a white woman named Peggy and the child she had with an enslaved man who managed to pay for her stay. Even before the first fire, Hughson had been taken to court for being a fence: receiving goods that slaves stole and reselling them. Caesar and Prince, who sold the stolen goods to him, were said to hold meetings where they pretended to be Freemasons—a real secret society to which people such as George Washington and Benjamin Franklin belonged. Were they having fun imitating the silly rituals of their owners, or were they conducting more ominous rites of their own? Rumor had it that Hughson himself had urged the two to "burn the houses of them that have the most money, and kill them all."

What was going on at Hughson's place?

Indentured servants were not enslaved, but they had very few rights until they paid off or served a term of a set amount of years. The court offered Hughson's indentured servant Mary Burton an end to her indenture if she would tell all she knew. She talked about the stolen goods sales but had nothing to say about fires, until she was threatened with prison. Then she claimed she had heard Hughson and several slaves plotting the fire in the fort. Caesar and Prince were convicted of theft and hanged. Peggy, Hughson's tenant, saw that she was in danger and began to confess, as did some of the slaves being held in the city hall jail.

Two enslaved people were quickly convicted of plotting the fire and were condemned to be burned at the stake. Facing that horrible death, they offered

confessions and named others—
which, in the end, did not change their
fate. Being burned alive was reserved
for slaves, so Hughson and Peggy were
hung. The pace of accusation and trial
now quickened as one enslaved person
after another understood: Confess and
name names and you will be hanged.
Resist and you will have a slow, painful death in the flames.

Horsmanden saw further proof
of the necessity and righteousness
of his cause in every new convic-
tion. But as the alleged conspiracy
seemed to become larger and larger,
he grew certain that it was part of a
grand scheme orchestrated by a white
person of far more influence than
Hughson (and certainly not a woman
like Peggy), and for global not local

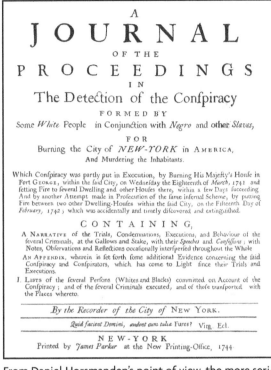

From Daniel Horsmanden's point of view, the more serious the "conspiracy" in New York, and the more people
he convicted, the more important he would be.

reasons. Which white people would want to destroy English New York? To
Horsmanden, the answer seemed obvious: Catholics. John Ury, a music teacher
who had just shown up in town, was rumored to be a priest in disguise. Here,
here was the key to it all—the devil behind all the evils. Ury was quickly tried and
hanged. As the executions sped by, four whites and seventeen Black people were
hanged, thirteen enslaved people were burned, and seventy-two white people
were exiled from New York. Thirty-four deaths.

"I am a stranger to you" began the anonymous letter received by a high official that summer. Apparently a Bostonian, this outsider was moved to write as
he read about the burning of enslaved people. These "horrible executions among
you upon this occasion puts me in mind of our New England Witchcraft in the
year 1692." Naming other people could spare an enslaved person the fire, but the

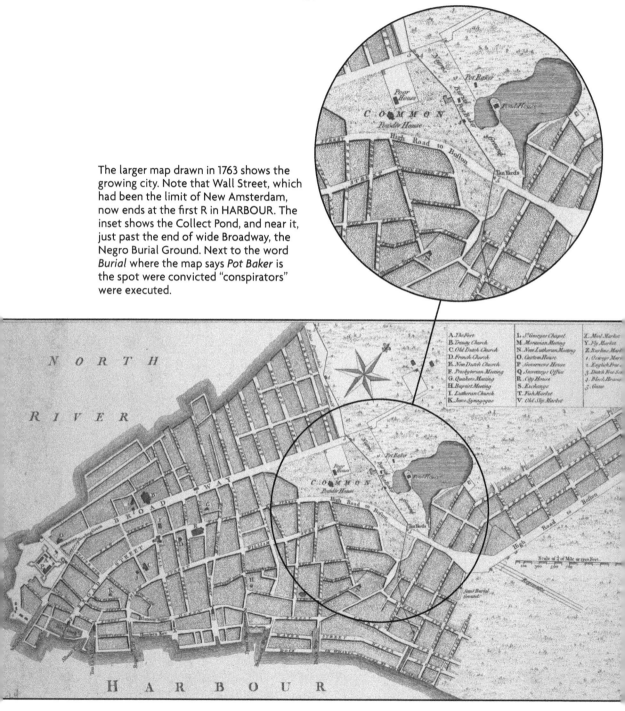

The larger map drawn in 1763 shows the growing city. Note that Wall Street, which had been the limit of New Amsterdam, now ends at the first R in HARBOUR. The inset shows the Collect Pond, and near it, just past the end of wide Broadway, the Negro Burial Ground. Next to the word *Burial* where the map says *Pot Baker* is the spot were convicted "conspirators" were executed.

court would neither hear nor weigh anything a slave said against a white person. Enslaved people could only testify in court against other enslaved people, and indeed, much of the evidence that sent slaves to their death came solely from fellow slaves. The Bostonian thought that such evidence was as dubious as the spirits that were said to have been flying around the courthouse in Salem's famous witch trials. "It makes me suspect that your present case, & ours heretofore are much the same and that Negro & Spectre evidence will turn out alike." After all, "any body would chuse rather to be hanged than to be burnt." The letter writer suspected that the New York trials would end when elites were named.

Maybe the Bostonian was right. As Mary Burton, Hughson's former indentured servant, kept adding to her story, she indicated that "some people in ruffles" (wealthy, important) had been in on the plotting at Hughson's tavern. No one pursued that idea, and the trials did indeed come to a close.

The fires stopped. But what had actually happened back in March and April? Were slaves conspiring? Were low-level thieves setting fires to hide evidence or distract attention? Were slaves holding dark ceremonies, or having a bit of fun imitating and mocking their masters? Was the angry talk of "Fire, Fire" or "kill them all" a sign of frustration and resentment, or an actual incitement to murder? A history written in 1827 thought that "hostility to the Catholic religion" biased the judge in a fashion "very unfriendly to the fair development of truth." In the 1960s, though, some historians came to think that an important rebellion of the enslaved really did take place in 1741. Today, most authorities agree that we cannot know why each fire started. We do know that as the trials went on, some people did not trust the court or believe the fatal confessions. New York City had become another Salem, Massachusetts—but in Salem supposed witches were hanged, while in New York enslaved people were burned.

During his trial at city hall, John Hughson spoke of hatred of "them that have the most money"—the elite symbolized by Trinity Church at the other end of Wall Street from the Meal Market. From Leisler's clash with the city's grandees down to grumbling in taverns, signs of a growing chasm between rich and poor accompanied New York's increasing wealth and trade. As Mary Burton sent one enslaved person after another to a gruesome death, she described the grind at the bottom of the city's social scale: the poorest whites, some of them immigrants from Ireland, scraping by to rise, or not fall, by turning against Black people who had even less. New York, the city of finance where experts exchanged one form of money for another, rested on an explosive base of the poor, the indentured, the enslaved. And yet even at that volatile touch point of the desperate, there was the interracial couple. Black and white people were meeting, having children, starting families. The city could not stand still: one person, one group was always pressing against another, creating friction and contact. And it was all there to be found in the buildings, and trials, of Wall Street.

The next act in the drama of freedom and slavery again unfolded in city hall and farther along Wall Street, closer to the docks.

CHAPTER 5

Revolution

TWO SIDES OF A CITY IN FERMENT

War was good for New York City in the 1700s, and from 1740 on, England and France battled almost continuously in Europe, in India, in Africa, and especially in North America and the Caribbean. The more British ships that needed to be provisioned and loaded, the more soldiers and sailors requiring equipment, the better for New York. And when the conflict flared in the Caribbean, there was an extra road to riches for an enterprising white man. Just as in the days of Captain Kidd, he could buy a ship, call himself a privateer, attack French vessels sailing among the islands, and take home prizes. Between 1756 and 1763, when this Anglo-French conflict spanned the globe, 128 privateers hauled eighty captured ships worth 1 million British pounds (more than 220 million modern American dollars) into New York's port. Fortune-hunting privateers were no longer pillars of society, as Kidd had been, but they could arrive in the city with little more than will and determination and make money, as did Isaac Sears from Connecticut, where his father gathered oysters, and Alexander McDougall, fresh off the boat from Scotland.

Sears and McDougall were assertive, outspoken leaders and soon found men of similar temperament. By the mid-1760s, the new "senseless people"—workers who did not take kindly to orders from England or from the New York grandees of their time—called themselves the Sons of Liberty. Groups with a similar name were forming in all the colonies and sharing ideas in letters.

Parliament and King George III had imposed a "stamp tax" on the colonies—the colonists now had to purchase a new stamp to place on any legal document or even newspaper. The tax itself was not so high that it was difficult to pay. Indeed, the leaders of the colonies all agreed that if Parliament simply came to the legislatures of each colony and asked them to raise a certain sum of money, that would be fine. The issue was not money. It was freedom and slavery.

As the colonists saw it, if England could tax them without giving them any voice or vote, they were like helpless children or, worse, like people powerless to help themselves: slaves. Patrick Henry in Virginia was the first to object to the tax. James Otis in Massachusetts joined him, and he suggested that representatives from all the colonies meet in New York. Philadelphia was a larger city, but the meeting was set for New York. In October 1765, twenty-seven men from nine colonies arrived in the city (in four colonies, governors wary of the meeting did not allow a delegation to be selected). The representatives met at city hall—and around town. As the clock neared four, they would retire to convenient taverns to continue their discussions, eat what was then called "dinner," and hammer out positions. Those informal meetings were as important as any of the resolutions they managed to pass; the Stamp Act Congress, as this assembly was called, was only the second time in the entire history of British North America that the separate colonies had met together (the first had been arranged by Benjamin Franklin in 1754 as the Seven Years' War loomed). The tavern discussions, like the Sons of Liberty letters, gave people who lived in colonies with distinct laws and traditions a dawning sense of being part of something larger. They were not just transplanted Europeans living in far-flung locations. Together they might be something else: Americans.

New York fosters mixture—and clash. Led by Sears and McDougall, the Sons of Liberty were not interested in formulating well-crafted and respectful petitions to beg humble consideration from Parliament. They would force change with their fists and fury.

On October 23, the *Edward* landed in New York carrying boxes of stamps. Two thousand enraged New Yorkers were there to meet the ship, howling against the loss of liberty that the tax represented. When night fell, sailors snuck seven boxes of stamps off the ship and hurried them into the nearby fort. Once word got out, posters began appearing around town warning everyone against using the stamps: "The first man that either distributes or makes use of stamped paper, let him take care of his house, person and effects. We dare." The posters were signed "Vox Populi"—the voice of the people. The angry, violent crowd of people, that is—not the elegant delegates of the Stamp Act Congress still debating at city hall.

Wall Street embodied the stable, moderate side of the modernizing city. Indeed, in 1762, streetlights were set up in town, the pillory in front of city hall was dismantled, and the Meal Market was closed down. When the market was in its prime, though, a coffee shop opened up right next to it as a place for captains and traders to gather. By the 1750s, the Merchants Coffee House was one of the most popular spots in New York and a gathering place for those impatient for change. If you wanted news straight from ships landing in the city, or, equally, if you wanted to stage a protest to send a message to town leaders, the Merchants Coffee House was the place to go.

The Merchants Coffee House, near the Meal Market and the docks, was a true center of New York in the period leading up to the revolution. This image is from the Frederick Hill history of Wall Street.

Crafted speeches and angry mobs were not the only possible methods of opposing the stamps. On October 31, some key New Yorkers suggested a new way to fight back. After talking it over at the Merchants Coffee House, they decided that they would stop buying goods from England. The *New York Gazette* announced a policy of nonimportation: "It is better to wear a homespun coat than lose our liberty." Instead of buying imported fabrics, local women could weave their own. Some two hundred merchants agreed to boycott English imports. As businessmen, they expected that Parliament would listen to economic reason, even if it ignored protests about liberty and freedom. This American innovation—fighting a hated policy by choosing what you buy or don't buy—has the great advantage that it allows everyone, women, children, even enslaved people, to make a difference. Politicians can say what they want, but everyone with a coin can vote with what they decide to boycott or to buy.

The next day, the Stamp Act went into effect. The city mourned: ships flew their flags at half-mast; buildings were hung with black fabric; at the Merchants Coffee House, game boards were similarly clothed in black. The city was treating the new law as the death of freedom. Daylight hours ticked by; the city stood ominously silent. Then came night and time for the crowd, the mob, to speak.

Near the fort at the foot of Manhattan, the Sons of Liberty built an effigy of New York's lieutenant governor, Cadwallader Colden—the one official in the colony who was determined to enforce the Stamp Act. His image, and one of the devil set beside him, went up in flames. Rattling cowbells and screaming, the men ran down and menaced the fort, then burned Colden's expensive coach. One group of some three hundred men peeled off to pillage and burn the possessions of a British officer who had threatened to "cram the Stamps down their throats." New York was on the edge of turning from riot to revolution.

A poster tacked up at the Merchants Coffee House called for a direct attack on the fort on November 5. Colden stalled for time, holding off enforcement of the Stamp Act until a newly appointed governor arrived. And indeed, Sir Henry Moore, fresh from his post in Jamaica, managed to cool tempers on all sides. The crisis passed.

As 1765 limped to an end, there were two different revolutions brewing in the city. At city hall, the Stamp Act Congress had begun linking the colonies together and creating a sense of shared legal principles, especially among the wealthy, educated, white elite: New York as center of connection. On the streets and down at the Merchants Coffee House, sailors, artisans, and laborers were finding their own sense of community and voice in rage, violence, and shared fury: New York as center of conflict.

For the moment, elites, mobs, and women spinning cloth shared a common purpose in opposing Parliament. But there were those among the grandees who feared the crowds more than the crown, and those among massed men whose anger could easily leap from English laws to Catholics to the rich. And unheard in the protests were women, enslaved people, and free people of color who had to calculate what all this ferment would mean for them.

This image of a pro-British Tory being mocked and assailed by a crowd of colonists was once seen as a sign of the New Yorkers' unquenchable passion for liberty. It is that, but it also shows the turn to vigilante mob violence that is a more disturbing strand in American history, up to the present day.

FROM PROTEST TO WAR

The Stamp Act protests and nonimportation plan worked—sort of. Urged by minister William Pitt (whose name is honored in the city of Pittsburgh), Parliament rescinded the Stamp Tax. New Yorkers celebrated by building a statue of Pitt and giving it a place of honor on Wall Street. But Pitt and Parliament only agreed to eliminate this one tax. At the same time, they passed a law asserting that they had the power to tax the colonies as they saw fit. Tensions continued to rise, and 1770 saw the first true armed clashes of the revolution, starting on January 19, 1770, when an angry crowd of New Yorkers fought hand to hand with British troops in the Battle of Golden Hill, six weeks before the now better-known "massacre" in Boston. Soon enough, Parliament passed new taxes, this time on

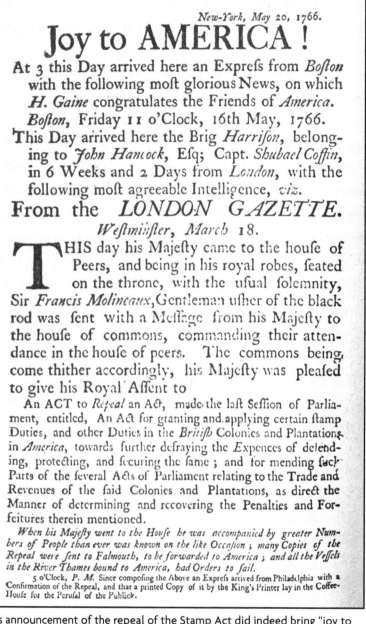

New-York, May 20, 1766.

Joy to AMERICA !

At 3 this Day arrived here an Exprefs from *Bofton* with the following moft glorious News, on which *H. Gaine* congratulates the Friends of *America*. *Bofton*, Friday 11 o'Clock, 16th May, 1766.

This Day arrived here the Brig *Harrifon*, belonging to *John Hancock*, Efq; Capt. *Shubael Coffin*, in 6 Weeks and 2 Days from *London*, with the following moft agreeable Intelligence, *viz.*

From the *LONDON GAZETTE.*

Weftminfter, March 18.

THIS day his Majefty came to the houfe of Peers, and being in his royal robes, feated on the throne, with the ufual folemnity, Sir *Francis Molineaux*, Gentleman ufher of the black rod was fent with a Meffage from his Majefty to the houfe of commons, commanding their attendance in the houfe of peers. The commons being, come thither accordingly, his Majefty was pleafed to give his Royal Affent to

An ACT to *Repeal* an Act, made the laft Seffion of Parliament, entitled, An Act for granting and applying certain ftamp Duties, and other Duties in the *Britifh* Colonies and Plantations, in *America*, towards further defraying the *Expences* of defending, protecting, and fecuring the fame ; and for mending fuch Parts of the feveral Acts of Parliament relating to the Trade and Revenues of the faid Colonies and Plantations, as direct the Manner of determining and recovering the Penalties and Forfeitures therein mentioned.

When his Majefty went to the Houfe he was accompanied by greater Numbers of People than ever was known on the like Occafion ; many Copies of the Repeal were fent to Falmouth, to be forwarded to America ; and all the Veffels in the River Thames bound to America, had Orders to fail.

5 o'Clock, *P. M.* Since compofing the Above an Exprefs arrived from Philadelphia with a Confirmation of the Repeal, and that a printed Copy of it by the King's Printer lay in the Coffee-Houfe for the Perufal of the Publick.

This announcement of the repeal of the Stamp Act did indeed bring "joy to Americans." But at the same time the British government insisted on its right to declare other taxes when it chose to do so—which would eventually lead to war.

tea. By September 1773, ships filled with a half million pounds of the leaves were on their way to Boston, New York, and down the coast. Drink that tea and the colonists would be accepting the very principle that they saw as the essence of subjugation: taxation without representation.

The Boston Tea Party in December 1773 may be more famous, but New York was equally determined to reject the tea. In April 1774, an angry crowd met in front of the Merchants Coffee House. The captain of one tea-carrying ship met the Sons of Liberty at the same coffeehouse, where he was warned that "for the safety of your cargo, your vessel, and your persons," it would be wise to turn back and go home. He did. A second ship landed, and, just as in Boston, mildly disguised colonists dumped its tea into the water.

King George decided to punish the colonists, and by 1775, a conflict between motherland and its rebellious children seemed inevitable. That April, New Yorkers gathered—as one would by now expect—at the Coffee House (still in the same spot, now with a slightly different name) to get word about the initial battles in Lexington and Concord, Massachusetts. Come summer, as the city awaited the arrival of George Washington, general of the newly created Continental Army, a committee first of sixty men and later one hundred ran the city from inside the Coffee House. Outside, New York's angry crowds roiled, surged, and made demands.

NEW YORK LOST

New York played a central role in the American Revolution—but not in the way that either the British or the Americans expected. The British thought it would be the most important spot to conquer. European wars were won when one side captured the other's capital city, which made Philadelphia and New York key objectives. With control of New York's port and the Hudson River link to Canada, the king's men thought they would have an easy time of crushing the rebellion. John Adams agreed—he believed that the city was "a kind of key to the whole continent"—and George Washington made defending the city his great stand to hold off the invading enemy. The largest single battle of the war was the aptly named Battle of Brooklyn. There, General Washington made the crucial strategic discovery that would save his cause: he could win by losing—or at least by not fighting.

Washington had somewhere between 13,500 and 23,000 men with him, depending on how many deserted, finished their enrollment, or signed up. By August 1776, the British had 32,000 soldiers and 10,000 sailors and marines assembled in Staten Island, the largest European overseas armed force ever assembled.

Starting on August 26, the well-trained British forces raced across Long Island, defeating Washington's men all along the way and trapping his army in Brooklyn. With the British at their back and the East River looming in front of them, the Americans could not retreat. Washington had already lost some 1,200 men in the day's fighting. If the British—who had come through almost unscathed—charged, the Americans would surely be forced to surrender.

But the British hesitated.

According to one story, Native Americans helped Washington by calling out their war cries, which set dogs barking and disguised the sound of marching men. Then, under cover of night, Washington was able to ferry his troops to Manhattan. The Americans had lost, badly, but they had not been forced to surrender. That would be the key to the entire war: so long as Washington's forces could avoid major clashes but keep fighting, the British would have to keep chasing them. And every so often, the Americans could steal a victory—and raise their spirits. That would first happen in Harlem.

Washington's army was safe in Manhattan, but demoralized, injured, and in disarray. Six thousand of his men who lived in nearby Connecticut simply went home. The Americans retreated north, up the island, while the British followed them across the river. Frightened, the Americans began running hither and yon. Near what is now Forty-Second Street, Washington saw his men "flying in every direction and in the greatest confusion." Furious, he screamed, "Good God! Have I got such troops as those?" He had to be led away—to make sure he was not captured. Guided by calm officers such as Lieutenant Aaron Burr, the army headed north, reaching Harlem Heights. The British trailed behind.

On September 16, small units of the two armies clashed on a farm near what is now 106th Street and West End Avenue, and the Americans slipped away

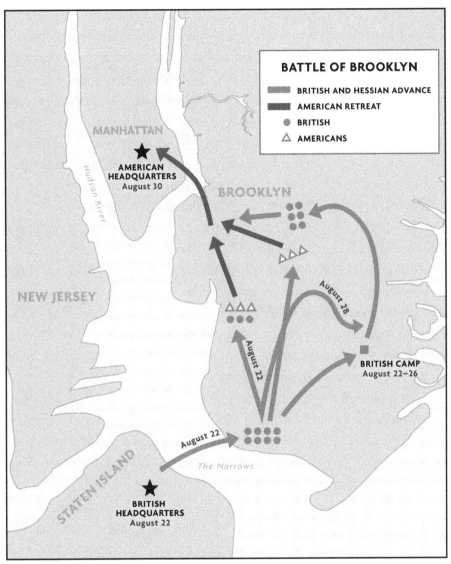

BATTLE OF BROOKLYN

▬ BRITISH AND HESSIAN ADVANCE
▬ AMERICAN RETREAT
● BRITISH
△ AMERICANS

MANHATTAN

AMERICAN
HEADQUARTERS
August 30

Hudson River

BROOKLYN

NEW JERSEY

August 28

August 22

BRITISH CAMP
August 22–26

August 22

The Narrows

STATEN ISLAND

BRITISH
HEADQUARTERS
August 22

George Washington hoped to block the large British and Hessian army in Brooklyn, but he left one path largely unguarded. On the night of August 26 and into the following morning, fourteen thousand British soldiers swept past the five American defenders. By late afternoon, the British had total victory. But Washington and his men managed to escape to Manhattan and New Jersey, to fight another day.

again, near to 125th Street. The contemptuous British sounded the horn for a fox hunt—as if their enemies were mere prey—and gave chase. This was the ultimate insult, especially for fox-hunting Virginians like Washington. The Americans' unit, though, was now close to their main force, and Washington agreed to counterattack. Instead of gleefully pursuing weak Americans, the British unit was suddenly at bay. In two hours of fighting, the British lost fourteen men and had to retreat. As Joseph Reed, one of Washington's aides, wrote to his wife, "You can hardly conceive the change it has made in our army. The men have recovered their spirits and feel a confidence which before they had quite lost."

Battles in New York left the Americans defeated but able to retreat to fight another day. The skirmish in Harlem had given them a model—quick attacks, sneak attacks, could raise morale and hurt the enemy. The British victory in Brooklyn made New York a Tory town—the capital of Loyalist America. British soldiers showed their views by chopping the head and arms off of the likeness of William Pitt—the Parliamentarian who had defended the colonies—leaving the statue on Wall Street mutilated. British New York suited wealthy New Yorkers such as Oliver De Lancey and William Bayard, who had never been happy about the push toward independence. The grandees won; the "mob" was silenced.

In a pattern that would continue into the next century, the rule of a pro-British elite offered some benefits for African Americans. In order to undermine their enemies, the British military offered freedom to any enslaved man who ran away and joined them—though the freedom the British offered was a wartime strategy, not a rejection of slavery. They continued to hold slave auctions and did not free the enslaved of Loyalist Americans. Indeed, throughout the war, more African Americans chose to fight for the new nation than for the king. Still, in British New York, free African Americans were known to attend "Ethiopian Balls" where they conversed with British officers—to the horror of the rebelling colonists. As enslaved people slipped away to freedom in New York—including some previously in service to Patrick Henry and George Washington—it became a more African American city. So long, that is, as it remained British.

There was a perfect weapon the Americans could use against British New York—the very one that had caused so much fear in the 1741 slave trials: fire.

This engraving of the city in flames was created close to the time of the event by Franz Xaver Habermann, a German artist.

Washington considered, but rejected, a plan to burn the city—and then an accident (or conspiracy, though current evidence favors chance) set the city aflame on September 21, 1776. The fire started near the tip of Manhattan, then spread through wooden buildings along the west side. Trinity Church was topped by a wooden steeple. When flames reached the steeple, it looked like "a vast pyramid of fire," and in just a few minutes the church was destroyed. By the time the fire burned out, one hundred buildings, fully a quarter of the homes in the city, were gone.

Loyalists in New York who cast their lot with the British remained to dance and dine with British officers in the charred city, and profit from supplying an army. African Americans had to decide whether to accept freedom from the calculating British or remain enslaved to Americans who claimed their own cause was freedom. New York had been the prize at the start of the war, but then sat on the sidelines until it was over.

SNAPSHOT

New York and Independence

During the Revolutionary War, the city's population declines from 25,000 to 12,000. Somewhere between 4,000 and 11,000 American prisoners die while held captive by the British in the city.

1784 The first boat sets off from the city for China; the *Empress of China* brings a 25 percent profit for investors.

1786 Society of St. Tammany created; first Roman Catholic church in the city opens.

1789 George Washington inaugurated at Federal Hall; New York is national capital.

1790 First United States Census. Manhattan's population: 33,121, 10 percent of African descent. Kings County's population: 4,494, 33 percent of African descent. Richmond County's (Staten Island) population: 3,835, 23 percent of African descent. The population of the areas that will later form Greater New York (Manhattan, Brooklyn, Queens, the Bronx, and Staten Island) is 49,401.

National capital moved to Philadelphia (and then, a decade later, to Washington, DC).

1792 Agreement that will create the New York Stock Exchange signed.

1795 Yellow fever sends people to Greenwich.

1796 First African American church opens.

1797 New York port surpasses Philadelphia in volume of imports and exports.

1800 The population of the areas that will later form Greater New York is 79,216. Manhattan's population: 60,515, 10 percent (6,382) of African descent and 2,868 enslaved. Kings County's population: 5,740, 1,811 of African descent. Richmond County's (Staten Island) population: 4,564, 758 of African descent. New York's total population is about 10 percent of London's 880,000, similar to Lima or Liverpool.

There are now more than forty docks on the East River and just more than ten on the Hudson.

1804 Hamilton-Burr duel.

1806 125th Street surveyed and laid out.

1809 Washington Irving's history of the city, in the voice of Diedrich Knickerbocker, is published.

1810 Manhattan's population: 96,373, 10 percent (9,823) of African descent and 1,686 enslaved. Manhattan surpasses Philadelphia as the most populous city in the nation. The population of the areas that will later form Greater New York is 119,734.

1811 The plan for the grid of streets and avenues in Manhattan is approved.

1814 Steam ferry shuttling between Manhattan and Brooklyn begins service.

1817 New York Stock & Exchange opens at 40 Wall Street (name changed in 1863).

CHAPTER 6

Capital

THE FIRST TRIUMPH—EVACUATION DAY, NOVEMBER 25, 1783

"In this place, and at this moment of exultation and triumph, while the Ensigns of Slavery still linger in our sight, we look up to you, our deliverer." With these words, the victorious General George Washington, pausing at Cape's Tavern on Broadway and Wall Street, was welcomed back to New York. Standing beside Washington was General George Clinton, governor of New York State, with his young nephew De Witt cheering from the sidelines. In careful ranks just ahead of them, the British army (the "Ensigns of Slavery") departed. For the next hundred years, Evacuation Day was an official holiday in the city—the moment of transition and liberation, for some.

The British, and the Great Fire of 1776, left behind a devastated city of ghosts. As a returning patriot noticed, once-proud Trinity Church was a "ghastly" shell, as dead as the "surrounding graves." Fragments of buildings created "grim shadows," giving streets an "unearthly aspect." Homes that soldiers had used as living quarters looked "as if they had been inhabited by savages or wild beasts." Angry rebels entering the ravaged city hunted for lingering enemies. They wanted their homes back and rent money for the time they had been occupied by British troops. American prisoners had been crammed into prison ships and Livingston's Sugar House, where they were starved and left to die from disease, abuse, and neglect. Somewhere between four thousand and eleven thousand prisoners lost their lives. Their friends and relatives clamored for revenge.

Loyalists who had reveled in the British occupation during the war were terrified. By Evacuation Day, some forty thousand Loyalists—from nearby areas as well as the city itself—had boarded ships in New York and left to start new lives in Canada or England.

"I am totally ruined," lamented William Bayard as he prepared to sail off to England. The De Lanceys—long one of the most influential families in the colony—realized they would lose their vast real estate holdings along the East River.

As the Loyalists fled, the Sons of Liberty saw their moment. A political party of "mechanics" (workers) swept the elections in December and demanded that any Loyalists who remained in the city lose their right to vote, and even to engage in "trade and commerce." The people were hungry to turn the tables on the grandees, but what of those the Loyalists had protected?

About four thousand departing people, one-tenth of the total civilian evacuation, were African Americans—many of whom had escaped to the city to take up the British offer of freedom. Washington was but one of many slaveholders who came to New York and demanded that what he considered his property be returned to him. Guy Carleton, the British general who was turning the city over to the rebels, refused. He felt honor bound to respect the deal made during the war. From the point of view of Washington's triumphant army, the British soldiers were "ensigns of slavery." From the point of view of African Americans, slaveholders were retaking control. For the next hundred and twenty years, New York City would become less and less African American and more and more white. Within the city, radical groups such as the "mechanics" were made up of white workers. White advocates for African American rights tended to be elites. Greater voice for white workers meant less support for African Americans. This tension would run through the entire history of the city.

By 1784, a timeline for abolishing slavery was adopted by all of New York State's neighbors except New Jersey. The following year, abolitionists met in New York City—yet again at the Merchants Coffee House. Some of the most prominent people in the state were there, including Alexander Hamilton, Governor Clinton, the city's mayor, and John Jay, a close associate of General Washington's. The group's efforts to free enslaved people and protect those still in bondage from

New-York, Nov. 24, 1783.

The Committee appointed to conduct the Order of receiving their Excellencies Governor CLINTON and General WASHINGTON,

BEG Leave to inform their Fellow-Citizens, that the Troops, under the Command of Major-General KNOX, will take Poſſeſſion of the City at the Hour agreed on, Tueſday next ; as ſoon as this may be performed, he will requeſt the Citizens who may be aſſembled on Horſeback, at the Bowling-Green, the lower End of the Broad-Way, to accompany him to meet their Excellencies Governor CLINTON and General WASHINGTON, at the Bull's Head, in the Bowery---the Citizens on Foot to aſſemble at or near the Tea-water-Pump at Freſh-water.

ORDER OF PROCESSION.

A Party of Horſe will precede their Excellencies and be on their flanks---after the General and Governor, will follow the Lieutenant-Governor and Members of the Council for the temporary Government of the Southern Parts of the State---The Gentlemen on Horſe-back, eight in Front---thoſe on Foot, in the Rear of the Horſe, in like Manner.   Their Excellencies, after paſſing down Queen-Street, and the Line of Troops up the Broadway, will a-light at CAPE'S Tavern.

The Committee hope to ſee their Fellow-Citizens, conduct themſelves with Decency and Decorum on this joyful Occaſion.

CITIZENS TAKE CARE!!!

THE Inhabitants are hereby informed, that Permiſſion has been obtained from the Commandant, to form themſelves in patroles this night, and that every order requiſite will be given to the guards, as well to aid and aſſiſt, as to give protection to the patroles : And that the counterſign will be given to THOMAS TUCKER, No. 51, Water Street, from whom it can be obtained, if neceſſary.

This official proclamation informed New Yorkers where General Washington would land and how he would progress through the city. Note the mention of the "tea-water pump" at the end of the first paragraph. Fresh water would soon become an issue in Manhattan.

abuse were slow to gain traction, but by 1790 one-third of the Black people in New York City were free. And in 1799, New York State ruled that children born after July 4 would be free once they reached adulthood.

A few free Black families managed to hold on to the "Negro Farms" they had been granted back in Dutch times outside of the old wall, near a stream called Minetta (apparently an English version of the Dutch *mintje kill*, or "tiny stream") that ran to the Hudson. But exercising the right to land meant having to be able to pay taxes and upkeep on it. And that was difficult, as the jobs open to free Black people were very limited.

Demonstrating an early version of its endless ability to regenerate, New York quickly got back on its feet. Within two years of Evacuation Day, its population doubled as Americans exiled during the war returned and were joined by people eager to rise with the new nation. Two young lawyers—Aaron Burr and Alexander Hamilton—found homes on Wall Street with their families and set about seeking clients. Siding with the more radical workers, Burr favored confiscating some of the Loyalist properties and selling them off. Siding with the wealthy, Hamilton argued that letting old Loyalists vote, build business, even prosper was good for everyone, even workers. The more money in the community and the more buying and selling, the better. As he defended their rights, Hamilton also convinced wealthy people who distrusted and disliked the new nation to help shape it, rather than plot to make it fail. Put profit ahead of vengeance, he preached, and the bustling city listened.

THE SECOND TRIUMPH—INAUGURATION

The thirteen former colonies were free of British rule, but how should they govern themselves? Should there be an executive, a president, and if so, what should that person be called—not His Majesty like a king, surely? What should the nation's money be, and where should it be created? Each former colony had its own currency, and every trading ship brought in English, Spanish, and French coins. How should the government itself be organized, and where would it meet? Where was the nation's capital?

Initially, the states created Articles of Confederation, which left them as largely separate entities, but by September 1788 a new constitution was written and adopted, bringing the United States together under a central government. Under the new constitution, George Washington was elected as the nation's first president. He, and Congress, headed for New York City—for the moment, the nation's headquarters. Philadelphia, still the larger city, had proven too dangerous when crowds of soldiers surrounded Congress, demanding back pay for their service during the war. Pierre Charles L'Enfant was asked to redesign city hall as Federal Hall, to be the center of all government. L'Enfant chose a simple, elegant design that harked back to ancient Greece and Rome. The America he envisioned was rational, clear, and democratic—no showy signs of aristocratic wealth and power. Wall Street was about to change from being the most fashionable street in a British city to the center of politics, government, and finance for a new nation. But first it had to welcome the new chief.

In April 1789, Washington traveled north from Virginia via Philadelphia. On the twenty-first, as he crossed the bridge to Trenton, New Jersey, girls dressed in white spread flowers ahead of him. An arch overhead was supported by thirteen columns and read THE DEFENDER OF THE MOTHERS WILL BE THE PROTECTOR OF THE DAUGHTERS, with the dates of important battles that had been fought nearby

First published in 1790, this is the only original image of Washington's inauguration. Historians have noticed that it focuses entirely on the dignitaries, not the watching crowds at street level. The building is a redesigned version of the old city hall, and the link to ancient Greece and Rome seen in the clean, spare look and columns was deliberate.

at Trenton and Princeton. By the twenty-third, he reached Elizabethtown, where a fifty-foot boat rowed by thirteen oarsmen dressed in white waited to deliver him to New York City.

The presidential boat, accompanied by two others filled with singers chanting songs written for the occasion, landed at Wall Street around two in the afternoon. Washington made his way to a rented house to rest. The city had seven more days to prepare for his inauguration.

Inauguration Day was cloudy, which discouraged no one. Celebratory gunfire woke the city that morning, and the streets began to fill early. Boats bringing visitors from nearby states clogged the harbor. Church bells began ringing at nine, calling people to pray for their new president. By twelve thirty, a delegation—including John Adams, who had already been sworn in as vice president—went to meet Washington at his home. Washington had made one symbolic choice of his own—his clothes were made entirely of American cloth from a Connecticut mill.

The one surviving image shows him on the balcony of L'Enfant's redesigned building, surrounded by dignitaries. Missing from the image are the crowds of people that jammed the street below. Missing at the start of the ceremony was a Bible on which Washington could swear to uphold his oath of office. No one had remembered to bring one, so Robert Livingston—who, like Washington, was a Freemason—sent someone to rush over to a local Masonic lodge to pick one up. Standing on top of a classmate's house across the street, Eliza Susan Morton noticed that the Bible rested on a table covered with red velvet. Finally, with everyone, and everything, in place, George Washington swore, "I will faithfully execute the office of the President of the United States and will, to the best of my ability, preserve, protect, and defend the Constitution of the United States." The crowd roared, bells rang out across the city—and it was done. America had its constitution and its president. And, for the moment, its capital city: New York.

CHAPTER 7

Money

Did New York deserve the honor of hosting the nation's government? A busy port town that already featured Federal Hall, it could be seen as a midpoint between the flinty New Englanders and the proud southern slaveholding squires. One plan envisioned turning the tip of Manhattan into a federal district, with a presidential home on nearby Governors Island. But was New York even American at all? A visiting Frenchman thought that "if there is one city on the American continent which above all others displays English luxury, it is New York." Some of the city's wealthiest women were rumored to want to be called "lady," as if they were British aristocrats. Alexander Hamilton disagreed. He thought the city's very wealth and financial power was just what the new nation needed.

Hamilton worked with furious intensity. As the Broadway musical *Hamilton* explains, he didn't want to waste his "shot"—his chance to shape the new nation. Hamilton was convinced that the country needed to prove to potential investors—both at home and overseas—that it was trustworthy. His America was like Hamilton himself: a young immigrant land that needed to demonstrate its worth. He wanted an America like New York City, where money could make the man. This was precisely the opposite of what some other key leaders—such as Thomas Jefferson and James Madison—thought.

Jefferson and Madison, both Virginian slaveholders, wanted an America made up of self-sufficient farmers, who could decide for themselves how to spend their money and use their time. The man himself was more important than his wealth. A strong central government might, for example, impose taxes or abolish slavery. To these founders, America's obligation was to established, independent Americans like themselves. Hadn't America just fought a war to diminish the control of large and distant governments?

Take currency. During the war, the Continental Congress had printed money that no one valued, and so it had taken 167 Continental dollars to buy a dollar's worth of gold. After the war ended, sharp-eyed businessmen had sought out soldiers and offered to pay them for their Continental currency—at a huge discount. They might offer fifteen cents for every Continental dollar. The businessmen were making two bets: the soldiers and their families would be desperate and eager to sell, and the new government would eventually fully fund the Continental bills. One old dollar would be worth one new dollar to the person smart enough—or rich enough—to hold the Continentals until the government made that offer.

To people such as Jefferson and Madison, this was a betrayal of the revolution.

Examples of colonial currency. The variety of images and denominations shows the lack of a single central authority.

The soldiers who'd risked their lives deserved every penny. Speculators deserved nothing. Hamilton saw it differently. It would be too difficult to find every soldier and give him back his money. And a deal was a deal. If you made a bad bargain, that was your decision. To him, the government needed to show all creditors that it would make good on its debts. All debts from the war—whether from individual states or the bills issued by the Continental Congress—should be collected together and paid by the new American national government.

Which should laws favor, people or principle? Individuals who had sacrificed for the nation—and then made bad, or desperate, financial decisions? Or a central government that set rules and played by them, even if that left the wealthy or powerful to reap profits at the expense of those heroes? Hamilton saw Jefferson and Madison as hypocrites. An anonymous article that some historians think he wrote asked, "Who talk most about liberty and equality . . . ? Is it not those who hold the bill of rights in one hand and a whip for affrighted slaves in the other?" The rural slaveholders saw Hamilton as accumulating dangerous—almost royal—power in "Hamiltonopolis," a city of scheming financiers eager to fleece honest, hardworking people.

TRADING THE CAPITAL FOR CAPITAL

Over the course of the spring and summer of 1790, the prospects for Hamilton's debt plan were poor. According to Jefferson, it was in this moment of peril that Hamilton came to his home for a dinner that would reshape the future of New York City—and, in some ways, the country. On the night of June 20, Hamilton, Jefferson, and Madison sat together to eat and talk. Hamilton then made an offer—a swap: if they would agree to his debt plan, he would support their idea to move the nation's capital first from New York to Philadelphia, then, once the site was prepared, to a new location along the Potomac River between Maryland and Virginia. America's government would be planted in the South, the slaveholding South of Jefferson and Madison, near their plantations in Virginia—not the North of businessmen, traders, financiers, and abolitionists. In time, the same L'Enfant who had designed Federal Hall would indeed plan out what is today Washington, DC.

The dinner deal—if we believe Jefferson's account—held. Hamilton's plan passed Congress, and New York lost its chance to be—like London or Paris—the single financial, cultural, and political capital of a nation. In the long run, that may have served New York best, for it could concentrate on what it already did well: making money and telling stories through art and media.

From a modern point of view, it is easy to criticize the southern slaveholders. But Hamilton's side of the compromise equally reflected his limitations, and the proof played out in his beloved New York. The country now had a central bank and an agreement to cover old debts. Down the street from the new central bank, a frenzy of deals was playing out upstairs in the Long Room of the Merchants Coffee House, which, according to Madison, was now "an eternal buzz with gamblers." Hamilton saw danger ahead. He feared the "scriptomania" that was gripping New Yorkers—a mad dash to get in on these new deals. He had reason to worry.

If the magic of New York is the ability to make something out of nothing—to turn opposites and conflicts into creation and new beginnings—it comes in both good and bad versions. For the capital of finance can also be the capital of financial games, where schemers make endless wealth seem to appear and then disappear, taking people's lives and safe savings with it.

One of Hamilton's closest associates was William Duer. Duer was a patriot and known as the most lavish and generous host in town. He was also deep in plots to fool investors and reap millions. "Speculation"—betting that the price of something would soon rise—was on everyone's minds. For some, such as George Washington, buying vast parcels of land was the surest pathway to fortune. For Duer, the golden road lay in the new bank. Duer organized a group of wealthy men to buy and shuffle bank shares in a way that promised to balloon their resale value. The instant the stock they controlled went on sale, everyone scrambled to buy it. "The merchant," one skeptic noticed, "the lawyer, the physician and the mechanic, appear to be equally striving to accumulate large fortunes." New York, and the nation, were experiencing their first stock bubble.

Just as Bankmania grew, and grew, and grew, the government announced that Duer owed $250,000 to the treasury. He had put every cent of his own, plus endless amounts of borrowed money, into his investment schemes. Duer himself owed another $750,000 and had no assets. The total amount of money tied up in the bank speculation was equal to the savings of "almost every person in the city, from the richest merchants to even the poorest women and the little shopkeepers." The proposed bank collapsed before it opened and New York reeled from its first stock market crash. This was exactly what Jefferson and Madison warned about—pieces of paper manipulated by greedy men with back channels to power that destroyed the livelihoods of good, honest farmers.

As New Yorkers nursed their financial wounds and threatened Duer with terrible punishments, investors realized that they needed a more structured way to buy and sell stocks. And so, on May 17, 1792, twenty-four men standing beside a tree at 68 Wall Street signed an agreement. They were establishing the very first rules for what would become the New York Stock Exchange. The signers were a portrait of the opportunities New York afforded. There were American Protestants and Jews originally from Spain and Portugal, new immigrants and old New England families who dated back to the *Mayflower*, businessmen who had sided with the British and backers of the revolution, slaveholders and abolitionists. Theoretically, the stock exchange was an equalizer: a man (no woman held a seat on the exchange until Muriel Siebert in 1967) who was good with figures and had a strong stomach for risk could do well, whether he could trace his ancestry back to Dutch New York or had just gotten off a boat. Wall Street was the perfect expression of James Graham's motto; here money would make the man. But in another sense, it centered on a small circle of white men who knew one another quite well (the first African American member was Joseph L. Searles III, seated in 1970). By 1793, the stock exchange had moved down the block to the Tontine Coffee House, at the corner of Wall and Water Streets.

Stock trading was going to be one engine of the city's future. Although it could be volatile, causing panics and crashes, it would also create wealth. And while many in the rest of the country would see the wheeling and dealing of Wall Street as the polar opposite of America's small-town Main Street, Wall Street would be New York's own Main Street—the center of the economy that kept the city growing. There were to be two sides of New York: one in which a white man

After traders established the rules for buying and selling stocks in a meeting at 68 Wall Street, they moved to the Tontine Coffee House at 82 Wall Street. A tontine is an agreement in which participants contribute to a common fund and receive dividends from it during their lives. As the original 203 members of this tontine died off, more money was available to the survivors, until the last seven inheritors divided up what was left in 1870.

who was clever or ruthless enough could rise, and another in which the wealthiest insiders shuffled power among themselves.

The conflict over Hamilton's debt plan had another consequence for New York and the nation. When Washington was elected, he hoped the nation would be united, working together to create a new kind of republic in which men of virtue would vote, and govern, for the good of all. But as politicians separated themselves into those who shared Hamilton's vision of a strong central government eager to support business, and those who agreed with Jefferson in believing that America ought to have a minimal government and be governed to favor the farmer, the worker, and the individual, they formed the first political parties—Hamilton's Federalists versus Jeffersonian Democratic-Republicans. Despite Washington's hopes, politics in the new nation would be just as heated and vicious as it had been in the colonies. In New York City, political rivalry influenced even how its citizens would find water to drink.

WATER

The sugar trade made a great deal of money for New Yorkers, but it came with a price: disease. Starting in the 1690s, every few years a bad disease season would hit the cane fields and shortly thereafter an epidemic would break out in New York. We now know that mosquitoes carried diseases, including yellow fever, from the islands to the United States via shipments of cargo. At the time, though, no one knew what caused these "malignant fevers" or how they were transmitted.

In 1793, the strange fever hit Philadelphia, and New Yorkers began to argue about what caused it. Like anti-immigrant politicians today, Federalists implied that foreigners had brought it. Democratic-Republicans blamed the smells coming from stagnant water in the city. Two years later, the same fever reached New York. Over the summer, fever claimed 732 lives. The crisis year came in 1798: more than two thousand New Yorkers, some 5 percent of the total population, were killed by the illness no one could prevent. A committee blamed "deep damp cellars, sunken yards . . . filthy and stagnant water . . . and the want of an adequate supply of pure and wholesome water."

The lack of clean water did not create the fever, but it did contribute to health problems. Before Europeans arrived, the Munsee had avoided this issue by building their fields and settlements near Manhattan's natural springs. The Dutch and later the English clustered at the tip of the island where, instead of using natural springs, they dug wells. Yet the growing population of pigs, goats, dogs, and horses—not to speak of people with their chamber pots—rendered local water unsightly, malodorous, and soon deadly. Enterprising individuals could venture up the island to the Collect Pond, scoop up fresh water, and return to sell the precious liquid by the ladle. Soon enough, though, the pond was overused and became polluted. New Yorkers learned to boil their water for tea or brew it into beer. The more the city grew, the less satisfactory wells, boiled drinks, and water sales proved to be. One solution was to move away from the growing city, but not too far away. Farther up the island, the appealing, green, and wealthy area of Greenwich, later Greenwich Village, grew as a country retreat. Greenwich was removed from crowding and disease, seated beside the flowing Hudson, and gifted with its own springs. Aaron Burr bought a lavish home on Richmond Hill

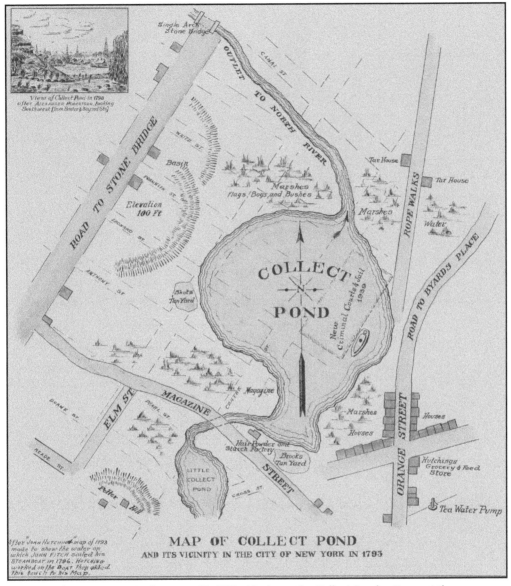

Based on a map originally created in 1793, this shows the Collect Pond as it was at the time. Now entirely gone, it is largely covered by Foley Square. Orange Street is now called Baxter Street, Magazine Street is Pearl Street, and modern Elk Street was once Elm. The next incarnation of the area was as the notorious Five Points.

This is a section of the hollowed wooden logs that were used as water pipes in the city. The tall perpendicular piece served as a gate that could be raised or lowered to control the flow.

in Greenwich that had served as Washington's headquarters at the beginning of the war, and he borrowed thousands upon thousands of dollars to furnish it. When another fever hit in 1805, fully one-third of the city's seventy-five thousand residents relocated to Greenwich. Hamilton, in turn, built a home even farther up the island in Harlem

Escaping disease was a privilege of the rich. As John Lambert noted when yet another epidemic hit in 1822, "Very few are left in the confined parts of town except the poorer classes and the negroes." He added that the latter were "of great service in this dreadful crisis." This imbalance in who is exposed to pandemics and who takes the necessary—and dangerous—role of a first responder remains to this day.

The Collect Pond now had many neighbors who used the water for every need. "It's like a fair every day with whites, and blacks, washing their clothes, blankets, and things . . . sudds and filth are emptied into this pond, besides dead dogs, cats." Worse yet, the nearby businesses used the pond as a giant sewer for the noxious waste they produced. Not only was the water in the pond unhealthy, but the smelly runoff flowing east and west was a kind of liquid barrier confining the growing city to the tip of Manhattan Island. After the deadly year of 1798, the city decided the entire poisonous mess of the pond and the streams and swamps it fed would have to go. Knocking down a hill gave them enough stones to fill the pond. When draining did not go as well as planned, a canal was added—and then covered to create Canal Street. The process of remaking Manhattan into a product of human engineering began.

MANHATTAN COMPANY

Farmers versus bankers, those who blamed diseases on smells and those who blamed immigrants: the growing split between the Democratic-Republicans and Federalists was not just a matter of who won this election or that. You could immediately tell which party a man belonged to by how he acted: Democratic-Republicans were happy to shake hands; Federalists did not like being touched and would bow. This difference in styles was so deep, it seemed that the victory of one would be the destruction of the other. An "in" party could create a stranglehold that even included banks. Hamilton and the Federalists had created the two banks that merchants in New York could use. Democratic-Republicans began to feel that they could never get loans. New bank charters had to be approved by legislative bodies currently controlled by the Federalists. It seemed the Democratic-Republicans were trapped: they could neither use existing banks nor open new ones.

Aaron Burr was clever enough to find a way out of the bind. As each outbreak of fever seemed to make clear, New York City needed to solve its water crisis. Burr offered to create a company that would lay strong pipes to a distant water supply. Once the bill to create the Manhattan Company was being considered by the state legislature, Burr offered a small addition: if the company had extra money, it could use it in any legal way it saw fit. In other words, it was a bank. The Manhattan Company eventually merged with the Chase Bank and still exists today as Chase. It was so fully a bank that it did very little to remedy the city's water problems, but that had never been its real purpose. Burr's supposed water company was a political tool, and it had struck a powerful blow in the conflict of two parties—and in the titanic clash of two brilliant rivals.

HERO AND NEMESIS

Aaron Burr and Alexander Hamilton were so perfectly opposite and yet identical that they seem to have been two halves of the same person—the way a superhero and his or her nemesis can be precise mirror images of each other.

Alike: Physically, they were both short for their time, Hamilton at five foot seven and Burr at five foot six. Men in a hurry, each one was relentlessly driven by the passion to leave behind his horrid childhood. Each seized the moment of the revolution to distinguish himself as a leader, Burr in battle, Hamilton as Washington's aide. Equally notorious for their pursuit of women, they made their names as extremely hardworking and skilled lawyers while living as neighbors on Wall Street. They were each set, dead set, on winning—in battle, in court, in the contest of life for fame, in the eyes of women. They were each set, dead set, on obliterating the other.

Different: Burr was born to privilege. His grandfather was Jonathan Edwards, the most powerful and influential preacher in America, and his father was one of the founders of Princeton University. But by the time he was two, his parents, two grandparents, and even a great-grandparent were all lost to disease. Reared by a distant uncle, Burr rejected religion and trusted only, solely, himself. Perhaps growing up so isolated made him especially careful with words, or, as he described himself, "a grave, silent, strange sort of animal." Hamilton intensely distrusted Burr's silences, seeing him as a calculating sphinx who "has not principle, public, or private." The lesson of Burr's terrible childhood was that nothing lasts, no ideal, no law; nothing matters but will, energy, calculation, and skill. You cannot hold back the ravages of fate—you must battle always, alone and for yourself. At age eleven, Burr applied to Princeton but was rejected as being too young. For the next two years, he studied eighteen hours a day, barely stopping to eat, and at thirteen he applied again, this time asking to be admitted as a junior. There was a new regime at the university with a new curriculum; they let him in as a sophomore.

Hamilton was the illegitimate son of an impoverished mother on the small Caribbean island of Nevis. He grew up with nothing, but his intelligence and way with words were soon recognized. Brash, outspoken, brilliant, Hamilton used words as weapons to slash his opponents. "In politics, as in war," he believed, "the first blow is half the battle." He was given schooling, then a job; when he wrote a powerful description of the devastation a storm brought to the island, it drew attention that led him to New York. The lesson of Hamilton's terrible childhood was that you must build firm foundations that last—family, wealth, connections, ideals, principles that cannot be swept away. Against the hurricane, only clarity, eloquence, and perfect planning can endure.

During the revolution, Burr clashed with Washington and the dislike was mutual. His first combat in the war was the campaign to take over Canada. Burr endured extreme hardship and showed not only courage and leadership in combat but valor, as when he risked enemy fire to carry the fallen body of a general back to his men. To the end of his tortured life, his former battle brothers were his most faithful supporters. Much later, seeing himself as a kind of North American Napoleon, he attempted to lead forces to take parts of Mexico and the Southwest as a kingdom of his own. For Burr, there were no boundaries, even of the nation. Given that the United States was about to gain some of that land through the Louisiana Purchase, and much of the rest would later be won in the Mexican War, Burr was not entirely wrong to question where the United States began or ended. To him, it ended wherever he could successfully plant his flag.

Hamilton worked so closely with Washington that the general served as a kind of adoptive father. Hamilton became Washington's treasury secretary and wrote farsighted papers envisioning the new nation's future financial success and mapping out a pathway to get there. If Burr, chasing glory in the Southwest, was the bad son ready to tear apart Washington's legacy, Hamilton was the good son attempting to enshrine it.

The inward and grim Aaron Burr, paired here with an image of his lavish home on Richmond Hill in Greenwich (now Greenwich Village)

Wealth, standing, power, and public ideals against will, organization, and private calculation—Hamilton against Burr would be the next act of the Federalists and the Democratic-Republicans, the grandees and the senseless people. For while Hamilton had principles he allied with privilege, Burr found allies among those excluded from power.

In 1783, officers who had fought in the war created the Society of the Cincinnati, with admission limited to officers who had served with honor and their firstborn sons. (It was named after a Roman general who gave up power and returned to his farm. The city in Ohio also named after him did not yet exist.) One of its original members, Hamilton liked the idea of linking leading figures together—he saw this as a way to strengthen national bonds. But was the society a move to create a military aristocracy, a separate caste of knights perennially ruling over the common people? Burr—seeing it as a political organization likely to favor Hamilton and the Federalists—joined forces with the Society of St. Tammany, a group that emphasized the virtues and values of white, male American workers. (It was named after a legendary Lenape leader who had been gracious to European newcomers.) Tammany later became the voice of Irish immigrants and their families.

For the next hundred and eighty years, Tammany captured large swaths of the white, immigrant, working-class vote and influenced or sometimes outright controlled elections in the city. Burr showed them the way.

It was not easy to vote in New York City. Not only did you need to be white and male, but you had to own property. Even beyond that, wealth gave extra advantages: until 1804, a man could vote in as many parts of the city as he (or his wife) held property. Hamilton had married a Schuyler and was thus part of one of the richest and most powerful families in the state. Burr had to hustle to find his voting base.

The spring 1800 elections for state offices were vitally important to both Hamilton's Federalists and the Democratic-Republicans favored by Burr. The Federalists made sure that the president would be chosen by electors (as is still true today), and that these influential men would themselves be selected by the state assembly. Burr proposed a bill that would at least let the entire voting public choose the electors. The Federalists had the assembly votes to defeat that plan and assumed they would win the city and state elections, and that New York's electoral votes would give them the presidency. They reckoned without Aaron Burr.

The confident and dashing Alexander Hamilton as romanticized in this painting by John Trumbull.

Burr realized that there was a way to combat the advantages of the wealthy and powerful: "superior *Management*" (italics in the original). Like modern campaign organizers, he collected lists of all voters, sent party faithful to get out the vote, and on election day made his headquarters into a hub gathering information from everywhere in the city. He even figured out a way to allow people without property to vote: he bundled together groups of these workingmen and granted them joint ownership of a piece of land. Guided by Burr's brilliant planning, the Democratic-Republicans won every one of the city's assembly races, giving his party thirteen precious electoral votes. Hamilton was so disturbed by the outcome that he privately suggested the state legislature vote on the presidency before the new winners took office. He knew that would be illegal and undemocratic but thought the issues were so important that "it will not do to be overscrupulous."

With the victory Burr achieved in New York City's assembly races, the Democratic-Republican Party, headed by Jefferson and Burr, won the presidency. But under the rules at the time, the two men received the same number of electoral votes. That left it to Congress to choose between them. After many rounds of balloting, the representatives picked Jefferson. The "grave, silent" Burr could not abide the constant stream of what felt like personal insults that had come from Hamilton, and he was sure that Hamilton, through his endless, cutting disparagements, had tipped the House against him.

Hamilton had, in fact, made clear to everyone he could reach that he saw Burr as a threat to the nation.

As a public man, he is one of the worst sort—a friend to nothing but as it suits his interest and ambition. Determined to climb to the highest honours of the State, and as much higher as circumstances may permit—he cares nothing about the means of effecting his purpose. 'Tis evident that he aims at putting himself at the head of what he calls the "popular party" as affording the best tools for an ambitious man to work with. . . . In a word, if we have an embryo-Caesar in the United States 'tis Burr.

Burr felt Hamilton had insulted his honor and demanded an apology or a duel. Hamilton thought his remarks were just standard political warfare, nothing personal, and he had no need to show regret. That clash of words continued as Burr ran for governor of New York four years later, and the difference between Hamilton, the verbal swordsman, and Burr, the man who always cautiously weighed his words, led the two men to the morning of July 11, 1804.

In rowboats they crossed the Hudson from around Forty-Second Street to Weehawken, New Jersey, and faced each other with loaded pistols.

Hamilton did not believe in dueling but felt he could not refuse when Burr challenged him. He tried to satisfy honor without risking either of their lives by firing first—and deliberately missing, hitting an overhanging tree. He wanted Burr to see that—and in effect call off the duel. But Burr took the opposite road: a skilled marksman, he aimed, fired, and ended Hamilton's life. That shot was also the end of Burr's political career and the end of an era. Burr spent the rest of his life scrambling from one scheme to another, falling ever further out of sight. Hamilton left a legacy of some of the most important writing about the principles of law, economy, and government in the nation's history—and election rules designed to keep power away from the mass of voters. The man who almost became president wound up as an afterthought to the man he killed, but he, too, left a legacy: a structure of political organization that gave white working people a voice in New York just as the city was about to enter the age of strategy and planning.

Building the City

Union Square

1800–1890

∼

In which politics splits the city, planning expands it, the port grows, and Manhattan spreads uptown. Immigration redefines it, shopping is transformed, and at the explosive touch points of Black and white people, rioting, theft, borrowing, and blending create a new American popular culture and a new form of city center.

SNAPSHOT

New York of Wealth and Poverty: The Age of Canals, Sailing Ships, and Irish and German Immigration

1817–25 Erie Canal built.

1818 First regular shipping line connecting New York and Liverpool, England, begins service.

1819 Financial panic.

1820 Manhattan's population: 123,706, 10,886 of African descent and 518 enslaved. The total population of the areas that will later form Greater New York is 152,056.

1822 A law eliminating the property qualification for white male voters while increasing the amount of property required for African American voters is passed and goes into effect in 1827.

1827 All enslaved people in New York emancipated.

1828 Washington Square created.

1830 Manhattan's population: 202,589, 13,976 of African descent. The total population of the areas that will later form Greater New York is 242,278.

1832 Cholera epidemic.

1832–38 A horse-drawn railroad runs along Bowery/Fourth Avenue from Prince Street to Thirty-Second Street; steam engines take over above Thirty-Second Street.

1833 The New York port is the largest shipbuilder in the nation.

Union Square oval is created as center of wealthy residential area.

1834 Brooklyn incorporates as a city; when William Lloyd Garrison creates an organization in the city to oppose slavery in the South, anti-abolitionists riot against it.

1835 The Great Fire destroys 693 buildings in the Wall Street area.

Approximately 22,000 seamen on 2,008 vessels enter the city's port.

1836 Many strikes in the city, including by longshoremen.

1837 Financial panic, many businesses in the city fail, power of organized labor weakens.

One-sixth of Manhattan built up with buildings and paved streets.

1838 The first steam-powered transatlantic ships reach New York from England; the trip can be made in two weeks.

1839 Work begins on the High Bridge to bring water from the Croton River to the city.

1840 Manhattan's population: 312,710, 16,358 of African descent. The total population of the areas that will later form Greater New York is 391,114.

1844 Clipper ships, built in and launched from New York, create faster China trade, as some complete the trip more quickly than steam-powered ships.

Anti-immigrant publisher James Harper is elected mayor.

1845–49 Irish famine.

1847–51 Railroad line built linking New York City and Albany.

1848 Revolutions in Europe spur German immigration.

1850 Manhattan's population: 515,547, 13,815 of African descent. The total population of the areas that will later form Greater New York is 696,115.

1855 Immigration blooms: 97,572 people who had been born in German-speaking lands live in New York, as do 175,735 Irish immigrants. Manhattan's population: 629,904. The city's foreign-born population (322,460) outnumbers those born in the United States (307,444).

Castle Garden at the tip of Manhattan is adapted to process immigrants. It will be the city's reception point until 1890.

Approximately 55,000 seamen from 3,773 vessels enter the city's port.

1855–65 Steamships registered in foreign lands come to dominate shipping in and out of New York's port; as clipper ships fade, New York becomes less of a center of shipbuilding.

1856 Approximately 150 Chinese, most likely sailors, live in the city.

1857 Work begins on creating Central Park.

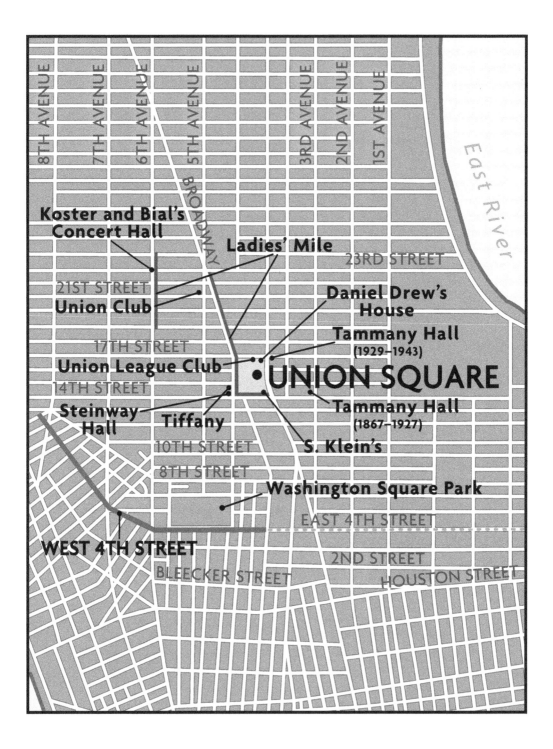

CHAPTER 8

Redrawing the Map

By 1807, the city's soon-to-leave-office mayor, DeWitt Clinton, sent a proposal to create a city planning commission to the soon-to-take-office state senator DeWitt Clinton. In both roles, Clinton liked ambitious enterprises for improving his city and his state. By 1811, the future grid for all of Manhattan up to 155th Street was mapped out. Wall Street was the home of finance. Greenwich was a country retreat. The plan imposed a rigid grid of lots all across the island with almost no gaps for things like parks, but the planners argued that the nearby rivers offered enough air and recreation. With one major adjustment to come, the pattern for living and working in Manhattan was determined. In effect, the commissioners created a giant Monopoly board, and now players would compete to buy properties, build hotels, and charge rents. The plan envisioned, but also created, Manhattan's future.

You can get a sense of how long the city fathers expected it would take for their grid to fill in by how they built their new city hall half a mile north of Wall Street. The side facing south, where nearly everybody lived, was clad in marble. The back, which faced north, was just plain brownstone. Since no one, certainly no one important, would live on that side anytime soon, there was no need to waste money making it look fancy.

According to one count, before 1811, Manhattan featured 573 distinct hills. An early Dutch visitor reported that "the whole country has a waving surface, and in some places high hills and protruding mountains." In order to create the

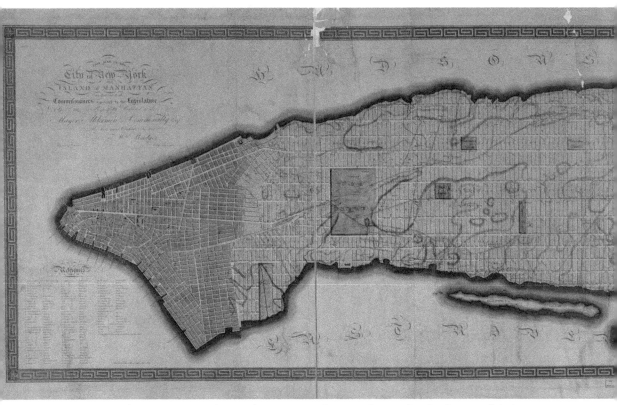

The Commissioners' Map of 1811. New York City is clustered in the dense and darker region at the tip of Manhattan, but this map lays out the entire grid for the city's planned expansion up the island to 155th Street.

neat rectangular blocks spelled out in the 1811 plan, the city was going to have to flatten most of the waves. Despite all that work, anyone who walks or bikes the island today can still feel some of the effects of its original geography.

The marshes, ponds, and streams are gone—marked only by names that hint of places where water once ran. The larger slopes, though, are still there. If you walk uptown in the east Thirties, you can still feel the climb to Murray Hill—named after an eighteenth-century Quaker who built a home and farm there. If you bike uptown on the east side of Central Park (which stretches from East Fifty-Ninth to 110th Street), you know you are going uphill. If you stand in Morningside Park on 110th Street and look north, you clearly see the hills

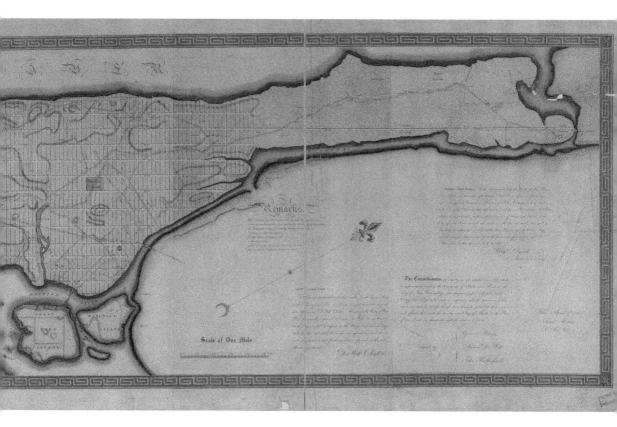

that lead to an area that is raised above the rest of Manhattan in a flat and once fertile plain, where in 1658 the Dutch colonial administration established a village: New Haarlem.

In the 1811 plan, that village was to become part of New York City's new grid. There was something about planning in 1811 that had special resonance. The new nation was like a toddler learning to walk—feeling its limbs, testing its power, seeing what it was capable of doing. But the next year, America and England went to war again—which delayed the work begun in 1811. That war showed that the United States was not a temporary blip, an unstable aberration that would soon return to its proper colonial status. This new country, indeed this new kind of nation, would survive and grow. And so, after the war of 1812 ended in 1815, American leaders returned to their civic planning. And the biggest plan of all came from Clinton and New York.

A GAP BECOMES A SQUARE

Union Square has never been geometrically a square. In that 1811 grid, there was one spot that could not quite be worked out. What is now called Broadway was once Bloomingdale Road and dated back to the 1700s. Created by centuries of people, horses, and carts, not the designs of surveyors and city planners, it started out as a diagonal cutting across from east to west as it headed from south to north. Where the diagonal crossed the straight lines of the grid at the Bowery (or Fourth Avenue), bounded by Tenth and Seventeenth Streets, there was an empty triangle. More avenues crossed here than anywhere on the island, so it was dubbed Union (as in "joining") Place. In 1811, just as the city had decided to leave marble off of the back of city hall, it did not have to think about the odd space of Union Place—it was a hilly nowhere.

What politicians could not envision was crystal clear to a real estate developer. Samuel Ruggles convinced the city that he could get wealthy people to move into the blank parts of the map if he gave them private spaces. First, a park was laid out, bounded by Nineteenth and Twenty-Second Streets and Third and Fourth Avenues and surrounded with a fence: Gramercy Park. To this day, it is a private preserve that is accessible only to neighbors who have a key. Ruggles then planned out a park with a central fountain at Union Place. This elegant greensward (renamed Union Square) was a sedate, orderly place suited to the strolling respectable homeowners who lived near it. The park oval was surrounded by a fence, then split into neatly laid-out quadrants planted with precise rows of trees. As the avenues flowed downtown from Union Square, residents were within easy walking distance of St. Mark's Church, where old Peter Stuyvesant was buried, or the tony Grace Church, or the eminently respectable homes facing Washington Square. Like Gramercy Park and this original plan for Union Square, Washington Square, once a site for hangings and a potter's field where poor people were buried, was now the calm, refined centerpiece of a wealthy neighborhood. Henry James, who was born on Washington Place, wrote a novel evoking the Washington Square of his childhood: "The ideal of quiet and of genteel retirement, in 1835, was found in Washington Square." The area, he continued, "has a kind of established repose which is not of frequent occurrence in other quarters of the long, shrill city."

The exclusive homes and buildings of Greenwich, Washington Square, and Union Square had become especially appealing to rich New Yorkers and became a symbol of belonging to the elite. Gone were the days of salty privateers sponsoring churches. The elite were associated with cultivation and refinement, manners, grace, and a library filled with leather-bound books.

Genteel homes required staff to clean, cook, shop, and help with children. In 1855, thirty-three thousand women in Manhattan were domestics, working in other people's homes. The overwhelming majority—some 93 percent—were Irish or German immigrants, while the largest group of native-born domestic workers were African Americans. The "calm" of Union Square, Washington Square, Gramercy Park, and other similarly wealthy neighborhoods was created and maintained by women whose own families were invisible to their employers.

Union Square: A New Kind of City Center

This photo essay is a visual tour of Union Square over the nineteenth century. The images show the location as it evolved from being a blank spot on the map to an entirely new kind of city center—encompassing transportation, shopping, entertainment, politics, and protests.

This engraving made by James Smillie shows "the Union of Broadway & the Bowery" as the hilly dirt road it was in the 1830s.

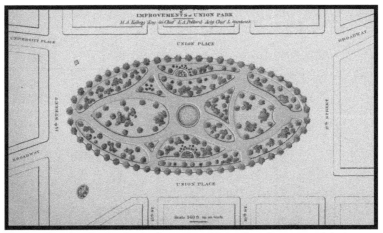

The clean, formal oval in this plan for the revision of Union Place gives a sense of the image of the elite, quiet neighborhood the park was meant to anchor.

The statue of George Washington was added to Union Square in 1856 and located as in this image on the southeast end of the square. It was moved to its current location in 1929.

Drawn in 1849 by C. Bachmann, this bird's-eye view looks down from the formal oval of Union Square across the heart of Manhattan to the port. St. Mark's church, where Peter Stuyvesant was buried, is the white building at the center left; Fifth Avenue is lined with trees and leads to Washington Square Park.

By the late 1860s, Union Square was a hub of transportation—see the trolleys lined up along Broadway—and shopping, as the awnings over the many stores suggest.

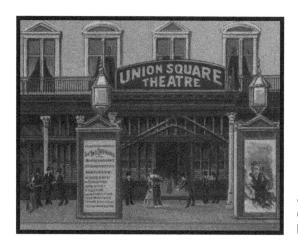

A decade later, the many ways people could reach the square made it a natural home for popular entertainment.

Political organizations, such as the Tammany Society, ringed the square and nearby streets, and when Tony Pastor brought his new version of "variety" to the bustling area, it gave birth to what would be called vaudeville. The candidates listed on the banner were the Democratic nominees for president and vice president in 1904.

CHAPTER 9

Private Homes and Public Shopping

NOVEMBER 4, 1825

The *Seneca Chief*, a boat with a flat bottom built to navigate through canals, was out of its element floating toward the tip of Manhattan. A larger boat carrying Governor DeWitt Clinton sailed out to meet it—but not to assist the smaller craft. Clinton was on his way to collect the green barrels of Lake Erie water bound by glittering hoops that the *Seneca Chief* had carried along the new Erie Canal and down the Hudson River. Cannon lined the entire route, booming in a carefully planned sequence that took three hours and twenty minutes, from the first blast near Buffalo down to New York City and then back to Lake Erie. Trailing the *Seneca Chief* was *Noah's Ark*, a boat that a local paper reported was filled with "creeping things" and larger animals such as "a bear, two eagles, two fawns," as well as birds and even fish—all representative of the West, to which, thanks to the new canal, the city was now connected. In a symbolic "wedding of the waters," Clinton opened and upended the barrels, spilling the Lake Erie water into New York Harbor (except some that was sealed in special vials for dignitaries). The "Festival of Connection" was the fulfillment of Clinton's dreams, and the guarantee of the city's future.

As the *Seneca Chief* neared the city, bands gathered on boats serenaded it and cannon boomed out greetings. Once it safely docked, the whole town turned out to congratulate and celebrate the guests. The Erie Canal was open for business, and that business would flow in and through New York City. It would no longer cost $120 and take three weeks to ship a ton of goods from New York to Buffalo. Now that the canal was open, the time was cut to eight days and the price to six dollars. As farmers, miners, and ranchers spread west across the continent, they would be shipping everything they grew, and buying everything they needed, through New York. New York City would no longer be just one eastern port scrambling to catch up with Philadelphia; as Clinton predicted, the city was about to become "the greatest commercial emporium in the world." Manhattan, he envisioned, would be "one vast city" that would be "covered with inhabitants."

For all the celebration, canals are not built by themselves without painful labor or grave consequences. Carving the waterway took eight years of brutal, backbreaking effort from working-class white and African American men who had to cut down trees, pull up tree stumps, and hack through hard rock with picks and shovels—dynamite had not yet been invented. As this army of laborers pushed ahead, they were splintering the lands of four Native nations: the Mohawk, the Onondaga, the Cayuga, and the Seneca. At each stage, the state attempted to dispossess and remove the people. In fact, the Native nations have endured, though often not on their original homelands. Native peoples paid a price for New York's growth. In turn, the wealth that the canal brought to New York split the city apart, for the age of planning that allowed New York to build the canal was also the dawning of the age of factories and machines.

Back in the 1700s, it had been common for a wealthy merchant or shop owner to live in the same building as his business. Meals, conversations, and breaks served to bridge the lives of owner and employee. Young workers learned artisanal skills that might, in time, allow them to open their own workshops and businesses. By the 1800s, the elite no longer lived at their places of business and were looking for cheap labor to run their factories, not apprentices who would slowly master crafts. When the novelist Herman Melville was a child, his father, Allan, was doing well in his business. The family moved to a new home uptown. "Its distance from my store," Allan wrote, "nearly two miles, will compel me to dine [apart] from my family most of the time." As they strolled their elite neighborhoods, young men of the 1820s and '30s affected British and Scottish accents, saying "dawnce" for *dance*, "cawn't" for *can't*, "fathaw" for *father*, and such. By

The ships gathered here on Lake Erie began the naval procession down to New York that culminated in the wedding of the waters.

contrast, a decade later, in the 1840s, the very symbol of a working-class white young man was Mose, the Bowery B'hoy. Mose was a fictional character known for his own slang, being ready for a fight ("spillin' for a muss"), hating immigrants, and being bonded to his gang.

Grandees and workers had been clashing in the city since Leisler. Now where New Yorkers lived, where they worked, how they moved around the city, and even how they spoke continually reinforced the sense that they lived separated, even opposed, lives. This was the side of the city that handled division through distance.

REAL ESTATE

Throughout much of the nineteenth century, May 1 was the wildest day in New York City. All rental agreements ended on that date, so every person or family who wanted, or desperately needed, a new place to live packed up, left, and rushed to their new lodgings. The streets were so clogged with luggage and hustling families that Moving Day was an official holiday. Then as now, real estate was the city's obsession.

As late as 1827, the streets of lower Manhattan were still seen as "irregular, narrow, crooked, and badly adapted to the comfort of the inhabitants." North of that tangle, though, streets were laid out as far as modern Houston Street (which is essentially the lower edge or Zero Street in the north-south number sequence). Eager surveyors translated the 1811 map into a physical reality by planting 1,549 stone markers showing exactly where key intersections of streets and avenues would one day appear. Savvy investors realized that there was a lot of money to be made by buying appealing locations that the next wave of New Yorkers would need to occupy. After all, New York was the fastest-growing area in the entire country; fed by the Erie Canal boom as well as Irish and German immigration, between 1820 and 1860, the city's population leapt from 123,000 to 813,000—all those people needed to live somewhere.

John Jacob Astor was the smartest investor of all. After making a first fortune trading with China, he used his profits to switch to real estate. He bought land throughout Manhattan, then leased or sold the plots to builders eager to put up housing just ahead of avid buyers and renters. He would ride around the farms that still filled most of Manhattan and snap up the soon-to-be-valuable acreage, but he also knew when to buy farther downtown. As Aaron Burr's fortunes faded, Astor bought up his fancy home and the extensive property that made up the heart of what would become Greenwich Village. Astor didn't invest his money on actual buildings or changing markets—he bought the land and held it until the next plunger took the risk. In 1835 alone, the total value of real estate in the city rose from $143 million to $233 million. Astor's mastery of city real estate worked so well that by 1830 he was said to be America's wealthiest person.

New Yorkers spread across and up the island in a recurring pattern: the wealthy sought out appealing, private spaces with nice sight lines while poor people lived where they could afford it. As the city expanded, it needed new modes of transportation. The wealthy owned their own horse-drawn carriages, or could buy space on the stagecoaches that congregated in the downtown business district. When the Melvilles moved uptown, it cost Allan eight cents to take the stage to work each day. By 1829, larger horse-drawn "omnibuses" plied set routes between elite businesses and fancy neighborhoods. The omnibus was a twelve-seat carriage that, according to one 1870s guidebook, charged ten cents a ride and so catered to the middle class and the wealthy. Transportation was not just a way to get from place to place; it was a sign of who you were and what you could afford.

In 1832, railroad companies began the dance with realtors that would continue to this day and transform the city. Wherever tracks were laid, new areas were opened up to development. In the next twenty years, railroad companies built seven lines running the length of the island, from close to the Hudson River on the west to Second Avenue parallel to the East River. At first, though, these railroad cars were pulled by horses, not locomotives. The grid was filling in; upper Manhattan was now in play. But when trains began using locomotives, rich people objected to the noise and smoke disturbing their quiet homes. The city passed a law mandating that from Twenty-Seventh Street south, trains must be pulled by horses, not engines. In 1854, the switching spot from horses to locomotives was moved farther uptown to Forty-Second Street. Horse-drawn trains competed with the horse-drawn omnibus for the city's riders. More people than ever could move, if they could afford the fare.

If you picture the city as a living, growing organism, the buses and trains were the ligaments connecting its spreading parts. But spread also allowed distance—and the rich to move away from the poor.

STOCKS

Every railroad that laid tracks around the country, to and from New York and beyond, had two major roles: one as a provider of transportation, and another as a vehicle for financial speculation—stock trading. Near the corner of Seventeenth Street, 41 Union Square was the home of Daniel Drew, Wall Street's master of the short sell. If, for instance, a stock sold at one hundred dollars, he would borrow a share from one person and sell it to another, betting that before he had to buy another share to return the stock to its original owner, its price would decline to, say, ninety-five dollars. If his guess—or more likely inside knowledge—panned out, he'd make five dollars on each share. Short-selling worked especially well in Drew's day because there were no rules on Wall Street, and one vast project after another—such as building the railroads crisscrossing the United States and running up and down Manhattan—needed funding.

In the early decades of the twenty-first century, money from America and Europe poured into China and India as those countries "developed." In the 1800s, investors in England saw America as the place to earn big profits. Those English investors were an ocean away from the actual management of American railroads, whereas Drew sat on the board of directors of the Erie Railroad—a key route leading to and from New York City. Not only did this give him advanced warning of events that could change the price of Erie Railroad stocks, but he could also use his perch to manipulate the stock prices directly. As the saying went, "When Uncle Dan'l says 'Up,' Erie goes up. When Uncle Dan'l says 'Down,' Erie goes down. When Uncle Dan'l says 'Wiggle-waggle,' Erie bobs both ways."

There were no laws to prevent Drew from manipulating the market. The only check on Drew was his archrival, a trader as powerful, skilled, and determined as he—Cornelius Vanderbilt. This was exactly the kind of insider trading Thomas Jefferson had warned about in his battles with Alexander Hamilton: the dark magic of making money out of thin air. Indeed, an 1837 stock market panic caused the booming Manhattan real estate market to crash, losing some $40 million in value, bankrupting hundreds of businesses, and causing approximately one-third of the city's workers to lose their jobs. Even the often disdainful former mayor Philip Hone wondered "how the poor man manages to get a dinner for his family." The entire nation fell into a depression that lasted through the next five years. Banking and railroads finally put the market, and thus the city, back on its feet

The unregulated stock market carried the city—rich, middle class, and poor—on its roller-coaster ride of boom and bust. These financial games gave working people jobs on the upswing, but they only emphasized the divide between those devastated by the downswing and those who could ride out the market's cycles.

This interior view of A. T. Stewart's department store shows that this building was a palace devoted to shopping.

SHOPPING

By the 1850s, the city was the grand mart of consumer goods, filled with ever more elaborate palaces of commerce. The man who led the way was A. T. Stewart.

Stewart arrived in New York from Ireland in 1820. Although he was still a teenager, he had a small inheritance and brought enough money to open a fabric store three years later. By 1832, he began an important practice that was new to America: everything he offered for sale came with a set price. This freed women "from distrust of their own power as hagglers or bargain-makers." Shopping was becoming less a negotiation in a marketplace and more a kind of tourism, a free exploration of items on offer. Stewart ran frequent sales and stationed barkers on the streets to approach women and pitch the latest offering. He was treating selling goods the same way the master showman P. T. Barnum was revolutionizing entertainment.

As Barnum realized, "everything depended upon getting people to think, and talk and become curious and excited over and about" his acts and curios. Barnum had opened his American Museum on Broadway and Ann Street in 1841, displaying everything from a model of Niagara Falls to a "Feejee mermaid" and a flea circus. Five years later, Stewart unveiled his marble palace just a few blocks from Barnum on Broadway and Chambers Street. His immense store was the first shop in the city to leave street level—it had a first and a second floor. The building itself was faced in marble and featured fifteen glass windows. A shopper (almost always a woman) could feel elegant simply by coming to Stewart's.

This was the city's first department store. Shoppers could find many different kinds of products in carefully organized selling sections—or departments. Set prices eliminated haggling, and the department store meant shoppers did not have to go from store to store to find what they needed. Stewart's made shopping not a chore but an experience.

In 1862, Stewart closed his Chambers Street store and created an even more magnificent one uptown on Broadway and Tenth Street. Once again, the store had two floors, now served by five steam elevators. At the center was a giant glass dome supported by sixteen iron columns. "Standing beneath the dome," the *New York Daily Press* observed, "and gazing up through story after story till the eye reaches the top, one is made dizzy and bewildered by the sight." Writing in a women's magazine, Alice B. Haven added her own description. Looking at all of the women around her, she saw a "restless, ever-changing throng, like a waving tulip-bed, or the glittering of a kaleidoscope, with an ascending hum that marks a hive of human activity and industry."

Armies of women laboring on sewing machines created the ready-made clothes available at Stewart's.

The second floor featured another innovation: not only were there fabrics to buy but women at work with sewing machines. Shoppers could now purchase ready-made clothing instead of having to order new clothes from a tailor or make them at home. While clothing "sizes" did not exist yet, what a person wore was increasingly a product of a great many hands sewing pieces of cloth into pre-set patterns. As one social critic wrote, "There is no reason why manufacturing houses should not supply every article worn at the cost of material and labor."

In one way, Stewart was making shopping more rational, more organized, less personal. In another, he was encouraging women to make buying into a kind of vacation, a trip to a pleasure palace designed in every square inch to let them gaze and to entice them to yearn. One after another, retailers such as Lord and Taylor, Macy's, and Arnold Constable copied Stewart by building their own department store palaces, moving one street after another uptown along what became known as Ladies' Mile—Broadway from Fourteenth to Twenty-Third Streets—passing both uptown along Sixth Avenue and directly through Union Square. The buildings around the square began to fill with elegant retailers such as Tiffany selling jewelry and Steinway offering the best pianos.

The new stores created yet another new feature: window displays. At Stewart's, a passerby could gaze inside to see the store. But in his successors' stores, windows became a kind of theater, a picture-show display of the wonders on sale. Windows "extend[ed] for miles on miles, ever diversified and varied; a perfect kaleidoscope of silks and velvets, laces and jewels, rich books and music, paintings and statuary, rifles and racquets, confections and amber-like bottles, *cloisonnée* and cut-glass, everything imaginable for use or luxury, massed in perfect affluence, and displayed in the most attractive way possible." The department stores along Ladies' Mile leading to Union Square were a kind of amusement park centered on the glory of sales.

Crowds of window-shoppers (a new term) filled the streets, spending, as the *Tribune* reported, "their lives in sauntering through Broadway during fashionable hours seeing and being seen." The ever-changing throng that Haven saw at Stewart's was becoming a feature of New York's own streets.

The New Yorkers who would promenade along Ladies' Mile had less and less to do with the most vulnerable New Yorkers. Invisibility worked—for the rich. As one reformer put it, "Union Square or the Avenues know as little of Water Street or Cherry Street as if they were different cities." He was referring to the desperate people moving into homes built over what had once been the Collect Pond. That area was to become the most notorious neighborhood in the city: the Five Points.

THE FIVE POINTS: PLAGUES OF DISEASE AND FIRE

In 1825, the year of the Erie Canal, the two-story wooden homes built on the land-fill over the former Collect Pond housed the poorest New Yorkers. Understanding that neighborhood is similar to the task of decoding the tale Washington Irving told about the sale of Manhattan Island: one history maps how the neighborhood was described in legend, another attempts to recover what life was actually like. Both are important.

Between the 1820s and '50s, residents of the Five Points included an ever-growing population of immigrants from Ireland and Germany and a significant minority of African Americans that grew smaller over the years. After New York State finally and completely abolished slavery in 1827, African American men were relegated to the most physical and menial jobs in the city—chimney sweep, sailor, barber. African American women took in laundry or sold hot corn on the streets. Irish men and women also earned their livelihoods with physical work, taking jobs as laborers, tailors, shoemakers, domestics, and seamstresses. Landlords found they could make money from even such impoverished tenants by splitting up their rental homes into ever smaller apartments. This was doubly profitable, as more tenants crammed into tiny spaces meant more rent the landlord could collect, while the more dilapidated the building, the less the owner paid in taxes.

There was a kind of grim logic to the Five Points: businessmen were figuring out that instead of training skilled workers to complete tasks, they could divide work up into a great many small steps. The more knowledge a craftsperson possessed, the more leverage he or she would have in being paid. By contrast, the many small tasks could be farmed out to the cheapest labor, such as poor people, women, immigrants, even children. Those ready-made clothes on display in the department stores were made this way. As businesses needed fewer skilled workers and more low-wage employees, landlords provided ever-worse cheap housing for men and families living on the edge of desperation. This is a constant theme in a growing city with limited housing stock: *where* poor people can live also defines a great deal of *how* they can live.

As the tumbledown houses-turned-apartments filled with Catholic immigrants and Black New Yorkers, white Protestants moved away. The Five Points neighborhood seemed to repel anyone who did not absolutely need to live there, especially when heavy rain filled basements with water and the air with noxious smells. If Union Square was built in the image of the upper-class London the "best" New Yorkers sought to emulate, the Five Points symbolized the rotting underside of life those same New Yorkers were determined to escape. Yet the Five Points was in the heart of New York, close to centers of business such as Wall Street. A letter to the *Evening Post* in 1832 expressed alarm at a "race of beings of all colours, ages, sexes and nations . . . inhabiting the most populous and central part of the city." Many critiques like this one expressed bigotry toward immigrants and people of color, who were often compelled to live in crowded homes with poor sanitation that left them extremely vulnerable to disease. And as we learned in 2020, once an epidemic begins, no one is safe.

Cholera, a disease spread by a bacterium that lives in food and water, spread around the world and hit New York in late June 1832. The rich fled the city: that summer, more than one hundred thousand people, about half the population, escaped to nearby farms, rented homes, and vacation spots. The poor had no choice but to stay behind, and some 3,513 lives were lost in the epidemic. Preachers blamed the dying for being sinful. Reformers scolded them for drinking too much. Former mayor Philip Hone thought the poor brought the disease on themselves, as they did their own poverty, their "wretchedness and want." Yet even those who could run away and sneer at the victims recognized a problem. The city still had no supply of clear, fresh drinking water.

The cholera epidemic finally convinced enough leaders that an expanding New York City bursting with a growing population needed water. Construction of the new water system was approved in June 1835. But the managers of Burr's old Manhattan Company were not ready to give up their monopoly and fought back; the project stalled. There was a price for greed. The lack of water left the city open to its old enemy: fire.

December 16, 1835, was a freezing-cold, windy day—and a terrifying night. At 9 p.m., fire broke out way downtown, near Hone's son's business. "How shall I record the events of last night," Hone asked his diary, "or attempt to describe the most awful calamity which has ever visited these United States." He was not exaggerating. Reading at home in his library, Hone heard a fire alarm and rushed to see the flames, and to either help put them out or protect his son's store. "When I arrived at the spot the scene exceeded all description; the progress of the flames, like flashes of lightning, communicated in every direction." The fire burned for sixteen hours and destroyed seventeen acres of lower Manhattan, including 674 buildings. The flames burned so brightly on the clear night that they could be seen from Philadelphia to New Haven, Connecticut. The damage was so severe in part because so many firemen had died in the cholera epidemic a few years before, and because the limited water supply had frozen.

Finally, in 1837, New York addressed the problem that had been growing since the days of the British. The Croton River in upstate New York was dammed to create a reservoir. Then forty miles of pipe were laid, including a section that crossed the Harlem River along the High Bridge. Croton water gushed through the pipes to Forty-Second Street, where the main branch of the New York Public Library sits today. That spot had been a potter's field filled with the bodies of more than one hundred thousand people who had died too poor to have their own graves. The corpses were dug up and shipped to Wards Island near the city to make way for a giant reservoir. This mammoth container held the water for the lower city—and, as of October 1842, burst forth in dancing sprays from that ceremonial fountain at the center of Union Square. When rich and poor lived in separate sealed-off neighborhoods, New Yorkers were poisoned and ravaged by fire; when the city worked together, it exploded into new life.

CHAPTER 10

The Wickedest House on the Wickedest Street

IRISH NEW YORK

The Irish had been coming to New York since the days of British rule; indeed, DeWitt Clinton's own ancestors were from Ireland. Like the Clintons, many of these early Irish immigrants were Protestants, and neither the poorest nor the least educated to arrive in the city. That had changed by the 1830s, when thirty thousand people a year were landing in New York on ships from Ireland, most of them poor and Catholic. They found a city ready to use their labor but not to accept their faith. Anti-Catholic feeling had run through the history of colonial New York, and Protestant New Yorkers saw Catholicism as at odds with the essence of being American. Former mayor Hone called the Irish "the most ignorant, and consequently the most obstinate, white men in the world."

Until 1806, you could not serve in city government unless you swore an oath condemning the Catholic mass and the worship of Mary and other saints. While Clinton helped to end that practice in New York (it remained in effect in England until 1829), public schools in the city were run by a private Protestant organization until 1842. As more and more Irish Catholic children entered public schools, they were given Protestant Bibles to read, sang Protestant hymns, and read textbooks that Catholic leaders interpreted as having anti-Catholic passages. The idea was that Protestantism, democracy, and self-disciplined hard work were all connected. To become real Americans, the Irish would have to convert, or at least become less attached to their priests and their churches and more similar to American Protestants.

Even New Yorkers such as the inventor Samuel F. B. Morse and the inclusive and open-minded poet Walt Whitman were avid anti-Catholics. Morse claimed to have uncovered a new international Catholic conspiracy against "the Liberties of the United States." Whitman thought that diminishing Protestant control of public schools would allow teachers to spread "Catholic superstition." Harper Brothers, then and now a leading book publisher, found a public eager to read the racy, made-up confessions of a supposed former nun. For people like Hone, Morse, and Whitman, the proof of the problem with the Irish was in the Five Points.

Between 1845 and 1851, famine ravaged Ireland. The island's population declined by half, losing 20 percent of its people to starvation and disease. Another 30 percent—or one and a half million mothers, fathers, children, and elders—left. Of those emigrants, some six hundred thousand came to New York City. Between the Irish and the Germans (who also arrived in large numbers in this period, expanding the Protestant, Catholic, and Jewish communities in the city), New York's population boomed from 371,000 in 1845 to 630,000 a decade later. Many of the most desperate and disadvantaged Irish and Germans shoe-horned themselves into the miserable housing in the Five Points.

Charles Dickens, who came to New York as a tourist, used his novelistic skill to characterize the neighborhood: "This is the place: these narrow ways, diverging to the right and left, and reeking everywhere with dirt and filth. . . . Debauchery has made the very houses prematurely old. See how the rotten beams are tumbling down, and how the patched and broken windows seem to scowl dimly, like eyes that have been hurt in drunken frays." To Dickens, the buildings themselves reflected what he saw as the alcoholic indulgences of their miserable inhabitants. One building, in particular, emblemized the rotting neighborhood.

In 1792, when the Collect Pond was a reliable source of water, a brewery was built on its shoreline. By 1837, the water was long gone and the building was converted into what one sensationalist magazine called "the wickedest house on the wickedest street that ever existed in New York." The Old Brewery was said

to be the site of daily thefts, violent fights, murders, and the voices of "wailing children." While hard evidence about life in the building is limited, we know that it was indeed horribly overcrowded. In 1850, 221 people were spread over just thirty-five apartments, meaning more than six shared each small space. A visiting writer described a "doorless apartment beyond, of the size of a kennel . . . occupied by a woman and her daughter, and the daughter's child, lying together on the floor, and covered by rags and clothes of no distinguishable color, the rubbish of bones and dirt only displaced by their emaciated limbs. The sight was too sickening to endure."

Extreme poverty, filth, and crime seemed to be the normal condition within the Old Brewery, and yet none of these abysmal conditions is what most disturbed visitors. "Every house," a writer claimed, "was a filthy brothel." A reformer agreed: "Every house was a brothel, and every brothel a hell." Studies of police reports seem to confirm this impression: desperately poor families living one on top of the other did turn to prostitution. Men sold the labor of their strong arms and backs. Women sold the skill of their hands. Daughters had to sell themselves. To those horrified by the Five Points, the prevalence of prostitution was a blazing moral indictment. It was proof of the bestial, immoral condition of the Irish. And yet in their eyes, even this was not the absolute bottom-most rung of the Five Points hell.

One sight in the Five Points seemed to shock observers more than any other: "white women, and black and yellow men, and black and yellow women, with white men, all in a state of gross intoxication, and exhibiting indecencies revolting to virtue and humanity." Black and white people ("yellow" meant mixed race in this writing) were mixing in Five Points—much as they had in John Hughson's tavern one hundred years earlier. The rules of early nineteenth-century society were ignored; even the color line was not respected. The pressure of poverty, need, and crowding was so great that lives could be recombined in ways that were not acceptable anywhere else. New Yorkers fortunate enough to live elsewhere saw this as the absolute proof of the degraded, subhuman life that unfolded in the Five Points.

Dickens, like the shocked reporter and the disgusted reformer, created vivid word pictures of the Five Points that linger to this day. But in the 1990s, archaeologists began exploring in the area and found places where residents of the old neighborhood had dumped their garbage. Sorting through the cracked bits of broken clay tobacco pipes and shattered plates, they made very interesting discoveries. Households in the Five Points seemed to have had crockery and tea sets that were either mass-produced copies or secondhand versions of items that would be found in farmhouses of the time, and just a notch below those of middle-class households. The actual families were determined to live—and to show guests—a proper, respectable life. The area was poor, overcrowded, and dirty.

The Five Points: Tourism and Warning

These images show how the Five Points was depicted by artists and editorial illustrators. *Frank Leslie's Illustrated Newspaper* shows the apparent misery and poverty of the slum neighborhood. The standing man is meant to be Irish, as well as both glum and passive—doing nothing for the besieged mothers and beseeching children.

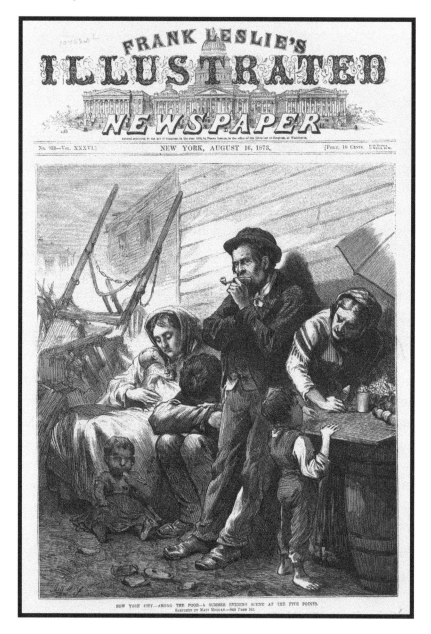

The Old Brewery was described as the "headquarters of crime" in the city.

This image of a "rum shop" highlights how degraded the people in The Five Points were by featuring a drunken woman.

Publications like *Sights and Sensations of New York* of the city were meant to entice readers while also warning what could befall someone who drank, gambled, and wound up being robbed or worse.

Drawn in 1827, this image is the most standard image of the area: with mobs, fighting, drinking, chaos, and, at the edges, African Americans and an elegant gentleman near a possibly drunken woman.

This drawing of Pete Williams's dance hall in the Five Points contains an important clue. To the left is an interracial couple, a white woman dancing along with an African American man (with his hand raised). We don't know how accurate the image is, but it hints at the world of connections across boundaries of race that actually took place in the city.

But the extreme descriptions of it were designed to serve as an example to middle-class and wealthier families. The Five Points was used as a threat, a warning of how far people could fall if they strayed from the Protestant straight and narrow. The immigrant, the working family, and worst yet, the interracial couple were cast as the immoral dangers threatening the city.

To twenty-first-century eyes, of course, forming families across racial lines is normal and the abhorrence of it is what needs to be explained. Middle-class New Yorkers professed revulsion and contempt for the Five Points, but there is another side to the story. For if there were so many brothels, who were the customers? Why did visitors, from Dickens on, feel the need to visit a chamber of horrors only to register their disgust? Even if they came to condemn, they also created interest across the city's separated neighborhoods. When Black and white New Yorkers met, new families were born. For all its truly grim sides, the Five Points was also a site of tourism and transformation.

Dickens led his readers into the deepest depths of the Five Points: Almack's, a dance space named after a fashionable club in London. A mixed-race woman met him at the door, and he then heard a Black fiddler and tambourine player. Fans crushed in to see "a lively young negro, who is the wit of the assembly, and the greatest dancer known." William Henry Lane, known as Master Juba, was a spectacular dancer, as Dickens recorded: "Single shuffle, double shuffle, cut and cross-cut; snapping his fingers, rolling his eyes, turning in his knees, presenting the backs of his legs in front, spinning about on his toes and heels like nothing but the man's fingers on the tambourine; dancing with two left legs, two right legs, two wooden legs, two wire legs, two spring legs—all sorts of legs and no legs—what is this to him?" Applause cascaded over Master Juba when he finished his electrifying act.

Deep in the heart of the "wolf's den," New York was making possible entirely new forms of art. Soon promoters began staging dance competitions, Master Juba against the Irish jig dancer John Diamond. We don't know who won—but whoever did, Irish audiences saw new ways to move. Black audiences saw Irish jigs. Out of this conflict, and this blend, tap dancing was invented. And that was only the start of the creative energy that was born when Black and white people were pressed so closely together. They could copy one another, steal from one another, learn from one another. That is how the city creates transformation: by pressing people so close together they cannot escape clashing, and they also cannot escape being curious.

BLACKING UP: "BITTEN BY THE TARANTULA"

Perhaps the pathway to what would become America's most popular form of entertainment began as early as 1820, when young African Americans held dance competitions near the waterfront in lower Manhattan at the Catherine Market. This was a poor area where, as in the Five Points, African Americans, white Americans, and mixed-race families found homes. Young men known for their "suppleness" arrived from New Jersey—and made sure they would be noticed by tying their hair into bands (like dreadlocks) weighted with pieces of lead. Dancers from Long Island used dried eel skins to hold their hair in ponytails.

This drawing of William Henry Lane gives a hint of the combination of controlled elegance and lyrical power in his dances—and you can see the links to Irish clog dancing and what later became tap.

Some of the dancers were free, some still enslaved. New York had the largest population of free African Americans in the country, and dancing as powerfully, as expressively, as possible, long hair flying, might have felt like a kind of freedom. While the young men enjoyed competing to show their skills, white people gathered to enjoy the spectacle.

Or maybe the new art form began upstate as the Erie Canal was being built, when Irish and African American men labored, and relaxed, side by side. At the Catherine Market and along the tracks of the canals, Black people danced and sang in public, and white people watched closely. Soon enough, they began imitating the steps. There was admiration in the imitation: a sense that these musicians and dancers were the most alive and exciting performers you could see anywhere. Sometimes white performers who planned on copying the moves and using them in their acts even paid the original dancers for the use of their steps. Everyone, white and Black, knew that a white crowd might gather to watch Black dancers at a market, but white audiences in actual theaters would not pay to see Black performers. Whites simply would not accept Black people as stars, as entertainers to be admired in formal settings. Pleasure and prejudice combined in white responses to Black skill and talent.

Some whites felt that Black people should not appear in front of white audiences at all, that it would be offensive to white eyes to even look at a Black person performing. If white men came to the Five Points to see Master Juba, then that was their choice. And indeed, even he had to appear at times with his face painted an exaggerated form of black, so that audiences might think he was a white person pretending to be Black person, and thus he would not be disturbed. Yet as the crowds at the Catherine Market and Master Juba's performances showed, white people wanted to experience Black music and dance. White performers thought of ways to please that public.

A key moment arrived one day in the 1830s when a performer named Thomas Dartmouth Rice came onstage at the Park Theater in New York and tried out an act. Rice, who was white, had blackened his face with burnt cork and painted on exaggerated red lips. To the tune of "Jump Jim Crow," he performed a circling dance, leading up to a heel-clicking leap. Legend has it Rice copied the dance (and borrowed the tattered clothes) of a Black person he met in Lexington, Kentucky. His New York audience loved it and demanded more. As the *New York Tribune* reported (all quotes within the quote are the actual lyrics of the song), "Mr. T. D. Rice made his debut in a dramatic sketch entitled 'Jim Crow,' and from that moment everybody was 'doing just so,' and continued 'doing just so' for months, and even years afterward. Never was there such an excitement in the musical or dramatic world; nothing was talked of, nothing written of, and nothing dreamed of, but 'Jim Crow.' The most sober citizens began to 'wheel about, and turn about, and jump Jim Crow.' It seemed as though the entire population had been bitten by the tarantula."

Rice wasn't the first white performer to use cork to darken his skin to play a Black character. That is where New York enters the story. By creating such a hit act in the city, Rice launched the classic form of blackface minstrelsy—and created what the great jazz musician and historian Wynton Marsalis calls the "longest-running form of American popular music." In their history of jazz, Ken Burns and Geoffrey Ward extend Marsalis's claim: "For almost a century, the minstrel show would be the most popular form of entertainment in America, a ritualized blend of lively music, knockabout comedy, sophisticated elegance, the reinforcement of ugly and persistent stereotypes—and simultaneous unabashed enthusiasm for the music and dance of the country's most despised minority."

Frederick Douglass hated everything about minstrels and minstrelsy. He saw the performers as "the filthy scum of white society, who have stolen from us a complexion denied to them by nature, in which to make money, and pander to the corrupt taste of their white fellow citizens." The actors were indeed painting themselves as the most extreme stereotype of Black Americans. Minstrel shows featured the "plantation darky," a portrait of enslaved people as white audiences wanted to see them: happy-go-lucky children of nature whose foolish squabbles and misunderstandings took place in illiterate dialect, unquestionably in need of a white master's benevolent guiding hand.

Minstrelsy let white audiences believe that this is what Black people really were: entertaining but lesser beings. Most people in the white audiences rarely saw, and never spoke with, African Americans. The more popular minstrelsy became, the more it confirmed to those audiences that what they were seeing onstage was the truth about Black people. It is no coincidence that after the end of slavery, the term "Jim Crow" was used to refer to laws establishing and enforcing racial segregation. The name came from minstrelsy, as did other stereotypes and insults. One of the stock characters soon added to minstrel shows was

"Zip Coon"—the overdressed, foolishly pretentious city character—and "coon" was an insulting name for Black people. Minstrelsy shaped the false stumbling, humble, foolish part—the mask—Black people were forced to play in front of white people.

Minstrelsy quickly spread across the country—from New York to New England and through all the major eastern and southern cities, then to the California gold fields and San Francisco stages, with stops all along the growing rail lines and even at the White House to entertain presidents Tyler, Polk, Fillmore, Pierce, and Lincoln. Onstage, Black people were humiliated to the joy of audiences who—even if they were immigrants, poor, Irish, or otherwise usually the victims of prejudice themselves—became "white" or at least "not Black" for the night. And at the door, anyone seen as being a Black person was kept out—African Americans were not allowed to sit in the audience at minstrel shows.

African Americans, enslaved or free, were actually adapting African traditions—playing complex drumming rhythms, inventing stringed instruments such as the banjo, singing in call-and-response dialogues—and making creative use of European songs and sounds. Indeed, white and Black musicians learned from and borrowed from one another. The audience for blackface minstrels enjoyed the music but had no interest in exploring the origins of African American music and dance. Instead, they were eager to believe that the songs and movements were so lively, so much fun, because Black people were so simple, so close to nature, so primitive. Minstrelsy reinforced stereotypes that persist to this day.

And yet that is only part of the story. Minstrelsy was more alive, more dynamic, more exciting than other styles of music and performance of the time. White workers who were increasingly hemmed in by low-paying jobs, lectured to drink less and fight less, to be more like the elite Protestants of Union Square, could come to a minstrel show and let loose. Enjoying a minstrel act could be a kind of rebellion. A white worker could say, or at least feel, that he, too, would like to jump, to sing, to dance, to be foolish, wild, and free. And that attraction to turning the world upside down could even extend through the minstrel mask back to Black people. The original lyrics to "Jump Jim Crow" included lines that

The Many Layers of Blackface Minstrelsy—Where Stereotype, Appropriation, and Admiration Mixed

Blackface minstrelsy is a difficult and complex—yet crucially important—strand in American history. White people used blackface to portray Black people as inferior in appearance, speech, and action. Yet white performers were actually imitating Black innovation and skill in music and dance and using what they saw as Black styles to express themselves. Black performers began using minstrelsy for their own purposes after the Civil War.

This scene from a play was drawn in 1848. The typical Bowery character "Mose" is the man in the top hat watching the African American man dance. But the image is based on an 1820 sketch of "dancing for eels at the Catherine Market." What people saw on the street had, in thirty years, become theater.

Billy Van was a comedian and the blackface character he played was meant to be as silly, as ridiculous, as "primitive" as possible. Yet you could say the sober, neatly groomed Billy on the left was in "white face" while the comedic minstrel was his inner self.

The poster on the right captures the key moment when T. D. Rice danced "Jump Jim Crow." As late as 1946, the Disney film *Song of the South* featured a crow named Jim who was drawn in exactly the same pose as the one in the center of the poster. The Boston Minstrels poster gives a sense of the mix of pleasure in minstrel music and prejudice that white audiences savored.

recognized the "wish for freedom . . . shining" in Black people's eyes. And Rice, after his career as Jim Crow, wore blackface to play Uncle Tom in the touring abolitionist theater version of *Uncle Tom's Cabin.*

Minstrelsy allowed white audiences to experience a translated, appropriated form of African American culture. Even the exaggerated and ridiculed finery of Zip Coon's clothing was based on the ways in which African Americans in New York were making use of fashion. In 1832, a British visitor remarked that he "repeatedly saw coloured females in the height of fashion in Broadway." And the same year, a Swedish tourist added that on a Sunday, the city's streets were "given up to the African world, it was a high treat to witness the switching of canes and important strut of one sex, and the affected dangling of parasols and reticules of the other."

While everything about minstrelsy told white audiences that they were superior to Black people, at the very same time, minstrelsy gave those audiences a sense that they needed, they grew from, they even depended upon Black people. You can see this most clearly by comparing the United States to the rest of the world: when the Afrikaners (the descendants of Dutch people who arrived in South Africa around the same time as other Dutch settled in New Amsterdam) enforced apartheid, or strict racial segregation, they never listened to African music. The only white people who did were opponents of apartheid. The Nazis attempted to ban all Jewish music, Jewish musicians, even Jewish influence in music. For all of the racism, segregation, and prejudice in the United States, white Americans did something different.

Minstrelsy's enduring popularity forces us to look at it very closely to make sense of this nation. Blackface minstrelsy allowed a white audience to have some translated, distorted form of contact with Black music, Black dance, Black life. And audiences wanted and needed that connection. This may sound so strange as to be impossible. Yet, as Wynton Marsalis has said of minstrelsy and jazz, "the last thing in the world a jazz musician wanted to do was to be a minstrel; however, the music in the minstrel show, the banjo music, the music with grooves, the music that depicted different human circumstances, jazz musicians definitely came out of that environment." Minstrelsy demeaned Black people and yet also made their music, their creativity, however mangled and mistranslated, central to American life.

After the Civil War, African Americans began to form their own touring minstrel groups, blackening their faces, adding the same exaggerated features, and performing the same demeaning skits, yet also being paid for demonstrating their talents. As African Americans began creating their own acts, even Frederick Douglass saw some value in minstrelsy: "It is something gained, when the colored man in any form can appear before a white audience."

Blackface minstrelsy was the first time a new kind of popular culture music and dance was born in America. It abused Black people while stealing from them. Yet it also was the beginning of a kind of mixing created here, out of the peoples of this land. New York was a seedbed of minstrelsy and spread this new art to the nation. When Commodore Perry landed in Japan, the Japanese performed a traditional drama to share their culture. He put on a blackface minstrel show to feature ours. For some in the city, though, the very closeness of Black and white that contributed to minstrelsy was a threat that must be stamped out.

CHAPTER 11

Can the City Hold Together?

FAULT LINES: VOTING

In 1821, Irish voters and their supporters, including the Tammany Society, had reason to celebrate. Though the law would not fully take effect for another five years, New York State agreed to allow any white man to vote—he no longer needed to own property, as when Burr "bundled" votes to defeat the Federalists. Wealthy Protestants who saw those same new voters as a "noisy rabble" were furious. It was as if the struggle that began with Leisler was finally settled: the people now had electoral power over the grandees. This new electorate was, though, carefully limited. As of 1827, any enslaved person born on or after July 4, 1799, would be forever free; the 1821 law *increased* the property qualification for Black voters, so few of those African Americans would have a say in governing the state.

The voting rules clash showed the fatal New York trap: Some wealthy Protestants wanted to disenfranchise, or totally reform and transform, the Catholic Irish. But these were the same civic leaders who were leading the fight against slavery everywhere. Any move by elites to aid African Americans was seen as a threat by the Irish; any move by the Irish to rise or to fight the prevailing prejudice they faced involved distancing themselves from Blacks. Any benefit to one group was damaging to the other.

The New York elite took its lead from England in both disdaining the Irish and hating slavery, which England ended for all of its colonies in 1833. As the lawyer George Templeton Strong confided to his diary, "England is right about the lower class of Irish. They are brutal, base, cruel, cowards." Peter Williams Jr., an African American religious leader, tried to mobilize the negative view of immigrants to speak for his own people: "We are natives of this country, we ask only to be treated as well as foreigners."

For their part, the Irish could not stand the moralism of the rich people who had literally starved them to death in Ireland, paid them minimal wages in America, and forced their children to read Protestant texts, yet spoke passionately about the needs of Black people. "Irishmen have no [more] bitter enemies, Catholics no fiercer foes, than are nine-tenths of the American Abolitionists," wrote one Irish American publication in 1843. "Dark, sullen, ferocious bigots as they are, they abhor the name of Ireland and Catholicity." Faced with what they saw as such obnoxious and powerful enemies, the Irish made use of Tammany to fight political battles. And they turned their rage, their fury, against Black people. The more the Irish were seen as bestial, subhuman, and sinful, the more they were determined to show that they were totally different from African Americans—who were often described as having those same traits.

FAULT LINES: AMALGAMATION

On the sweltering night of July 9, 1834 (not coincidentally a year after England abolished slavery), New York was home to three connected white riots—against the very idea of ending slavery and the possibility of racial mixture. Arthur Tappan, a wealthy abolitionist, was falsely rumored to have married an African American, and Henry Ludlow, an abolitionist minister active in the Underground Railroad, was said to be holding interracial marriage ceremonies. A crowd of some one hundred attacked the home of Tappan's brother Lewis, also an active abolitionist. Smashing through windows and knocking down doors, they crashed into the house, pulled out paintings and furniture, and tossed them to the streets. Blocks away, a mob that may have been as large as three thousand was set to disrupt an abolitionist meeting scheduled to take place at the Chatham Street Chapel. The meeting had already been cancelled, so rioters from both locations streamed together down to the Bowery Theatre in order to harass a British actor

AN AMALGAMATION POLKA.

Drawn in 1845 by Edward Williams Clay, this image shows prominent abolitionists, both Black and white, dancing together, as if to speak for Black rights was to want to mix and intermarry.

they disliked. The theater manager was only able to calm the crowd by waving an American flag and bringing a singer onstage to sing the blackface minstrel role of Zip Coon, which assured the crowd that the manager shared their views.

While Tappan and Ludlow were advocates of Black rights, they lived in wealthy white neighborhoods. In the Five Points, Black people and white people were crushed together. White rioters warned white people to put a lit candle in their windows—then drove some five hundred Black and mixed-race people out of their tiny apartments and into the streets and parks. From then on, African Americans began moving out of the Five Points toward Greenwich Village and beyond.

Amalgamation—that is, the mixing of Black people and white people in churches, in the abolitionist cause, perhaps even in families, and thus children— became a word of extreme abuse in New York of the 1830s. The white horror at the thought of amalgamation belied the fact that it was white slaveholders who continually abused, and had children with, enslaved Black women. And indeed, it was in the Five Points neighborhood where Black people were driven out of their homes that white and Black people had chosen to live together, and to form families. The horror expressed at the thought of mixture was a fiendish mirror image of the actual connections between white and Black people.

Riots pitting working-class white people against African Americans and elite Protestants were one expression of the deep fault lines in the city. Racially segregated public transportation was another. As African Americans fled from the Five Points, more and more of them moved to lower Greenwich. By the 1850s, the area near Carmine Street and Sixth Avenue became known as Little Africa. Every fifth horse-drawn car that served the neighborhood carried a sign saying "Colored persons allowed in this car." A dark-skinned person could enter a white

In this 1864 cartoon, Abraham Lincoln is shown as Othello. One commentator says that he is so into the part he has "blackened himself all over," as if to oppose slavery was to become Black.

car—unless a single white passenger objected, in which case he or she had to leave. Until, that is, July 1854.

That month, Elizabeth Jennings boarded a horse-drawn railroad car on Third Avenue. The conductor warned her that she might have to leave. "I'm a respectable person, born and brought up in New York," she responded. The conductor spat back, "I was born in Ireland and you've got to get out of this car." It took the conductor, the driver, and a policeman to drag her away. But Jennings—backed by her well-respected father, white abolitionists such as Horace Greeley, and a young attorney named Chester A. Arthur (who would later become president)—took the rail line to court and won. By 1856, after another court fight, New York's public transportation was no longer segregated. But as with the mobs, this conflict revealed the contesting groups: wealthy Protestant abolitionists, like Greeley and Arthur, exerting control; Irish immigrants, like the conductor, keeping a tentative hold on their place in the city; and African Americans, like Elizabeth Jennings, battling for the most minimal respect and opportunity.

FAULT LINES: DOCKS

New Amsterdam began as a port, and by 1860, New York City (Manhattan) was the largest port in the nation by far. Just across the East River, Brooklyn was the third-largest city in the United States (after New York and Philadelphia), with its own growing set of ship companies. Lower Manhattan, especially along the East River, bristled with docks. Since the 1830s, New York had been the largest shipbuilder in the nation, with steamships coming and going, including regular routes across the Atlantic. In the next decade, New York began building and launching the speedy, tall-masted clipper ships that captured the wind and could cover the fourteen thousand miles to China in as few as seventy-four days. When gold was discovered in California, clipper ships built in New York and sailing from its wharves carried endless loads of eager prospectors—and the milk, coffee, flour, and clothes they would need once they landed.

Every steam or clipper ship that was built in the city required shipments of special wood and metal, and trained carpenters. In 1860, some sixty-six thousand seamen arriving on nearly four thousand ships landed in the city—needing food, lodging, drink, and entertainment. New York's port now featured a "sailor-town" of boarding houses, taverns, restaurants, and hiring halls for sailors. These mariners arrived from everywhere in the world and included a wide variety of ethnicities and races. The historian Johnathan Thayer calls the streets by the docks a "melting pot for all humanity." The port of New York, it would seem, could provide endless opportunity for a person with strong arms and a willingness to work. But that did not prove to be true.

Every boat that launched or landed needed to be loaded and unloaded. In the days before trucks and elevators, teams of men straining every muscle were required to drag, haul, and lift cargo using only ropes, pulleys, and levers. The word *longshoreman* is a shortened version of "along the shore," perhaps from a phrase called out from landing ships in colonial days: "Long shore!" That shout was an alert to all the men near the pier that a boat was about pull in and would need hands to unload it. Even as the port grew, working the docks meant living nearby and on call but never being sure when you would be needed. Local bosses called stevedores would pull together a crew as needed from the available men—which gave them a great deal of power. In turn, owners did everything they could to limit the wages and rights of the men working the docks. By the 1850s, the longshoremen's bustling but dangerous, low-paid, and never secure world of work was overwhelmingly white and Irish. The men knew one another and shared family connections, Catholicism, support for Tammany, and membership in the Democratic Party. A much smaller set of African American men also lived near the docks and found steady work there.

In the 1850s, the white longshoremen took a step to improve their lives: they formed the Longshoremen's United Benevolent Society and set rules for who could work on the docks—"such white laborers as they see fit to permit upon the premises." As one African American paper reported, "The influx of white laborers has expelled the Negro almost en masse from the exercise of the ordinary branches of labor."

Cynical politicians and newspaper writers kept warning the Irish that if slavery in the South ended, a wave of African Americans—protected and promoted by their rich Protestant allies—would take their jobs and lower their wages.

Painted by William J. Bennett in 1828, this view of South Street from Maiden Lane shows the density of ships arriving in New York's port and how close they came to the street. The port was a mixing place of sailors and goods from throughout the world, but also a site of friction over control of the docks.

In fact, the two groups were not competing for the same work. Poor African Americans were even more restricted in the jobs they could take than the Irish. They were confined to the work no one else wanted or would do, while the Irish found work as both skilled and unskilled laborers. The clash at the bottom of New York's social ladder was not really over jobs but over status. Who is better? Who is worse? Who is the least civilized, the least American, the least deserving? To rise in the city seemed to require forcing others to be beneath you.

The battle lines that were dividing America of the 1840s and '50s ran directly through New York: native-born Americans condemning immigrants; Protestants and Catholics in wars of words; the Irish furious at Blacks; abolitionists and defenders of slavery hating one another; and the steep and growing divides among rich, middle class, and poor. In 1848, revolutions broke out across Europe as the rule of kings and noble families was challenged in one city and country after another. For the moment, the royals managed to hold on to power, which sent the frustrated revolutionaries rushing across the ocean to New York. Some of these veterans of 1848 believed that wealth should be forcibly taken from owners and given to workers. New York, the city where money ruled, also housed critics of the entire capitalist system. Faced with racial conflict, political radicalism, and working-class riots, what could the city do?

THE PARK

The landscape architect Andrew Jackson Downing had an idea for healing the city. He thought parks could bring the city together: workers would walk beside gentlemen and learn to admire and copy their graces. Downing's idea soon gathered support, but each segment of the city had its own idea of what a park should be. Wealthy people who owned land wanted a park placed so that their properties would become more valuable. Spokesmen for the Irish were eager for open space near the Five Points. A German newspaper pushed for many small parks scattered in a variety of neighborhoods, not one near the richest in the city. People who owned property way uptown on the west side saw a park as a way to evict the 270 members of the well-established Black community of Seneca Village and the 1,600 German farmers who were already building their own settlements on empty land. Finally, in 1853, the uptown, wealthier New Yorkers won out. The park would indeed be far uptown: between Fifty-Ninth and 106th Streets (later expanded to 110th) and between Fifth and Eighth Avenues. This site forced the Black and German communities to lose their homes and to move.

Downing died in a boating accident, so a new designer was needed. When a contest for the best plan was held, Frederick Law Olmsted and another architect, Calvert Vaux, won. Their vision of the park matched Downing's original image. It would be a place that was "attractive as to force into contact the good and the bad, the gentlemanly and the rowdy." This contact, though, was to flow in one direction—the "rowdy" would be trained to admire and emulate the "gentlemanly."

The park, for example, featured a "bridle path"—a little over five miles laid

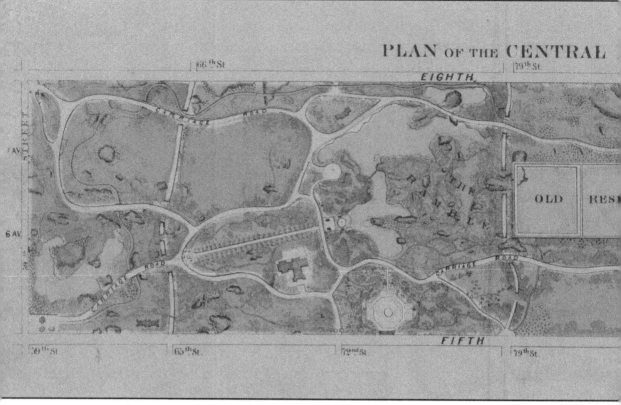

PLAN OF THE CENTRAL

This 1860 map shows the plan for the park, as well as the sites of the old and new reservoirs. Seneca Village, the African American settlement that was eliminated to create the park, was between 82nd and 89th Streets and between Seventh and Eighth Avenues.

out so that men and women who stabled or rented horses could enjoy a pleasant ride. A magazine writer in 1887 acknowledged that "most park users could not afford" the appropriate clothing, from black leather boots to trim riding hats. But the article reassured readers that "the spectacle of their betters on parade served an uplifting, or at least entertaining, purpose." Those not in the mood to saddle up and ride could make use of the six miles of paths designed for carriages—if they could afford to own or rent a fine coach and set of horses.

From the ideal of healing the city through riding paths, Central Park was born.

Central Park was designed to be a place of transformation that would weave together the divided city but only by "uplifting" the poor, not serving their needs. There was no plan for places to play games or open spaces to hold rallies. When the park opened in the winter of 1858, there was no public transportation inexpensive enough to allow a poor New Yorker to get there. Since New York was still a city of separated neighborhoods, this left Central Park as a preserve where elites could enjoy skating on frozen ponds or promenading along its twenty-eight miles of pleasant walkways. If a park could not heal the city, how would New York survive when the nation broke apart?

SNAPSHOT

New York in the Civil War and Reconstruction:
Railroads, Telegraph, New Wealth

1860 South Carolina secedes from the Union after the election of Abraham Lincoln.

Manhattan's population: 813,669 (12,574 of African descent). Kings County's population: 279,122 (4,999 of African descent)—making Brooklyn the third-largest city in the country after New York and Philadelphia. The population of the areas that will later form Greater New York is 1,174,779.

Approximately 66,000 sailors on 3,982 vessels enter the city's port.

1861 Ten more southern states secede from the Union.

Fort Sumter fired on by Confederates; Civil War begins.

1861–65 New York serves as a supply base for the Union army.

1863 Draft riots erupt in the city on July 13–16.

1864 Cornelius Vanderbilt gains control of the Hudson River Railroad.

1866 First successful transatlantic cable.

1867 Vanderbilt gains control of the New York Central Railroad.

Construction begins on first elevated railroad (el), which will link lower Manhattan to Thirtieth Street by 1870.

1869 On September 24, Jay Gould and Jim Fisk's attempt to control the price of gold collapses when President Grant intervenes; Wall Street crashes.

Transcontinental railroad completed with joining of Union Pacific and Central Pacific.

1870 Manhattan's population: 942,292 (13,072 of African descent). Kings County's population: 419,921 (5,653 of African descent).

William M. (Boss) Tweed controls the city; focus of port shifts from docks on the East River to those on the Hudson River.

1871 The first Grand Central Depot is built and handles eighty-five trains a day.

1873 The New York Central Railroad handles as much freight as the Erie Canal.

Wall Street firm headed by Jay Cooke fails and financial panic follows.

Tweed arrested.

1878 Els built on Sixth and Third Avenues.

1879 The very first telephone exchange opens at 82 Nassau Street; the first city phone directory, listing 252 names, was published the previous October.

1880 Manhattan's population: 1,206,299 (19,663 of African descent); Kings County's population: 599,495 (9,153 of African descent). The population of the areas that will later form Greater New York is 1,911,698.

CHAPTER 12

New York's Civil War

IS NEW YORK CITY PART OF THE UNITED STATES?

The election of Abraham Lincoln made a civil war seem inevitable. If the nation divided, where would New York City fit? Lincoln won the state of New York but lost the city by thirty thousand votes. A proposal to end the property qualification that still disenfranchised 80 percent of African American voters was defeated in the city by an even larger majority.

On January 7, 1861, New York's mayor, Fernando Wood, declared his sense of where the city belonged in the clash of North and South: "With our aggrieved brethren of the Slave States, we have friendly relations and a common sympathy." Wood suggested that the city might follow the Confederacy in leaving the Union and invite California with its gold to do so as well.

Wood was allied with the city's poor white voters, but that was not his only, or even main, reason for floating the startling idea. New York's economy was married to the slave South. As late as the 1850s, slavers were illegally setting sail from the city and coming back with human cargo. In 1856, Walt Whitman revealed that "this hellish traffic has been carried on from this port at least for twenty years." The number of ships was not large, but the willingness of the city, its police, and its judges to look the other way was a sign of how much the slave economy meant to the city. And the South knew it.

"What would become of the great metropolis, New York," a southern magazine asked, if it did not have cotton to ship, slave plantations to finance and outfit? "The ships would rot at her docks; grass would grow in Wall Street and Broadway." Many of the city's wealthiest, most established leaders agreed. Some of these men were descendants of colonial grandees; others had made their fortunes more recently in New York's active and churning economy. They shared a common sympathy for the South and hatred for Lincoln. Many belonged to the Union Club on Fifth Avenue and Twenty-First Street, not far from Union Square.

Mayor, old money, new money, Irish immigrants—could the city unite against Lincoln, against the Union, and either join the slave South or become an independent city-state-port serving the cotton economy?

No. The moment word reached the city that shots had been fired at Fort Sumter and the Civil War had begun, the mood of Gotham entirely switched. Once the issue was not rights for African Americans but holding the nation together, the city united behind that cause. George Templeton Strong felt the shift and wrote in his diary, "Change in public feeling marked, and a thing to thank God for. We begin to look like a United North." Buildings and window displays everywhere, even the floor of the stock exchange, now sported Union flags, and the head of the chamber of commerce swore that "there can be no neutrality now—we are either for the country or its enemies." Mayor Wood, never known for having firm convictions, came out for the Union and against the South. The new mood of the city was to be declared in a mass rally at Union Square on April 20.

How many people could possibly crowd into the park? By some counts, 100,000; by others, up to 250,000. New York gathered to greet Major Robert Anderson, who had defended Fort Sumter, and to see the tattered Union flag he brought back. Defense of the nation rallied the city, and not just to defeat the South. "Now," wrote Jane Woolsey, who would go on to serve as a nurse during the war along with her mother and sisters, "we don't feel that the social fabric is falling to pieces at all, but that it is getting gloriously mended." Perhaps war could do what Central Park couldn't—bring the factions of the city together.

The Tammany Society itself recruited a division to fight for the Union: the Forty-Second New York, many of whose members hailed from the Five Points. By 1863, a new generation of business and professional leaders, including the

With this image we begin to enter the era of photography. It was taken in Union Square during the rally on April 20, 1861, and nearly every inch of the park was filled with people.

merchant prince A. T. Stewart and park designer Frederick Law Olmsted, created the Union League Club to counter the grandees of the Union Club and to support the Union. The Union League built their headquarters on Seventeenth Street facing Union Square. Supplying the Union army soon took the place of handling southern cotton, and New York seemed to settle down—until it exploded.

"DOWN WITH THE RICH MEN"

By March 1863, the Union army knew it was going to need more soldiers. Some enlistments were expiring, the pace of casualties was rising, and the war was not going well—which further discouraged men from signing up. Rather than wait to see who would volunteer, Congress passed a law making all white men between twenty-five and thirty-five, and unmarried men between thirty-five and forty-five, eligible to be drafted. Once a list was compiled, a lottery would determine who had to set off to war. There was, though, an out. Everyone knew that some people would try to evade serving. The new bill created an official way to accomplish that: find a substitute who was willing to go in your stead, or pay three hundred dollars (about six thousand dollars today), and you were exempt.

If you were for the war and in favor of the government taking over where states were too divided, weak, or corrupt to act, this was a good plan. And if you were well-off, this all seemed rational and clear. If you were poor and you had no way of gathering three hundred extra dollars, this was horribly unfair. The draft law almost perfectly—terribly—fit the New York trap. Lincoln had announced the Emancipation Proclamation, which would take effect on January 3, 1863. The kind of men who formed the Union League could see an efficient national government gathering the army it needed to defeat the rebellious South and free African Americans from slavery. The Irish workers found it doubly unfair—they had to fight a rich man's war, and they had to risk their lives to free Black people. It was as if Black people were rising above the helpless Irish, uplifted by their safe, rich, Protestant friends.

Monday, July 13, the new draft was to begin, and the city was strangely quiet. Hundreds of men due to report for work as early as 6 a.m. at machine shops, on the docks, in construction, could not be found. At eight, the missing men appeared, together, marching up Manhattan's West Side, urging their fellow workers to leave their jobs and join them. What began as a peaceful protest—complete with NO DRAFT posters—changed mood as they reached the East Side. Marchers tore down telegraph poles, pulled up railroad tracks, and began beating up people they recognized as opponents.

A fire company that had lost one member to the new draft burst into the office where the selection was taking place, chanting, "Down with the rich men." The firemen smashed the lottery wheel and set the place on fire.

As Monday stretched on, perhaps as many as fifty thousand men, women, and children rushed to the Upper East Side to join the protests, to cheer them on, to watch. The mood of the city was so dangerous that the draft was suspended, which accomplished nothing. Empty and unguarded draft sites were perfect targets. Two hundred men led by Patrick Merry, an Irish laborer, burned a draft office on Twenty-Ninth Street and Broadway and ransacked a nearby jewelry store, leaving with as many valuables as they could grab before beating up an African American fruit seller. Merry's rampage hit targets associated with the draft, the rich, and the Black people—as if he and his men were trying to wipe out everything in the city they hated with one violent blow. Other rioters broke into the homes of rich Republicans, ripping apart "pictures with gilt frames . . . sofas, chairs, clocks."

The torrent of violence and hate reached a climax when a mob set fire to the Colored Orphan Asylum at Forty-Third Street and Fifth Avenue, exposing all 237 children to the flames.

Not content with trying to burn the children alive, the vicious mob set out to break into the building, hacking at the doors with axes. The doors held just long enough for the asylum's superintendent, William Davis, to lead most of the children out. An Irish protester pleaded for the rest, shouting, "If there's a man among you, with a heart within him, come and help these poor children." The crowd beat him, but another man named Paddy M'Caffrey and his fellow workers and firemen protected the last twenty children and got them to safety.

This was a racial purge sweeping through the city. Those who took to the streets were trying to erase African Americans—by lynching one if they could catch him, or through brutal intimidations. Longshoremen announced that "the colored people must and shall be driven" from the docks. Younger men, even gangs of boys, set upon any Black people—or mixed couples—they could find to beat or kill them. "The laboring classes there," wrote a journalist about one poor white section of the city, "appear to be of the opinion that the negroes are the sole cause of all their trouble, and many even say that were it not for the negroes there

People were horrified by the fury of the draft riots, especially by the burning of the Colored Orphan Asylum (top). The rage in the crowds is evident in the lower image—the conflicts and pressures in the city that had been building for decades exploded.

would be no war and no necessity for a draft." The draft protests opened the flood-gates of the city's violent passions: the poor against the rich, immigrants against Black people, factory workers against owners, pro-Southerners against aboli-tionists. Though they did not approve of the rioters, the elites themselves were divided—Union Club members who hated the draft and Union League mem-bers who supported it. New York City was having its own civil war—with each segment of the city making its own way through the growing chaos. Every indi-vidual had to make a choice: while many of the rioters were Irish, M'Caffrey saved Black children and Irish policemen were fiercely attacked by the mobs. Black men were lynched—hanged, burned, and mutilated—but where they could, Black people fought back and defended themselves.

By Monday night, the fire companies pulled back. By Tuesday, most German Americans sided with Lincoln's Republicans against the riots. But by Tuesday night, the mayor asked for men to be sent from Gettysburg to restore order.

New York's leaders did not approve of the violence—this was not the kind of pogrom where officials look the other way while mobs attack the vulnerable. But they hesitated, afraid that if they declared martial law and turned the city over to the army, they would fuel the most extreme anti-government emotions. Besides, the battle of Gettysburg had ended two weeks before and New York in flames would be just the encouragement the South might need to fight on, or for the British to intervene and support their cause.

By Wednesday, the marauding bands were made up of poorer men who worked in factories—the skilled workers had stayed home. So had the poor-est Irish Americans of the Five Points. Six thousand federal troops arrived by Wednesday night and brought their grim, battle-hardened discipline to the streets of New York. By late Thursday, the riots were over.

While estimates at the time said hundreds, even thousands, died, histori-ans can only account for 119 deaths, most of whom were rioters shot by federal troops. Whatever the actual death toll, this was by far the nation's worst urban clash.

And yet, by August 19, the draft began again—and while ten thousand troops arrived to keep the peace, there were no protests at all.

William Marcy Tweed, a rising star in Tammany, had found a way out of the crisis. If the law said anyone could pay three hundred dollars to get out of the draft, there was a simple way to make sure this would not discriminate against the poor: create a fund that would supply the money to anyone who requested it. The city agreed to a $3 million bond providing the base of what would eventually grow to $14 million. The decision of whether to serve and collect a nice bonus or to stay at home became a matter of personal choice, not personal finances.

Tweed's plan was the beginning of a New York in which money could heal all wounds. Money from the city, from the state, from the nation, was filtered through and handed out by the organized power of Tammany Hall and its soon-to-be grand sachem, its leader, William Tweed. In that sense, the rioters had made their point—wealth should not decide life or death. Even if they were poor, they could organize and make demands.

The other resolution to the draft crisis came, as the *Times* wrote, some eight months later on March 5, 1864, once again at Union Square, in front of the Union League Club.

The square was filled—up to one hundred thousand people took up every spot—to watch a regiment of soldiers receive their special flags. The men assembled in perfect formation in front of the club had one thing in common: every one of the soldiers was Black. This new regiment had been recruited by the Union League itself, the new generation of elite leaders of the city. The women of the Union League came forward to honor the brave soldiers, pledging to "anxiously watch your career, glorying in your heroism, ministering to you when wounded and ill, and honoring your martyrdom with benedictions and tears." In a city, indeed a nation, where *amalgamation* had been a curse word, elite white women were blessing Black soldiers and promising to honor or heal them.

The Civil War left New York with Tammany and Tweed in power with plans to build a new headquarters around the corner from Union Square, and the Union League with its support for African Americans perched on the square. The end of national combat opened the next act of the contest across the park for control of the city.

CHAPTER 13

Across the Square

On the auspicious date of July 4, 1868, the Democratic Party opened its national convention in the spacious new location of Tammany Hall: 141 East Fourteenth Street just off Union Square. The Tammany Society was happy to show off its mammoth auditorium and its power in the city; the Democrats were just as eager to meet in New York. The party prided itself on being the voice of working people standing up to the wealthy and the defender of immigrants against prejudiced nativists. Tammany, the voice of New York's Irish immigrants, was a perfect host. The convention was open to new ideas: Susan B. Anthony arrived and praised the party for having fought for "the removal of the 'property qualification' from all white men, and thereby placed the poorest ditch-digger on a political level with the proudest millionaire. And now you have an opportunity to confer a similar boon on the women of the country." Democrats were receptive to Anthony (though they did not adopt her idea), especially as she had alluded to the principle the party thought was the key to its success: it was the party of white rule.

Now, with the war over, many Republicans believed that all adult male Americans must be treated as equal citizens with equal voting rights. That meant the South needed to be watched over by federal troops to protect the rights of formerly enslaved people. New York, whose white electorate continued to disenfranchise its own Black citizens by insisting that they—and only they— must own property in order to vote, was a good place for the Democratic Party to meet.

As the 1868 presidential election approached, Democrats, with support from the nearby Tammany Society, filled Union Square. The true center of the city, the square was the natural place for all causes to gather and to show their strength.

The year before, the Democrats had scored a series of electoral successes throughout the North running on their platform of white racism. Banners blaring the party's position—WHITE MEN SHALL RULE AMERICA—decorated lively rallies. Voters, they sensed correctly, accepted that the war had ended slavery, but just as firmly believed Black people were inferior and did not deserve full and equal voting rights. The party was eager to use those victories as a map to winning the presidency. Samuel J. Tilden, a prominent New York lawyer who would be the Democratic candidate for president in 1876, sent out a message urging that "our position must be *condemnation and reversal of negro suffrage in the states*" (italics in the original). The Democrats were sure that white voters did not see the end of slavery as being the same as accepting African Americans as equal citizens.

A key step in taking the elections lay in winning New York State, and there the Tammany Society's power in the city could be crucial. Tammany came through by giving up to sixty thousand Irish immigrants almost instant citizenship so that they could vote the party line. But even as the nominating convention was taking place, Tweed had his eye on his own grand goals: gaining control of every aspect of the city's finances. Anything that needed to be built, maintained, or approved would go through him or his loyal allies. And that meant the Festival of Greed could begin.

THE FESTIVAL OF GREED

Daniel Drew, the stock trader who lived on Union Square, had new allies in competing with Cornelius Vanderbilt on Wall Street—the sharp traders Jim Fisk and Jay Gould. Fights over control of railroad lines were not just questions of who owned the most stock. Legal issues often arose—which meant that whoever owned the most corrupt legislators and judges was likely to get rulings in his favor. The pathways to New York's corrupt politicians and judges went through Tweed. Fisk's and Gould's money gave Tweed an ever-growing war chest. He, in turn, used the money for new bribes to get laws passed that gave him more power.

Tweed was similar to many wealthy men of his time; that is, while he was relatively tall at five foot eleven, he was also round, weighing in somewhere between 280 and 320 pounds. Hungry for food, for wealth, for power, he was the kind of man who got everything he wanted—and more. The city was expanding uptown along the East Side toward Harlem, which meant erecting new buildings, laying new water, sewer, and gas pipes, and constructing new streets and avenues. Tweed and his friends bought property just ahead of where developers were coming and cashed in by owning the land the developers would need. He then made sure to be properly bribed to give out every contract he and his allies approved. According to one account, Tweed played so many angles that he made as much as $5.5 million (about $110 million today) in just one particularly lucrative morning. When the city decided to rent out space in Tammany Hall, he charged over $36,000—conveniently adding a zero to the usual fee. The space itself was not even suited to the purpose the city had in mind. Inflating the price of a contract that should not have been given in the first place was characteristic of Tweed: think big, think bigger, grab what you get, don't look back.

Tweed did not think there was anything wrong with what he was doing.

He insisted, with some justification, that "New York politics were always dishonest—long before my time." Indeed, he saw himself as performing a kind of service. A city as divided between Protestant and Catholic, rich and poor, immigrant and native as New York could never function just through voting. It needed the grease of "bribery or patronage or corruption." He was not entirely wrong. Even as he siphoned off millions upon millions of dollars, he made sure the growing city was built well. His streets used the latest technologies, his sewage lines were carefully researched, the three- and four-story homes that were being built for middle-class families featured modern toilets and clean Croton water. He orchestrated plans for an immense system of trains that would ride on elevated platforms up Third Avenue and down Sixth Avenue, covering the length of Manhattan. Union Leaguers and

Thomas Nast's caricatures of "Boss" Tweed made fun of and captured the web of patronage and larceny that surrounded him and his supporters.

even journalists happily invested in the city's new transportation systems, starting with those initially favored by Tweed. Tweed was masterminding the next stage of city growth, with side payments to himself every inch along the way.

Across the square, almost everything Tweed, Tammany, and the Democratic Party did revolted the men of the Union League. They worked to protect Black voters in the South, to eliminate the property rule for Black voters in New York, to challenge the Tammany naturalization machine that instantly turned Irish immigrants into voters, and to bring Tweed to justice. The reformers had two useful allies: Congress and the press.

The Democrats were wrong about the 1868 presidential election. Staying quiet about his views on Black suffrage, General Grant was elected president, and Congress was in Republican hands. By February 1870, Congress passed and the states ratified the Fifteenth Amendment, which gave equal voting rights to all

Tammany and the Democrats supported Irish immigrants against the prejudice of elite Protestants and Republicans, but also made use of their power in the city to grant quick citizenship to incoming newcomers in exchange for their loyalty and their votes.

men, no matter how some states wanted to resist. In the next election, federal supervisors would come to New York, as they did to the South, to make sure African Americans could vote—and instant citizens could not. While the percentage of African Americans in New York had been declining throughout the nineteenth century, when they could finally vote, some eleven thousand new voices would be added to any election. That was not good news for Tammany Hall.

John Davenport, a former Union officer, was put in charge of making sure that the November 1870 elections in the city would comply with the Fifteenth Amendment. Davenport also happened to be the legal counsel to the Union League. In order to watch over the polling places, he made use of federal marshals, men empowered to enforce the law. Hiring about two hundred African Americans as part of his crew of marshals, Davenport made his views visible and clear. Instead of being excluded from voting, African Americans would now be patrolling the voting places as the arm of national law and power. When New York City police tried to intimidate and even arrest the newly deputized marshals, Davenport arrested the policemen. Tweed, of course, bailed out the patrolmen, but a judge ruled against them. The integrated team of marshals took to the streets to supervise the election.

The *New York Times* was as eager to expose Tweed as were the Union Leaguers. That gave a voice to any witnesses who had evidence and were willing to share it. At the same time, the political cartoonist Thomas Nast drew clever, biting satires for *Harper's Weekly* magazine that reached people who might not spend the time to read lengthy exposés. "I don't care much what the papers write about me," Tweed grumbled, "my constituents can't read. But—dammit!—they can see pictures." As in the colonial days of Zenger, the press was going to battle with power.

For those who could read, the *Times* had the evidence. An ambitious former ally of Tweed's named James O'Brien had demanded a payoff of $350,000 ($7 million today) to keep his head down. Tweed refused. O'Brien managed to obtain copies of Tweed's actual account books and snuck them to the paper. There it was in print, graft on a grand scale: a new courthouse that was budgeted at $250,000 in 1858 was finally finished in 1872 at a cost of $12 million— $9 million of which sluiced directly to Tweed and company. And graft on the smallest scale: the city paid Tweed's dog walker one hundred dollars a month as an interpreter, though perhaps aside from a sensitivity to barks and yelps, he could neither read nor write in any language. By November 1873, the cartoons and exposés did their work. The city turned against its former leader and Tweed was brought to trial. The Festival of Greed he had overseen ended.

The Union League versus Tweed was Hamilton and Burr all over again. Hamilton had warned of leaders who might use the "popular party" to become an "embryo-Caesar." Tweed had done just that—using Irish votes to establish himself as an embryo-Midas: his hands touched everything that was built in the growing city, and every touch yielded gold for him and his allies. Burr, in turn, had found a way to give power to powerless workers, those excluded by the kinds of voting rules Hamilton favored. Tweed and Tammany really did give the Irish, and the white working class, a voice in the city. By contrast, E. L. Godkin, the editor of the prominent magazine the *Nation*, railed against "ignorant" Irish Catholics and insisted that it was time for "the Anglo-Saxon race" to run the city.

To him, that meant British Protestants, not Irish Catholics. Nast, the cartoonist, marched with Irish Protestants in a parade meant to insult and humiliate Irish Catholics.

In 1876, neither Democrat Tilden nor Republican Rutherford B. Hayes garnered enough electoral votes to become president. That left it to Congress to sort out. The Republicans made a deal: they would abandon African Americans in the South, leaving the former Confederate states to the control of local whites, in exchange for the presidency. Increasingly the attention of the Republican Party shifted from African American rights to absolute support for business and wealth. The new face of wealthy, elite New York and America was J. P. Morgan. Morgan's father was a successful American banker with headquarters in London. His son made money during the Civil War by buying rifles from the government for $3.50 each, loaning enough money to a middleman to buy them from him at $11.50 each, improve them, and then sell them back to the government at $22 each. When the army sued, the courts ruled for Morgan—business was business and a bad deal was still a deal. Cornelius Vanderbilt's son and heir William, who invested with Morgan, expressed the new elite's sense of superiority as forcefully as possible. "The public," he exclaimed, "be damned."

There was just one place in the city where Union Leaguers and Tammany supporters might meet, and it, too, was found near Union Square.

In 1868, Dan Bryant's Minstrels, one of the most popular and longstanding minstrel groups in the country, made the auditorium in Tammany Hall their new home. Union Square was about to become the center of entertainment for the city. You could get there by horse-drawn train, omnibus, carriage, foot, and soon the el, and it was filled with crowds.

The horse-drawn trains and omnibuses could not meet the needs of the expanding city. After Tweed's fall, a new group of investors took on the challenge of fixing the city's transportation, and within a decade steam-powered "elevated" (el) trains were clattering along tracks built above Second, Third, Sixth, and Ninth Avenues at up to twelve miles per hour. There was a price for the speed of the el—the novelist William Dean Howells, who was used to Boston's quiet streets, warned that "no experience of noise can enable you to conceive of the furious din. . . . The noise is not only deafening, it is bewildering." Not only were the trains noisy and, on steep curves, dangerous, but the structure of steel cast avenues in shadow, making stretches of Manhattan seem like a vast insect encased in its exoskeleton. But a trip to Union Square made it all worthwhile.

VARIETY

Starting in the 1830s, saloon concerts gave men in New York places to drink, shout, and enjoy boisterous entertainment designed just for them and considered inappropriate for women.

Tony Pastor started his career in show business in 1849 when he was just twelve, singing in blackface at Barnum's museum. As he grew up, Pastor went on tour as a circus clown, sang at temperance meetings, and by the Civil War, was writing his own songs. Pastor was on the side of the worker, the little man, and the Irish against the rich—but also white people over Black people. His blackface songs were in exaggerated dialect, portraying Black people as illiterate and foolish. His songs for poor whites had real sting. Commenting, for example, on the Draft Riot, he wrote:

> We are coming, Father Abraham
> Three Hundred dollars more;
> We're rich enough to stay at home,
> Let them go out that's poor.

In lyrics that sound like a modern criticism of the wealthiest 1 percent, he said:

> The Upper Ten Thousand in mansions reside,
> With fronts of brown stone, and with stoops high and wide
> While the lower Ten Thousand in poverty deep,
> In cellars and garrets, are huddled like sheep.

For all his criticism of the wealthy, Pastor was a canny businessman, and after the war he came to a crucial realization about entertainment in the city. He

As this bill from Tony Pastor's theater shows, he offered a sequence, or "variety," of acts: Dutch Deception, Irish Comic Extravaganza, French Sisters. The performers reflected, and made fun of, the variety of people in the city. The audience was also a mixture, though it did not include African Americans. The beautiful singer and actress Lillian Russell was a star of her day.

"determined that if women could be induced to attend, the patronage could be materially extended." That is, if the elements society considered inappropriate for women—racy, coarse acts, the heavy drinking, and the raucous crowd—could be toned down, women as well as men, the rich and the poor, could attend the same shows. Saloon concerts typically had many acts and were thus called "variety" shows. Pastor intended to have a similar mix of comedy, song, minstrelsy, and animal acts but in a new, more tempered key. Pastor would present mixed fare for a mixed public. This was New York as a place of transformation at work. Though he did not employ the term, Pastor's new brand of performance took on its own name: vaudeville. In 1881, he moved his theater into the auditorium in Tammany Hall. This was a perfect location for reaching out to a wide audience, and soon Union Square became the hub of vaudeville for the nation, and the world.

A songwriter named Edward Marks explained how music circulated through Pastor's. After an "initial break in the beer hall, a song might work up to the smaller variety houses, and finally to Tony Pastor's, on Fourteenth Street, or Koster and Bial's, whence some British singer might carry it home to London. If it scored there, it might come back here as a society sensation." Koster and Bial were promoters who had a music hall of their own on Twenty-Third Street.

Performers gathered in Union Square, going from one talent booking office to another, looking to be placed on the roster for a New York or touring vaude-ville company. The old elite oval had become the hiring hall for aspiring perform-ers. These shows very often made fun of the Irish, the Jews, the Italians, always the Black people, American Indians, feminists, reformers—they were demean-ing and insulting in every way. Yet they were also a vehicle for performers who were themselves from every kind of background to make a career in show busi-ness. There is a direct line of performers and routines from vaudeville to musical theater, film, TV, and even stand-up comedy today.

Stretching ever northward from Union Square, one block after another along Broadway was filled with theaters and companies booking talent to tour the nation in vaudeville groups. Called the "Rialto" after a famous neighborhood in Venice, this swath of Manhattan was the theatrical heart of the nation. In the 1880s, there were more than a hundred companies based in the Rialto that sent performers from New York across the country. By 1904, that number crossed four hundred. Any tourist visiting the city had to go to the Rialto to visit the legendary stages. Any local theater throughout the United States was thrilled to feature a touring company based along the same Manhattan streets. Vaudeville was New York's machine of popular culture at work. Drawing on the ethnic, reli-gious, racial, class, and gender conflicts and connections of the city, vaudeville made insulting fun of nearly everyone and engaged audiences across the land.

The Union Square of Tammany and Tiffany, of Daniel Drew's home, of the Union League and the Union Club, of the eager patrons of first Dan Bryant's minstrel shows and then Tony Pastor's variety productions was something new in the world. For the first time, the center of a city was not city hall, as it had been on the old Wall Street; was not a church like Trinity; was not an open market. Union Square was none of these and all of these—it was where many of the forces rising, pushing, suffering, triumphing in the city all met. It was the heartbeat of a city that was about to change. The next wave of immigrants was about to arrive, to live in their own new neighborhoods, linked by new forms of transportation, and the city would soon find a new center.

SNAPSHOT

The Golden Door—The New Waves of Immigration Begin

1881   Steel steamships begin to replace iron-hulled vessels.

Anti-Semitism and pogroms in Russia push ever more Jews to immigrate to the United States. By 1910, 1.4 million Jews will have moved to the city, of whom 1.1 million will remain as residents.

Cuban poet and advocate of independence José Martí comes to New York and works to free his homeland and Puerto Rico from Spanish rule.

1882   Thomas Edison opens the world's first electric power generation station at 257 Pearl Street in Lower Manhattan.

1883   Approximately nineteen thousand vessels reach the New York port annually.

1884   The New York Central Railway is carrying twice as much freight as the Erie Canal.

1886   Statue of Liberty completed and opened to the public.

1890   Manhattan's population: 1,515,301, 23,601 of African descent. The population of the areas that will later form Greater New York is 2,507,414.

1892   Ellis Island immigration center opens.

1895   New York Public Library created by combining the Astor, Lenox, and Tilden collections.

CHAPTER **14**

"The Streets Belonged to Us"

May 1, 1890

Mounted on a white horse was a tall man whose glossy black hair and dark eyes gave him a look of biblical power and authority. With his resonant voice and command of Jewish learning, Joseph Barondess might have been a rabbi, as his father had been back in the Ukraine, or an actor, as he trained to be in America, but he was a labor leader. Trailing behind Barondess were some nine thousand Jewish workers marching uptown from the Lower East Side to Union Square. The army of protesters were demanding that their workday be limited to eight hours, a cause they shared with workers of all backgrounds.

Labor began using the square as a gathering place just after the Civil War in 1866. Those gatherings increased in 1872 when the designers of Central Park reconfigured the genteel oval of Union Square to include a platform for speakers and an open space for meetings. On September 5, 1882, the very first Labor Day demonstration was held there, with unions carrying signs declaring that LABOR BUILT THIS REPUBLIC AND LABOR SHALL RULE IT, NO MONEY MONOPOLY. Four years later, on May 1, International Workers' Day was first celebrated in New York and throughout the country. The "union" in Union Square was no longer a reference to crossed avenues or elite clubs—it meant the place where the voice of working people, of the Left, would demand to be heard.

Ever since the "mechanics" party of Burr's time, workers in the city had tried many ways of organizing to fight for their rights. Some groups bonded in being white, others in being German, or Irish, or male, skilled artisans or unskilled masses. Some chose to craft alliances with Tammany or the Democratic Party, others to form their own parties or, as the ideas of Karl Marx spread in Europe and America, to demand revolutionary change. In June 1872, some one hundred thousand workers—inspired in part by a radical uprising in Paris two years earlier—marched through the city to demand an eight-hour workday. A year later, a major economic panic set off a four-year depression that left up to a quarter of the city's workers without jobs. New York was becoming a national center of discussion, planning, and strikes as working people fought for their place in society. Labor was a potent force in the city, and Union Square was its main staging ground.

The rally led by Barondess carried yet another message: New York was becoming a homeland, *the* homeland, of poor working-class Jews from Eastern Europe. In that sense, "union" was not just organized labor; it was the expression of a common lot in life. Barondess led a union of people who made clothing on sewing machines, and in 1900, 90 percent of those workers in New York were Jewish.

The Statue of Liberty was dedicated on October 28, 1886. In the next twenty-eight years (until World War I interrupted sea travel and then restrictive immigration laws were passed), seventeen million immigrants arrived in the United States, the vast majority of them through New York Harbor. This was by far the largest movement of people in the history of the world. The new arrivals changed the city, the nation, the world, and themselves. One strand of these new immigrants were Jewish workers such as those who marched with the charismatic Barondess to Union Square.

Ellis Island opened as an entry point and inspection station for immigrants in 1892. More than twelve million people passed through its doors before it closed in 1954.

Throughout the nineteenth century, German Jews followed the Spanish and Portuguese Jews of Stuyvesant's day in making New York their new home. By the late nineteenth century, the German Jews were relatively well established in the city: they spoke English and owned businesses or worked in skilled trades or professions. In 1870, there were about 60,000 Jewish people in a city of 940,000—a small but solid community. By 1900, the Jewish population swelled to 290,000; almost all the new arrivals came from Russia or other parts of Eastern Europe.

Starting in 1881, a series of anti-Semitic attacks sponsored by the Russian authorities launched a period of crisis for Russian Jews. A regular flow of steamships made moving to New York one possible solution for escaping the pogroms. Yet there were many paths for Jews to consider: immigrating to Palestine (the biblical Holy Land), plotting for revolutionary change in Russia, trusting miracle-working rabbis, building new businesses. All of these options were being considered and discussed. Between 1900 and 1910, over one million Eastern European Jewish immigrants landed

Lewis Hine's 1905 photo captures one of the millions of Russian Jewish immigrants who arrived at Ellis Island. Hine was a sociologist who used photographs not just to document people and events but as tools to promote social change.

in New York City. In Europe and in America, the keynote of Jewish life was ferment, searching, seeking answers. That fever was inflamed on the streets of the Lower East Side, home to five hundred thousand Jews.

THE JEWISH LOWER EAST SIDE: CRAMMED TOGETHER, SPLITTING APART

The Jewish Lower East Side ran roughly from the Bowery on the west to the East River, and from East Broadway on the south to East Houston on the north; it included such streets as Orchard, Hester, Delancey, Forsyth, Allen, and Grand. Three-quarters of New York's Jews lived in roughly that area in 1892. To New

The Lower East Side was the initial home for many Jewish immigrants arriving from Eastern Europe. In 1910, for example, the blocks between Delancey and Rivington Streets, from Allen to the river, housed thirty synagogues, with another twenty-two between Grand and Hester. Jews lived, worked, shopped, studied, played, and prayed on these dense streets.

Yorkers from long-standing families, the influx of Eastern European Jews made their city unrecognizable. The *New York Herald* wrote that the Jewish neighborhood "is as unknown a country as Central Africa." William Crary Brownell, the gentlemanly editor of books by leading authors such as Edith Wharton and Henry James, saw the spread of posters with text in Hebrew and Yiddish as a kind of barbed wire blocking his sight: "Broadway beneath Tenth Street is a forest of signs which obscure the thoroughfare, conceal the buildings, overhang the sidewalks." James himself literally sputtered in print trying to find the words for what he was seeing when he returned from England to visit his native New York. He called the new neighborhood "something fantastic, and *abracadabrandt*, belonging to no known language." (The French word he slightly modified is suggestive of magic, of abracadabra, and means "incredible, preposterous.") For both men, the problem was not simply that strange languages now covered once-familiar streets but, rather, that wholly unfamiliar lives were unfolding in their city. It was as if some spell had wiped away the known and replaced it with the phantasmagorical, the bizarre.

For the arriving Jews, the "forest of signs" was the most comforting assurance of welcome. Right outside the doors of their apartment buildings, they would find a version of the world they had left behind. Inside was another matter. The new immigrant neighborhoods were just like the old Five Points: so crowded that the term *crowded* itself is far too mild. *Crammed* is not just more evocative; it is more accurate. In 1895, there were sections of New York near the Lower East Side in which eight hundred people lived on each acre of land, more than in any other place—city, town, or village—on earth. Five years later, there were blocks in the heart of the Jewish neighborhood with more than double that population, some 1,750 people per acre.

Jews often came in a staggered sequence: a father or son arrived first and strove to earn enough money to send for his wife and children, then parents or relatives. This did not always go as planned; the first male might disappear into the new country, to remarry or struggle with failure he could not admit. But as a rule, Jews came as families and formed families once in America. Poor immigrants could not afford the rent on their own, so they took in boarders, often a new set of men arriving to earn enough to bring their own families. A two-bedroom apartment might have four or five adults and two, three, or more children from infants to teenagers together. One survey in 1908 found that half of the families had three or four people sleeping in a single room, and for nearly a quarter of the families, one room was home to five or more. And that was only a count of those who lived in those tight spaces. Until an 1892 act forbade it (and since the law was not well enforced, long after), sewing clothing often took place in the home and involved the entire family. Home was literally a fraction of apartment space in which to eat, sleep, and work—with a smelly public toilet somewhere in, or just outside, the building. "Privacy in the home," one writer recalled, "was practically unknown."

This sardine-like living had two opposite effects. So many Jewish immigrants, and soon their children, lived similar lives of similar labor under similar

Hester Street: The Jewish Lower East Side

Three scenes on Hester Street over a decade give a sense of the density of people in the neighborhood.

The image at left is a Jacob Rils photograph that he took in 1890. The crowded street was the only place children could play. The sign on the top left of the picture is in Yiddish—a form of middle German written in Hebrew characters.

Opposite: The corner of Hester and Norfolk Streets eight years later, when shopping has spread off of the curbs

The photograph below, taken in 1902, gives a wide vista of the layers of people walking, shopping, selling, and driving carts through the same streets.

conditions that it was very easy to think of themselves as a group. These shared experiences made group solutions—unions, Socialism, organizations of people from the same regions, synagogues—appealing. But especially for the young, there was something between the crammed apartments and the group events: the streets.

Whenever people tumbled out of those clogged apartments, they filled the streets: to shop, to play, to talk, and to watch. Rows of peddlers with their carts filled both sides of a street, with layers of shoppers passing among them. Anzia Yezierska, the great novelist of the female Jewish immigrant experience, described the scene: "Hester Street roared like a carnival. . . . Women with market baskets jammed against each other at the pushcarts, their eyes bright with the zest of bargain hunting."

For the young, the streets were a living social network. Irving Howe, the chronicler of the Lower East Side, said of his own childhood, "The streets were ours. Everyplace else—home, school, shop—belonged to the grownups. But the streets belonged to us." A few boys might be playing stickball in an alleyway, while girls watched both the game and the infants and toddlers roaming about, and yet other groups of passersby streamed along the sidewalks. You can still almost hear the density of whispers, confidences, rumors, stories that must have swirled through those streets. Common challenges brought a sense of unity, but the streets, Howe wrote, "spoke of freedom." Girls' lives were much more confined than boys', yet Yezierska echoed Howe's words: "Choked for ages in the airless oppression of Russia, the Promised land rose up—wings for my stifled spirit—sunlight burning through my darkness—freedom singing to me in my prison." "I am a Russian Jewess," Yezierska wrote in a novel, "a flame—a longing. A soul consumed with hunger for heights beyond reach. I am the ache of unvoiced dreams, the clamor of suppressed desires."

America brought Jews freedom *from* the oppressions of the tsar and the pervasive anti-Semitism in Russian society. Yet America also brought Jewish young people freedom *to* explore, or at least imagine, new ways of living. To parents, New York's restless streets brought a new kind of danger for their children: Would they become unrecognizable as they became American?

THEATER AND SONG: BECOMING AMERICAN

As Jews filled the Lower East Side, they began to find new ways to hold together and to make sense of their new lives. Great cantors—men (and today also women) who sing prayers as part of synagogue services—began to make records and to appear on stages as musical stars. Prayers in Hebrew, often expressing intense longing and suffering, were becoming one form of popular culture.

Plays in Yiddish—the common language of Eastern European Jews—performed a kind of magic. An audience hearing its own language, and seeing nostalgic versions of its own stories onstage, had a space that belonged entirely to them. Yiddish plays allowed the Jews to feel less alone in the new land, the relentless city. At the same time, by experiencing the plays together, the audience could celebrate being here, now. Actors became stars—in Yiddish, but, for some, soon in English on Broadway and then in film. Plays filled with sad songs about the old country served as a gateway into the new.

The Jewish neighborhood was a great churn of people, work, ideas, conflict that took in immigrants and, in generational waves, sent families, women, men, ideas, creations back out into the city and the nation. The Lower East Side was another example of New York as a place of transformation, not a stable home but a slowly, inexorably rotating turnstile. New York crushes people together but gives space for those squeezed newcomers to create art, to create culture, to speak, to sing.

ITALIAN NEW YORK

As late as 1850, there were almost no Italians in New York—just 833 people claimed that heritage. Starting in the 1880s, desperately poor Southern Italian men came to America to look for a way to better themselves. Back home, as one immigrant recalled, "It was work and work hard with no hope of any future. . . . [N]o prospect of ever going beyond the fifth grade or ever becoming other than what one started out to be." Their brothers or cousins were making similar journeys to Argentina, Belgium—anywhere they could find a job. Indeed, in 1890, four times as many Italians lived in Buenos Aires as in New York. Still, each year in the 1880s, some 30,000 Italians landed in New York, and in the next decade

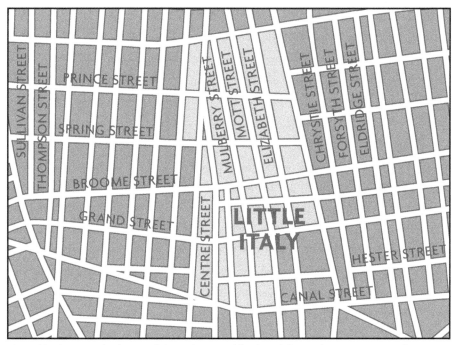

These blocks were the heart of the Italian neighborhood, but Italian immigrants also spread west across to Sullivan and Thompson Streets and then north into Little Africa and what would come to be called Greenwich Village.

that grew to 65,000 annually. By 1900, there were 250,000 Italians in the city, and, for the first time, more Italians came to North than South America. In the decade between 1898 and 1909, almost two million Italians arrived in the United States. The majority of the Italians who landed in New York did not expect to stay. They hoped to make enough money to buy land back home and establish their families there. Between one-third and one-half of this wave of Italians did leave—but the rest stayed and helped to change the city.

Pascal D'Angelo was sixteen when he arrived in 1910, expecting to earn money and then return home. Like many of the single men who came to America, he found jobs in manual labor outside of the city. When he finally returned to New York City in 1914, he saw it for the first time: "On my first arrival in America," he wrote, "I had hurried through New York as through some wild vision." On his return, he noticed how pale and cold the New Yorkers seemed, and "how lovely and yet repulsive this enchanted city was." He caught New York perfectly: a place that was simultaneously lovely and repulsive, and in that strange, dynamic intersection of opposites, enchanted—magical.

While D'Angelo was typical of the single Italian men, by the late nineteenth century more and more Italian men brought over their mothers, wives, and daughters and built their lives in New York. The growing Southern Italian sections of Manhattan were not as concentrated as the Jewish Lower East Side. One cluster was in what came to be called Little Italy—along Mulberry, Mott, Centre, and Elizabeth Streets. Another group moved into the Little Africa section of Greenwich Village that Elizabeth Jennings lived in when she integrated New York City transportation. As late as the 1960s, Bleecker Street between Seventh Avenue and Sixth Avenue (where it crosses Carmine) hosted Zito's bakery, where those who arrived at the right moment could buy hot loaves of bread fresh from the oven. Cafés sold Italian pastries, and grocers offered baskets of cipollini (tiny white) onions and blocks of Parmesan cheese to be sold in chunks or grated to sprinkle over pasta.

As Italian families took root in New York, they worked in a limited range of jobs. Giuseppe Giacosa, an Italian author who had written the lyrics for many popular operas, visited the city in 1892. He noted that "there are many Italians in New York and Brooklyn, supplying a large part of the stonemasons, sculptors, stucco workers, painters, many many barbers, waiters, nearly all the fruit merchants, from the many who are established in fine stores to those who go around with baskets and carts." Some of the foods the Italians sold—garlic, pasta, tomato sauce—were initially seen as foreign and unfamiliar by native-born Americans. That negative view of anything Italian created a problem for children born in the city. "We were becoming Americans," the educator Leonard Covello (born Coviello) wrote, "by learning to be ashamed of our parents." In time, generations of Italians would help change what it meant to be American.

The Heart of Little Italy

Three aspects of the Italian immigrant experience

Lewis Hine took this photograph on Ellis Island in 1905 and noted that the family's concerned expressions were because some of their luggage had been lost. The lack of a husband might well have been because he had come earlier to work.

This Italian family opened a bread store on the East Side, while the man on the right sells watches from his store.

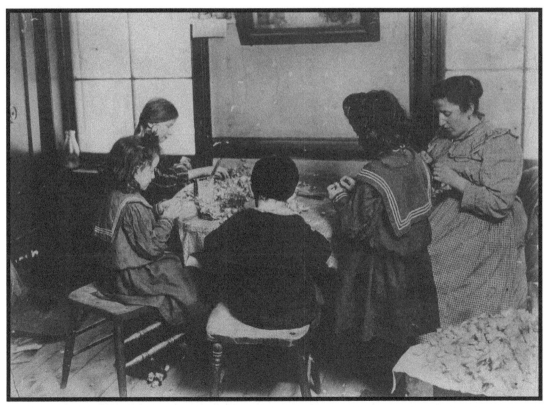

Hine took this image three years later, in 1908. It shows an Italian family at 122 Sullivan Street in what is now SoHo. The four children, ages six, seven, nine, and ten, worked afternoons and evenings to help the family earn four cents for every package of artificial violets they pieced together. Italian girls and women often worked in the home, while Jewish immigrant women worked in sweatshops outside of the home.

The City Electric

42nd Street

1900–1920s

In which the mixture of people and lives in New York City

allows it to invent, perform, own, broadcast, publish, and distribute

the words and music that transform the nation

and, eventually, the world.

SNAPSHOT

Greater New York—the Golden Door Opens Wider, and Then Shuts

1898   Greater New York is created by uniting the five boroughs. New York is now second only to London in the size of its population.

1899   Between 1899 and 1910, 1.9 million Italians come to the United States, most planning to return to Italy, others looking for a new home.

1900   With 3,437,202 people, New York's population has inched past Paris and is about half the population of London; 60,666 of the city's residents claim African heritage, approximately 490,000 are Jewish, and 220,000 are Italian.

1903   Williamsburg Bridge completed.

1904   Interborough Rapid Transit (IRT), the city's first subway line, opens.

1907   A British ship crosses the Atlantic from New York in under five days.

Motors replace horses as the power source for city buses.

1909   Manhattan and Queensborough Bridges completed.

1910   New York City's population is 4,766,883. Between 1 and 1.2 million are Jewish, and 545,000 are Italian; 2.3 percent of Manhattan's residents are of African descent.

1913   The Woolworth Building, the tallest in the world, opens.

Spanish-language newspaper *La Prensa* begins publication in New York.

On February 17, the Armory Show opens, bringing European abstract art to America.

1915 The New York Central Railroad carries 64 million tons of the city's freight while the Erie Canal handles just 2 million tons.

1917 America enters World War I, and 1.5 million soldiers leave for Europe via New York City.

1919 During the Red Summer, anti-Black riots break out in cities across the United States. Claude McKay writes "If We Must Die."

1920 New York City's population is 5,620,048; approximately 1.6 million are Jews, and 41,094 could be defined as Hispanic. Manhattan's population is 2,284,103; 109,133, or 5 percent, are of African descent, the first time the percentage has been that large since 1850.

New York City is considered the world's busiest seaport.

1921–29 Laws passed in Congress severely limit immigration to the United States, with especially low quotas for everyone other than Northern Europeans.

1927 Holland Tunnel opens. Charles Lindbergh completes a solo flight to Paris.

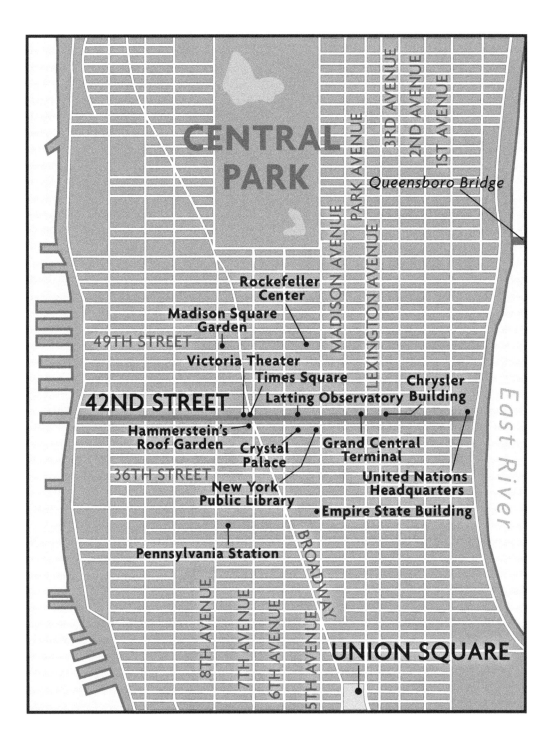

CENTRAL PARK

3RD AVENUE
2ND AVENUE
1ST AVENUE

PARK AVENUE

Queensboro Bridge

MADISON AVENUE

LEXINGTON AVENUE

Rockefeller
Center

Madison Square
Garden

49TH STREET

Victoria Theater

Times Square

Chrysler
Building

42ND STREET

Latting Observatory

Hammerstein's
Roof Garden

Crystal
Palace

Grand Central
Terminal

36TH STREET

United Nations
Headquarters

New York
Public Library

Empire State Building

Pennsylvania Station

East River

Broadway

8TH AVENUE
7TH AVENUE
6TH AVENUE
5TH AVENUE

UNION SQUARE

CHAPTER 15

Greater New York

With the sky invisible and a fine, cold, stinging rain pelting from it, with ceaseless showers of fire and stars of all the colors of the rainbow, and huge fountains of shining silver and gold, sparkling, glowing, and flashing vividly amid the blackness around and above, with the crash of cannon and the roar of exploding bombs punctuating with quick periods the minor din of steam whistles, braying horns, and shouting men, the clash and throb of a huge brass band dominant over it all, and the mellow, distant chimes of Trinity Church heard now and then at intervals; with a cloud of smoke hanging low, tinted now red, now green, as the colors of the fire below changed with many flash lights throwing their long shafts of white everywhere, intersecting each other, making eccentric evolutions in the darkness, and finally concentrating in a great glare, the flag of Greater New York was officially unfurled over the New York City Hall at midnight by a touch of a button by the Mayor of San Francisco, 3,700 miles away, and the second city of the world came into existence.

As the *New York Times* recorded, thousands of New Yorkers braved the rain on December 31, 1897, to gather in Union Square to begin the celebration of the megalopolis that was about to be born. There was much to celebrate. By 1896, Brooklyn had over one million residents. New York City had crossed the Harlem

River at Manhattan's northern edge by adding what would become the western Bronx. Queens and Staten Island were still filled with farms and small villages. At the stroke of midnight, these five disparate regions would be combined, raising Greater New York's population from less than two million to nearly three and a half million. The city that had once been scattered buildings behind a wooden wall now trailed only London in population. And London could not rest easy: thousands of immigrants were arriving daily at New York's open door.

It was fitting that the celebration began at Union Square, and Tony Pastor himself judged a contest of the bands. The square had been the center of an island city made up of separate walking neighborhoods. A sprawling new metropolis for the new century would be the home of masses in motion. Over the next decade, and all across the city, planners designed projects for people on the move, proclaiming and creating the "greatness" of Greater New York. Three new bridges arose to link Manhattan with Queens and Brooklyn, while a tunnel was carved under the Hudson to tie New Jersey to the expanding urban center. A new station for the Pennsylvania Railroad arose between Thirtieth and Thirty-Fourth Streets, a vast marble gateway to the city.

Until the Civil War, New York really was Lower Manhattan up to about Fortieth Street, a city in which church steeples stood out against the skyline as the highest points human effort could reach. The one hint of the city's future came in 1852. The Crystal Palace was built on Forty-Second Street to display the vast array of objects and goods being churned out by modern machines, transported by steamships and railroads, gouged out of the earth by drills and the endless labor of armies of men. Next to the glass palace was the Latting Observatory. A 350-foot wooden tower,

Taken in 1908, this photo of Wall Street to Trinity Church gives a sense of how the narrow, bustling street had developed since colonial days.

Drawn in 1853, this lithograph shows the Crystal Palace with the Latting Observatory on the left. The tower with its steam-powered elevator was a hint of Manhattan's vertical future.

the Latting was the tallest building in America, and it was graced with a new device. Visitors could ride a steam-powered elevator up the first two levels, then climb out to use handy telescopes to view sites from Staten Island to New Jersey. The palace burned down, but the stretch upward aided by ever-safer elevators was the city's future.

After the Civil War, the scale of the city changed. Increasingly, New York City was defined by size: large hustling crowds, buildings reaching to the sky. This push upward was aided by an accident of the city's geography; much of Manhattan's bedrock consists of schist, a strong and firm stone that is especially well suited to securing the foundation of tall buildings. "Skyscrapers," the architectural critic Lewis Mumford claimed, took their name from "the topmost sail" of clipper ships. You could see the ever-taller buildings as monuments to the power of human ambition. Mumford had just the opposite reaction; he hated the growing towers, which he thought stole "space and light and sun" from the people. That was just the start of what he disliked in the new city of money and size.

For the poorest New Yorkers, builders put up tenements designed to house

Between 1913, when it was completed, and 1930, the Woolworth Building on lower Broadway near city hall was the tallest building in the world.

as many renters as possible in apartments with very little air or light. Mumford called these "grim" and "dreary." By contrast, on Wall Street, financial institutions advertised their strength and solidity with substantial office buildings faced with stone. In the boardrooms, lawyers and businessmen were consolidating companies into new corporations that did business across the nation and located their headquarters in New York. Office buildings—with elevators linking warrens of offices—were both the humming headquarters of national and international businesses and displays of the host company's importance. By 1913, for example, the Woolworth Building, rising 732 feet in the air, was the tallest building in the world.

To Mumford, these office-hives were the soulless expression of the "paper city, buried in its newspapers in the morning, intent through the day on its journals and ledgers and briefs and Dear-sir-in-reply-to-yours-of-even-date, picking at its newly invented typewriters and mimeographs and adding machines, manifolding and filing, watching the ticker tape flow from the glib automatons." New York, he thought, had become a dystopia where size, money, and Wall Street calculations ruled. Everyone could be bought; human feeling was erased by monstrous buildings that eclipsed the sky. And yet even as he described the nightmare city, he recognized that New York provided a home for individuals with vision: Walt Whitman, the gay poet; Herman Melville, the inspired author; the Roeblings, who imagined and built the Brooklyn Bridge; experimental painters such as Albert Pinkham Ryder. And while Mumford did not mention this, those crammed apartment buildings and anonymous office jobs allowed people who did not fit in their gossipy hometowns to come to New York and create new lives: single women who did not want to rush into marriage, men attracted to men and women attracted to women, revolutionaries determined to change society.

In the new Greater New York, the intense pressure of work, money, speed, and scale was overwhelming and freeing—and even both at the same time. For the city was not just a collection of individuals; it was the home of crowds with their own needs. The wide thoroughfare of Forty-Second Street was the heart of the new interconnected city, marked east to west by three magnificent new creations: a palace, a temple, and a pathway—all designed to serve the people.

The palace was built because of a terrible accident. By 1902, trains rushed in and out of New York's main terminal, Grand Central on Forty-Second Street and Fourth Avenue, every forty-five seconds. On January 8, a train arriving from Westchester plowed into one already in the station, killing fifteen people. The tunnel into the station was so dense with smoke from trains coming and going that the engineer could not see the warning signals. Prompted by that fatal crash, the Vanderbilt family decided it was time to tear down the station and rebuild it. The new station would serve only electric trains—clearing smoke from tunnels—and would be its own architectural wonder. Grand Central Terminal

This image of Grand Central Terminal gives a sense of its palatial grandeur. Central train stations like this in major cities were not meant to be simple traffic hubs. The traveler could feel important just by being there. The large clock in the middle of the station floor was, and is, a landmark used as a meeting place.

was designed to be *grand*—large, with soaring high stone ceilings: a place that made passengers feel important just by being there. Switching to electric also meant that trains could run underground in the city, freeing the land above to be developed into office and apartment buildings. The imperial station was finally completed and ready to welcome the public on February 2, 1913.

The temple was created through an agreement uniting three legacies into one glorious gift: a library that would be free and that everyone could use. In his will, the immensely wealthy John Jacob Astor donated enough money to start a reference library near where he lived on what is now called Astor Place in the East Village. James Lenox, a wealthy book lover, gave his personal collection that included extremely rare books to a second library designed for scholars. Samuel J. Tilden, who almost became president on the Democratic ticket in 1876, insisted that the money he put aside in his will be used to create a truly public library. In 1895, all three libraries agreed to pool their resources and their collections and build one great home for books and readers: the New York Public Library. This plan created something new for the city—free access to knowledge and imagination.

The ideal place for the library was the block between Fortieth and Forty-Second Streets facing Fifth Avenue, occupied by the no-longer-needed Croton Reservoir. Water now flowed directly into the city in tubes. The old reservoir was used mainly for pleasant rambles along its high walls. In 1900, five hundred workmen began the labor of smashing it apart. It took two years to remove the old reservoir walls, and another nine to finish the library building, using the stones from the walls as part of the foundation. On May 23, 1911, the cathedral of reading, thinking, and learning—the largest building built out of marble in the entire country—opened. Ten years earlier, though, another benefactor, the steel magnate Andrew Carnegie, had donated enough money to create branch libraries around the city. Readers could either find books in their own neighborhoods or come to Forty-Second Street to read in a library that honored their intelligence and curiosity in the same way that Grand Central Terminal valued their bustling lives.

The subway changed the city. On October 27, 1904, Mayor George B.

The main building of the New York Public Library is a destination of its own. The third-floor reading room features a blue ceiling painted with constellations and long, well-lit wooden tables. You sit surrounded by knowledge.

McClellan Jr. (son of the Civil War general of the same name) was about to begin a joyride. For four years, twelve thousand men had been digging down through Manhattan's hard rock, carving out tunnels and laying track. Now, "in the name of the people," the mayor declared "the subway open." He led two hundred august passengers down the steps of the city hall station, the first stop on the city's first subway line, and onto the train. Though he had no experience driving trains, the mayor insisted he must be the motorman in charge. Racing at up to forty-five miles per hour, he somehow safely guided the subway all the way to its last stop at 145th Street in less than half an hour. A new mode of transportation for a new New York.

Digging and blasting through Manhattan stone to build Grand Central and then the first subway lines gave work to the tens of thousands of Italian men now arriving every year. That manpower was, in a sense, the invisible, the ghost presence behind the changing city, though we can recover a few stories. Thomas Moro, a current New Yorker, heard that his great-grandfather "would get up very early in the morning about 4:30 a.m., put on his long johns because of the draft in the tunnels, put these heavy black boots on that were already covered in dust and mud, and walk out the door with his metal lunch box."

The original city hall subway stop is no longer used but was designed to be not just practical but beautiful. The ornate tiling was created by Rafael Guastavino Moreno, an immigrant who arrived from Spain in 1881.

The city's first subway line ran uptown on the east side from city hall, across Forty-Second Street to the west, then farther north on the west side. The stop at Forty-Second Street and Seventh Avenue, then, was the central node of the whole system. It linked east and west, north and south. Finally, the people of the city were able to move around, quickly, cheaply, and throughout much of the island.

Fast, inexpensive subways meant that people could live in one spot and work in another. Developers loved the idea, because now vast areas of the united city could be developed—turned from empty land into big profit. People concerned about the dense immigrant neighborhoods were thrilled that new homes would be built that could relieve the overcrowding. Some of these reformers were focused on improving the health and safety of the new New Yorkers. Others, such as former mayor Abram Hewitt, looked down on the new immigrants. They were eager to break up the immigrant enclaves so that the new arrivals would be less concentrated and more ready to become "American." What the old Protestant elite had tried to do with the famine Irish, a new generation of reformers attempted with the arriving Italians and Jews.

The subways did change the Lower East Side. By 1916, less than a quarter of the city's Jews still lived there and the majority of Italians lived uptown in East Harlem. Yet the movement the subways made possible also changed what it meant to be American. The center of change was Forty-Second Street. One immigrant inventor had a vision of how to turn the area starting north from Forty-Second Street and Seventh Avenue into the most intoxicating center of entertainment, amusement, and his passion: the opera.

CHAPTER 16

The Immortal

In 1864, Oscar Hammerstein I (not to be confused with his now more-famous grandson the Broadway musical lyricist) landed in the city. He was fifteen, penniless, Jewish, and escaping from a well-off but abusive father back in Germany. After he found work sweeping floors in a factory that employed people to roll tobacco into cigarettes and cigars, he discovered that he had a talent for inventing labor-saving devices that were immensely useful in the tobacco business. The intrepid young man began to make money and fell in love with Rosa Blau, a coworker, and they were married. He was the perfect image of the rags-to-riches immigrant New Yorker.

The year before Hammerstein landed in the city, thirteen-year-old Samuel Gompers (the family name was Gomperts, but Samuel later changed it) and his family arrived from London. The cigarette- and cigar-rolling business launched Gompers's career as well, but in a path distinctly different from Hammerstein's. Gompers had begun working at home rolling cigars at the age of ten, and he devoted his life to organizing tobacco workers and, more broadly, to the union movement. Tobacco workers learned to roll cigars without looking, and so, Gompers recalled, they had time to "think, talk, listen, or sing." One person might read out loud to the others, inspiring all to organize and plan together. By 1875, he was elected president of his union, and in 1886 he helped to found the American Federation of Labor (AFL). The AFL was one of the most enduring and powerful labor organizations uniting workers across the country, and he served as its head for thirty-nine of its first forty years. Gompers believed that workers who shared specific skills needed strong, well-funded unions that would fight for concrete gains such as shorter hours and better pay—not a radical transformation of society. Gompers and the AFL offered a path to better working conditions in the new city and the new century. Hammerstein offered a path to entertainment and pleasure.

Hammerstein did not care about money in the slightest. He later took to wearing a tall top hat at all times, and a family tale says that his sons needed to remember to stash some bills in the hat when he went out so that he'd have a few dollars on him. As he began to make his way in New York, he was determined—or more accurately, he was fanatically, maniacally determined—to be involved with opera in the growing city.

In Neal Shusterman's dystopic novel *Scythe*, two teenagers are given tickets to an opera to understand the conflicts and emotions of an earlier age—war, vengeance, murder, love. As the novel suggests, opera is the Olympics of music: it requires superhuman effort and skill to hit the notes and sustain the melodic lines. Opera fans in Hammerstein's day experienced performances with the intensity others felt at a baseball game or prizefight. This was especially true as New York City became the immigrant hub of the world. While all of these poor immigrants worked endlessly long hours, they also needed some relief, some entertainment. They needed opera: opera told their stories.

Despite the grand history of the Roman Empire, there was no nation of Italy until 1871. The peninsula was divided up among kingdoms that were the heritage of centuries of conquest by one empire or another. Popular operas by Giuseppe Verdi rallied the people of Italy against the many monarchs to form a nation. In the slogan "Viva Verdi," his name even doubled as an acronym for *Vittorio Emanuele Re d'Italia*, and indeed Victor Emmanuel of Sardinia did come to be the first king (*re* means "king" in Italian) of a united Italy. Early in the nineteenth century, Germany was even more divided than Italy. The three hundred or more distinct territories, principalities, and kingdoms narrowed to thirty-eight by 1815. It was only, again, by 1871 that a united Germany with a single leader—Kaiser (the German equivalent of the Roman *caesar* or Russian *tsar*) Wilhelm—was created. In this very period (between 1853 and 1874), Richard Wagner composed a cycle of four operas—based on the legends that also inspired *The Lord of the Rings*—that were meant to forge a German national identity.

To be Italian and love Verdi or to be German and devoted to Wagner was to both adore a form of art and feel the deepest pride in your language, culture, and birthright. Opera not only provided a language but created a common experience—a kind of nightly ritual—for many of New York's new immigrants, much as the Yiddish theater did for the Eastern European Jews.

Hammerstein set out to be the man to link those magnificent works with this endlessly growing audience.

FROM THE HARLEM OPERA HOUSE TO LONGACRE SQUARE

Ever since the 1870s, when the railroad lines and then the el spread through the city, the development of New York began moving north, along Central Park. Still, one area of the city remained almost untouched: Harlem. The descendants of Alexander Hamilton still owned the home and land where he had moved his family to escape disease. Other farms and estates tracing back even to Dutch times were only now being broken up and sold. Goats roamed empty lots in a section of the city that seemed a world away from the bustle of Union Square. By the 1880s, this was sure to change. Smart investors realized Harlem was a place to build homes for those on the rise—the German Jews, for example, who wanted nothing to do with the new Eastern European arrivals. By 1887, a German Jewish congregation purchased a church on 125th Street and named it Temple Israel of Harlem. Upscale Jewish department stores, Blumstein's and Koch's, followed with stores on the same block. Hammerstein began buying land and building in Harlem. He built twenty-four apartment buildings and fifty houses there, as well as his own new lavish home at 44 West 120th Street. Harlem and a constant stream of new inventions were making his fortune.

In 1889, Hammerstein opened what he saw as the crowning jewel of Harlem: the Harlem Opera House at 207 West 125th Street. Seating 1,375 people and decorated in lavish mirrors, gold paint, and marble walls, this was the largest theater in the entire city. Fine art—a sculpture of Wagner, a painting of Queen

Oscar Hammerstein, left, in his signature top hat, conversing with the Italian conductor Cleofonte Campanini, who would go on to lead the Chicago Opera. Opera was Hammerstein's consuming passion.

Elizabeth I listening to Shakespeare—set the tone for the audience. Though he had no training as an architect, Hammerstein designed his own theaters and dreamed up useful inventions to improve the acoustics and create air-conditioning for his auditoriums. You get a sense, though, of what did not matter to him by the one element he left out of his new opera house: he forgot to include a box office, where people would pay for their tickets.

Having one large Harlem theater only convinced Hammerstein that he should have two. In 1890, he sold the profitable Harlem apartment buildings and used the money to open the Columbus at 114 East 125th Street. The Columbus Theatre was even larger than its sister, with room for 1,649 customers, and became the uptown home of vaudeville, minstrelsy, and musical comedy. Hammerstein bookended 125th Street with immense theaters and made entertainment central to Harlem. That was just a start.

After trying one theater at Forty-Second Street and Sixth Avenue and another at Thirty-Fourth and Broadway, he made the great plunge—into the mud, rank smells, and darkness (there was only one streetlamp to light many blocks) of Thieves Lair, beside Longacre Square.

If Harlem was overrun with goats, Longacre was filled with horses, as this later historical account from the 1920s makes clear: "The sound of the black-smiths' hammer mingled with the tinkle of the horse-car bell. Stables abounded, and here and there a red flag indicated a horse auction. Florid men, wearing white stocks and horseshoe pins, stood about discussing the merits of equine bargains, for in those days my lady drove to the play behind a pair of spanking high-steppers, and horse-sense ruled. By night this district, now ablaze, was as dark as Egypt, save for the dim lights of an occasional livery-stable, a corner saloon, or a city street lamp."

Longacre was named after a street in London where horse-drawn carriages were built. At the uptown end of the neglected land was the American Horse Exchange (between Fiftieth and Fifty-First Streets and Broadway), where elite New Yorkers could appraise and purchase thoroughbreds; after fire and rebuilding, today it is the Winter Garden Theatre. At the downtown end, near Forty-Second Street, was an area called Great Kill (from the Dutch *kil*, meaning "stream"), a muddy nothing. Hammerstein, who came to be called Oscar the Immortal, knew this was just the place to build a theater, two theaters, ultimately, seven theaters. Having transformed Harlem's main street, he was about to turn Forty-Second Street into the new, true heart of the city.

LONGACRE

As the story goes, in 1894 or '95, Hammerstein stood amid the odors and mud of Forty-Second Street at the crossing of Seventh Avenue and Broadway. He gazed past the parade of suspicious characters and horses relieving themselves on the street and saw what the intersection could be. He knew that you build where it is easiest for people to go. Forty-Second Street would be the center of the city because anyone, everyone, could get there. On the east side, trains coming into the city landed in Grand Central Terminal and electric streetlights had been installed all the way to that corner. Trolley lines going up and down and across the island met there, and the Ninth Avenue el was nearby.

A new city, a world city, was taking shape, and Hammerstein had located its heart.

In 1898, Hammerstein opened the Olympia on Broadway between Forty-Fourth and Forty-Fifth Streets. This was more an entertainment complex than a mere theater, as it housed three different auditoriums as well as places to walk, smoke, and buy a drink. Facing the street was a giant electric sign advertising yet another attraction: HAMMERSTEIN'S ROOF GARDEN.

Built to draw crowds, the Olympia featured all sorts of acts new to the stage, including the Cherry Sisters, two totally untalented young women from Iowa who performed vaudeville that audiences loved to boo. Hammerstein placed a net in front of them so they would be protected when people threw fruit and vegetables (initially supplied by the producer himself) at them. People loved hating the act. In 1898, he brought in Isham's Octoroons, which featured a chorus line of Black women, opera arias, and more suggestive fare. Across the street from the Olympia, at the Casino Theatre, *Clorindy, or the Origin of the Cakewalk*—with text and lyrics by the poet Paul Laurence Dunbar and music by the classically trained Will Marion Cook—was the second (by a few months, to a minstrel musical) Broadway show to be entirely written and composed by African Americans.

In 1896, Dunbar had written a poem defining, from the inside, what it was like to have the stereotypes of blackface minstrelsy imposed upon a person:

We wear the mask that grins and lies,
It hides our cheeks and shades our eyes,—
This debt we pay to human guile;
With torn and bleeding hearts we smile,
And mouth with myriad subtleties.

Why should the world be over-wise,
In counting all our tears and sighs?
Nay, let them only see us, while
We wear the mask.

We smile, but, O great Christ, our cries
To thee from tortured souls arise.
We sing, but oh the clay is vile
Beneath our feet, and long the mile;
But let the world dream otherwise,
We wear the mask!

Now in *Clorindy*, Dunbar was taking the next step: turning prejudice upside down. On southern plantations, African Americans had seen white people dancing their European minuets and quadrilles and then invented their own livelier, perhaps mocking, versions of the steps. The white masters enjoyed watching—and making fun of—the slave dances and staged contests, giving the performers a slice of cake as a prize (thus the phrase "winning in a cakewalk"). First white and then Black blackface minstrel groups added versions of the high-stepping

In this image of African American dancers performing a cakewalk, there is a combination of elegance and showmanship, a distinct step away from the most extreme distortions of blackface minstrelsy.

There was no mechanical air-conditioning in the early twentieth century, which made rooftop locations with open windows especially appealing sites for performances. Hammerstein connected the "Venetian Terrace" he had built on top of the Victoria Theater with his nearby Theatre Republic to create the Paradise Roof Garden.

cakewalk to their routines. Dunbar and Cook were taking hold of this legacy and making it their own with *Clorindy*. Five years later, they again collaborated on a Broadway show and featured a cakewalk song titled "Swing Along." The song told the dancers to "lift your heads up high" and that "white folks jealous when you'se walking two by two." Instead of hiding behind a blackface mask, Black people would swing along with pride.

While the dialect, characterizations, dancing, and humor of these shows aimed to please white audiences, the need to fill stages and provide new acts was creating a small opening for Black artists. From a den in the Five Points where Master Juba danced, through the decades of blackface minstrelsy, to the newly minted stages of Forty-Second Street, Manhattan provided a tiny but growing window of opportunity for the display of African American talent. At first, vaudeville bookers tried to make sure that at most only one African American act would be included in their nightly offerings. But the performers were too popular to be so tightly regulated.

Hammerstein kept experimenting with different kinds of entertainment in his giant house, and by 1898 he was totally broke. The Immortal met defeat by charging forward with double, triple the energy and risk. He sold his Harlem home to finance yet another theater, the Victoria, and took to sleeping in apartments within his theaters. Located on Forty-Second Street and Seventh Avenue, the Victoria was in a prime spot. Hammerstein soon opened another playhouse, the Republic, next door and connected the two with the Paradise Roof Garden. His Forty-Second Street was becoming a night-out entertainment complex for browsing, eating, drinking, walking, dancing, and seeing shows. By 1905, New York's new subways were the most used system in the world, and Forty-Second Street was the most popular station. Everyone could get to Hammerstein's theaters, and everyone did, though African Americans needed to go to court to be allowed to sit where they liked. In New York, at times, the courts even ruled in their favor. Whether through the power of Black talent, the determination of Black customers, or the growing size of Black audiences, music, theater, and dance in New York were beginning to become avenues of opportunity for African Americans.

Eight blocks downtown, Thirty-Fourth Street was called Herald Square, after the *New York Herald* newspaper, whose headquarters were nearby. In 1904, the *New York Times* moved into its own new building, the Times Tower on Forty-Second Street, giving its name to the growing center spreading out beneath its shadow: Times Square. On New Year's Eve of 1907, the newspaper celebrated by having a giant lighted ball descend as a huge crowd gathered and counted down the seconds. This was the final way in which Times Square was a new kind of city center: It wasn't just that masses of people went there. Now the crowd itself was part of the reason for going. You went to be part of the throng, the hubbub of the city electric.

Hammerstein did not live to become New York's master of opera. When he died in 1919, he was once again out of money. But his ambition left a glittering trail: he built ten theaters in New York, Philadelphia, and London, opened Harlem to top-flight entertainment, and made Times Square the beacon to dreamers from all over the nation, and the world.

CHAPTER **17**

"Come On and Hear"

At Forty-second Street . . . when the doors of all shops are open, the windows of nearly all restaurants wide to the gaze of the idlest passer-by. Here is the great city, and it is lush and dreamy. A May or June moon will be hanging like a burnished silver disc between the high walls aloft. A hundred, a thousand electric signs will blink and wink. And the floods of citizens and visitors in summer clothes and with gay hats; the street cars jouncing their endless carloads on indifferent errands; the taxis and private cars fluttering about like jeweled flies. The very gasoline contributes a distinct perfume. Life bubbles, sparkles; chatters gay, incoherent stuff. Such is Broadway.

—Theodore Dreiser

The "lush" street the novelist recalled was a kind of dreamland of appetites. Patrons entered Rector's restaurant on Forty-Fourth Street through a new innovation, a revolving door, spinning out of the common street into never-never land. Diamond Jim Brady was said to spend his evenings there polishing off several platters of oysters before consuming six crabs, two ducks, another six or seven lobsters, a steak, and a turtle, and he did make sure to eat his vegetables. Brady's eating was legendary, but that style of excess was so common that Rector's and its competitors were called "lobster palaces." Rich men came to declare their wealth through their appetites, bulging stomachs, and indulgences—which were not limited to food. They also pursued the young women appearing in the shows filling Hammerstein's theaters.

Rector's and others began to feature singers and other acts as well as food. The beer gardens linking theaters did the same. This nonstop, enchanted land of pleasure began to shuffle the city's hierarchies of rich and poor, men and women, even—in music if not in seating—Black and white. For by 1912, music suggested dancing, and dancing could lead anywhere. One anonymous author noted that high-society people were coming to restaurants that offered dancing. This created a "hodge-podge of people in which respectable young married and unmarried women, and even debutantes, dance, not only under the same roof, but in the same room with women of the town." "The spirit of caste and convention is disappearing," the *Nation* noted in 1913. "Ideals are mingling in delightful promiscuity. . . . There you have the modern synthesis of New York as revealed in the neighborhood of Forty-second street."

At night, the most elite young women of the city were dancing next to women who had to sell their bodies. In the afternoons, "the modern synthesis" took place in a different way: at "tea dances," single women could pay for a professional dance partner. One mother was so outraged when Eugenia, her teenage daughter, became addicted to these dances and began showering a paid partner with presents that she took her daughter to court. "If I didn't go to at least six cabarets a night," the mother quoted her wayward daughter as saying, "I would lose my social standing." The judge sternly warned Eugenia that "the best friend you have is your mother," and the chastened nineteen-year-old agreed that "I was wrong and mother was right." While the case was all over the newspapers, and officially confirmed the nineteenth-century idea that mother knew best, the twentieth-century days and nights of dancing continued.

Eugenia and the other white women who were rushing out to twirl in Times Square were learning dances that had roots in African American and Latin American culture but had been adapted by white dancing duos such as Vernon and Irene Castle. The Castles were elegant, graceful, chaste, and light on their feet, but they needed music with the proper bounce and lilt. They hired the African American composer and band leader James Reese Europe to be their musical director. Europe mixed white and Black musical traditions, sending the Castles and their fans spinning across the dance floor to the lilting beat of ragtime.

RAGTIME

The catchy lyrics, intoxicating melodies, and dance crazes that began on Forty-Second Street were the machine of Manhattan at work: Yiddish-speaking immigrants of the Jewish Lower East Side swirled together with Irish performers and the syncopations that the African Americans brought to New York to create tunes by day and dazzling spectacles at night. Blazing with the new speed and dash of electric lights and endless nights, Forty-Second Street sparkled. That churning, kaleidoscopic thoroughfare had its own rhythm: ragtime.

Ragtime asked piano players to master Western chords and African American syncopation at the same time. The great ragtime pianist and composer Scott Joplin thought that "there has been ragtime music in America ever since the Negro race has been here." He meant that African Americans had always experimented with taking Western musical forms and ragging, or adapting, them to more complex rhythms. Ragtime music added an extra, unexpected beat to familiar rhythms, and by the late 1800s, more and more people, Black and white, found the combination irresistible. The musical critic Hiram Moderwell recalled "hearing a negro quartet singing 'Waiting for the Robert E. Lee,' in a café, and I felt my blood thumping in time, my muscles twitching to the rhythm." "When the Band Plays Ragtime," a 1902 song by James Weldon Johnson, who also cowrote "Lift Every Voice and Sing," captures that beat:

> When the band plays ragtime
> It sets your feet on springs
> When the band plays ragtime
> You feel like you've got wings,
> I declare you jes can't he'p it,
> You've jes got to kinder step it,
> When the band plays ragtime.

The first four lines flow like any popular song, but in the fifth and sixth "can't he'p it" and "kinder step it" make you stop, hesitate, and then leap forward in the last line, thrilled by that little unexpected pause.

Scott Joplin published his own "Maple Leaf Rag" in 1899, and it was first recorded four years later. Most Americans, though, learned new songs by buying the sheet music and playing them at home. Tin Pan Alley—located on Forty-Second Street—was the nation's capital for publishing and promoting sheet music. By 1913, the sheet music of that one piano piece sold a million copies.

By 1911, with Forty-Second Street in full blare, ragtime was popular everywhere. The editor of one music magazine noted, "The most popular music of the day is that known as 'rag-time.' From New York to California and from the great lakes to the gulf ragtime music of all styles is the rage." Twentieth-century Americans were hearing that speed and bounce and it sounded like their lives, like their busy days and high-living nights. Ragtime was the pulse of being alive.

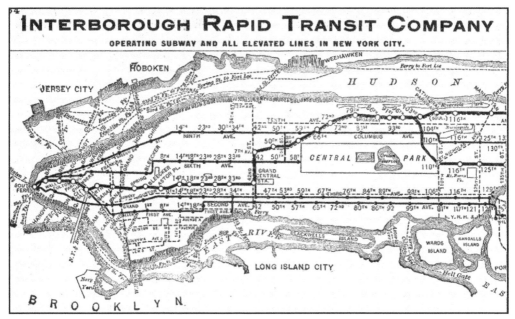

The IRT was the city's first subway line, and it crossed from the east to the west side on 42nd Street. That made the 42nd and Seventh Avenue station the stop that was easiest to reach from anywhere on the Manhattan island. New York had its new center.

African Americans had found the beat of the new century, of New York. In fact, ragtime was so well known that every tinkling piano celebrated it—in one song:

> Come on and hear
> Come on and hear
> Alexander's ragtime band.

It took just a few months for "Alexander's Ragtime Band" to match the million-copy lifetime sales of "Maple Leaf Rag," and it quickly became the century's new bestseller. Yet experts debate whether it deserves to be called "ragtime" at all, and it was not written by an African American. Instead, a Jewish man born in Siberia and raised on Cherry Street, the heart of Jewish immigrant New York, wrote it. Irving Berlin had his offices, actually two offices for two parts of his career, on Forty-Second Street, the center of New York as the engine of transformation.

Berlin's family arrived in America with very little money when he was four, and his father died four years later. The young boy quit school and set out to bring money to the family selling newspapers on the streets and in cafés and singing for tips. At fourteen, he left home to make his own way. Soon enough he reached Tony Pastor's at Union Square. Music publishers had noticed the popularity of Pastor's and used it as a way to spread the word about their songs. First a "plugger" would perform the song on a piano to interest a performer. Then, when the singer sang it onstage, "boomers"—carefully planted in the audience—would cheer wildly. Berlin began as a boomer at Pastor's—low on the ladder of musical success, yet inside the hit-making machine.

Irving's next step allows us to add a then tiny but still important group to the New York mix: he got a job as a singing waiter in Chinatown. The first Chinese arrived in New York as sailors, and the community grew as a form of refuge. Prejudice and violence drove Chinese workers out of the American West, where they had built the railroads. New York was a landing spot for the men—almost all were men—where they could find work and a degree of safety. The first Chinese lived in the Five Points, where some married Irish women. In 1882, the Chinese

Exclusion Act—a national law that banned Chinese workers from coming to America—limited the growth of the neighborhood, which had moved to Mott and Pell Streets. But over time, Chinese men and women found ways, legal and not, to enter the country and build their community. The Russian owner of the Chinese restaurant where Berlin worked noticed him and invited him to try writing a song, which he did. By the time he was nineteen, in 1907, Berlin was being paid a weekly salary to write songs for a Union Square music publisher, and three years later he crafted "Alexander"—his first giant hit.

Berlin had the gift of knowing what people wanted to hear and giving them those words and melodies in

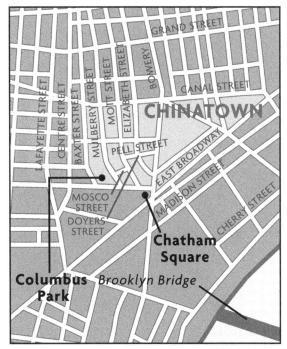

This map outlines the heart of traditional Chinatown in Manhattan. But the neighborhood has expanded (up to Grand Street) and contracted in the ebb and flow of different immigration waves and housing costs.

such a perfect package that listeners felt they had always known that song—as if they were born hearing it. In a career that lasted almost the entire length of the twentieth century, he wrote twenty-five songs that reached number one on the sales charts. Standards such as "God Bless America," "There's No Business Like Show Business," "Oh! How I Hate to Get Up in the Morning," and "White Christmas" are just a tiny fraction of the classic songs he created.

Berlin was extremely talented, but his success was also a portrait of his moment. The Jews of the Lower East Side were accustomed to being a minority in a majority culture. They had centuries of experience in simultaneously resisting the pressure to convert and watching the moods of their gentile neighbors very carefully. In America, there were once again Christians eager to convert Jews or, at least, to make Jews less distinct. But the culture that was bursting forth in New

Right: The Chinese Exclusion Act of 1882 made it extremely difficult for people from China to come to America, and since most who were already here were men, New York's small Chinatown was largely a bachelor community. Nevertheless, Chinese men did find partners, sometimes, as in the Five Points, with Irish women, and started families. This image dates from 1909.

Below: Apparently taken on Chinese New Year, this early twentieth-century image shows how, despite prejudice against Chinese people, Chinatown had become a tourist attraction. New York's ethnic neighborhoods enticed the curious.

York was not quiet and churchgoing; it was ragtime, vaudeville, Times Square. Ethnic artists could become popular by sounding all-American and could be seen as all-American by being popular—no immigrant groups had ever had that chance before. On Forty-Second Street, even being Irish was no longer considered too immigrant or Catholic; it was the epitome of all-American.

George M. Cohan, the child of a family of Irish vaudevillians, wrote and performed songs that were the essence of being a high-spirited American, such as "I'm a Yankee Doodle Dandy," "You're a Grand Old Flag," and, during World War I, "Over There." The irresistible dances hurtling Cohan across the stage were the direct descendants of the style invented by Master Juba in the Five Points a century earlier. Cohan even glorified Times Square itself in "Give My Regards to Broadway," telling "the gang at Forty-Second street that I will soon be there."

Forty-Second Street created, sold, and performed the music, songs, dances, and theater for the entire nation. Through sheet music, records, dance steps, and touring companies, the New York mixture of Black people and white people, immigrant and old-line American, reached across the country. Times Square was today's Hollywood plus Broadway plus television plus the music and videos of the internet all in one place blazing with light.

The electric sign advertising Hammerstein's Roof Garden was the first hint of what would become, after a change in city laws in 1916, the illuminated billboards of Times Square. A French writer saw the "immense blaze of legends and pictures, most of them in motion" as "the finest free show on earth," while a visitor from England stood in wonder watching "zig-zag lightnings strike an acre of signboard." The Heatherbloom company hired the genius of electric signs, O. J. Gude, to create one that would be a sensation. The sign showed a girl made of light who seemed to walk through sheets of rain, shielded by her umbrella, as wind blew in from behind her, showing off her petticoat. The sign was a little story in light, and crowds stopped to stare, to view it over and over again as a kind of modern miracle. Electric signs were only one of the many kinds of new entertainment being born on and close to Times Square.

Like Irving Berlin, David Sarnoff grew up in an immigrant Jewish household so poor that even as a child he needed to earn money to support the family.

By 1909, Hammerstein's Victoria Theater stood on 42nd Street and Seventh Avenue as an entertainment amusement park offering everything from Gertrude Hoffmann's scandalous "Visions of Salome" to the airy rooftop garden. The Victoria was the enticing entrée to the ever-expanding theater district.

After hustling selling newspapers, at fifteen he got a job sweeping the floors at the Marconi Wireless Telegraph Company of America. Guglielmo Marconi had done the seemingly impossible: find a way to send and receive telegraph signals through the air. Sarnoff was an ace telegraph operator—though his claim to have been the only person on land to have received a distress signal from the sinking *Titanic* was not true. And wireless telegraphy was only a start.

One hundred thousand people jostled for space in Times Square on July 2, 1921, to listen to loudspeakers on the Times building broadcasting the very first boxing match ever carried on Marconi's next invention: radio. Jack Dempsey knocked out Georges Carpentier and the nation went radio-mad. Within two years, there were 556 stations across the forty-eight states, and half a million homes featured the new invention. Sarnoff rose with radio, becoming head of the Radio Corporation of America (RCA) and then the network of stations he created: the National Broadcasting Company (NBC). RCA went on to buy Victor, the largest maker of phonograph records.

Sarnoff's New York was the headquarters of radio, of records, and its theaters were the place to see premieres of the next new medium: full-length movies.

The very first fully talking picture was *The Jazz Singer* (1927), which opened on Broadway between Fifty-First and Fifty-Second Streets. The movie was about a Jewish young man who chooses jazz over religious singing—and actor Al Jolson delivered the key song about his "mammy" in full blackface. In Times Square, the blurring and borrowing across ethnic and racial lines included theft, stereotyping, and an absolute assumption that the general audience, the popular audience, was white.

And yet, Times Square brought opportunity to African Americans. The two key crossing points came in one great, tragic star and a revolutionary play. Born on New Providence island in the Bahamas, Egbert Austin Williams was part of an important but neglected strand in America's immigration history: West Indians who began arriving in New York near the turn of the century. Intelligent and eager to rise, Bert was accepted into Stanford to study engineering, but could not afford the tuition. He began performing out west with George Walker to earn money—and found he had an exceptional gift.

Williams and Walker called themselves the "Two Real Coons" and appeared in blackface—two more African Americans forced to humiliate themselves to please white audiences. Williams's signature song was "Nobody," and his character was a man for whom everything went wrong. He was such a brilliant performer that audiences saw both the humor and the tragedy in his character. As W. C. Fields, one of the most famous comedians of the time, said, "He was the funniest man I ever met, and the saddest." Booker T. Washington went a step further, insisting, "He has done more for our race than I have. He has smiled his way into people's hearts; I have been obliged to fight my way." Washington's insight was a forecast of a theme in the future of American race relations in which the popularity of Black musicians, athletes, and movie stars made at least those stars visible to the white majority. Williams began to headline on his own, the first African American performer to do so. And then he appeared in *Shuffle Along*.

When it opened at the Cort Theatre in 1921, *Shuffle Along* was an all-Black musical—featuring Bert Williams, among others, with music by the Black composers and lyricists Eubie Blake and Noble Sissle—for the first time built around a love story between two Black characters. Blake and Sissle had already

Bert Williams turned prejudice upside down. While he sang and acted about being "nobody" (matched by his look of poverty and defeat in this costume), he was such a compelling talent that he made audiences love him. He showed the heart and humanity beneath the blackface mask.

performed together onstage in elegant clothes and were among the initial African American artists to appear without blackface. The show was full of firsts. The great singer, actor, and athlete Paul Robeson was part of the cast, as was the dancer Josephine Baker. Florence Mills was one of the stars, and though she is no longer well known, when she died in 1927, some 250,000 people filled Harlem's streets to honor her as the funeral procession passed by.

The young poet Langston Hughes rushed to New York just to see this "honey of a show. Swift, bright funny, rollicking, and gay, with a dozen danceable, singable tunes." Night after night he came back, to see it again and again. Not only was there novelty onstage, but African Americans were allowed to sit in the orchestra section with whites—which was so revolutionary only one other theater in the city (the Lafayette in Harlem) allowed it and President Woodrow Wilson had tried to pass a law limiting those prime seats to white patrons. There was blackface even in this all-Black show. And the musicians in the orchestra had to memorize the score. Blake explained, "We did that because it was expected of us. People didn't

Shuffle Along featured a love story between a Black man and woman, which had never before been featured on Broadway, or—most likely—any stage in the country. Harry Truman adopted a song from the show as his campaign song when he ran for president in 1948.

believe that Black people could read music—they wanted to think that our ability was just natural talent." But even with these restrictions, African Americans were stepping out of the straitjacket of white stereotypes, into their own creativity and power. *Shuffle Along*, Hughes wrote, "gave just the proper push . . . to that Negro vogue of the 20's, that spread to books, African sculpture, music, and dancing." And that was, in part, because in one downtown neighborhood, Greenwich Village, all of the dominant attitudes in America were being questioned, while in Harlem, New York was becoming the "Negro capital of the world."

42nd Street: A Glowing New City Center

Times Square transformed night. The bright lights of theater marquees and ever larger and more compelling electric-light advertisements bloomed in the darkness and made walking along the streets feel like the invitation to an adventure. Each decade added a new layer of shining display.

In 1908, movies were displayed on the Times Tower, whose beacon was a kind of lighthouse calling all to come. The crowd was part of the appeal, as was the New Year's ball drop in the same location.

Twenty years later, this image of theaters was sold to tourists as a taste of the city's attractions.

By 1934, advertisements for beer, cars, and cigarettes, as well as shows, lit up night town.

In 1953, even the new form of entertainment that would compete with Broadway theaters needed Times Square to entice the public.

Difference

West 4th Street, 125th Street

1900–1930s

In which the city is pulling in opposite directions: the radicals of Greenwich Village question money, gender, power, and art, making New York the nation's "gay capital"; eugenicists seek to seal the borders of a white nation; and Harlem becomes the world center of the New Negro.

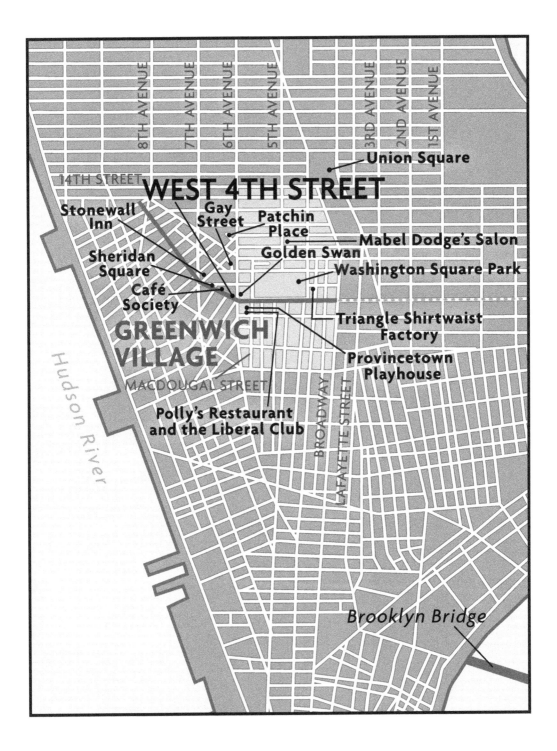

8TH AVENUE · 7TH AVENUE · 6TH AVENUE · 5TH AVENUE · 3RD AVENUE · 2ND AVENUE · 1ST AVENUE

Union Square

14TH STREET

WEST 4TH STREET

Stonewall
Inn

Gay
Street

Patchin
Place

Mabel Dodge's Salon

Sheridan
Square

Golden Swan

Washington Square Park

Café
Society

GREENWICH
VILLAGE

Triangle Shirtwaist
Factory

Provincetown
Playhouse

MACDOUGAL STREET

BROADWAY

LAFAYETTE STREET

Hudson River

Polly's Restaurant
and the Liberal Club

Brooklyn Bridge

CHAPTER 18

"Our Whole Big Human Selves"

> When I speak of Greenwich Village I have no geographical conception
> in view. The term Greenwich Village is to me a spiritual zone of mind....
> The city which hasn't a Greenwich Village is to be pitied. It has no life,
> no illusion, no art.
>
> —Hippolyte Havel

The Village was the capital of revolutionary thinking and living in America—the place to attack old ideas and experiment with new ones—and West Fourth Street was a pathway snaking through the Village.

In 1806, Elizabeth Schuyler Hamilton, Alexander's widow, helped to found a society to care for orphans in Greenwich, the village rich people used as a retreat from the city. The following year, a building went up to house the children and a lane running next to it was called Asylum Street. When the asylum was torn down in 1833, the road gained a new name: West Fourth Street. Even though the city had mapped out its rational grid plan in 1811, Greenwich was allowed to keep its own haphazard thoroughfares. Because West Fourth followed an older pattern, its name had nothing to do with the numbers of nearby streets. Near the Hudson River, West Fourth improbably begins at Thirteenth Street and continues to cross Twelfth, Eleventh, and Tenth Streets angling south and east before turning sharply eastward when it meets Seventh Avenue at Sheridan Square.

The Village did and still does feel like a little hamlet distinct from the rest of Manhattan—and not just because its warren of angled, crisscrossing streets is the opposite of the island's neatly mapped rectangles. Buildings in the West Village on and near West Fourth were built in the early or mid-nineteenth century as single- or dual-family homes made out of brownstone—not the gleaming skyscrapers seen elsewhere. A guidebook written in 1939 described the Village in words that had been true long before and are not far from what you can see today. It noted the "winding streets" and "houses with steep roofs, often of slate, with old chimney pots; old brass knobs on handsome doors; high-ceilinged rooms, small-paned windows; carved mantels over huge fireplaces."

In the early twentieth century, some of the larger buildings as well as single- and dual-family homes were broken up into apartments. Artists, poets, and believers in radical causes began noticing the apartments for rent in the Village at what seemed to them very low prices. The fact that Village buildings were older, sometimes odd, and almost fairy-tale-like in their eccentricity suited these free-thinkers. In the skyscrapered, soulless, money-focused city, such people craved an island of their own. These new Villagers tried out ways of thinking, creating, and living that were inexpressible in almost every other part of the country. That did not make them perfect people—their affairs, addictions, and egos are as legendary as their creations. But they truly led us into the world we live in, and aspire to, now.

In the poorer parts of the Village, five- to six-story buildings honeycombed into small apartments were already filled with Irish laborers, Italian immigrants, and African Americans. The growing Italian population crossing from Little Italy was pushing out the African Americans who lived near Minetta Lane. But, as ever in the city, closeness also brought couples together. In 1900, several apartment houses along Minetta Lane were integrated, with white families from Germany, Russia, Belgium, and France living side by side with Black families from Africa, Bermuda, and Barbados. This small section of the Village was an extreme exception in a country in which segregation had been officially approved by the Supreme Court. A census of the block from that year even lists five mixed-race couples. By 1920, one of those families had moved slightly north to Gay Street.

Gay Street is a tiny angled lane perhaps named after the owner of a stable on the block in the 1830s. Built for the families of artisans, the brick three-story houses were solid and trim. Nine Gay Street was the home of a multigenerational mixed Irish and African American family that had relocated from Minetta Lane: the Austins. The Austin clan was led by Annie—who was Irish—and included her three mixed-race children and six grandchildren.

Throughout the city's history there had been mixed Irish–African American couples, but they had always been described by outsiders as the most degenerate expression of the lowest of the low. There was prejudice in the Village and in the almost entirely segregated city. But in the Village, Black and interracial families were living near a new generation of the nation's most creative men and women. Breaking the boundaries between Black and white was not despised or hidden; it was part of life.

West Fourth Street continues east from Seventh to Sixth Avenue. In the early 1900s, the elevated train ran over Sixth Avenue, creating a noisy, dark cavern beneath the steel. Where West Fourth crosses Sixth Avenue stood Cadigan's bar, which an inspector wrote was "so full of those of both sexes and races that there was no vacant place." Across Sixth Avenue was another bar named the Golden Swan, but everyone knew it as the Hell Hole. The bar was the home territory of an Irish gang called the Hudson Dusters, which made it feel "at once alive and deadly," but a group of male and female radical intellectuals and artists liked the "smoky" feeling of the place. A young Irish American named Eugene O'Neill would go there to drink himself into oblivion alongside other men trying to escape into their blurry dreams. One of O'Neill's drinking buddies was Joe Smith, an African American employee of the bar whose girlfriend was white, and who was known to be both a local political force and gang leader. Smith, another Villager recalled, had the "air of a ruler." Many years later, O'Neill would weave Joe's story into *The Iceman Cometh*, a tragic play that remains a cornerstone of American theater. Instead of condemning the kind of lost souls who drank away their lives at the Hell Hole, O'Neill explored the deepest truths of being American through their stories.

O'Neill was America's first great playwright. His talent—and his courage in exploring the darkness within us—transformed serious theater. Five of his plays focused in one way or another on African American lives. He often used dialect

John Sloan was an accomplished artist who knew the Village well, drew images for *The Masses*, and captured many scenes of city life. This etching of the Golden Swan featured Eugene O'Neill himself seated at the upper right.

and language that, even in the 1920s, some African Americans found offensive. Yet his were the first plays by a serious white author to focus on racism, to feature a Black actor, to include an interracial cast, and to treat the inner life of an African American as important. Lives mixed, lives crossed, in the Village, and O'Neill's plays showed it.

"WE ARE FREE WHO LIVE IN WASHINGTON SQUARE"

After West Fourth Street crosses Sixth Avenue, it moves on to become the southern edge of Washington Square. By the early 1900s, the garment manufacturing trade that employed so many immigrants, especially Jewish and Italian young women, had moved out of the Lower East Side's tenement apartments. Now sweatshops clustered at the eastern end of Washington Square at

Washington Place. Immigrant women worked sixty- to seventy-hour weeks for miserable wages in these sweatshops, where they were forbidden to talk with their neighbors and lost a half day's pay if a boss thought they took too many bathroom breaks.

On November 22, 1909, the Great Hall of Cooper Union, located in what is now the East Village due east of Washington Square, was filled with women. These garment workers were debating whether to go on strike for better conditions, and the city's labor leaders, men such as Samuel Gompers, were scheduled to lead the meeting. Women, the men were sure, would not have the toughness and determination to win a strike. "I want to say a few words," twenty-three-year-old Clara Lemlich announced in Yiddish as she pushed her way toward the podium. "I am one of those who feels and suffers from the things described here. I move that we go on a general strike." The hall erupted in cheers and she won the day. The strike involved up to forty thousand immigrant women and lasted through the next February. And it drew the support of some Villagers, almost all of whom were middle-class or wealthy college-educated women. While one strand of labor activity in the city was led by cautious leaders such as Gompers who slowly won gains for unions centered on specific skills, another was now bubbling up through the militant voices of women allied with their middle-class sisters in the Village. The Villagers, in turn, became active voices in protests for women's suffrage—one cause inspiring another.

On March 25, 1911, fire broke out at the Triangle Shirtwaist factory on Washington Place. "They're burning! They're jumping out of windows," one Villager screamed to another over a crackling phone line. "A great swirling, billowing cloud of smoke . . . swept like a giant streamer out of Washington Square," reported Martha Bruere as the top three floors of the building were consumed in flames. Women ran up to her and told what they were seeing: "Tears were running from their eyes and they were white and shaking as they caught me by the arm. 'Oh,' shrieked one of them, 'they are jumping. Jumping from ten stories up! They are going through the air like bundles of clothes and the firemen can't stop them.'" The factory owners had bolted the exit doors so they could examine each worker as she left daily to prevent theft. But now as fire spread, women could only be consumed in the flames or leap to their deaths from the windows. One hundred and forty-six perished.

Tragedy—abetted by cruel, criminal owners and just across the park from the homes of reformers and radicals—helped forge the labor activism of the Village. Women who wanted to help their sisters, who demanded a voice and a vote, who were determined to record, report, and improve the conditions of the working poor became ever more of a force in the Village. And that was only the beginning. By 1912, the press began writing about Villagers as the new "bohemians"—American versions of the passionate, madcap, artistic rebels of Paris.

If Forty-Second Street was about music, dance, songs, plays, and food packaged to please and to sell, the Village set out to be the opposite: the utopia of being yourself. John Reed grew up in Portland, Oregon, studied at Harvard, and came to New York as a dashing writer, reporter, and poet. Most of all, he was seeking newness, life, energy, adventure, change. You can hear that in the draft manifesto for the socialist magazine *The Masses* he wrote in 1913:

"We refuse to commit ourselves to any course of action except this: *to do with the Masses exactly what we please. . . .* The broad purpose of *The Masses* is . . . to everlastingly attack old systems, old morals, old prejudices—the whole weight of outworn thought that dead men have saddled up us; and to set up many new ones in their places. . . . We intend to be arrogant, impertinent, in bad taste, but not vulgar. We will not be bound by one creed or theory or social reform, but will express them all, providing they be radical" (italics in the original).

Number 42 Washington Square South housed a large gathering of the intellectual artists, including Reed. He described 42 in a poem:

Yet we are free who live in Washington Square,
We dare to think as Uptown wouldn't dare,
Blazing our nights with arguments uproarious;
What care we for a dull old world censorious
When each is sure he'll fashion something glorious?
Blessed are thou, Anarchic Liberty
Who asketh nought but joy of such as we!

Reed and his fellow Village radicals knew that they were defying the expectations of their parents, of mainstream America, of "a dull old world censorious." They were playful in their radicalism, but that did not mean they were any less serious. The handsome, dashing, fearless Reed was seen by many as the Village's leading man—the hero of radicalism.

When Reed and his fellow creators of *The Masses* wanted to find colleagues, all they had to do was walk west on Washington Square South back to MacDougal Street (which forms the western edge of Washington Square) and turn left. Just as coffeehouses and

This is the view across Washington Square Park in the early twentieth century when a trolley ran through the park. Fifth Avenue begins just past the arch.

taverns gave men a place to gather in colonial days, the tearooms and playhouses of MacDougal just south of the square were the hotbeds of new thought for the men and now women of the Village.

Polly's Restaurant at 137 MacDougal was one of these headquarters until 1916, when Polly Holladay moved her café to Sheridan Square. Polly charged little for food and didn't mind if you couldn't pay. Paintings by experimental artists as well as semi-nude self-portraits by seventeen-year-old Clara Tice hung on the walls, attracting the attention of the city's censors. Polly's lover, the arch-anarchist revolutionary Hippolyte Havel, would finish his chores as an excellent cook, walk up to patrons, and call them "bourgeois pigs." Havel was the former lover and still friend of the most important, galvanizing female radical of all: Emma Goldman. Goldman was an anarchist who opposed all governments, an idealistic Marxist who wanted wealth to be shared, a feminist who argued passionately for women's rights to birth control and for all forms of love: "If two people care for each other, they have a right to live together as long as that love exists."

The art, the cheap meals, Havel's curses—all made for the perfect bohemian

The scene at Polly's restaurant with a note written by Jessie Tarbox Beals. Beals was a photographer who captured the personalities and sights of the Village and understood the value of selling its bohemian oddness as a tourist attraction.

atmosphere. Polly's sat just beneath the Liberal Club, which defined itself as a "meeting place for those interested in new ideas." Not just ideas: pianists played ragtime, poets read, even the famous Swiss psychologist and colleague of Sigmund Freud, Carl Jung, came to speak.

The Liberal Club had originally met near the much more sedate Gramercy Park. Henrietta Rodman, a New York City schoolteacher, changed that. At the time, a woman who married and had a child was not allowed to return to teach. Rodman, supported by the club, led protests against this rule (which was still enforced in some other parts of the country until the 1960s)—and won. Removing an antiquated law, though, was just one example of her devotion to change. Rodman wore sandals, did not take her husband's name, worked to create shared living spaces so women could hold jobs while others cared for their children, campaigned to make birth control information widely available, and

Five women getting ready for a festive Liberal Club dance. The bare feet and combination of ancient Greek dress and Egyptian headdress might have been a nod to Isadora Duncan, who wore similar loose clothing when she danced, or simply given the women a way to feel free and different from the world of their parents and other censorious, corseted peers.

advocated having many affairs. Why, she demanded, should the membership of the Liberal Club be entirely white? Faced with Rodman's protests, the Liberal Club split, and she led a faction down to MacDougal Street just above Polly's. On February 17, 1914, Rodman was one of a group of Village women who spoke on a panel on "What Feminism Means to Me." Marie Jenney Howe spoke for all when she said, "We're sick of being specialized to sex. We intend simply to be ourselves, not just our little female selves, but our whole, big, human selves."

Howe and Rodman used the Liberal Club site to host a series of pathbreaking meetings that lasted until the 1940s yet are still somewhat mysterious to historians. Members of the Heterodoxy Club were sworn to secrecy and did not keep notes of their meetings. This all-female organization was interested in personal liberation and was a welcome home to a great many aspects of female experience. Elisabeth Irwin and Katharine Susan Anthony were a lesbian couple who lived on Bank Street in the Village with their adopted children. They were one of several same-sex couples in Heterodoxy. Grace Nail Johnson, James Weldon Johnson's wife, was the only African American member.

Next door to the Liberal Club was the Washington Square Bookshop. In fact, the club and store were so linked that a hole was cut in the wall between them so each became an extension of the other. One afternoon, the lively crew at Polly's decided to use the bookstore to stage a play. They continued their theatrical experiments at the Provincetown, Massachusetts, home of *The Masses* contributor and labor activist Mary Heaton Vorse, and then they turned a stable next door to the café at 139 MacDougal Street into the Provincetown Playhouse. Many of the Village radicals wrote material for the playhouse, but two playwrights were exceptional. Susan Glaspell used theater to explore—and to reveal onstage—the tensions and pressures women felt, confined by marriage, by law, even by patterns of female relationships. For O'Neill, the playhouse offered a passageway from trying to escape his demons in drink to exploring his experiences in a series of brilliant plays. The openness of the Provincetown group—led by Glaspell's husband, George "Jig" Cram Cook—gave O'Neill the freedom to write, explore, and find his fearless voice. He went from one challenge to another. His *All God's Chillun Got Wings* starred the all-American athlete, singer, and actor Paul Robeson, explored interracial marriage, and was condemned by New York's mayor because it featured Black and white children together on the stage. To officials in New York and throughout the nation, mixing races was illegal. To O'Neill and the Village radicals, it was life.

Revolutionaries of all sorts would debate actions in the clubs and ideas in the teahouses, write and illustrate articles for *The Masses*, create books to be published and featured in the store, and write plays to be performed across the street. If they strolled farther east on Fourth Street, they would reach 27 East Fourth, the headquarters of the Industrial Workers of the World, the radical labor movement. Or they could cross Washington Square Park, head north up Fifth Avenue, and land at Mabel Dodge's salon.

THE SALON

A wealthy American heiress who had recently held court in an Italian villa, Mabel Dodge decided in May 1913 to host a series of gatherings where "both men and women can meet to eat and drink and talk together." She wanted it to be a place for "Socialists, Trade-Unionists, Anarchists, Suffragists, Poets, Relations, Lawyers, Murderers, 'Old Friends,' Psychoanalysts, I.W.W.'s, Single Taxers, Birth Controlists, Newspapermen, Artists, Modern Artists, Clubwomen, Woman's-Place-is-in-the-home Women, Clergymen, and just plain men . . . stammering in an unaccustomed freedom a kind of speech called Free."

There were real risk-taking pioneers at the salon, such as Emma Goldman, the eloquent anarchist, and Alexander Berkman, her lover who had been sent to prison for attempting to murder the wealthy Henry Clay Frick. The one-eyed radical labor leader Big Bill Haywood came to the parties, as did Margaret Sanger, who was leading the fight for contraception and for a woman's right to her passions and desires. The freewheeling conversations inspired Dodge to devote herself to an explosive exhibit that changed the history of art in America.

On February 15, 1913, Dodge achieved her greatest success. With her active support, a show of the most exciting—and challenging—European and American abstract art opened at the Sixty-Ninth Regiment Armory on Twenty-Fifth Street and Lexington Avenue. The show was a triumph of publicity. Day after day, the newspapers told stories of how crazy the art was and ran cartoons showing people literally standing on their heads trying to make sense of the squares, cubes, and wild colors. The more experts mocked the abstract works by Picasso, Braque, Duchamp, and Brancusi as capable of driving viewers insane, the more New Yorkers flocked to the sold-out show. Soon enough gallery owners and collectors began featuring the latest European art styles—Cubism, Futurism, Constructivism, Dada, Vorticism—on their walls. And two new museums—the Whitney (which began in 1918 as the Whitney Studio Club on Eighth Street in the Village) and the Museum of Modern Art (1929)—gave experimental art an American home. Through art, the Village was changing the city. Until, that is, the city turned against the Village.

CHAPTER 19

War

EUGENICS: BREEDING WHITENESS

World War I split New York apart, exposing fault lines as deep as the clashes that led to riots during the Civil War. Even as the lively Villagers were thumbing their noses at capitalism, celebrating diversity, supporting strikes, and speaking out as women, precisely the opposite views were gathering strength in other parts of the city. One side of New York was opening to new people, new ways of thinking and living, while another was closing down, sealing in, and insisting on its version of American greatness.

In a city whose port, docks, and many businesses depended on international trade, the outbreak of war in 1914 was initially a disaster. America was the largest debtor nation in the world, owing more money to others—for example, European investors—than any other country. As Europeans called in their debts to pay for weapons and stopped buying American products, New York, the center of finance and trade, was in real trouble. But as the war continued, ambitious, smart businessmen in the city, such as the banker Thomas Lamont, came to a realization. The more Europeans destroyed one another, the more opportunity for America to become an international financial power. "Many people," Lamont noted, "seem to believe that New York is to supersede London as the money center of the world." And as the war continued year after year, the Europeans needed more and more American arms and supplies. The city was abuzz with shops making weapons to send across the Atlantic. As Lamont predicted, by the time peace was declared in 1918, America was no longer the world's largest debtor but the world's largest creditor. Frank Vanderlip—like Lamont, a banker with global ambitions—fairly glowed with a vision of the city's future: "We have an opportunity now to become the wellspring of capital for the world." New York was international in that it was an immigrant city, and it was open to new ideas and new art. But it was also, increasingly, a center of international money.

Former president Theodore Roosevelt's energy, his nose for publicity and feel for crowds, his drive to take on and clash with his enemies, was the bustling city itself embodied in a person. Through his father's family, he could trace his history back to Dutch ancestors who arrived in the city in the 1600s. His New York, though, was not the city of the Villagers. Roosevelt was obsessed with ideas of masculine force and racial purity. To Roosevelt, being American meant becoming as much like white, Protestant, Northern European men as possible. That meant everyone must "act as Americans . . . not as Irish Americans, German Americans, Native Americans." Immigrants could not "cling to the speech, the customs, the ways of life, and the habits of thought of the Old World which they have left." If America and its immigrant city was a melting pot, the temperature must be high enough to burn away any remnants of other cultures.

Roosevelt eagerly accepted those immigrants willing to strip away their pasts and be totally transformed. The story of America was the tale of the glorious founding fathers and mothers, and in endless pageants and parades, schools, towns, and cities could create new Americans by reaffirming the greatness of the heroes of the American Revolution. Roosevelt, though, was allied with others who had more extreme views. Eugenicists believed that humanity needed to be carefully bred, like dogs, flowers, or horses, to favor the best race: whites. Immigration, other than from a few favored "white" nations, must be stopped. Roosevelt's friend Madison Grant argued that for America to continue to be "an asylum for the oppressed" would lead to its destruction. "We cannot forever absorb this influx of the scum of the earth," insisted William Earl Dodge Stokes, another wealthy New Yorker. America's future, they were certain, depended on blocking Southern Italians, Eastern European Jews, and everyone in the "Asiatic Barred Zone," which extended from Russia through to the Pacific islands. The

THE ONLY WAY TO HANDLE IT.

This 1921 anti-European-immigrant cartoon shows the very same hostility toward those seeking to come to the United States that has more recently been directed against immigrants and refugees from Central and South America.

story of America was about white heroes and the threats to them from weaker races. What then of Black people already in America?

When the Rough Riders fought in Cuba during the Spanish-American War, Roosevelt had served with the African American Buffalo Soldiers, and he thought African Americans deserved to be officers in the regular army. President Roosevelt had invited Booker T. Washington to dine with his family at the White House, which outraged more extreme racists. As with immigrants, he respected individual African Americans who fit his mold of uplift and achievement. But he was passionately against racial mixing.

The white race, Roosevelt believed, had exceptional traits that could only be preserved and fostered through having purebred children. Picking a side in World War I might not seem to pose an obvious choice for someone devoted to the idea that Northern European white people were a superior race, since England and Germany were on opposite sides. But Henry Fairfield Osborn, another friend of Roosevelt's and the head of the American Museum of Natural History, decided that Germans were not really white. Instead, they had been debased when they were invaded centuries ago by Central Asians. Germans were now defined as "Huns"—descendants of Attila—not true Nordics. England, thus, was the defender of white civilization and deserved America's enthusiastic support.

Even as Roosevelt found a contorted racial logic for supporting England, other New Yorkers were choosing their own sides. German Americans were still a significant section of the city's population and many sided with Germany, until America entered the war. Jews who had fled from the tsar's pogroms could not imagine fighting as Russia's ally. Russia's 1917 revolution took that country out of the war but created a new set of conflicts: Should Jews support the Soviets? Irish Americans determined to see their ancestral homeland free itself from English rule were eager to defeat the nation that had been their ancient oppressor. By contrast, many of the city's elite admired the English, married their daughters to English nobles, and filled their homes with artifacts and symbols of English history. The slaughter in Europe inflamed New York's old tensions between native and immigrant, rich and poor.

Roosevelt had something in common with men on both sides of the conflict, a love for war. To them, the quest for triumph and glory was a virile, masculine urge necessary to the health of men and nations. "The nation," he announced in one of his most famous speeches, "that has trained itself to a career of unwarlike and isolated ease is bound, in the end, to go down before other nations which have not lost the manly and adventurous qualities." Friedrich von Bernhardi, a German general, agreed. War is "an indispensable factor of culture in which a truly civilized nation finds the highest expression of strength and vitality." Fighting, tasting blood, was a chance to face, in the hail of bullets, the kind of crisis in which a man's soul was forged. According to this view, European colonists taking over Africa and Asia, following in the footsteps of the conquerors of the Americas, demonstrated the racial superiority of whites—who were merely fulfilling their evolutionary destiny. While real men needed combat, true women devoted themselves to rearing the children who would guarantee the continued dominance of whites. A white woman who did not have children, Roosevelt argued, was like a man too cowardly to fight. The theory of evolution was distorted into a vision of man the warrior and woman the breeder in which "races" were like animal species competing to survive and thrive.

When President Woodrow Wilson led the United States into war, he was determined to unite the nation behind the effort and to silence dissent. Emma Goldman, Alexander Berkman, and Big Bill Haywood, who had sparkled at Dodge's salon, were quickly arrested and shipped off to jail. For German

Americans, it became dangerous to be seen as allied in any way with the nation's enemy. German classical music disappeared from concert halls and German light opera vanished from Broadway theaters. Jews, anxious to be accepted in America, realized that that meant supporting the war. African Americans, too, wanted to prove their worth as soldiers. They would have to fight two battles, combatting bombs and bullets while the army command undermined them daily. While the French admired and honored Black soldiers, the Americans sent a secret message to the French warning against encouraging "intolerable pretensions to equality" by such acts as eating with, shaking hands with, and casually conversing with Black soldiers. Most of all, the men should have no contact with French women.

"I LOVE MYSELF"

The Village was a living rejection of the entire world of Roosevelt, Osborne, and Grant. In words that could as easily be written in the twenty-first century, John Reed insisted that the war only served to distract workers from their real struggle: "The country is rapidly being scared into a heroic mood. The workingman will do well to realize that his enemy is not Germany, nor Japan: his enemy is that 2% of the people of the United states who own 60% of the national wealth." Max Eastman, who managed *The Masses* and was just as radical, handsome, and engaged in dramatic romantic affairs as Reed, shared that antiwar view. The federal government did not see the publishing of antiwar sentiments as free speech and in a series of trials managed to force the paper to suspend publication long enough to go out of business. Reed sped off to Russia in 1917 to report on the revolution, hurriedly wrote *Ten Days That Shook the World* while back in the Village, and then returned to the Soviet Union, where he died. (The movie *Reds* tells this story very well.)

The Village announced that the anti-immigrant forces, the supporters of race purity, the "patriots" rushing off to fight were wrong: about virility, masculinity, and war; about women; about labor, immigration, and what it meant to be American. Being different was right, even glorious. Some of the women of Heterodoxy lived nearby in an unusual spot. Off Tenth Street, half a block west

Patchin Place is particularly odd in that it looks like a roadway framed with sidewalks but is a tiny blocked alleyway no vehicle could enter.

of Sixth Avenue, is the alleyway entrance to one of the very few dead-end streets in Manhattan. Two rows of light-brown three-story buildings, each with its own sidewalk, face each other across a tiny roadway—strange since the alley has a gate and cars are not allowed to enter. This enclosed space is called Patchin Place, and though before 1917 it lacked electricity, running water, or indoor toilets, in its odd sense of being a hideaway community it was the essence of what the Village offered. Patchin Place became the home of many famous Village authors, including the poet E. E. Cummings and the novelists Theodore Dreiser and

The Village: Selling Freedom and Living It

The early Village had a playful aspect, with stores and cafés that were deliberately eccentric. Villagers were billing themselves as nonconformists, which allowed them to live unconventional lives. Women (generally white and middle class) had a degree of independence in the Village—whether in running their own businesses or in creating their own relationships—that was extremely rare in the rest of the country.

Right: In 1902 Jessie Tarbox Beals became America's first female news photographer. By 1917, she had moved to the Village and supported herself by opening a shop where she sold her images of the Village to tourists. Her portraits of Villagers stressed the independence of women like herself who were making their own lives.

Below left: The two titles framing Beals's image of this café suggest two aspects of the Village: the Will o' the Wisp tearoom in her written caption sounds English and cozy, while "idee chic" in the banner over the doorway suggests French and modern.

Below right: Born in what is now Romania as Marie Marchand, Romany Marie ran a series of cafés that were centers of Village cultural and intellectual life. She famously cared more for rich conversation than for making sure her often-broke patrons were able to pay.

A BUSY CORNER IN GREENWICH VILLAGE
WILL O' THE WISP TEA ROOM
IDEE CHIC
ALADDIN TEA ROOM

ROMANY MARIE'S IN GREENWICH VILLAGE
— AS VIVID AS A SCARLET BIRD AGAINST A MOUNTAIN PINE ! —

A Beals portrait of Grace Godwin in her "Garret." The sign reads "This place ain't bohemian"—which of course meant that she hoped customers and guests would see it as just that.

Godwin's Garrett captures many layers of the Village. The "garret" was created by a con-man entrepreneur who called himself Bruno Guido. He had noticed that the space, on Washington Square South, faced the last stop on the 5th Avenue bus, exactly at the height where passengers could see it. He turned it into a stage set of the Bohemian Village and sold his own magazines to tourists—which did feature real Village talents such as Djuna Barnes and Hart Crane. When he left the Village, Grace Godwin took over the garret, using it as a restaurant and place to sell her creations as well as a home. Godwin, though, tried to exclude Black people, which was illegal and showed that independence was not always the same as openness.

Tall and striking, Djuna Barnes was a visible presence that touched on many aspects of the Village: she dressed all in black with a hat and cape and would wear makeup in startling blue, green, or purple. She ate at Polly's, the Provincetown Players put on her plays, and she joined in the Mabel Dodge salon. Barnes's love life, involving men and women, was public knowledge. In order to support herself, Barnes studied drawing and then illustrated stories she wrote as an independent reporter. Her experimental fiction and poetry are still read today.

In Paris (where this image was taken), Barnes was part of a circle of writers that included James Joyce and the lesbian couple Jane Heap and Margaret Anderson who were the first to publish Joyce's pathbreaking novel *Ulysses*.

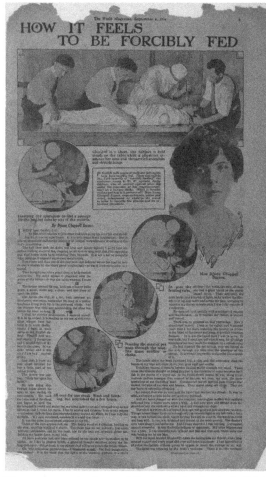

When women went on hunger strikes to call attention to the fight to win the right to vote, they were forcibly fed. Barnes put herself through the process to let readers see it.

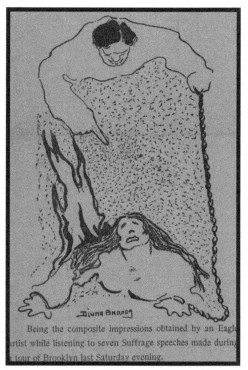

Covering a meeting of suffragists, Barnes captured how they saw male domination.

The Task Is Sordid and Hard, but It Must Be Done—So After an Early Breakfast Out Sets the Bohemian.

By DJUNA BARNES

Illustrated by the Author

"After all, one must be faithful to one's bracelets."

While her drawing of the Oscar Wilde-like Village Bohemian is satirical, Barnes was drawn to homosexual men and was astutely aware of the blurring of gender lines on the streets around her.

Djuna Barnes. First, though, it was a place where women who lived there gathered to speak intimately and openly. The only two men regularly invited were the essayist Randolph Bourne and his friend Carl Zigrosser. Bourne had a disfigured face and severely hunched back, and a brilliant mind.

Bourne looked out across the Village, across New York, and saw a vision of "transnational America." The Jews, the Irish, the Chinese, the Germans—these were not inferior races who needed to be melted down in a pot and remade as copies of George and Martha Washington. Their cultures, their worldviews, their foods, even their disagreements with the descendants of colonial families were life, energy: the true fruits of democracy. Bourne told all of the new New Yorkers: you don't have to *become* American; you, in your difference, *are* America. The true story of America was the streets of New York.

In the years after World War I, Bourne's allies seemed to lose the fight. By 1924, Congress passed and the president signed laws that blocked immigration in exactly the ways the eugenicists had wanted. In the coming years, those very laws served to trap Jews in Europe as Hitler consigned them to the gas chambers. But in places like the Village, being "different" continued to be celebrated.

Even as Roosevelt and others like him spoke for a sharp division between hyper-masculine men and women duty bound to motherhood, the Village was known to be "the home of 'pansies' and 'Lesbians.'" Long-haired effeminate men and short-haired masculine women were the very symbol of Village openness. As in any city, there had always been gathering places for New Yorkers attracted to the same sex. During the large influx of single Italian men, for example, a lively world of same-sex activity took shape, though often the Italians did not think of themselves as attracted to men and planned to marry women on their return to Italy. By contrast, two American men, one of whom often wore dresses, announced that they were a married couple. The Village was a public space for those exploring who they were and how they wanted to present themselves.

Liberal Club dances had been the playful highlight of the Village's prewar days. By 1918, a suspicious investigator at a club dance reported that men "wear expensive gowns, employ rouge . . . and in short make up an appearance which looks for everything like a young lady." In 1925, a few doors down from Polly's original home on MacDougal, Eva Kotchever—who punningly called herself Eve Addams—opened a tearoom in which men were "admitted but not welcome." These locations, and others like them in Harlem and on Forty-Second Street, were well known and easily visible. So much so that George Chauncey, the modern historian who recovered this history, says that New York came to be recognized as the " 'gay capital' of the nation."

You didn't even have to go to a dance or cross-dress to experience the Village's radical openness to different ways of being male and female. The Washington Square Bookshop shelved the latest studies from Europe on sex and sexuality. The British author Edward Carpenter showed that throughout history some of the most creative, accomplished people, such as Michelangelo, had been attracted to members of the same sex. One such book was an anthology created by Carpenter that featured poems by a selection of the most famous male authors from the ancient Greeks to the present, all expressing seemingly forbidden feelings for other men. Countee Cullen, the African American poet, read the book and on March 3, 1923, recommended it to his friend, Alain Locke, a professor of philosophy at Howard University: "I read it through in one setting. . . . It opened up for me soul windows which had been closed; it threw a noble and evident light on what I had begun to believe, because of what the world believes, ignoble and unnatural. I love myself in it."

Countee Cullen and Alain Locke—two men at the center of the Harlem Renaissance. Claiming a heritage of achievement as a gay man was like claiming a heritage of honor as an African American: the Village and Harlem inspired one another.

CHAPTER 20

"The Pulse of the Negro World"

Everybody comes to New York. New York puts everybody in his place. Harlem is the Negroes' place. Negroes from the south whose ancestors were African slaves for generation on generation. Negroes whose ancestors were African, and Indian, and pale-face. Negroes from the west, the east, the north. Negroes from Africa, the West Indies, the Bahamas, the Central and South Americas, Cuba, Jamaica, everywhere. Ethiopia has stretched forth her wings.

—Wallace Thurman, *American Monthly*, May 1927

MARCH 21, 1924
The Civic Club, 14 West Twelfth Street

The gala took place in the Village because no other fancy hall in the city was open to a fully integrated audience of men and women, Black and white. But it was all about Harlem. One year after getting Countee Cullen's letter, Alain Locke hosted an evening to celebrate the "Debut of the Younger School of Negro Writers." This dinner was the triumphant announcement of what Locke called "the New Negro."

Locke had gone to Harvard, been the first African American Rhodes Scholar, and earned his PhD in philosophy. In celebrating the powerful voices of new writers, he was announcing a new historical moment for Black people, for America. "For generations," he later wrote, "the Negro has been more of a formula than a human being—a something to be argued about, condemned or defended, to be 'kept down,' or 'in his place,' or 'helped up.'" In a sentence, he captured a century of American history, from blackface minstrelsy to abolitionist philanthropy. This legacy had hidden Black people, even from themselves: "His shadow, so to speak, has been more real to him than his personality." But now "the pulse of the Negro world has begun to beat in Harlem." Black thinkers, artists, writers, and musicians were connecting with Africa, with African peoples everywhere, in a shared sense of "self-respect" and "race pride." The writers and artists gathered in the room were the voices of an African American "spiritual coming of age."

The evening had originally been planned to honor Jessie Fauset's new novel, and while she was not pleased that the focus shifted from her alone to a generation, she was actually responsible for many of these new voices. As the literary editor of the NAACP's magazine *The Crisis*, Fauset had hosted literary salons in Harlem and had been the first person to publish poetry by Langston Hughes and Gwendolyn Brooks. Hughes credited her as a key "midwife" of the entire New Negro literature.

The most glittering stars of the Black writing world attended the event, including W. E. B. Du Bois, also a Harvard PhD, editor of *The Crisis*, and the nation's Black intellectual leader; the diplomat and author James Weldon Johnson, who was the head of the NAACP; and Johnson's assistant national secretary (and successor), Walter White. Seated beside these key thinkers were white authors such as Eugene O'Neill and editors from prominent book and magazine publishers—who soon began publishing works by the artists Locke heralded. Indeed, one year later, an issue of *Survey Graphic* was entirely devoted to "Harlem—the Mecca of the New Negro" and included works by Cullen, Hughes, Claude McKay, Zora Neale Hurston, and Fauset, an essay by Locke, and drawings by the Harlem artist Aaron Douglas. Johnson called the book version of that issue "one of the most important books on the Negro ever published." The Harlem Renaissance had officially begun.

Locke believed that through art—novels, poems, essays, paintings, sculptures, music, theater—African Americans in Harlem could drop the mask, could wipe away the shadow placed over them by the white world. They could erase the grinning lips of blackface, end the silence imposed by violence and prejudice, and

The cover of the issue of *Survey Graphic* celebrating "The New Negro" featured an image of the great singer Roland Hayes, who was one of the first African American artists who was recorded and honored for singing European classical music. This was one of a series of striking portraits of key figures in the Harlem Renaissance drawn by the German-born Winold Reiss.

declare themselves as modern, creative, alive, and strong. At its best, the Harlem Renaissance was one grand red-carpet announcement of the strength and power of Americans of African descent. This was especially true for fiction. The ever-expanding Black community in Harlem produced the talent; access to the kinds of editors and publishers who attended the Civic Club dinner created the opportunity. As Johnson wrote in 1930, "Within the past ten years more fiction has been published by Negro writers than had been brought out by them in the preceding two hundred and fifty years. And every bit of this fiction . . . has been written by writers of the Harlem group"—a perfect example of New York as the media capital bringing new voices to the nation. But life is not that simple. African American Harlem itself was a product of prejudice.

Harlem had been a Jewish neighborhood featuring Hammerstein's theaters bookending 125th Street and a growing immigrant Italian section on its east side. Now it was being heralded as a Black mecca. As so often happened in New York City, the change came due to real estate.

In 1908, the Harlem Property Owners' Improvement Corporation made a bold suggestion: having tried unsuccessfully to resegregate the city's transportation systems and to block African Americans from using the public library on 135th Street, the white landlords moved on to a more drastic proposal—a twenty-four-foot-high fence to be built along 136th Street to keep African Americans out of upper Harlem. This early effort to wall off migration fortunately failed.

The fight over the color of Harlem had been going on since the beginning of the century. At that time, there were a couple of buildings on 125th Street named after white abolitionists that were entirely filled with Black renters. All of the rest of Harlem was white, and Manhattan's African American neighborhoods were on the West Side—one called the Tenderloin in the Twenties and Thirties, and another named San Juan Hill (after the same campaign in Cuba where the Buffalo Soldiers fought alongside Roosevelt) in the Fifties and low Sixties.

The damaging force behind the creation of Black Harlem was white New Yorkers' determination to live in all-white areas. Philip Payton, a smart African American real estate entrepreneur, known as "the father of colored Harlem," realized that once he advertised a building as open to Black renters, he could count on two results: whites would leave, and he could raise the rent to incoming Black

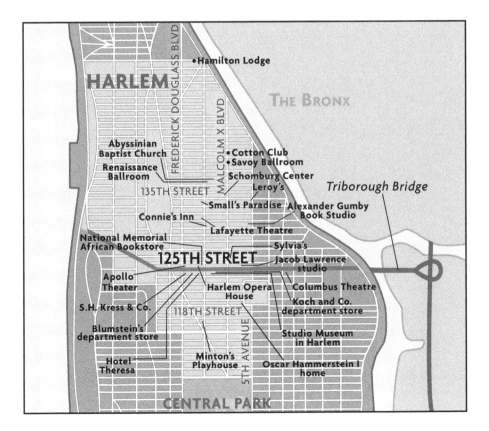

Home to Harlem

Many images of Harlem were meant to entice white visitors to see it either as a wild, primitive, and yet ultra-modern place where they could let loose or as a new version of the Five Points: a site of degradation and decay. But for an ever-growing African American population, it was home. These were taken in the 1930s.

Friends sitting on the stoop in front of an apartment house on a summer's day

Above: A row of stores along a Harlem avenue

Right: Stopping for a shoe shine on 135th Street and Lenox Avenue

Below: A fruit stand on 133rd Street and Madison Avenue with a picketing striker in front

people. As James Weldon Johnson explained, "The whole movement, in the eyes of the whites, took on the aspect of an 'invasion'; they became panic stricken and began fleeing as from a plague. The presence of one colored family in a block, no matter how well-bred and orderly, was sufficient to precipitate a flight." (Johnson knew this story well as his wife, Grace, was the daughter of Payton's partner John Nail.)

Since African Americans were shut out of most of the city, large, appealing apartments in Harlem seemed ideal—and worth the cost. The American South was for African Americans what Russia was for Jews—a place of prejudice, violence, and hopelessness. More and more young African Americans rushed north to New York. At the same time, a smaller wave of immigrants from the Caribbean reached the city. Together, the two streams increased the Black population from 60,000 to 90,000 in the first ten years of the new century, then nearly doubled it to 152,000 by 1920, and doubled it again to 327,000 in 1930. The Great Migration of African Americans from the South to northern cities and, especially, to New York was the Jewish and Italian immigration all over again—but within the United States. The newcomers needed places to live, and real estate professionals such as Payton kept using the same formula.

On the positive side, Harlem was becoming a vibrant hub for African American life, with welcoming streets, churches, and parks. By 1918, more people of African descent lived in Harlem than in any other city in the world. On the negative side, African Americans were frozen out of many jobs, unions, and professions citywide, yet were trapped into paying a premium for living in Harlem, where the large theaters along 125th Street were still segregated. Harlem gave African Americans a place to breathe, to think, to create, to be alive—at a price.

African American Harlem was not just a location; it was a cause, an idea, of Black empowerment. As the memoirist Eddy Harris put it, "Harlem is a state of mind." On July 2, 1917, a white-against-Black race riot broke out in East St. Louis, leaving nine whites and hundreds of African Americans dead. Marcus Garvey, a Jamaican immigrant living in Harlem, indicted the nation: "This is a massacre that will go down in history as one of the bloodiest outrages against mankind for which any class of people could be held guilty." From that moment on, Garvey would be a key voice in Harlem, advocating that Black people separate from white society and follow him and return to Africa. One response to the nation's prevailing white racism was for African Americans to turn inward, to build their own independent businesses, schools—even, perhaps, to create their own separate nation. As Locke explained, "This deep feeling of race is at present the mainspring of Negro life."

The NAACP took a different approach to the East St. Louis attacks: it organized a silent march of African American women and children all dressed in white. On July 28, 1917, nearly ten thousand protesters walked down Fifth Avenue—the most elegant thoroughfare in New York—from Fifty-Ninth to Twenty-Third Street, demonstrating their poise and grace and indicting the bestial white violence. With Garvey's rhetoric and the NAACP's march, African Americans were becoming more assertive. As the uptown streets filled with members of the African diaspora—from the Caribbean, from the South, from the rest of New York—Harlem became the voice of all Americans of African descent. Some would speak in political speeches, others in sermons, and yet more in writing, music, and art.

The silent protest displayed the composure and grace of the city's African Americans as opposed to the murderous violence of white mobs in other parts of the country.

On February 17, 1919, two years after the silent protest down Fifth Avenue, came the opposite kind of march. The twelve hundred members of the 369th Infantry Regiment—the Harlem Hellfighters—paraded up Fifth Avenue to Harlem in the loudest, most joyous celebration. The African American unit had served a longer continuous stretch in combat than any other American World War I outfit and received the highest honors from the French military. The regiment was equally famous for its unique military band, led by the same James Reese Europe whose music animated the Castles' dancing. As one New York paper reported, they were "the proudest band of blowers and pounders that ever reeled off a marching melody."

When Europe and his band turned west from Fifth Avenue on 110th Street and marched up Lenox Avenue, they began playing "Here Comes My Daddy Now"—announcing to all Harlem that its men were home. The *New York Times* described the scene: "The Hellfighters marched between two howling walls of humanity. . . . From the rooftops thousands stood and whooped things up."

In the rest of the country, the return of Black soldiers was not as warmly welcomed. Over the "red summer" of 1919, white-against-Black race riots took place in cities including Chicago and Washington, DC, and most horribly in Elaine County, Arkansas, where an unknown number of African Americans (counts range between twenty-five and two hundred) were murdered. For the first time, though, where they could, African Americans fought back with their own guns against raging whites. Claude McKay fought with words. He was born in Jamaica, where his skill as a writer earned him enough money to come to the United States to study. In the summer of 1919, a poem "exploded" out of him responding to the murders. Max Eastman (then editor of *The Liberator*, a successor to *The Masses*) immediately published it.

> If we must die, let it not be like hogs
> Hunted and penned in an inglorious spot,
> While round us bark the mad and hungry dogs,
> Making their mock at our accursèd lot.
> If we must die, O let us nobly die,

So that our precious blood may not be shed

In vain; then even the monsters we defy

Shall be constrained to honor us though dead!

O kinsmen! we must meet the common foe!

Though far outnumbered let us show us brave,

And for their thousand blows deal one death-blow!

What though before us lies the open grave?

Like men we'll face the murderous, cowardly pack,

Pressed to the wall, dying, but fighting back!

"If We Must Die" was the voice of all Harlem—of all African American people who knew they must not let the "shadow" of racism, even the most bloody violence, silence their voices, their "race pride." One side of the Harlem Renaissance came about because African Americans were hemmed in—by segregated housing and jobs in New York and by lynching and murder in the whole country. Another side was a result of the creative explosion as African Americans found their voices and their power. New York, as it had with minstrelsy and then vaudeville, found talent and publicized it to the nation— this time in print and music.

Playing in Harlem, James P. Johnson gave the piano a new voice and the 1920s a new soundtrack. Born in New Jersey, Johnson studied classical music and then invented (or perhaps perfected) "stride," a piano style that took ragtime and sped it up into thundering cascades of sound. While the right hand played a melody, the left explored (or, you could say, would "stride") all over the keyboard. This was very difficult, complex, and compelling. Johnson composed the music for the dance that was the essence of the "Roaring Twenties," the Charleston, though he also crafted blues, orchestral music, the score for an O'Neill play, and a one-act opera, *De Organizer*, to a Langston Hughes text. Piano playing in Harlem grew ever faster, like the pace of city life, and ever more a display of a master's astonishing skill. Pianists would compete in "cutting" contests to see who was best, and Johnson would always win, though Willie "The Lion" Smith (who was said to be half Jewish) gave him a run for his money.

Ragtime had spread across the nation through sheet music and, later, recordings. Stride was recorded as well, but in the 1920s more and more white people streamed up to Harlem to hear it played live. Where could you hear the best stride? Smith played at Leroy's on 135th Street, the rare establishment allowing only Black customers, so long as they were attired in formal dress, to attend. Connie's Inn at 131st Street was the opposite of Leroy's: only white customers were welcome to listen to Johnson's protégé Thomas Wright "Fats" Waller's scintillating notes. Hurtig and Seamon's Music Hall on 125th Street was similarly segregated, though the separate nightclub downstairs eventually let Black patrons in—so long as they entered through the back door on 126th Street.

The Cotton Club on 142nd Street was for whites only. Indeed, from its name to the plantation-style decorations that featured murals of cotton fields and slave quarters, everything about the club echoed the themes of minstrelsy and the divisions of race. All the female dancers had to be light-skinned African Americans. Yet the artist who brought crowds to the club was Edward Kennedy "Duke" Ellington. Always cool and composed, he played the piano, but his real instrument was his band. Recognizing the gifts of his players and masterfully blending them, he created music played in clubs that you could dance to—or just listen to and admire. From 1927 to 1932, and on and off after that, his headquarters in New York was the Cotton Club. Many of the tunes and stage shows used jungle themes—signaling to white audiences that a trip up to Harlem would be sexy, primitive, wild. By contrast, Ellington and his band were groomed and dressed in tuxedos and, however vibrant their music, there was an overriding elegance—which the Duke embodied. Ellington took music from the virtuosity of stride to the architecture of jazz.

Outside of the Savoy Ballroom, where Black people and white people were welcome to dance, and even dance together, and Small's Paradise on 135th Street, the clubs of Harlem sold music—and adventure—to white audiences, who were eager to come. In 1920, the United States decided to ban the sale of alcohol. Prohibition was meant not only to diminish drinking but to curb the immoral behaviors linked to bars and taverns and the lavish restaurants on Forty-Second Street where rich men entertained showgirls. One by one the lobster palaces

Though the Cotton Club gave African American artists such as Duke Ellington and Cab Calloway a home base, it was designed, in every aspect, to appeal to a white audience.

and rooftop beer gardens closed. But adults responded to a ban they detested by defying it. The effort to uplift moral standards by banning alcohol had precisely the opposite effect.

New York City filled with speakeasies—mildly disguised or slightly hidden drinking spots. Since these bars were illegal, control of the liquor trade and much of the city's nightlife fell to gangsters, who could supply bootlegged liquor, were happy to host "immoral" behavior, and could bribe nosy policemen. The more white New Yorkers grew accustomed to defying the law and rubbing shoulders with criminals, the more appealing it was to throw all caution to the wind, to disdain all previous conventions of behavior and decorum. White adults wanted to go wild—and what better way to do that than by taking a subway or car up to Harlem, to the Black neighborhood. As one guidebook put it, using the stereotypes its writers assumed white readers shared, in Harlem visitors could

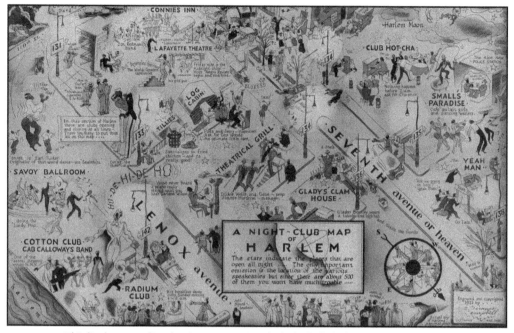

This lively map of Harlem's attractions included Gladys' Clam House, where, suited in a white tuxedo, Gladys Bentley displayed her musical talent and openly flirted with women in the audience.

see African Americans' "unfailing sense of rhythm, their vocal quality, something primitive, animal-like, and graceful." Uptown, visitors could hear Black music, dance and drink the night away, and return at dawn to their white jobs in white businesses in white parts of town. To slumming outsiders, Harlem was deliciously "hot."

Claude McKay—whose poem had helped begin the Harlem Renaissance—very quickly felt that Harlem was just "an all-white picnic ground with no apparent gain to the blacks." And yet, in these clubs, whites for the first time sat very close to Black musicians and dancers and experienced their skill and talent. Even though the halls were segregated and framed as entertainment for whites, many in the audience saw the lie of racial separation and white superiority. Packed close together in clubs, some whites felt a new sense, a new seed: difference is not ranking, it is exciting, interesting, it is life. And Black artists had a platform to develop and share their creations. The Harlem clubs spread the experience of Black excellence and the thrill of mixture. And that was only the start. Ellington's performances at the Cotton Club were broadcast live on radio and captured on record. This was the New York story: what was created in the city was shared everywhere. Everyone with a radio or record player could hear Harlem's music, and Harlem's music announced a new voice, a new art, to America and the world. Harlem made room for African American artistry—while all too often affirming racial separation.

One hint that McKay was wrong and that the explosion of Black creativity in Harlem was not just a show for white eyes comes in the fascinating and little-known figure of Alexander Gumby. Gumby arrived in the city in 1904 and worked where he could: as a bellhop, as a butler, in a post office. However, he dressed as a dandy. Richard Bruce Nugent, a gay Harlemite and author, described Gumby's "fancy clothes, a perennial walking stick, pale yellow kid gloves and a diamond stick-pin." Gumby was also gay and a direct link between the gender-nonconforming worlds of the Village and Harlem. He held gatherings at his studio on 131st Street, which was such a center of art and social life that the Baltimore *Afro-American* announced that "one really didn't know Harlem till one knew Gumby." Gumby himself called his salon "the first unpremeditated interracial movement in Harlem." The studio was meant to foster conversation and displayed the some three thousand rare books relating to Black history that he collected, art, and his remarkable scrapbooks. In over three hundred volumes, he pasted down images and stories relating to slavery, Black leaders and thinkers, Africa, Black sports heroes, basketball, dance, theater, the Village, his own studio, interracial marriage, and every other topic that interested him. As the scrapbooks became known, they were used as the centerpieces for Black history weeks in several eastern cities. Gumby was partially bankrolled by a wealthy lover who lost money in the stock market crash and so the salon ended, but he continued filling his scrapbooks throughout his life and remained an active figure in Harlem until he died in 1961.

McKay was right that the clubs were filled with white patrons, but they were not the only places in Harlem to hear music. When a person in Harlem had trouble meeting bills, he or she would host a rent party in an apartment.

Harlem Renaissance

Harlem was a true home for a flowering of African American creative talent, with some of the stars shown here: authors James Weldon Johnson and Zora Neale Hurston; poets Countee Cullen and Langston Hughes; painter Jacob Lawrence; singer Billie Holiday; and Paul Robeson, equally talented as a singer and actor. This explosion of talent occurred in Harlem because it was the first place to offer a wide range of African American artists both a nurturing Black community and access to white sponsors and publishers.

James Weldon Johnson

Jacob Lawrence

Countee Cullen

Langston Hughes

Billie Holiday

Paul Robeson

Zora Neale Hurston

Or sometimes a party would begin because some of the great pianists came by. Ellington recalled that Johnson's agent, Lippy Boyette, would knock on someone's door and announce he was with "James P." "These magic words opened anybody's door and we would sit and play all night long." Anyone—Black, white, Harlemite, or visitor—was welcome, if he or she had the small admission fee. Guests came for good food, homemade liquor, and exciting music. Rent parties meant that live stride and jazz really were Harlem's music—not just a performance in a segregated club for visiting whites. There was, though, a second story in the rent party: people needed to fill their homes with guests because for many, times were tight. Even as the nation seemed to enter flush days in the 1920s, only 6 percent of the city's African American men were professionals—and almost all of those doctors and lawyers were employed in Harlem working with poor African American clients and patients. The vast majority of African Americans were confined to low-paying jobs, often in white parts of the city. Black men received less pay than whites for comparable work, and a great many women worked as maids or laundresses for even less than their husbands. There were almost no good jobs uptown.

Harlem's center was 125th Street, a wide thoroughfare graced with theaters and the two grand department stores, Koch's and Blumstein's. No African Americans were employed in Blumstein's until 1929; indeed, as late as the mid-1930s, only one hundred out of the four thousand people employed on Harlem's main street were African American. African American customers were not even allowed to try on clothes in either department store. With such limited job prospects, often both parents needed to work far from home to support a family. That left children and teenagers on their own; juvenile crime in Harlem quadrupled between 1914 and 1930. Worse yet, by the 1930s, 60 percent of Harlem's children were defined as "malnourished" by the city. School was no solution. Harlem's public schools were overcrowded and in terrible condition.

A rent party was a great night of sounds exploding with the best jazz piano-playing in the world. Yet it was also a harsh necessity. Harlem offered pure possibility if you looked at it from the outside, and real confinement if you had no choice but to live there. And sometimes Harlem broke all the rules.

The Hamilton Lodge Ball held on 155th Street was, by universal acclaim, the "most unusual spectacle" ever witnessed. Though the annual event dated back to 1869, sometime in the 1920s it became a mammoth, spectacular, well-publicized drag ball. Men dressed as women, women dressed as men, surely also transgender people (though not identified as such at the time)—they all gathered for a grand night of "dancing, love-making, display, rivalry, drinking, and advertisement." "All the men who danced," one wide-eyed white visitor wrote, "were dressed as women, wearing plumes and jewels and decorations of every kind." Some eight hundred people, mainly African American, though whites also attended, came in 1925, and nearly double that number, fifteen hundred, the next year. By 1934, four thousand people were reported to have joined in the fun. As one observer saw it: "The ball was a melting pot, different, exotic and unorthodox but acceptable." *Acceptable* is too mild a word. Today, when a person is said to "come out," that means the individual stops hiding a true sexual orientation and admits it to the world. But in the era of the exuberant drag balls, to "come out" meant to be announced, presented to the world, just like a debutante. The singer Gladys Bentley came to the balls dressed, as she did when performing on stage, in a white tuxedo. Open about her attraction to women, she flirted with them during her popular show and doubtless at the ball. A person could come out in glory, in vivid display, at Harlem's Hamilton Lodge Ball.

Abram Hill, who would go on to help create the American Negro Theater, described a highlight of the annual ball—a contest for the man who displayed the "best feminine figure, beauty, and best looking gown." One special moment came when Jean La Marr, an African American with "decidedly brown skin . . . with almond eyes, flashing teeth, nifty feet and notoriously effeminate manners and carriage," won. Jean was wearing "an original creation of white chiffon created by Dan Hazel, Broadway designer." "Even here," Hill added, "Harlem displayed pride in the fact that a Negro had won first prize for the first time in the history of the annual affair."

The drag ball, like Ellington's jazz, the vibrant interracial rent parties, Gumby's scrapbooks, and the galaxy of authors Locke honored at the Civic Club, shows what Harlem made possible. Yet, once again, that is only half the story.

The annual Hamilton Lodge Ball was covered in Harlem's newspaper, the *Amsterdam News*, with lengthy articles and lively drawings.

White men and women drawn to the ball could come, but they could also attend similar smaller events in the Village or cruise popular spots in Times Square and return to "respectable" lives. The story was more complex for African Americans. In general, Harlem was more open, more accepting, of gender and life choices than was the white world. Yet after the ball, people from Harlem were still at home, as visible to their neighbors the next morning as they had been to the revelers the night before. While to a white man in drag "Harlem was wide open," African Americans with similar interests were condemned daily by Harlem's elite ministers, and, if they were arrested, the leading Harlem newspaper published their names, addresses, and occupations.

The split between the ministers in Harlem's best churches and the men in their glittering gowns at the Hamilton Lodge is just one side of a larger story. Even as the very best thinkers and artists in Harlem were establishing themselves, wave after wave of desperate, poor, and poorly educated African Americans kept arriving, fleeing from the grim South but locked out of the white neighborhoods of the city. Harlem was filled with American migrants, and its leaders were fighting desperately to preserve what they saw as the best of Harlem—with very little help from the city, state, or nation.

The City Suffers

Wall Street, 42nd Street, West 4th Street, 125th Street, Union Square
1930–1945

In which Wall Street crashes, the Broadway musical

tells the nation's stories, Forty-Second Street grinds,

Harlem explodes, labor radicalizes, and new voices

are heard in the Village, until New York is reborn as

the world city of the mid-twentieth century.

SNAPSHOT

New York in Depression and War: The Great Migration

1929 A major stock market crash occurs on October 29, Black Tuesday; the nation falls into the Great Depression.

1930 New York City's population: 6,930,446, which includes 1.7 million of Italian descent and approximately 1.8 million Jews. Manhattan's population: 1,867,312, which includes 224,670 of African descent, the highest percentage since the end of enslavement in the city. And 110,223 people in Manhattan are of Hispanic descent; 44,908 of those people are Puerto Rican.

Approximately 3 million people work in New York City, with most of the jobs in manufacturing, transportation, and communication; during the day, a ship arrives or leaves New York's port every ten minutes, making it the most active port in the world.

1931 The Empire State Building is the tallest building in the world; George Washington Bridge, the world's longest suspension bridge, links Upper Manhattan and Fort Lee, New Jersey.

1932 Approximately 828,000 New Yorkers receive public or private charity to get by.

1933 Fiorello LaGuardia wins contest for mayor.

1938 Approximately 300,000 people work in port-related jobs.

1939 World's Fair.

1940 New York City's population dips slightly over the previous year as some people move to nearby suburbs. The total population is 7,454,995; approximately 1.9 million are Jews and 134,252 are Hispanic, including 61,463 Puerto Ricans. Manhattan's population: 1,889,924, 298,365 or 15 percent of African descent.

1941 America enters World War II. New York City becomes the center for sending people and material to Europe.

1945 Air service between New York and Puerto Rico begins. The subway covers 554 miles and carries 7,750,000 people daily.

CHAPTER 21

"The Splendid Mirage"

> We were somewhere in North Africa when we heard a dull distant crash
> which echoed to the farthest wastes of the desert.
> —F. Scott Fitzgerald, writing about the stock market in "My Lost City"

At midday on Thursday, September 16, 1920, a horse pulling a loaded wagon covered with a cloth reached the corner of Wall and Nassau Streets. The driver stopped, hopped off, and, strangely, walked away. The bustling intersection in front of J.P. Morgan and Co., the richest, most powerful bank in the nation, was filled with people, so no one paid much attention to the man or the wagon. Precisely at noon, as the bells of nearby Trinity Church chimed the hour, a mammoth explosion obliterated the wagon and scattered shrapnel as high as the thirty-fourth floor of a nearby building, killing thirty-five people and injuring 130 more. Someone really hated Wall Street.

Why did Wall Street, and Morgan in particular, inspire such murderous rage? The bomber was never caught, so we can't give a precise answer, but there were plenty of people who shared that emotion. In a sense, Wall Street and Union Square spoke for two sides of the nation. Union Square was, increasingly, the headquarters of labor unions and the site of ever more left-wing demonstrations. The square was the most visible expression of the workers united, a collective with shared demands. J. P. Morgan, the man, had personally arranged the financing for major companies such as U.S. Steel and General Electric and organized the

A toppled car and some of the rubble left behind by
the 1920 Wall Street bombing

close network of banks that supported the entire US financial system—at great profit to himself. Though he had died in 1913, his company continued to play a similarly central and secretive role. Most recently, some felt Morgan's company had profited from World War I while average Americans went off to fight and die.

Was America the land of the many or the few, the workers or the banker? Suspicion for this bombing centered on Italian anarchists, but the labor activists in Union Square, radicals in the Village, midwestern farmers, Appalachian coal miners, and factory workers in cities across the nation had all, at times, been eager to bring down Wall Street. And yet Wall Street actually had provided the financing for every major beat in American history, from the corporations, transportation companies, and stores that kept the country growing to the wars that shaped the nation. The more roles Wall Street played, the more people were drawn into its orbit.

In 1865, the New York Stock Exchange had moved into an imposing new home on Wall Street. Wall Street had its first "million share day" in 1886 and tripled that total by 1901. The flood of trading that came from financing the Civil War and the postwar boom brought clusters of new business to the street: banks, stockbrokers, and exchanges sold commodities such as cotton or butter; life insurance companies sprang up; consulting firms such as the one that would become Dun and Bradstreet evaluated other companies; financial companies such as American Express enabled people to send money or credit from one place to another. The business of finance was the business of the city. Each new company that wanted to be near the center of money created a need for more workers, from lowly clerks to the wealthiest managers. Yet at the time, very few Americans directly invested in stocks or bonds. That changed with World War I.

Though the federal government began collecting income taxes in 1913, those payments covered only about one-third of the cost of going to war. In 1917, to make up the balance, Washington offered Liberty Bonds, expecting about 350,000 Americans to be willing to put up at least fifty dollars to earn interest when the bonds later matured. A massive public relations campaign involving eleven thousand billboards, sixty thousand female volunteers, announcements in fifteen hundred libraries, and slogans crafted by the best advertising and marketing minds of the day induced twenty million people to buy war bonds. For the vast majority of those buyers, this was the very first time they invested in a piece of paper with a promise, rather than purchasing a piece of land or physical product.

When those bonds came due in the 1920s, millions of Americans had extra cash and newfound confidence in investing. As "Sunny" Charles Mitchell of National City Bank (now Citibank) put it, the Liberty Bonds created "a large, new army of investors." Just when that flood of money became available, new companies were creating exciting consumer goods and services such as cars, radios, movies, household appliances, and phonographs. Americans rushed to buy on the layaway plan, paying only some now and a bit more every month, filling homes with goods and increasing the value of companies. Investing in stocks seemed to be a sure thing. So sure that you didn't actually have to pay the full value of the stock. You could buy on "margin"—putting up, say, $10 of the total $100 stock price, confident that if you sold the permanently rising stock for $120 you could easily cover the amount you were missing. Pressed by Mitchell to make ever more sales, National City's aggressive pitchmen spread throughout the country,

Posters such as this one were designed by the best advertising teams and created by famous artists. Buying bonds was treated as a patriotic duty.

creating in effect financial department stores where you could deposit savings, buy stocks, craft wills: entrust every current and future cent you earned to their wisdom.

People bought goods on the layaway plan and stocks on margin. Banks lent more money based on the apparent value of the stocks. Investors treated their ever-inflating but only partially paid-for stocks as their life savings while bankers secretly used the original deposits to purchase more stocks on margin—air building on air. The financial department stores not only sold investments but issued new bond issues—so that investors were trusting their broker to evaluate a bond the broker himself had created. Even as more and more individuals relied on rising stocks, behind the scenes the wealthiest and smartest investors, such as Mitchell himself, sold bonds they knew to be faulty and manipulated their own investments to escape paying income taxes.

The bubble kept growing. It seemed that value no longer had anything to do with how well a real company could do selling real products in real markets. Value was a form of faith where you would be a fool to ask too many questions.

Expansive companies flush with cash announced their importance with ever-taller buildings transforming the New York skyline. This was the paper city of money and corporations that Mumford had criticized, only growing much higher and faster. Forty-Second Street filled with buildings rising anywhere from forty to seventy stories. The owners of 40 Wall Street, across from the stock exchange, were determined to do better and build the world's tallest building. In 1930, they held a party to celebrate the triumph of their 927-foot-tall achievement. Even as they popped the champagne, the backers of the Chrysler Building on Forty-Second Street were plotting to pass them. Secretly, they pieced together four parts of a spire and hoisted it up to top their structure. Now the Chrysler Building, built to resemble the current models of Chrysler cars, was the world's first "supertall" skyscraper—that is, it reached to 1,064 feet high, past the 984-foot marker that is the divide between tall and supertall. Two years later, the Empire State Building topped out at 1,250 feet (1,454 including its spire), which gave it the title of world's tallest for the next thirty-nine years.

In a sense, the stock market was like the speakeasies and (for whites) the

Two skyscrapers dominated the new skyline: the tower of the Chrysler Building (left) was meant to echo the design of the company's new cars. The Empire State (right) was the tallest building in the world from 1931 to 1970.

Harlem jazz clubs: all old rules were gone, out the window. Life was one big spree with its "sunburst centre at Times Square." And in Times Square, the flood of money spurred new forms of creativity.

A NEW KIND OF THEATER, AND A NEW SONG

In 1927, a record-breaking 264 shows filled seventy-six Broadway theaters, and audiences witnessed the birth of a new art form: the Broadway musical. Watching blackface minstrelsy and vaudeville or European imports such as light operas in German or by the British team of Gilbert and Sullivan, Americans were used to enjoying actors sing and dance onstage. Sometimes the acts were linked by thin plots but those hardly mattered. In 1927, *Show Boat*, with text and lyrics by Oscar Hammerstein II (grandson of the creator of Forty-Second Street) and music by Jerome Kern, was entirely different. In this so-called book musical there was a true storyline, with songs that served to enhance and express key dramatic moments. Indeed, every show needed at least one hit song that was picked up by singers, featured in nightclubs, played on records, and turned into ever-new forms by jazz artists. Many musicals were meant to be pure fun. But while *Show Boat* was filled with appealing songs, it was about race and prejudice. *Show Boat* began a sequence of musicals stretching to *Hamilton* (which opened on Broadway in 2015) and beyond in which the combination of plot, song, music, and dance both entertains audiences and narrates our times.

In *Show Boat*, singer Julie La Verne is a light-skinned African American trying to pass as white. When she sings "Can't Help Lovin' Dat Man," she begins to give herself away. And when a Black character challenges her, asking her if she knows all the song's verses, she sings one that is clearly a blues riff—signaling to the Black actors onstage, and the entire audience, who she really is. The song inspires the white female lead to begin a wild dance, in a style meant to seem Black.

The most famous song from the show, though, is "Ol' Man River," first sung by Paul Robeson. The original lyrics showcased the weariness of Black workers tired of living and scared to die. But when Robeson sang it, he later changed the words to announce that he would always keep on fighting.

Starting with *Show Boat*, the New Yorkers who were disdained elsewhere—immigrants, Jews, the Irish, gays, lesbians, African Americans—had a popular vehicle in which they could rewrite the story of this land. New York, through Broadway with links to Hollywood, records, radio—and later television—was the nation's narrator. This mix and remix from the crosscurrents of life to new creation is the essence of New York at its best.

Going to see shows was just one way people in the city entertained themselves. As the novelist F. Scott Fitzgerald saw it, "New York . . . approached hysteria"—including a hysteria of spending by New Yorkers and guests: In 1918, there were 125,101 cars in New York. By 1931, there were 790,123 in the city—a total greater than in all of Europe. Tourists flocked to Manhattan to see its wonders. A French visitor described the glorious power of the city in 1929.

"New York dominates. . . . a city of rectangles, harsh and brilliant, the center of an intense life which it sends out in all directions. . . . New York is the only city in the world rich enough in money, vitality, and men to build itself anew in the last twenty years, the only city sufficiently wealthy to be modern."

The modern city was the home of skyscrapers and elevators, of radio and musical theater, of African American Harlem, the Bohemian Village, and fashion. When World War I made it more difficult for wealthy American women to buy clothes from Europe, American designers began creating their own styles. In the 1920s, the American look of clean, straight-lined, athletic clothing was made available for middle-class women. The new image of the short-haired "flapper" was featured in New York fashion magazines such as *Vogue*. The flappers' hats, skirts, dresses, and accessories (long necklaces) were designed, manufactured, and sold in New York. The world of fashion, from the designers to the magazines, was home to gay and lesbian creators. At the same time, Elsie de Wolfe, who dyed her hair blue and openly lived with her lesbian partner in Manhattan, essentially invented the profession of interior designer. New York was modern in its sleek buildings and sleek styles, and in its knowing acceptance of difference. But all of this glowing modernity rested on money, on Wall Street and its endless boom.

Paul Robeson in the original production of *Show Boat*. Robeson was the next step in African American male stardom on Broadway after Bert Williams: though "Ol' Man River" was a song of sorrow and pain, his depth and strength were unmistakable.

Then the music stopped and the bottom fell out of the entire stock market. No single cause burst the bubble. Rather, once stocks began to fall, everyone who had bought on margin rushed to sell at any price to cover their losses; crashing prices led banks—which held their own stocks bought on margin—to fail, wiping out life savings. The more money people and institutions lost, the more jobs

As news of the crashing stock market spread, people gathered in front of the Stock Exchange on Wall Street.

were cut, the more homes, cars, and consumer goods people could no longer afford, the more businesses failed, the more the economy slowed down. The government tried to protect American jobs by raising tariffs, making imports from Europe more expensive—which only served to spread the economic depression across the Atlantic and weakened the market for American goods.

If you were looking at the Dow Jones average price of thirty top stocks on Wall Street from September 1929 to July 1932, this is what you would see: September 3, 1929, 381.17; October 22, 325; October 23, 305; October 27, 299; October 28, 261; October 29, 230; November 13, 199; July 8, 1932, 42. It would take almost a quarter of a century for the Dow to return to where it stood in early September 1929.

Between 1929 and '31, income across the land declined by 30 percent and savings were cut in half, and by 1932, unemployment reached 23.6 percent, or nearly one-quarter of all employable Americans. The entire boom that began with Mitchell's "army" of Liberty Bond holders was wiped out, taking the "splendid mirage" of the glowing city with it. A decade after the 1920 bombing, many in a bitter nation shared the terrorist's fury at Wall Street.

CHAPTER 22

Depression New York

UNION SQUARE: THE RALLY AND THE RIOT
March 6, 1930

For "International Unemployment Day," the American Communist Party, some nine thousand members strong, organized a demonstration on its home turf of Union Square. The "people" were finally to have their say, as the elite, the rich, the grandees had failed, destroying the world economy with their greed. The city was reeling. So many New Yorkers could no longer afford to pay rent that any available space, from the fields of Central Park to warehouses by the docks, were filling up with huts, shanties, tents—temporary homes. At the square, the hammer-and-sickle flag of the Soviet Union was run up the flagpole first, to wave over the American flag, until the police demanded they be reversed. In the desperate city, the Union Square rally quickly grew. Loyal Communists made up just a fraction of the crowd as somewhere between thirty-five thousand and one hundred thousand people filled the square. When two thousand of the protesters broke off and marched down toward city hall, they were daring the police to stop them. For fifteen minutes, cops with clubs battered marchers and determined protesters fought back. The Party was pleased. A Communist leader thought the clash was a good step on the way to the "overthrow of capitalism and the establishment of a revolutionary workers' and farmers' government." He was wrong about the revolution, but right about the mood of the city.

In the year of the Union Square rally, machinists in Brooklyn decided to

Don Freeman's sketch of smiling men setting out like soldiers to shovel the city's snow

form a union—a particular kind of union. They allied with a larger Communist Party federation of unions, which, by 1935, decided to leave Gompers's old AFL. While the Industrial Workers of the World of the John Reed–Emma Goldman era no longer existed, many workers found the AFL too tame, too willing to seek compromise with bosses, and too limited in which workers it would organize. Angry workers were ready for a more militant, confrontational approach to management. The International Ladies Garment Workers Union (ILGWU), whose roots went back to Clara Lemlich and the radical women who went on strike in 1909, was also dissatisfied with the AFL and it, too, joined a new organization, the Congress for Industrial Organization (CIO).

When CIO unions went on strike, they were willing to totally disrupt the life of a company—taking over car manufacturing plants in Flint, Michigan, or, in New York, releasing mice to scamper across the floors of department stores. Influenced by, and at times run by, members of the Communist Party, they viewed labor and management as involved in a fundamental power struggle where owners had to be forced to give concessions to workers. Workers might have different kinds of jobs, from manual labor to office work, but they were united by being the people on guard against, in combat with, the bosses. Yet because New York was New York, there was a fundamental problem with the idea of class solidarity: so much of the city was organized around religion, ethnicity, and race. Unions often reflected a history, across generations, of one member of an ethnic group finding work for his or her close relatives and friends—from the same group. For all their belief in the workers united, many unions were entirely white, Irish, Jewish, or Italian. Even as New York became a home of ever more radical labor, it failed to grapple with the fundamental problem of race.

HARLEM: THE BATTLES OF 125TH STREET

> One Hundred and Twenty-fifth Street is Harlem's main street. . . .
> Anything that starts there will flash through Harlem as quick as lightning.
> —Claude McKay, "Harlem Runs Wild"

Harlem took the hardest hit when the market crashed. As the economy tightened, already underpaid Harlemites had to make do with less, and less, and even less. Prohibition was repealed in 1933, making the speakeasies and rent parties of Harlem less appealing to people from downtown. Only a quarter of the men in

Harlem had jobs at all, and new migrants kept arriving and needing work. Yet rents remained high since, in the segregated city, there were few places for an African American to go. Harlem's 165,000 people of color were forced to press in together. Just as in the worst days of the Lower East Side, Harlemites took in boarders to help with the rent, making Harlem now the most overcrowded neighborhood in the city. Even as Jews and Italians left their parents' dense neighborhoods in Manhattan to move up the island or to the outer boroughs, Harlem filled in with new migrants. The buildings from 138th to 139th Streets between Lenox and Eighth Avenues replaced the Lower East Side as the most densely populated area in the city. Worse yet, the crammed apartments were in increasingly bad condition with no central heating and toilets shared among many families. Low incomes, poor housing, and worsening

" KIN AIE AN LOOIE JUS' SAIELL ARUN' ?"

Don Freeman is best known today for *Corduroy* and his other picture books for children. Trained by the artist John Sloan (see 214), he loved sketching scenes of Manhattan life and between 1936 and 1941 published his drawings in a series of magazines he called *Newstand*. His images show the human heart of a suffering city.

conditions are a perfect formula for the spread of disease—which is why people, including babies, in Harlem were falling ill and dying at a rate 40 percent higher than in the rest of the city. Harlemites had reason to feel that the white city didn't care if they lived or died. Once white New Yorkers stopped treating Harlem as one big party, they could ignore it.

Extreme conditions encouraged extreme views. Marcus Garvey's idea that the African peoples of the world needed to unite and break off from whites seemed like a basic truth to a solid core of Harlemites. In the 1930s, the American Communist Party made a conscious effort to recruit African Americans, spear-headed by nominating James Ford for vice president in 1932—the first African American to be so honored. Communists argued that African Americans should have their own totally Black state in the South and separate from white society. A radical Socialist or Communist voice became a feature of Harlem life—most viv-idly through the irresistible appeal of the actor/singer/spokesman Paul Robeson. And a more active, militant voice began to be heard even in Harlem's most elite churches. In 1931, Adam Clayton Powell Jr., the handsome, eloquent young leader of Harlem's most prestigious house of worship, the Abyssinian Baptist Church, began to make his sermons and his congregation into a force for change on 125th Street.

By the summer of 1934, Powell and his church took a key role in the "Don't Buy Where You Can't Work" campaign. Picketers marched in front of Blumstein's department store carrying signs and forcing shoppers to think about why they would enter the store. A month after the campaign, Blumstein's agreed to hire a few Black salespeople at once with more to follow. Blumstein's eventually became the first store in the entire United States to feature an African American Santa Claus and to hang clothes on mannequins with African American features.

The slow shift of 125th Street away from being a white centerpiece of a Black neighborhood accelerated in the same year (1934) when a major theater changed ownership. Hurtig and Seamon's at 253 West 125th had already been renamed the Apollo but was still segregated and white. On January 26, the new owners showed they had another audience in mind when they began their tenure with "Jazz a la Carte" and offered to donate all profits of opening night to the children

The marquee of the Apollo showed the rise of Latin music and culture in the city as the Puerto Rican population in East Harlem grew.

of Harlem. Wednesday nights at the new Apollo opened the stage to newcomers. Broadcast on radio, Amateur Night at the Apollo became the country's greatest launching pad for new African American talent. Some of the most famous stars from the '30s to the '90s, such as Ella Fitzgerald, James Brown, the Jackson 5, Jimi Hendrix, and Lauryn Hill, were featured and launched there. But even successful protests at one visible store and new policies in a major theater go only so far when people are poor, hungry, sick, and sealed in by surrounding prejudice.

MARCH 19, 1935

People from Puerto Rico had been citizens of the United States since 1917, and many made their way to New York—to East Harlem—looking for work. By the mid-1920s, forty thousand people who spoke Spanish lived in the city, almost all of them Puerto Rican, Spanish, or Cuban. These immigrants did not quite fit any of the city's categories: they were not African American, though some were dark-skinned; almost all were Catholic, though their practice was quite different from that of the Irish or the Italians. Puerto Ricans began creating a neighborhood of their own wedged between the African Americans of Central Harlem and the Italians of East Harlem.

On this March day, a Puerto Rican teenager strolled into S. H. Kress—yet another segregated 125th Street department store, located directly across the street from the Apollo—and slipped a cheap penknife into his pocket. Quickly spotted, he was tackled by the staff before he could run out. The owner agreed to let the teenager off with a warning, and a policeman escorted him out the back door to 124th Street. Bystanders who had seen the police arrive were suspicious—what were they doing to the boy? They saw an ambulance arrive to treat the minor wounds from the tussle and suspected much worse. When a hearse pulled up nearby, a pure coincidence, the crowd was certain the police had murdered the young man. As rumors rushed through Harlem, the Communist Party passed out leaflets encouraging a massive demonstration at the store.

Harlem's anger, its fury, seemed to have a focus, a cause.

That night, Harlem erupted: 626 store windows were shattered, three African Americans were killed, two hundred people—white and Black—were injured. And the Harlem Renaissance was over. White-against-Black race riots have taken place throughout American history. This was different: a black community raging through its own neighborhood destroying property—attacking the stores of outsider owners, yes, but more like a storm, a hurricane, of pure frustration and pain. In the wake of the riot, the Cotton Club, the centerpiece of white slumming and Black talent, left Harlem and relocated to Forty-Eighth Street and Broadway.

As Alain Locke, who had heralded the beginning of the renaissance at the Civic Club, wrote, the riot was the voice of "this dark Harlem of semi-starvation, mass exploitation and seething unrest." From the point of view of white New York, Harlem was an increasingly dangerous slum. From the point of view of African Americans in Harlem, it was home. And the New York story of the lively jumble of people on its streets creating new kinds of art for the world continued beyond the old segregated clubs.

CHAPTER 23

"Sing, Sing, Sing"– Experiments in Integration

SING, SING, SING

American music's Jackie Robinson moment took place on January 16, 1938. Benny Goodman—a popular Jewish jazz clarinetist—headlined a concert at New York's most prestigious classical music venue: Carnegie Hall on Fifty-Seventh Street. While James Reese Europe had organized an evening there featuring his music in 1912, this was a rare event that treated American jazz as if it were of the same importance as European classical music. But it was the makeup of Goodman's band that made this night exceptional. Since 1936, Goodman had featured an integrated group including the African American pianist Teddy Wilson and vibraphonist Lionel Hampton (he would soon add the electric guitar pioneer Charlie Christian). Now on the famous stage where jazz was making its claim to excellence, Goodman was treating integration as simply normal and absolutely necessary. As the concert came to an end, the band played a song that practically propels you through the city's streets: "Sing, Sing, Sing." New York and the nation may have been mired in an economic depression, but the meeting place of Black and white in jazz was the racing pulse of modern life.

The Carnegie concert was just the beginning. Descended from a Vanderbilt, reporter and music producer John Hammond was a white Yale dropout who lived in the Village and had both the most astute taste in music and a true commitment to left-wing politics. He covered subjects in the African American world and created a magazine of his own in order to speak out against "discrimination in the recording companies, radio networks and musicians' unions." One day in February 1933, he was at Monette's Supper Club on 133rd Street when he heard a young, poor, singing waitress named Eleanora Fagan. Only a teenager, Fagan had already lived a very hard life, but Hammond heard the glory in her voice and arranged for her to record with Benny Goodman under her stage name: Billie Holiday. This was one of the very first times a Black singer was recorded backed by a white band. In 1935, she began to headline at the Apollo, and Hammond worked to create another special Carnegie Hall event.

On December 23, 1938, Hammond organized a mammoth concert called "From Spirituals to Swing." If Goodman's concert at the beginning of the year showed that jazz was art and integrated, Hammond's at the end revealed the history, richness, and variety of African American creativity. Beginning with a recording of drumming in Africa, the concert was a vivid declaration of the intelligence, complexity, depth, and history of African American musical art. Performers included other artists Hammond promoted, such as the pianist and bandleader Count Basie, the gospel star Sister Rosetta Tharpe, country blues and New Orleans jazz acts, and a set of pianists sharing a new style: boogie-woogie. The concert was a great success and repeated with a revised lineup the next year.

Alfred Lion, a rapt member of the audience, was inspired to create Blue Note Records to record the kind of music he was hearing—which was just one way the concert served as a cornerstone of America's musical future.

Five days after the concert, advised and in part bankrolled by Hammond, a former shoe salesman with strong left-wing views decided to open a fully integrated club of a new sort in the Village. Barney Josephson grew up in New Jersey, but his brother had been working with anti-fascists in Germany who were organizing against Hitler's regime. Josephson set out to create a café that would be a home base for integration. "I wanted," he later wrote, "a club where blacks and whites worked together behind the footlights and sat together out front." Café Society sat proudly at 1 Sheridan Square and was quickly seen as "a night club to take the stuffing out of stuffed shirts."

Josephson hated the segregation in New York's clubs. "One thing that bugged me about the Cotton Club was that blacks were limited to the back one-third of

Don Freeman played the trumpet well enough to sit in with professional jazz bands. He drew this sketch at the Savoy Ballroom, which was one of the rare locations in the city that allowed and encouraged interracial dancing.

the club, behind columns and partitions," he said. "It infuriated me that even in their own ghetto they had to take this. Of course, in any club below Harlem, which had black entertainment, such as the Kit Kat Club, a black couldn't even get in." Café Society in the Village was the next step beyond the Cotton Club. Performers at the club were written up in the most upscale magazines for the wealthy and fashionable. Some of the art on its walls was quickly copied to be displayed at the tony Fifth Avenue department store Bergdorf Goodman. In order to make sure the club didn't serve only the white and wealthy, Josephson took out advertisements in the Black press, inviting African American customers to come and enjoy the shows. The café was committed to integration on its stage and in its audience.

THE WEEKLY MAGAZINE

JAZZ INFORMATION

VOL. I, No. 9   NOVEMBER 7, 1939   TEN CENTS

SULLIVAN FORMS MIXED BAND

In 1939, having an integrated band was so novel that the press covered it as news. Joe Sullivan had been popular on the West Coast and then created his mixed group at Café Society. Teddy Wilson (left) appeared with Benny Goodman at Carnegie Hall before being a regular at Café Society downtown and then uptown.

Drummer Yank Porter in a super-sent pose. He and leader Teddy Wilson open at the new, uptown Cafe Society in the heart of New York's Blue Blood Night Club district on October 8th. The clarinetist is Jimmy Hamilton. Joe Sullivan and his new black and white band will replace Teddy at the original, downtown Cafe Society.

Café Society's advertisement shows the mix of Black (Mary Lou Williams) and white (Imogene Coca) artists it featured.

Boogie-Woogie Kings. . .Albert Ammons, Chicago boogie-woogie king, takes off on his own as Joe Turner, Kansas City blues chirper, shouts a vocal from atop the piano. Pete Johnson, also from Kansas City, stands by at the left, waiting his turn to perform b-w style. All three are featured with Billie Holiday and Frankie Newton at New York's Cafe Society.

Boogie-woogie was a fast, rhythmic piano style that can be seen as a precursor of rock n roll.

Lady Day, Billie Holiday, whose unforgettable renditions of "Strange Fruit" closed every show at Café Society downtown for nine months. This photo was taken by William Gottlieb, an excellent photographer of jazz artists.

One evening in 1939, a white New York City public high school teacher named Abel Meeropol, who shared Josephson's politics, came by the club to show a poem and some music he'd written. The United States Senate kept refusing to pass a bill outlawing lynching, and Meeropol couldn't get the image of a murdered Black man out of his mind. His song "Strange Fruit" is an indictment of the bestial brutality of lynching flung back in graphic rage. Josephson loved Meeropol's song. For nine months thereafter, Billie Holiday ended her set at Café Society with the song and Josephson carefully staged it to have maximum impact on the audience: "Lights out, just one small spinlight, and all service stopped. . . .

There were no encores after it. My instruction was walk off, period. People had to remember 'Strange Fruit,' get their insides burned with it.'"

Café Society was the vision of an America freed from the chains of racism. When Josephson served as a manager for African American artists who went to Hollywood, he wrote contracts that forbade the studios from using any racial stereotypes in the clothing, dialogue, or scenes with that star, and made sure they were paid top dollar. He was like a voice of twenty-first-century attitudes in a city and a nation that treated racism as not merely acceptable but indeed correct. The crossing of Black and white in New York led to the creation of a pathbreaking Broadway musical: *Porgy and Bess*. George Gershwin, the composer, had spent a month living next to the Charleston, South Carolina, community depicted in the show and insisted that it only be performed by an all-Black cast, which is one reason to call the original production a musical, not an opera. The Metropolitan Opera House would not permit even a single African American to appear on its stage.

The show was based on a book by a white southerner, who also wrote the text of the musical along with Ira Gershwin, George's brother. *Porgy and Bess* was a full-length piece set in a Black community filled with compelling songs and intense drama. From the moment the project was announced, it was controversial. White newspapers sent drama as well as musical critics to opening night—to decide what to make of it. Black newspapers were generally pleased to feature the classical training and high quality of the cast. And they were glad that the audience, which they assumed would be predominantly white, would have the chance to appreciate aspects of Black life and musical accomplishment.

Yet what to make of a musical about a Black community created by a team of white artists? Was this yet another form of minstrelsy? Virgil Thomson, a composer himself and a leading critic, summarized the conflicting reactions to the piece: "With a libretto that should never have been accepted on a subject that should never have been chosen, a man who should never have attempted it has written a work that has some power and importance." Duke Ellington was initially critical of Gershwin's work, saying, "It was not the music of Catfish Row or any other kind of Negroes." But over time he changed his mind. When he heard

The original cast of *Porgy and Bess*. The musical created a unique opportunity for the display of Black artistry and talent. From Robeson singing alone in *Show Boat* to an entire Black cast in *Porgy and Bess*, African Americans were beginning to have opportunities to strip away the stereotypes of blackface minstrelsy on Broadway.

a touring version in the 1950s, he wrote to the producers, calling "Gershwin the greatest" for having written the musical. Many famous African American singers and musicians including Louis Armstrong, Miles Davis, and Ella Fitzgerald embraced key songs from the musical, such as "Summertime," "A Woman Is a Sometime Thing," "It Ain't Necessarily So," and "I Loves You, Porgy." With some exceptions, African American actors and singers have been pleased to appear in a popular show that makes use of their talents. As James Weldon Johnson said of the original play version, "*Porgy* loomed high above every Negro drama that had ever been produced."

From a New York historical point of view, seeing *Porgy and Bess* as a white show about Black people is shortsighted. Gershwin wanted to write what he called a folk opera, an extended musical story that said something about the people of this land. This was a broad vision in which Black experience was central to American experience. Similarly, the dancer Jerry Robbins (who grew up as

Jerome Rabinowitz in Weehawken, New Jersey) filled a notebook with ideas for how to create a truly American dance. One idea was for a "Negro Ballet: South and North" that aimed to portray life along a southern river and in Harlem.

One reason Gershwin was so fluid in using jazz is that the pentatonic scale is used in some aspects of traditional Jewish and African American music. And he was so skilled in polyrhythms that he could hold his own with jazz pianists in Harlem and singers in a Black church in South Carolina. In the New York of the 1930s, it was possible to imagine sharing aspects of culture across racial lines as a common American heritage. Certainly, it was easier for Gershwin or Robbins to cross from white musical tradition to Black than for Ellington, James P. Johnson, and other classically trained African American composers such as William Grant Still and Will Marion Cook to cross from their Black musical heritage to European classical. African Americans had far fewer opportunities, and far less support, to create full-length classical pieces than did white composers.

Porgy and Bess remains central to America's musical heritage, a testimony to New York's crisscrossed cultures performed and critiqued by new generations up to the present.

FORTY-SECOND STREET: THE SLANG CAPITAL OF THE WORLD

On February 2, 1933, the Forty-Second Street Special—a railroad train—left Los Angeles carrying some of Hollywood's biggest stars to promote Warner Bros. Pictures' big new film: *42nd Street*. Even though none of them were in the movie, Tom Mix, the horse-riding cowboy hero, Bette Davis, the dramatic star, and Joe E. Brown, the comedian with the mile-wide grin, all came to New York City. As the train rode along, there were crowd-building preview screenings all across the country: Denver, Kansas City, Chicago, Toledo, and Memphis got to see the all-singing, all-dancing spectacle. The train reached Washington, DC, on March 4, just as Franklin Delano Roosevelt was inaugurated as president, before it pulled into Grand Central Terminal on March 9. The carefully planned launch worked perfectly and the movie became the second most popular film of the year. Something about *42nd Street* spoke to America.

Don Freeman's sketch captures the rundown, seedy side of 42nd Street.

The film was the love-story triumph of tap-dancing Ruby Keeler, the good-girl-who-becomes-a-star, backed by hundreds of young women dancing to Busby Berkeley's energetic choreography. But it also showed a gritty, chaotic street filled with tough guys and (in the slang of the time) hard-bitten dolls on the make. The feel-good, underdog-triumph plot, lavish production, and a darker side picturing the real Forty-Second Street as a place with just enough menace to make it interesting appealed to Depression-era audiences craving distraction.

The combination of Prohibition, the Depression, and then the repeal of Prohibition battered Forty-Second Street. First the lavish restaurants closed. Then, one by one, the theaters went from hosting plays to screening first-run movies to running cheaper double features as so-called grind houses. Then they hosted radio broadcasts, followed by striptease shows. Eventually they stood cold and empty. Ironically, because the economy was so weak, no one had the money or motivation to tear down the theaters and turn them into office buildings. The Depression preserved the Theater District as a kind of time capsule, even as the rest of the city later rebuilt. Instead of offering fancy nights on the town, Forty-Second Street became an amusement park filled with cheap and bizarre attractions. You can feel the chaos, grit, and liveliness in this description by Ward Morehouse, a Broadway veteran:

> It was offering palm readings and photos while-U-wait, live turtles and tropical fruit drinks, sheet music, nut fudge, jumbo malteds, hot waffles, ham and eggs, hot dogs, and hamburgers. A screeching amusement park bedlam that was somehow without a ferris wheel and a roller coaster, but that presented shooting galleries, bowling alleys, guess-your-weight stands, gypsy tea rooms, rug auctions, electric shoeshines, dance halls—fifty beautiful girls—chop suey, beer on draught, wines and liquors, oyster bars, bus-barkers, and there on the curb was the man with the giant telescope, ready to show you the craters of the moon.

Yes, Forty-Second Street was a tougher, less glamorous thoroughfare than it had been, but so much of America in the 1930s was struggling. And the street was the unquestioned center of almost all forms of entertainment. From 1937 to 1940, Broadway hosted a hit musical that was a sign of the times. *Pins and Needles* was sponsored by the ILGWU and featured actual garment workers as performers, with satirical songs about their strikes and sewing machines. The appealing songs' lively wit soon brought in audiences of all types. Broadway could turn anything—even union activism—into an all-singing, all-dancing hit.

Every major movie studio and record company had an office near Forty-Second Street. The cluster of remaining theaters kept the clubs, restaurants, and organizations for theater people going on nearby streets, as did two of New York's daily newspapers and three popular magazines. Tin Pan Alley still wrote the songs America sang. New York–centered radio knit the nation—and beyond. Living in the city from 1933 to 1935, the Argentinian tango star Carlos Gardel became what one expert calls "the first transnational Hispanic-American pop celebrity" by regularly broadcasting on radio and being recorded on film in the Astoria Studio in Queens. "Live from New York" was the call to everywhere announcing that something special was to follow: the music that made the country dance. In the decades before portable radios with headsets splintered us into individual soundtracks, sounds shared by groups clustered around a radio linked the nation.

As gangsters and showgirls, tourists, jazz musicians, and the children of immigrants filled the area, Forty-Second Street became the nation's great language factory. Walter Winchell, a local and national gossip columnist, listed the new words that were bubbling up from the clubs, theaters, and conversations of what he called "the slang capital of the world." Cascades of words and phrases such as *fan* (as in sports), *turkey* (as in flop), *wow 'em*, *upstage* (as in overshadow), *baloney* (as in false), *pushover*, and *plug* (as in shoot) came from the street, as did expressions such as "Yes, we have no bananas" and "Hello, sucker." Winchell was extremely popular first as a columnist and then on radio and later TV.

SPORTS AND THE VOICE OF FORTY-SECOND STREET

Sports in New York—the nation's media capital—defined athletics for the whole nation. The city featured three professional baseball teams (the Yankees, Giants, and Dodgers), and the Yankees and Giants were perennial pennant-winning rivals. The 1920s were the Babe Ruth "murderers' row" era of Yankee power and pride, which the media loved to cover, followed by the nearly equally storied era of Joe DiMaggio. Madison Square Garden—then located just at the uptown end of the Theater District on Eighth Avenue between Forty-Ninth and Fiftieth Streets—was the prime spot for everything else, from rodeos and the circus to college basketball.

On December 30, 1936, the Garden hosted what newspapers called "the game of the century." The best basketball team in the country, Long Island University, which had won forty-three games in a row, faced Stanford, the glory of the West. Stanford won, which was enough to draw headlines, but the real news was the strange way Stanford's Hank Luisetti scored his fifteen points. Instead of shooting a ball with two hands while planted on the ground—the "set shot" that every coach in the country favored—Luisetti used a one-handed jump shot. He was not the only player to try the shot, but until his breakout moment on the biggest stage, coaches insisted that players stay earthbound. The publicity around Luisetti began to change the game of basketball—now it was a jump-shot game. That's how New York worked: creators might arrive from anywhere, but New York is where they captured the national spotlight.

The language and lives of Forty-Second Street found their best voice through the characters and stories of Damon Runyon. Runyon was a sportswriter who arrived in New York from Kansas in 1910. His tales of guys and dolls with names like Nicely-Nicely Jones, Harry the Horse, and Sky Masterson were published in magazines to great success (editors could expect to sell an extra sixty thousand subscriptions if readers knew Runyon's work appeared in their magazine) and made into plays and some twenty movies. Runyon's world is still popular in the form of the musical and movie *Guys and Dolls*. His gift was to turn printed words into a kind of soundtrack—as if his stories were coming to you through the radio. You listen to his guiding voice and the characters' Broadway slang and it all sounds like a tale you are hearing from a friend—maybe an out-of-town uncle who is a bit different, but warm, and ready to let you into his interesting life. The gangsters and molls, gamblers and nightclub hosts came across as familiar, human, funny, and sad and trying to make the best of a crazy life. The Depression was a great equalizer—everyone had a hard time, everyone wanted a break—and Runyon put the jumbled-up, tough, heartbreaking, heartwarming world of Forty-Second Street at the center of the national imagination.

CHAPTER **24**

"Tear Down the Old"

The ninety-ninth mayor of New York was, in a sense, the city's first. Fiorello LaGuardia was both the essence of the city and the man who wrenched the city forward—and backward. You couldn't ask for a more perfect image of liberal New York: he was born in the Village to Italian parents—a Catholic father and Jewish mother. Because his father was a bandmaster in the army, he grew up where his dad was posted—on reservations in Arizona where he saw the conditions of Native Americans and experienced the prejudice directed against immigrants. He served as a translator on Ellis Island, where immigrants were processed before they entered the country, and was a combat pilot during World War I before returning to run for office—as a Republican in a New York City run by Boss Tweed's heirs, the Tammany Hall Democrats. LaGuardia, who spoke Yiddish as well as Italian and German, was short (five two), brave, hardworking, and determined to make life better for all New Yorkers. After becoming the very first Italian American elected to Congress, in 1933, LaGuardia—running as a "fusion" candidate linking both parties—was elected mayor for the first of three consecutive terms. The minute the result was confirmed, the new mayor ordered the arrest of Charles "Lucky" Luciano, a well-known mobster. Out with the old city, in with the new.

During the easy-money years of the gangsters and speakeasies, New York's mayor had been the nightclub-hopping "Gentleman" Jimmy Walker. Walker was the very symbol of a high-living city where rules were meant to

Fiorello LaGuardia's unmistakable life force came through whether on the radio or in person.

be broken—whether that meant the mayor siphoning off money for himself and his cronies or a city filled with places to buy illegal liquor. LaGuardia arrived in office just as a state commission was exposing Walker's crimes. The new mayor set out to clean up corruption in city government and city politics. That was just one way he was going to set the city right.

LaGuardia was a union man, ready to support even the radical groups affiliated with the CIO. The historian Joshua Freeman reminds us that even though the city held none of the nation's large industrial plants, New York was "by far the largest manufacturing center in the country." From the clothes everyone bought to the electronic devices in homes and factories, New York built what the nation used. All of this work meant there were millions of workers organized in ever more aggressive unions. New York's organized labor did not just want better wages or hours; many shared a vision of a government that provided for the people—homes, education, cheap public transportation, health care. LaGuardia agreed.

Franklin D. Roosevelt had been elected president in 1932—which made for a perfect partnership with LaGuardia. Both leaders believed that government had a key role to play in building a better society. As the mayor put it, announcing his first slum-clearance housing project, "Tear down the old, build up the new. Down with rotten antiquated rat holes. Down with hovels, down with disease, down with firetraps, let in the sun, let in the sky, a new day is dawning, a new life, a new America." New York's new housing sounded, and was meant to sound, a great deal like FDR's New Deal. The Harlem River Houses on 151st Street, for example, gave six hundred families new apartments in a well-planned complex.

The city's new parks commissioner, Robert Moses, shared the same belief in the power of government to improve lives. The city's parks were in terrible condition. Legend has it that staff at the Central Park Zoo carried guns, since it

was entirely plausible that lions might escape from
their decrepit cages. Moses's crew managed to exter-
minate some two hundred thousand rats in the park,
but he had his sights set on bigger plans. He aimed to
rebuild New York, and he did.

Moses built the highways and bridges that are
still used today to link the city's boroughs and to
access the surrounding airports (which he also built)
and suburbs. His grand plans and vast construction
projects marked the end of the old city designed for
horse-drawn vehicles and elevated trains and became
the blueprint of the new city of private cars. Yet his
plans also required tearing apart neighborhoods and
destroying communities, and they enforced his own
prejudices. While he was responsible for creating 255
parks around the city, only two were in Harlem and

Robert Moses in front of a map of the
greater city he was knitting together
with roads and bridges

neither were in its African American core. Instead, he built some six to seven
hundred basketball courts. Moses created beautiful beaches on Long Island by
adding immense amounts of new sand to older spots and planting beach grasses
to hold the dunes in place. Like the original designers of Central Park, he claimed
that he could bring all classes of people together by creating such appealing locations: "When you create parks in which rich and poor can enjoy, then, we feel
you are making democracy function." Yet some later critics have argued that
while he constructed convenient highways to bring New Yorkers to the shore, he
insisted that the bridges over the roads be built so low that only cars, not buses,
could pass. That ensured only those rich enough to have or hire a car could enjoy
the sand and waves. And he fought relentlessly and for decades to keep public
housing segregated. LaGuardia was different; he was on the side of the bus riders.

In newsreels from the time, Fiorello, the "Little Flower," looks either like
a bulldog boxer—in your face, direct, pushing ahead no matter what—or like
the comedian Lou Costello of the Abbott and Costello team (who developed
the hilarious "Who's on First" routine while headlining in a Forty-Second Street

theater). There was an almost comic roly-poly sweetness about the mayor, mixed in with that battling labor lawyer who hated the privilege of wealth and would fight for the little guy. When the newspaper delivery union went on strike in 1945, LaGuardia realized who would really be hurt: the children of the city who looked forward to reading the Sunday comics. He took to the radio to describe the strips and read the dialogue aloud so that the city's kids wouldn't miss out. With Moses at his side, LaGuardia was the voice of—most of—the city, rebuilding during the Depression and war.

LAGUARDIA'S NEW YORK
The Village (via Forty-Second Street)

On March 23, 1936, Mayor LaGuardia grabbed a shovel in Bryant Park behind the library on Forty-Second Street. He was starting the dig that would build a subway stop at the park—as part of a new line. The Sixth Avenue Line would replace the el, which was to be torn down, bringing light and air to the streets. A

Bryant Park under construction. The new Independent (IND) subway line had a stop right next to the park.

Don Freeman's cartoon showed another side of urban development: new buildings created nice apartments, but only for those who could afford the rent.

major stop on the railway was planned for West Fourth Street, where many lines could cross and passengers could transfer from one to another. Clearing away the el did more than let in the sun; it changed the neighborhood around the new stop. By 1935, the Hell Hole bar of O'Neill's day was gone and an odd empty rectangle remained next to the avenue. The city decided to fill it with a small public basketball court: the West Fourth Street Court, or "the Cage." The planners may not have thought this through, but putting a basketball court in the Village next to a subway stop for lines that connected directly to African American neighborhoods in Harlem and Brooklyn added a new form of linking to the city.

The National Basketball Association did not exist yet, but the city had a thriving world of professional players—divided by color. The Original Celtics were Jewish and Irish whites; the Harlem Rens (whose name came from their home court, the Renaissance Ballroom on 138th Street and Seventh Avenue) were the first team anywhere made up of and also owned, run, and managed by African Americans. The Original Celtics had dominated in the 1920s, while the Rens won the first World Championship of Professional Basketball in 1939. Subways began to create the possibility of mixed pickup games. Soon another park in Harlem would bring the best basketball players in the world uptown to try their luck at the Rucker Tournament. Subways and basketball courts were a kind of stitching that had the potential to weave the city together in new ways.

WORLD OF TOMORROW

LaGuardia and Moses wanted to announce their New York to the world as the city of the future—not a shattered victim (or, as some would see it, cause) of the Depression but the launching pad for new ways of living. The way to do it, they thought, was to host a grand World's Fair. The fair would be located out in Queens where there would be plenty of room to build and to host tourists from everywhere. With a grand opening on April 30, 1939, the fair was filled with displays of the inventions that would, indeed, soon change the world: television, color film, air conditioners, automatic dishwashers, and, in General Motors' World of Tomorrow, a vision of an entirely new kind of life.

The World's Fair: Image of the Future

The World's Fair set out to shift people's eyes away from the troubles of today to the "World of Tomorrow."

Above: Samuel Gottscho took this shot of the pool framing the Trylon and Peripshere, which were the symbols of the World's Fair.

Right: The 610-foot-tall Trylon and the Perisphere with its circumference of 628 feet were meant to be as striking, and modern, as the Eiffel Tower had been at the Paris Exposition of 1889.

The abstracted sweeping curves of the 950-foot spiral ramp or "helicline" led visitors out of the interior display of a perfect city of the future within the Perisphere.

An aerial view of the Trylon and Perisphere gives a sense of the whole fair ground.

In order to welcome the expected guests, the mayor set out to clean up the city—shutting down striptease acts, eliminating illegal liquor, and sweeping away that lively, visible world of bars and dances frequented by men in drag and women in men's suits and pants. The repeal of Prohibition was his weapon. Now instead of speakeasies run by gangsters, the city's bars would be licensed establishments patrolled by inspectors who had the power to define an effeminate man or masculine woman as "disorderly" and to treat the presence of supposed gay or lesbian or cross-dressed people as proof that it was a disreputable spot.

Whether in the Village, on Forty-Second Street, or in Harlem, police shut down gathering places where customers were evidently gay or lesbian in their clothing or behavior. If the owner of a bar or restaurant could be shown to have even "tolerated" the presence of obviously gender-nonconforming people, he or she was at risk of losing the license to sell liquor—which was necessary to stay in business. Even as jazz and progressive clubs such as Café Society—like subways and basketball—began to link the city, the anti-gay liquor license campaign did the opposite. Bars serving only gay customers became the new speakeasies: surviving through payoffs to inspectors, popping up here and there, known by insiders, shutting down and moving to new locations. For the next two decades, New York's gay and lesbian world moved underground. LaGuardia and Moses's world city was meant to be clean, well-managed, and safe—on their terms.

"HARLEM NEEDED SOMETHING TO SMASH"
August 1, 1943

On August 1, the day before his nineteenth birthday, the author James Baldwin was caught between life and death. His father was in the hospital dying, his mother in the maternity ward about to give birth. And all around him Harlem was "infected" by a strange mood. It was, he later wrote, "violently still." America had joined the fight against Hitler's racist policies, yet whether in the military or in the thousands of new jobs that were opening up in the defense industries, African Americans faced the same prejudice, the same restrictions, as they ever had. Their sons were being asked to risk their lives for a nation that told them to wait, wait again, wait for the war to be won, wait until we get around to tackling

In 1940, James Baldwin met Beauford Delaney at 181 Greene Street in the Village and experienced the "first walking, living proof, for me, that a Black man could be an artist." Delaney taught Baldwin "how to see, and how to trust what I saw." This Delaney portrait of the young Baldwin was painted in 1944. Delaney painted in a variety of styles, lived in the Village and later in Paris, and is now finally being recognized for his talent and importance.

the same racism at home that we are asking you to combat overseas. As Langston Hughes put it, "In America, Negroes do not need to be told what fascism is in action. We know." Harlem had seen even LaGuardia favor the rest of the city in jobs, new schools, and relief for the unemployed. Harlem was dry brush awaiting a match.

On that August day, Baldwin was downtown when Harlem exploded. At a hotel on 126th Street, a Black soldier tried to protect a Black woman as she was being arrested by a white policeman. The officer shot the soldier in the shoulder, but word spread that he'd been hit in the back, murdered. Rumor raced across Harlem and, as Baldwin recorded, "the mob fanned out, east and west across 125th Street" attacking white "bars, stores, pawnshops, restaurants"—every visible expression of "white power." Harlem "needed something to smash." By the time order was restored, one thousand people were arrested, fifteen hundred stores were broken into, and six people were dead, five of them killed by the police. Rage did not change Harlem's economy: eight out of ten of Harlem's businesses were still owned by whites. But it did announce that Harlem belonged to people who were proud of the world they had created and were sick of trying to please. The author Ralph Ellison recast the riot as a centerpiece of his National Book Award–winning novel *Invisible Man*. To white outsiders, Harlem seemed only dangerous and decrepit, much like the old Five Points. That was not how African Americans from throughout the country saw it.

The young painter Jacob Lawrence thought that the Depression "was actually a wonderful period in Harlem although we didn't know this at the time. Of course it wasn't wonderful for our parents. For them, it was a struggle, but for the younger people coming along like myself, there was a real vitality in the community." In 1937–38, inspired by his contacts with artists and poets in Harlem, he began something entirely new in American art. In forty-one panels he told a story from Black history: the life of Toussaint L'Ouverture, the leader of the Haitian revolution. No painter in America had ever made the history of the African diaspora his focus. To this day, the Haitian independence movement, the second successful revolution in the Americas, is hardly ever mentioned in schools. Then, in 1940, after opening a studio on 125th Street, Lawrence began to fill the sixty-one paintings he would use to tell the story he saw all around him: the Great Migration. "I thought about trains and people walking to the stations. I thought about field hands leaving their farms to become factory workers, and about families that sometimes got left behind. The choices made were hard ones, so I wanted to show what made the people get on those northbound trains. I also wanted to show just what it cost to ride them. Uprooting yourself from one way of life to make your way in another involves conflict and struggle. But out of the struggle comes a kind of power, and even beauty."

George Starling was one example of that migration. He arrived in Harlem in 1945 looking for a better life than being a fruit picker in Florida. To his eyes, Harlem was not a riot-torn ghetto. So many of the most famous African Americans lived there, and now he could spend his days beside them. On a Sunday, Harlemites in their best clothes would join the Stroll—an elegant ramble down Seventh Avenue, which James Weldon Johnson described this way:

> Strolling in Harlem does not mean merely walking along Lenox or upper Seventh Avenue or One Hundred and Thirty-fifth Street; it means that those streets are places for socializing. One puts on one's best clothes and fares forth to pass the time pleasantly with the friends and acquaintances and, most important of all, the strangers he is sure of meeting. One saunters along, he hails this one, exchanges a word or two with that one, stops for a short chat with the other one. He comes up to a laughing, chattering group, in which he may have only one friend or acquaintance, but that gives him the privilege of joining in. He does join in and takes part in the joking, the small talk and gossip, and makes new acquaintances.

For Harlemites, as for those exploring nonconforming sexuality and gender, New York was becoming a place to find warmth and community away from outsiders' eyes.

World City, Fractured City, World City

42nd Street, West 4th Street, Union Square, Wall Street, 125th Street

1945 – present

In which, facing the nation, New York begins as the hub of business, and, facing the world, it is the center of wealth and art, while on its streets the city begins to fracture, loses people to the suburbs, loses businesses, and almost goes bankrupt, only to revive to new wealth, new challenges, a terrible new assault, new citizens, and new forms of connection here and abroad.

SNAPSHOT

Postwar City

1950   New York City's population 7,891,957; 56 percent born in other countries or are of mixed native and immigrant parentage; approximately 2.1 million are Jewish; 750,000 are African American; 325,000 are Puerto Rican. Manhattan's population 1,960,101; 384,482 are African American. Brooklyn's population 2,738,175; 208,478 are African American.

1952   Lever House, first skyscraper in the International Style, built.

1954   Ellis Island immigration facility closed.

1955   More people cross Atlantic by air than ship.

1956   New form of shipping—loading goods in stackable metal containers—begins to be used at New York's ports.

1957   Lincoln Tunnel, the only three-tube underwater tunnel in the world, completed.

The New York Metropolitan area (which includes nearby suburbs) made up of nearly thirteen million people.

New York passes the Fair Housing Act, making discrimination in housing illegal.

Two New York professional baseball teams, the Brooklyn Dodgers and New York Giants, leave for California.

1960   New York City's population slips to 7,781,984; approximately 2.1 million are Jewish; 1,087,931 are African American; 757,231 are Hispanic, of whom 668,561 are Puerto Rican. Manhattan is approximately 23 percent African American, Brooklyn 14 percent.

1961–65   The Tammany Society loses control of the city's Democratic Party.

1964   World's Fair.

CHAPTER **25**

"Somewhere"

August 14, 1945

Throughout World War II, the giant cash register stood on Forty-Third Street beside a fifty-five-foot-tall replica of the Statue of Liberty, urging every passerby to buy war bonds—easy for the crowds of tourists, soldiers, sailors, and New Yorkers to see during the day. But at night, the Great White Way dimmed its lights. Military leaders did not want the glow of the giant advertisements and movie marquees to help any Nazi submarines that were lurking in New York harbor. The center of the city led by example, conserving energy just a bit, to show how we all needed to pull together for the war effort. Until now.

Some 750,000 people filled the avenues near Forty-Second Street as if it were a gigantic New Year's celebration. As afternoon turned toward evening, kissing broke out everywhere. A young sailor grabbed grandmothers, wives, daughters, a nurse, and pulled them over for a welcome—or unwelcome—smooch, captured on film by roving photographers. News girdled the Times Tower, the ticker giving updates on the day's events. At 7:03 p.m. came the words everyone was yearning to see:

★ ★ ★ OFFICIAL TRUMAN ANNOUNCES JAPANESE SURRENDER ★ ★ ★

Each star represented a branch of military service. A yell, a scream of relief, hope, triumph broke out that could be heard halfway up the island in the middle of

Times Square in Wartime

During World War II, Forty-Second Street took on new roles as the city's center. It led by example in dimming its famous lights at night. The ticker on the Times Building was one only way people could get news flashes of crucial events. News was public and shared, not seen on private screens. And when the war ended, New Yorkers rushed to celebrate together.

Right: Times Square at night

Below: People stopped in their tracks to read the news of the D-Day landing.

Left: The businessman and three sailors reading about the D-Day landing so perfectly capture the moment, this image almost seems like a scene from a movie.

Below: V-J Day in Times Square

Central Park. More, and more, and still more people rushed to the square until some two million people occupied every inch of space.

The war was finally over. The Depression was over. The fifteen years of suffering and sacrificing—over. Forty-Second Street was the place for that announcement, that celebration: New York was about to begin its reign as the only true world city. The victory was not only of the Allies over the fascists, but of New York and the New York idea. If you were an optimist and a New York fan, you could say that mixture, openness to immigration, everyone from every background pulling together, had won the war.

As Hitler rose to power, Europe's best thinkers, artists, and scientists had fled to America—some to receptive homes such as Black Mountain College in Asheville, North Carolina, but many to New York. The New School for Social Research, in the Village, welcomed them, as did Columbia University, where Enrico Fermi first split the atom, and nearby Princeton, where Albert Einstein worked at the Institute for Advanced Study. And it was these scientists, led by Einstein (and the aptly named Manhattan Project), who had developed the bomb that finally ended the war. America's golden door, the essence of New York, defeated the fascists.

What city was New York's rival? London, Paris, Rome, Berlin—the great capitals of Europe were in shambles, destroyed or impoverished by the war. Moscow was in the grip of Joseph Stalin, who wanted the city to shine but only to show the glories of Communism, not to let in new ideas. The megacities of Asia, Africa, and Latin America were decades away. The United Nations—the organization created after the war to make possible a future of peace and international cooperation—needed a home. It would be in America, but where? San Francisco? Philadelphia? New York didn't seem to have the room—until the philanthropist John D. Rockefeller Jr. donated the money to buy property near Forty-Second Street and the East River, saying, "New York is a center where people from all lands have always been welcomed. . . . It is my belief that this city affords an environment uniquely fitted to the task of the United Nations."

New York—and its heart, Forty-Second Street—stood alone as the center of the postwar world. And New York used all of its tools to tell its story. After

Show Boat, the next great Broadway musical was *Oklahoma!*, created by Oscar Hammerstein and his new partner, Richard Rodgers. It opened in 1943 and set a record for longest run that would last two decades. In *Oklahoma!*, Rodgers and Hammerstein perfected the "book musical," where song and dance, character and plot, worked together seamlessly to tell a story. After World War II, the team's next great show was *South Pacific*, which took on directly the themes of interracial love and prejudice. With songs like "You've Got to Be Carefully Taught," they set out to expose what Rodgers called "the superficiality of racial barriers." Broadway turned the lifestyles the city made possible into popular show tunes.

For all of its openness, when New York bid for the UN, the city faced a real problem: it had no place to house delegates of all shades, colors, faiths, and marital mixtures. Segregation in housing was still enforced in private buildings and in attractive city-run housing such as Stuyvesant Town. In order to host the UN, New York needed to create Parkway Village in Queens as a new, integrated garden community, where homes were built around a central green space. Families of all kinds were welcome there. Parkway, like *South Pacific* and the UN, offered one vision of the city's, and the world's, future.

For its part, Forty-Second Street gave birth to a new form of American ballet. Jerry Robbins finally found his American theme in watching how people—servicemen on leave and local New Yorkers—walked and dashed and flirted around Times Square. As a fellow dancer explained, Robbins wanted to capture "a special American look, a kind of looseness and ease—a special kind of running, like ballplayers." *Fancy Free* is about three sailors on leave in the city and the women they chase, dance, and flirt with, and who have their own fun with their suitors. It opened to twenty-two curtain calls and ecstatic reviews. The dance was then expanded into the Broadway musical and film *On the Town*—an all-singing, all-dancing love song to what Robbins called "my beautiful city." Just as Gershwin had insisted on an all-Black cast for his folk opera, Robbins knew that a musical about the city must have Black dancers. When the show opened, four Black members of the chorus partnered white women, for the first time in the city's history.

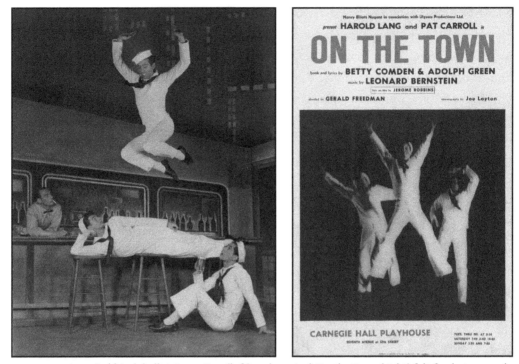

Jerry Robbins's ballet *Fancy Free* (left) and musical *On the Town* (right) felt fresh, true, and American — as if he had captured the life stories of people like the sailors seen in the Times Square shot on page 297.

New shows and new ballets were just one way New York shared its ideas and stories. Entertainment wasn't limited to the stage anymore. Televisions were starting to take over America's living rooms. New York was the home of the headquarters and studios of the TV networks that filled the blocks uptown from Forty-Second Street to Rockefeller Center.

New York, America, would now be the world's center, the home of the United Nations, the first truly global organization in human history—but which New York, and which America? The America that defeated Hitler's racism, or the America that segregated its military? The New York in which Brooklyn's Dodgers integrated baseball, or the New York in which the Yankees' chief scout rejected Willie Mays because "I got no use for him or any of them"? The America that forced Japan to surrender, or the America that interned Japanese Americans?

The New York of Café Society and integrated jazz, or the New York of the all-white Metropolitan Opera and housing discrimination?

New York the triumphant was eager to claim its place as the world city, yet its own deep divisions stood in the way, and the surrounding nation had a very different sense of what it was proudly declaring as the American Century. In New York, strong unions allied with a sequence of mayors were setting out to create a city that provided for working people throughout their lives. A completely different image of life was also taking shape in the city. Wall Street was ready for business—the business of building new homes, new roads, new cars, new schools for the babies that the kissing couples were sure to soon produce. The America of the postwar baby boom would spread out to the suburbs, away from the public, shared delights of Forty-Second Street to private homes, TVs, cars, and convenient shopping malls. And the America that never liked and never trusted left-wing, multiracial, immigrant New York would fill the halls of Congress.

Into the next century, New York was both the world city and the fractured city—breaking into separate niches within its borders, splintering off from the nation, and yet the prime symbol of the very global capitalist hegemony that parts of the world admired and others detested. New York was the sum of its history and parts as its moment of triumph and tragedy was about to begin.

CHAPTER 26

New York Center, Left, Far Left

WALL STREET

Postwar New York was the home of money.

A city without a rival in an expansive America, New York was the natural home for the nation's largest corporations. In 1951, 131 out of America's five hundred biggest businesses, and ten out of the top twenty-five, had their headquarters in the city. Giant corporations needed impressive and modern homes. Starting with the Lever House, Park Avenue in midtown began to fill with gleaming steel-and-glass rectangles. These skyscrapers did not resemble the Chrysler or Empire State Buildings, which declared their owners' status by building upward from wide bases to thin spires as if they were giant pyramids. Instead, built in the new International Style, they were meant to be clean, faceless—an expression of the modern. The new corporation was the home of the "man in the gray flannel suit"—the efficient middle manager who had gone to college after the war, his tuition paid for by a decision in Congress to provide for the education of people who had served in the military: the GI Bill.

The corporations ensconced in their shiny towers were doing well—which made Wall Street happy. Many in America believed that the old days of the robber-baron rich and the angry, poor workers were fading into memory and a new vision of the nation was taking hold: all would rise together. An ever-improving standard of living would eliminate the nation's divisions and heal its wounds; that was the promise of the 1950s. As the country's economy continued to grow, memories of the Depression faded. Individual investors (primarily in New York itself) and now, for the first time, women, began buying stocks. Growing families needed homes, which eager builders were supplying as fast as they could pour concrete. A family planned on buying a new car every few years, making General Motors, Ford, or Chrysler a good bet. Drug companies seemed to come up with a new miracle every day, which enticed investors to buy a stake in their innovations. Even the Cold War rivalry with the Soviet Union meant that the government would spend ever more on weapons, feeding the companies that manufactured them and providing money for research into computers and other new inventions. A growing country with an expanding economy sent the stock market higher and higher. Two years after the 1952 election of the Republican war-hero president Dwight D. Eisenhower, the stock market began an unprecedented fifteen-year boom, creating wealth for investors and ever more jobs for stockbrokers on Wall Street.

What could decorate the long blank walls of the new corporate rectangles? At 24 University Place, the Village was playing host to America's first homegrown, internationally recognized art movement: Abstract Expressionism. From the drip painter Jackson Pollock to the colorist Mark Rothko and the intense perfectionist Willem de Kooning, this set of painters and supportive art critics spent their nights at the Cedar Tavern on University Place. The Expressionists' work was photographed in *Life* magazine and shown to the country. Vast canvases that seemed to be simultaneously as personal as a dream and as grand as the postwar nation on the move were a kind of announcement that the New York art scene had supplanted Paris. If you wanted to be at the edge of the art world, you had to be there, in the city, in the Village, at the tavern. New York was the

Wall Street to Trinity Church—the same vista seen on page 176 is shown forty-two years later as the old street grows ever more dense with cars and people.

postwar global innovator—whether in its corporations or its art styles. Lee Krasner (who was married to Pollock), Elaine de Kooning, Helen Frankenthaler, and other women were there at the Cedar Tavern and were making their own artistic breakthroughs. But they had difficulty gaining equal visibility in the very male-oriented environment. The Village could host the rambunctious Abstract Expressionist crowd because New York was committed to a shared, public life.

Shortly after the war, as soldiers returned to work and families had money to spend, the cost of living rose throughout the country. In New York, where unions were so powerful and the voices of working people spoke more loudly than the interests of landlords, the city made the decision to limit how much rent an owner could charge for an apartment. The good of making it possible for young people to live in Manhattan, for artists to find space to work, for workers to live in clean, affordable buildings, for retirees to stay in their apartments, meant more to the city than the good of letting rents and profits rise. While the rest of the country scattered, New York clustered.

A city that welcomed young people and respected talent was a flourishing center for creativity. As children filled classrooms, New York publishers created the books, from the I Can Reads to Dr. Seuss's classics that became the common language of growing up. The editors and publishers of these books were most often smart, independent women (some of whom were in love with other women) whose only interest was an artist's ability to engage young people. Creators with Left or even Communist views, such as Crockett Johnson (*Harold and the Purple Crayon*) and Syd Hoff (*Danny and the Dinosaur*)—Hoff's satirical murals also graced the walls of Café Society—found a new voice in capturing the wit and subversion of childhood.

New York was the home of corporate America, but was corporate America suited to New York? The buildings, the jobs, the employees were meant to be uniform, normal, conformist—the opposite of the old city of Village radicals, Union Square labor rallies, and Harlem rent parties. Did those managers need to live in the city to work there? What of the women who had rushed to take jobs during the war when men were in the military and did not want to spend their lives as housewives? What of African Americans, who did not receive the same benefits

Syd Hoff's mural at Café Society made fun of the very patrons who looked at it.

from the GI Bill, especially after senators from segregationist states made sure their all-white officials would determine who qualified? What of those who could not marry or have families since they loved people of their own gender? Even as the city was the center of the 1950s image of prosperity, it was, on the margins and the edges, the center of opposition to that vision of American life.

UNION CITY
Union Square, May 1, 1946

Postwar New York was the home of labor.

With the war over, Union Square was ready to retake its place as the natural home for union rallies. On this date on which workers throughout the world celebrated their solidarity, somewhere between forty thousand and one hundred thousand people (counts varied) took four hours to march into and fill the square. As in 1930, the Communist Party was well represented, as were people who worked in stores, on ships, in offices, in the fur trades—with so many occupations present, the roster almost sounded like the old rhyme about the butcher, the baker, and the candlestick maker. New York was a union town.

The immigrant city where generations of newcomers simultaneously learned to hustle to find a way to make a living in a new land and relied on connections with relatives and countrymen was a perfect home for businesses—such as clothing—that needed to move quickly to keep up with trends. American men and women had money to spend, and soon children to clothe. Department store chains spread across the country to meet these needs. The clothes on their racks came from Manhattan. Making the shirts, dresses, and pants the whole country wore was not just a matter of selecting a design and manufacturing the items. The shirtmaker needed quick access to a button maker with the best styles, the milliner whose hats were just the right complement, the suit maker whose wares would frame the "look," and the sellers to guide buyers from store chains when they arrived in showrooms. Blocks away were the advertising agencies defining the next style with images in the popular magazines edited and published nearby. In Manhattan, not only was it easy to find every one of these interconnected businesses, but each type congregated on specific streets—as if the island were built to house medieval European guilds. In turn, though, the extremely close-knit trades were all organized into unions. And the largest one was the ILGWU.

Unions made up of people from similar backgrounds with similar skills were eager to at least protect and ideally improve every aspect of their members' lives. Subway fares must be kept extremely low so workers could easily move around the city. Public housing and city-run hospitals should be built to house and care for workers. The City University of New York must be free to educate the rising generation. The New York vision of inclusion even began to deal with race. In 1945, New York State was the first place in the country to pass a law forbidding discrimination in private employment "on the basis of race, creed, color, or national origin." But a state law went only so far. The ILGWU leadership, for example, remained rigidly Jewish, Italian, and male, even as its membership became increasingly Puerto Rican, African American, and overwhelmingly female.

Postwar New York was an experiment in building a city, a society, that was all business and all union at the same time. And it featured its own unique blend of peoples: in 1952, nearly half the city was Catholic (though the Irish, Italians, and Puerto Ricans each had their own version of the faith), a quarter was Jewish, and

Protestants were a clear minority. Whether the New York coalition of distinct groups of workers and stockbrokers, Catholics and Jews, children of immigrants and children of southern segregation, and female-dominated unions run by men could hold together or would splinter remained to be seen.

The rest of the country—where more and more white people rode in private cars, not public subways, lived in single-family homes, not shared apartment houses, sought out all-white suburbs, not mingled city neighborhoods, and were dominantly Protestant—liked what New York produced but was deeply suspicious of the city's social experiment. It seemed to smack of the great enemy, the great evil, the threat to American life: Communism.

UNION SQUARE, JULY 19, 1953

In tears, marching, holding signs, some five thousand people were watching the clock, waiting for a tragedy to unfold. The Soviets had managed to convince some American supporters to spy for them, even to steal atomic secrets so that they, too, would have nuclear weapons. Julius Rosenberg did exactly that—and was caught. His wife, Ethel, probably knew something of what he was doing, though it is not clear that she took an active part in the spying. But both had been tried

as betrayers of the nation, convicted, and sentenced to death. The very last appeal to the Supreme Court failed. Supporters were now gathered to mourn what they saw as a miscarriage of justice. Were their crimes deserving of death? Did Ethel even commit a crime? And what of their two boys, their children? The execution proceeded as planned. The crowd dispersed, leaving Union Square.

In the square where Communists had proudly led a rally six years earlier and had hoped to spark a revolution in 1930, the remaining faithful saw the party condemned

The Rosenbergs under arrest

as traitorous. All those unions that had worked with the Communist Party or been inspired by party organizers, all those workers who had come to rallies to walk side by side with party members, all who had been inspired by the ideal of a society of equals where everyone shared with everyone—all were now suspect. One by one, CIO unions distanced themselves from the party and drew closer to the safer and more moderate AFL. And in 1955, in Manhattan, the two rivals joined together to form the AFL-CIO. Unions remained strong in New York, allied with the city's powerful Democratic Party. Indeed, from 1954 to 1965, when Robert Wagner was the city's mayor, unions were one of the main voices in setting city policies. Yet the nation's suspicion of Communism did not end with the arrest of a few spies or the "cleansing" of the unions.

THE VILLAGE

The Rosenbergs' boys were adopted by a kindhearted public school teacher who admired their parents' politics: the same Abel Meeropol who had written "Strange Fruit." Indeed, the whole campaign against "Reds" was in a way a judgment of the Café Society world of integration. Before America entered the war, Leon Josephson had risked his life to help smuggle anti-fascists out of Nazi Germany, providing false passports if necessary. One would think that would make him an American hero, a freedom fighter. Yet, as his brother, Café Society owner Barney, knew, Leon was also a dedicated, principled Communist. To those suspicious of all Communists, an American Communist issuing false papers to Germans who might themselves be Communists looked very suspicious. Leon was called to Washington to testify before the House Un-American Activities Committee (HUAC). He refused to answer their questions. Leon was cited for contempt, and his appeal to the Supreme Court failed. New York's gossip columnists now turned on Barney's two clubs, Café Society downtown and uptown.

The cafés were suspicious, some said, because white and Black patrons sat together, danced together. Reviewers stopped coming to see shows. *Life* magazine, which frequently covered acts at the café, now sent a photographer to find evidence of Russian spies. Billie Holiday's eloquent renditions of "Strange Fruit" were treated as signs of radical, un-American beliefs. The "Red Scare" went beyond the café itself. Many of the artists who performed there shared Barney's or Leon's views. Their names began appearing in lists of artists to be "blacklisted"—kept off the stage. A nightclub is an expensive place to run— it needs publicity to promote acts and bring in curious customers. Simultaneously cut off from good press and attacked by right-wing critics, Barney was losing his audience. First, he sold his uptown branch. Then, on March 29, 1949, Café Society in Sheridan Square closed its doors.

Jerry Robbins had joined the Communist Party in the 1940s because he thought of it "as an organization which was very much for minorities and for advancing their causes." He had experienced anti-Semitism in America, felt an identification with African Americans, and, for a time, thought the party was

Walter Rosenblum, who took this photo in 1938, was a member of the Photo League, where he was influenced by Lewis Hine and studied with Paul Strand. They took images that celebrated the people of the city—a stark contrast to the sour suspicion of New Yorkers taking root in some parts of the nation.

an ally. He was also well known to be bisexual. In 1953, though he had long left the party, he was brought before HUAC and given a choice—name others he had known when he had been a party member or lose the chance to work and more. Even though Hollywood would not hire people HUAC blacklisted, Broadway would. But same-sex relationships were not merely condemned; they were illegal. With both his creative life and his freedom at risk, he gave names to the committee and earned the fury of the theater world, and everyone on the Left in the city.

New York as the beacon of integration and progressive ideas seemed to have no place in the Cold War America of HUAC. Could anti-Communism muffle the New York idea? No. Within the city, creativity is not so easily silenced.

The theory behind the blacklist was that the Communist Party was using media—films, music, plays—to infiltrate alien ideas into innocent American minds. By ruthlessly exposing these cultural traitors, these artistic spies, the blacklisters aimed to keep the country pure. Pure of Communists, that is; the suspicious investigators spent no time at all researching the many ways Nazis, Nazi sympathizers, and extreme white-nationalist racists had devoted their own time and money trying to influence American citizens. Starting in the early 1930s, the Far Left had actually set out to use culture to spread its ideas. "The special task of the Workers Music League," one manifesto read, "is the development of music as a weapon in the class struggle." The result, however, was comic disaster, not effective propaganda. Songbooks filled with lyrics about worker solidarity set to jarring music at best bored and most often annoyed real workers. By the mid-1930s though, alert left-leaning producers such as Alan Lomax, Charles Seeger, and later his son Pete realized that there already was a kind of music "of the people" in America: folk and blues.

The Village Vanguard—a club just a few blocks uptown from Café Society on Seventh Avenue—was run by Max Gordon and his wife, Lorraine. In their integrated club, they hosted Lead Belly, a Black singer who had served time in a Louisiana prison; Josh White, another skilled, appealing African American singer; and a white group called the Almanac Singers that included both Pete Seeger and the roving, talented singer-songwriter Woody Guthrie.

Irving Berlin wrote a first draft of "God Bless America" during World War I, then revised it as a kind of anthem to give the nation hope in the ominous Depression and pre–World War II days of 1938. As sung by the popular singer Kate Smith, the song was so universally embraced that it was played at both the 1940 Democratic and Republican conventions. That was the America of conformity and uniform values, the America that had no room for places like Café Society. Guthrie, whose guitar carried the slogan "This machine kills fascists," hated the song. He felt it celebrated the America of privilege and private property. This land, he insisted, did not belong to the wealthy or the devout but to everyone, even rambling hobos like him. On February 23, 1940, while staying in a hotel on Forty-Third Street and Sixth Avenue, he wrote his rebuttal song, "This Land Is Your Land." Guthrie recorded his song for Moe Asch, a record producer whose passion was to preserve the folk music of America and the entire world. Just as the city had given space to Paul Laurence Dunbar and Will Marion Cook to sing with pride, and to Broadway musicals to preach against racism, New York gave Guthrie a platform to reimagine the anthem of the nation.

In New York, some blacklisted musicians could still find work. Folk musicians could perform at small clubs like the Village Vanguard, record with out-of-the-mainstream record companies like Asch's Folkways, and broadcast on a few local New York radio programs. Even as Café Society was forced to close, the

Woody Guthrie (left) and Pete Seeger (right) treated folk songs as both lively music and political activism—giving voice to the people.

Bebop artists such as Thelonious Monk blazed their own intellectual artistic trails, leaving it to audiences to follow their leads.

Village—where the Weavers (a revised version of the Almanac Singers) lived in a collective—found its new voice in folk music. In 1957, just down MacDougal Street from where John Reed wrote and Heterodoxy met, Izzy Young opened the Folklore Center. The Center and nearby clubs on West Fourth Street drew aspiring singers from around the country and soon the attention of John Hammond.

Since the mid-1940s, uptown at Minton's Playhouse on 118th Street in Harlem a new generation of artists such as Thelonious Monk, Dizzy Gillespie, Charlie Parker, and Charlie Christian (who had played with Benny Goodman) was finding a new voice for jazz: bebop. Where swing had been upbeat and meant to please everyone struggling through the Depression by getting them to dance, bebop was personal, intellectual, ruminative. "Sing, Sing, Sing" had propelled fans out on the dance floor together; a piece like Monk's "'Round Midnight" went inside a listener's thoughts and feelings.

Folk music and bebop, like books for young readers, gave artists a way to flourish and to challenge the whitewashed image of America. And then there was Broadway.

FORTY-SECOND STREET

The Times Square district continued to create, produce, and air the TV shows the country watched. Broadway theaters featured a sequence of musicals that managed to entertain while inspiring the country with the best of the New York idea. Starting in 1949, a team of artists including the Jewish, bisexual Leonard Bernstein, the Jewish, bisexual choreographer Jerry Robbins (who had given in to HUAC), and the Jewish, gay, blacklisted Arthur Laurents set out to create a

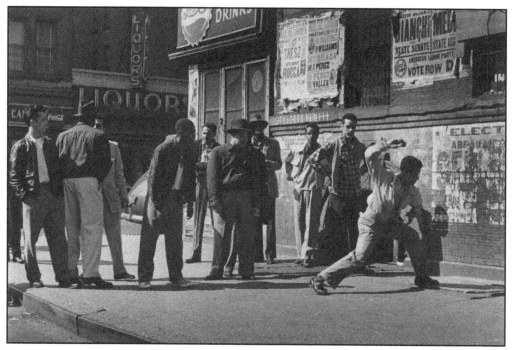

In 1952, Leo Goldstein, another member of the Photo League, captured life in Spanish Harlem—the rich social life that spilled out on streets, the challenges of living in a poor and neglected neighborhood.

modern, musical version of *Romeo and Juliet*. Their plan was to focus on the ill-fated love between an Orthodox Jewish man and an Italian Catholic woman on the Lower East Side. By 1956, inspired by clashes between Mexican Americans and whites in Los Angeles, and joined by the young Stephen Sondheim (a protégé of Oscar Hammerstein's), they decided to change the focus of their musical to a tragic conflict on the west side of Manhattan.

After World War II, New York began to become a Spanish-speaking city. The Puerto Rican population had tripled from twenty to sixty thousand before the war, then rose tenfold to more than six hundred thousand by 1960. These new New Yorkers were—like the Irish, Jews, Italians, and African Americans who came before them—generally poor, but they found work when the children and grandchildren of the earlier white immigrants moved up the career ladder to better-paying jobs. The industrial and hand labor that one set of immigrants had done in 1900 was taken on fifty years later by this new set of immigrants. Yet, as with African Americans, racism made the path to "rising" in America hazardous for Puerto Ricans.

West Side Story in 1957 was the perfect New York story. The clash of the nativist white gang—echoes of draft riots and the Five Points fury at amalgamation—and the newest newcomers, the Puerto Ricans, captured one long strand in the city's history. Yet the heart of the musical was the yearning for the other New York—the interracial families, the drag balls, the ideal of overcoming differences. When the star-crossed Tony and Maria sang "Somewhere there's a place for us," they were speaking about New York and Broadway itself, a place where outsiders—like the artists who invented the show—could be at home and create for the nation.

On December 5, 1957, New York took a first step to make "somewhere" mean the whole city: it became the very first place in the entire nation to pass a law making it illegal to discriminate against a buyer in selling a home or a tenant when renting an apartment. To that point, it was perfectly legal to create all-white neighborhoods or confine people of color to segregated areas such as Harlem. While 1957 seems terribly late, New York City was ahead of everywhere else in the country, as it had been twelve years earlier in banning discrimination in employment. Indeed, no federal law echoed its words until 1968. Yet that also meant that the clashes over integration in the city would be especially intense.

West Side Story captured the truths of the postwar city, which continued to be the cultural center of the nation and, in many ways, the world. Wall Street was generating wealth, and New York was proud of being the union city that provided for its working people and believed in equality. Yet was that true? Women filled unions, worked in offices, ran publishing divisions, were talented creators in every art form, and could be found in every artistic hangout yet were consistently overshadowed by men. The bustling city was built by all-white construction crews, was guarded by white police, while Black and brown Harlem seemed increasingly separated, neglected, and isolated. And both cities—the home of unions and the site of ethnic conflict—were out of touch with a nation racing away toward golden, suburban dreams.

West Side Story (below) turned the real lives that photographers such as Leo Goldstein captured in this 1950 image (left) into universal stories.

CHAPTER 27

Generations

May 28, 1957

The meeting took place in Chicago, but the shock wave hit New York. The Major League Baseball owners agreed that the Brooklyn Dodgers (the team with passionately loyal fans that had integrated baseball) and the New York Giants (headed by Willie Mays, known to play stickball on the city's streets) could move to California. The Dodgers to Los Angeles, the Giants to San Francisco. The New York ideal was being lost to the almighty dollar. As one fan wrote to Mayor Wagner, "I cannot impress upon you too much how important it is to keep the Dodgers in Brooklyn. . . . The Dodgers, being composed of Negroes, Spanish, and Whites, are a good example of how good you can get if everyone works together regardless of race or color." The ideal of shared effort was nothing compared with the reality of America on the move. Team owners realized that people were leaving their apartment houses and moving to California and wanted their teams to be near this growing fan base. And they were right; by 1964, California would pass New York as the nation's most populous state.

New York, the gateway to America, was losing the grandchildren of those European immigrants who had filled its streets. Indeed, in the decade of the 1950s, so many people moved out of the city that the millions of families having children could not keep pace and New York's population slightly dipped. Could it be that New York, with its crowds, subways, and ethnic neighborhoods, was the past and California, the Golden Land of sun, beaches, and cars, was the future?

In the early 1950s, popular television programs told stories about working-class families in New York—the Jewish Goldbergs in the show of the same name; the loudmouth bus driver Ralph Kramden (Jackie Gleason), his deadpan wife, Alice (Audrey Meadows), and his sewer worker pal Ed Norton (Art Carney) in *The Honeymooners*. Entertainers who began in vaudeville—such as Sid Caesar and Milton Berle—made the switch to television. By 1957, all such shows were gone—the New York story was not one the nation wanted to watch, and the New York comic was too raw for a national audience.

New York produced books for children, but starting in 1955, out in Burbank, California, *The Mickey Mouse Club* was filmed and broadcast on TV. That same year, Disney opened its major attraction: Disneyland in Anaheim, just next to Los Angeles. With Hollywood churning out films and Disneyland enticing children—and television studios—New York's cultural industry looked more and more like a fading giant.

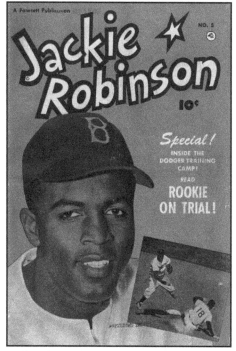

With Jackie Robinson, baseball joined Broadway and jazz in beginning to highlight the talents of African Americans.

Not yet. The very suburban, family-oriented quality of Disney and the new TV shows left room for New York to take risks. The city was still the main launching pad for talent, and by the mid-1950s some of what we now call the baby boomers were near-teenagers and looking for new sounds and new idols. As Madison Square Garden had announced the jump shot to basketball players across the country, New York's *Ed Sullivan Show* served as the TV pathway to stardom for Elvis Presley in 1956. Presley had previously appeared on two shows on other channels and scored well with audiences. Sullivan realized that to keep up in the ratings race, he needed to give Presley a unique platform: three appearances, including the season's premiere. Sixty million people watched him,

82 percent of the national TV audience, and rock and roll was launched as the soundtrack of adolescence.

By 1962, when the babies born after the war hit puberty, some 165 music businesses filled the Brill Building on Forty-Ninth Street and Broadway. The building was organized similarly to the way the garment trade functioned—companies could match quickly changing tastes since every specialized skill was housed just steps apart. The Brill Building was the nation's hit factory for teenage music—where an idea could become lyrics, music, a demo recording, and a radio deal in a single day. Blocks away, magazines covered popular culture, paid for by advertisements generated across town on Madison Avenue. When writers were ready to create full books, almost all of the country's major publishers were housed in the city. And a new generation of writers and poets found inspiration in the very decline and fall of Forty-Second Street.

Forty-Second Street was entirely ruled by the dollar. It would display whatever people would buy. As families filled their homes with TV sets, movie theaters lost their appeal. Owners desperate to draw crowds tried everything: a house devoted to horror, another for westerns, a third for foreign films, and for more and more theaters, as much nudity as they could get away with. In the late '40s and early '50s, Forty-Second Street became a place where you could find the niche, the genre, the style of movie you liked—so long as the films didn't cost much to show and you didn't mind watching in decaying, poorly maintained theaters.

The hunt for the dollar led straight to the lowest common denominator: sex. Bookstores began to fill emptied storefronts. Not because moviegoers were experiencing a sudden desire to become well-rounded individuals. The bookstores stocked pornographic magazines and erotic paperbacks just out of sight in back. By the 1960s, Forty-Second Street theaters ran the most explicit XXX movies while nearby stores offered coin-operated "peep show" machines that were totally unregulated. A paying customer could see whatever he (this was extremely male-oriented) wanted to see. The Deuce, as the street came to be known, was the symbol of everything wrong with New York. The formerly lively theater world of the Great White Way seemed almost emptied, hollowed out, a home only to the most marginal, the most desperate, the most criminal outsiders.

There was something almost biological happening in the city: as Forty-Second Street crumbled, it created a rich soil for a new birth of language and writing. The Beat poets and novelists took their name from that sense of being beaten down but also being on the rhythm, the beat, and even elevated—as in beatific. The Beats were defeated by surrounding culture, but also aimed to transcend it.

As the Deuce turned ever more to nudity and sex, it, like the old books on the Five Points, offered sensation and warning at the same time.

A novel of the time described a hangout on Forty-Second Street from the point of view of a Beat: "The place looked like some strange social club for grifters, dope passers, petty thieves, cheap, aging whores and derelicts." Horrible perhaps, yet the writer "somehow was not repulsed, but rather yearned to know it in its every aspect, the lives these people led, the emotions they endured, the fate into which they stumbled." Pascal D'Angelo had seen the turn-of-the-century city as "lovely," "repulsive," and "enchanted" at the same time. To the Beats, Forty-Second was the sublime essence of all three.

Beats such as the poet Allen Ginsberg and the novelist Jack Kerouac had been students at Columbia University. But they found their voice and their place amid the addicts and hustlers of Forty-Second Street. The Beats rejected, in every possible way, the values and ideas of HUAC, of suburban families, of corporate America. And yet their riffs began to appeal to other young people, college students, those who felt themselves to be outsiders. This was yet another form of New York mixture—high art and the lives of the criminal, the desperate. The Beats did not stay put—they moved on to San Francisco, Mexico, India, and back to the cafés of MacDougal Street and apartments in the East Village.

POSITIVELY FOURTH STREET

In the 1950s, the record producer John Hammond felt out of touch with the jazz world and turned his attention to folk music. All along West Fourth and

Feliks Topolski was a much-honored Polish-born British painter who had the gift of capturing a scene as he was seeing it. He visited New York in the 1960s, and his drawings, such as this one of Bob Dylan, vibrate with the energy of the time.

MacDougal Streets, in small cafés and bars such as Gerde's Folk City, Kettle of Fish, and the Gaslight, young people were strumming guitars, plucking zithers, buzzing on harmonicas, telling stories in song. As one version of the meeting goes, one day in 1961, Hammond went to listen to a blond Texan singer named Carolyn Hester. At her rehearsal, he heard a shaggy young man, barely twenty, who was not very good at playing the guitar or the harmonica, but Hammond found him "fascinating." Hammond invited the singer to his company's studio, where Bob Dylan performed some of his own songs. The producer signed him up right away.

Dylan and his girlfriend Suze Rotolo—whose parents had been Communists—lived on West Fourth Street near Sixth Avenue, and pictures of them taken a block away on Jones Street appeared on the cover of his second album, *The Freewheelin' Bob Dylan*. The album features Dylan's "Blowin' in the Wind," the song that became an anthem for his generation. Dylan had the unique ability to shape songs into dreams that hypnotize listeners and make them see the world through his eyes. His eyes were those of the nation's largest wave of young people, coming of age, setting out to change the world. Songs of protest bubbling up from the streets of the Village became the ballads, the anthems, of the new America.

Decaying Forty-Second Street had been fertile soil for the Beats (who in turn inspired Dylan). The folk revival that took place in the Village was yet another New York new birth. Rotolo's past fed Dylan, Hammond's ear gave him a national stage, and Dylan did the rest. His first songs echoed the style and politics of his hero Woody Guthrie; switching to electric guitar, he went on to spin surreal pageants that were a kind of soundtrack to many listeners' inner lives. If a generation of young people, white and Black, were going to join together in the fight for civil rights, in the mission to create a more inclusive nation, singers from the Village would give them voice and passion and courage.

Hammond went on to sign the Canadian poet Leonard Cohen and then the New Jersey rocker Bruce Springsteen. Dylan, Cohen, Springsteen: three poet shamans.

SEPTEMBER 22, 1964

New York's media machine promoted the music and politics of a new generation, but the buying power of teenagers posed a real threat to Broadway. What stories, what musicals, could speak to this moment of change? On this night, a musical once again by a team of Jewish writers, composers, directors, and scenic designers opened. While set in old Russia, *Fiddler on the Roof* captured the lives of the

The homes above Tevye's house in my father's sketch suggest the encircling world of tradition that *Fiddler on the Roof* explored.

creators' parents and grandparents. As the director Jerry Robbins said, it was "a glory for my Father—a celebration of & for him." Yet it was not just his father's story. Robbins kept pushing the creators to define what the show was about, and finally one said, "Tradition." *Fiddler* told one story that soon seemed to be everyone's story.

In an America where each day's headlines brought news of generational conflict, of women demanding to make their own choices, *Fiddler* captured experiences grandparents had lived, with echoes of conflicts grandchildren were experiencing. My father designed the sets; his father had been an important rabbi whose eldest son married a gentile. My grandfather treated my uncle as dead until they were reconciled on the rabbi's deathbed. What of the past forms us? What of the present demands we bend and change? What is giving up too much? When must we move and embrace the new? The show struck such a chord that its 3,242 performances set a new record for the longest-running musical in the city's history. In making art out of this past, *Fiddler* opened a new door: books and TV shows (such as *Roots*) and musicals (such as *A Chorus Line*) in which creators spoke to a broad public by exploring their own lives, their own heritages. Broadway did not need to speak to America with tuneful tales of Oklahoma, or the South Pacific, or an East Side story turned to the West Side. It could build new narratives for the nation out of the recalled—or researched—experiences of its own creators.

Fiddler was a pinnacle and a break. Audiences rushed in from the city, the suburbs, retirement homes in Florida, and ranch houses in California to experience this resonant, archetypal tale. The show toured the country and the world, was turned into a movie, and has been revived repeatedly everywhere from middle schools to Broadway once again. Every single day since it opened, it has been performed somewhere in the world. New York City created it, but soon enough audiences did not need the city to see it. Indeed, for them, often enough, change had meant leaving New York behind.

New York had money and cultural power, but the old splits—the masses and the grandees, advocates of mixture and defenders of separation, women demanding to be heard and men silencing them, the immigrant city and the all-American nation—were about to bring the city to its greatest moments of crisis. The union city was coming apart.

SNAPSHOT

Greatest Crises, Greatest Recoveries

1965 New York has the largest US factory workforce, at 1 million, and the largest manufacturing payroll.

On October 3, President Johnson signs law opening immigration to the United States from the entire world.

1966 The new Lindsay administration is faced with a transit strike.

1968 Container shipping makes up 12 percent of cargo in New York, up from less than 3 percent in 1965.

1970 New York City's population is 7,894,862; 1,668,115 are African American and 1,202,281 are Hispanic, including 811,843 from Puerto Rico—the next two largest Hispanic communities are Cuban with 84,179 and Dominican with 66,914. Manhattan's population is 1,539,233; 25 percent are African American. Brooklyn's population is 2,602,012; 25 percent are African American.

1975 Approximately 75 percent of the New York port's cargo is containerized; just 3 percent of jobs in the area near the port are linked to activity in the port (97 percent of work is in stores, restaurants, etc., not shipping).

City on the edge of financial collapse.

1977 The World Trade Center is completed; the towers are the tallest buildings in the world.

1980 New York City's population is 7,071,639; 1,784,337 are African Americans, and 1,406,024 are Hispanics, including 860,552 Puerto Ricans and 125,380 Dominicans, and 761,762 people of other races. The population of non-white or mixed people makes up 48.1 percent of the city's population.

1989 Los Angeles passes New York as the nation's main port.

1990 New York City's population rises slightly to 7,322,564, including 854,000 immigrants who have arrived since 1980.

1993 A bomb explodes at the World Trade Center, injuring over 1,000 people.

The African Burial Ground, dating back to colonial New York, is identified and called a city landmark.

2000 New York City's population reaches 8,008,278, including 1.2 million immigrants. In previous census forms, respondents were required to select a single heritage; starting in 2000 they could check as many as applied, which means numbers from 2000 forward do not precisely align with numbers from prior surveys. The city's population is 44 percent white; 26.59 percent African American; 9.9 percent Asian; 18.85 percent other or mixed; and 26.98 percent Hispanic, including 816,827 Puerto Ricans and 547,379 Dominicans; other large groups include Mexicans, Ecuadorans, and Colombians.

2001 The World Trade Center is attacked and destroyed on September 11.

2010 New York's population is 8,175,000, with 44 percent white; 25.55 percent African American; 12.77 percent Asian, with the three largest groups being Chinese, Bangladeshis, and Indians; and 28.58 percent Hispanic, with Puerto Ricans, Dominicans, and Mexicans the largest groups.

2014 The new World Trade Center complex opens on November 3.

2020 The COVID-19 pandemic ravages New York City.

CHAPTER 28

City on the Brink

DECEMBER 31, 1965

Two men faced off, holding the fate of New York City in their hands. Mike Quill, the head of the Transport Workers Union, was a tough Irishman who had long believed in confronting wealth and power. Though he was not an avowed Communist, he believed that labor must battle against capital, never trusting and never conceding anything to the bosses. He was threatening to strike, to shut down the city's subways and buses, unless the incoming mayor, John Vliet Lindsay, who was to begin his term the next day, gave his union members more money. Lindsay was a Yale-educated Upper East Side newcomer who could trace his roots back to Dutch New York. He knew the city could neither afford to pay Quill nor endure a lengthy strike—making the city look even more unappealing to the business and taxpayers it was already losing.

Quill detested Lindsay, whom he called "a juvenile, a lightweight, and a pipsqueak." "You have to grow up," Quill screamed. "You don't know anything about the working class."

"I am inheriting a bankrupt city with a multitude of problems," Lindsay managed to answer. "I therefore call upon you in the public interest to respect the city."

Quill slashed Lindsay with schoolyard insults; Lindsay replied in the elite language of "therefore," "upon," and "public interest." As the columnist Jimmy Breslin aptly put it, Lindsay looked across the table and saw the city's past. Quill looked at Lindsay and saw the Church of England, hated enemy of the Catholic Irish since time immemorial. The city was back to the battles of Hamilton's Federalists and Burr's Tammany, of the Protestant reformers and Catholic Irish.

At 5 a.m., the strike began. For the first thirteen days of 1966, the first thirteen days of Lindsay's new administration, the city was paralyzed: no buses or subways ran in New York.

The city was in trouble. Not only were corporations starting to move their headquarters out of Manhattan to locations with lower taxes, but more and more of the people who worked in the remaining big businesses lived outside of the city and commuted in. The highways and bridges Robert

The youthful Mayor Lindsay was a handsome, liberal Ivy League politician whose supporters saw him as a New York version of John F. Kennedy.

Moses built made it all too easy to dash in and out of town. Each well-paid executive who left cut into the city's tax base. Between 1960 and 1980, the city's population declined by some seven hundred thousand people, and the makeup of those who stayed entirely changed. A city that began the century as 98 percent white (Hispanics were not counted as a separate category at that time) was 50 percent white by 1980 and 48% non-white—many of whom worked in lower-paying jobs. Yet the city still tried to live by the LaGuardia/FDR vision of a government that provided for all. The city kept promising money to increase union salaries, to build housing, to improve health care, to expand the police department. Those promises were debts the city would have to pay, somehow, with its diminishing tax base.

Quill won his confrontation with Lindsay. When the strike ended, he got his union the increases and pensions he had demanded from the first. As Lindsay knew, agreeing to that contract guaranteed that every other union in the city

Commuters who sided with Lindsay detested Mike Quill for shutting down the subways.

would increase its demands. Good for hardworking union members. A disaster for the city. New York was relying on a national economy that was growing, for the moment, while living on money from the state, from the federal government, and on accounting tricks that paid today's bills by promising to pay more tomorrow with fantasy money that might never arrive. Growing welfare payments, union contracts, free college for New Yorkers, an expanding police department, and a shrinking tax base were like that moment in a cartoon where a character runs off the edge of a cliff and keeps pumping his legs for a split second before he realizes where he is and begins to crash.

The pull of the suburbs increased as press reports stressed the dangers of the city. Crime was rising; the annual murder rate rose from 631 in 1964 to 1,554 a decade later. But the sense of fear was more a result of sensational cases than statistics. When a man riding a subway with his wife and child tried to take an annoying drunk off the train at 125th Street, he was stabbed to death. Instead of linking the city, the subways came to seem like a warning: stick to your own territory. More and more New Yorkers began to question whether a street, even a whole neighborhood, was safe before crossing it. The more dangerous the city seemed, the less appealing it was for the working families who were its backbone.

As late as 1947, over a million New Yorkers worked making things with their hands and a popular author described the city as "the greatest manufacturing town on earth." From the artisans of the colonial city to the garment workers of the postwar period, from the longshoremen at the busy port to the construction teams putting up skyscrapers, New York had always been a city of physical work. Some of those jobs gave work to immigrants, to Puerto Ricans, to African Americans, to women, creating a base of employment. But by the 1960s, manufacturing jobs were leaving the city—cut in half by 1973. Just as clothing manufacturers had cut costs in the 1800s by having armies of cheap labor do the sewing, now they decided to leave unionized New York entirely. Low-tax states that had fewer regulations to protect workers and did not support unions courted business, as overseas factories would do once again in the twenty-first century. Companies' eagerness to produce as cheaply as possible undermined first New York's and later all of the United States' ability to provide manufacturing jobs.

Even when small businesses did well and began to grow, they would move away from taxes and old buildings to the expanses of nearby suburbs. A growing number of African American women did manage to stop working as domestics in white people's homes and find work in offices. But the best working-class jobs for men that remained—for example, in construction—were controlled by unions that passed along jobs from father to son and remained rigidly white. Even as working-class jobs disappeared, a new wave of immigrants arrived—poor African Americans from the South and Hispanics, primarily from Puerto Rico. There was less and less work for these newcomers, and their already poorly maintained neighborhoods suffered. The vicious cycle of urban decline came just as the whole nation grappled with race.

HARLEM
September 18, 1960

In 1930, Lewis Michaux began selling books on the corner of 125th Street and Seventh Avenue (what is now Adam Clayton Powell Jr. Boulevard), which he termed Harlem Square. His store was a kind of bookend to the public library branch now known as the Schomburg Center, which housed the materials on Africans and the African diaspora collected by Arturo Alfonso Schomburg across town on 135th Street and Lenox Avenue (now called Malcom X Boulevard). The large painted sign in front of the National Memorial African Bookstore announced this was "The House of Common Sense and the Home of Proper Propaganda" and that the world was populated with "2,000,000,000 (two billion) African and Nonwhite People." Michaux was a Garveyite long after Garvey was deported, and Harlem Square was the gathering place for speakers to mount stepladders and preach the gospel of Black nationalism. The store was more than that. It was a kind of library of books by, about, and for the children of the African diaspora and all of the world's people of color. The store and the corner were precisely the reverse of the racism that confined and demeaned African Americans: shelves filled with pride, honor, and forgotten history. Even as the more familiar southern civil rights movement led by Dr. Martin Luther King Jr. grew in the 1950s and '60s, the argument for separation—for African Americans to reject the hope of integration and build their own world—had new advocates in Harlem. You could find them congregating at Michaux's bookstore or down 125th at the Theresa Hotel.

On this day in September, Fidel Castro, the bearded revolutionary leader of Cuba, was in New York to address the United Nations. Rather than stay in a posh hotel near Forty-Second Street, he chose to come straight to Harlem, to the Theresa Hotel near Michaux's bookstore. Castro arrived to express solidarity with workers and people of color, and so he met twice with a rising star in Harlem: Malcom X. Malcolm was the electrifying voice of the Nation of Islam—a rejection of Dr. King's slow, nonviolent uplift toward voting rights, integration, and acceptance from white America. Malcolm was the voice of African American bitterness, rage, and self-determination. His intelligence, eloquence, and willingness to confront everyone from more accommodating African Americans to whites spoke for something many in Harlem

New York City was so liberal that Fidel Castro, the revolutionary leader of Cuba, stopped off to see the mayor and his wife when he arrived in town.

felt. Enough. Enough promises. Enough hope. Enough trying to please and be accepted by people filled with prejudice and hate. Many in Harlem were angry, despairing, in pain.

Harlem erupted again in 1964, when a white policeman shot and killed a Black teenager who, the officer claimed with no evidence, had slashed him with a knife. Looking back on the event, the Basketball Hall of Fame star Kareem Abdul-Jabbar—at the time a dominant player at a New York Catholic high school—registered his disgust. "It was not the death—that happened all the time—but the lie that was intolerable. It made all of Harlem face the fact that they didn't even have the strength to exact an acceptable apology." Over six days, angry Harlemites and the police threatened, and clashed with, one another. Though the fury passed, the officer was acquitted and Harlem remained tense as civil rights battles took place across the nation. While Lindsay stared across the table at Quill, coped with crime and budget deficits, and read one report after another about New York, the city in crisis, he monitored the pulse of Harlem.

From a distance, Harlem in the 1960s can be described with statistics of poverty, unemployment, addiction, decaying housing. Life was difficult. Yet for those living on its streets, it was also neighbors, relatives, conversations on stoops, gossip, stories, and friends. Michele Wallace, a scholar of film and author of *Black Macho and the Myth of the Superwoman*, recalled her childhood in Harlem of the 1960s before drugs took a toll on the neighborhood. "On crisp Sunday mornings we would walk down Seventh Avenue . . . with my grandmother. All along

Topolski chronicled the 1964 clash in Harlem, juxtaposing an American flag with the military-style police and the angry crowd.

The Young Lords were a Manhattan Puerto Rican activist group whose slogan was
¡Basta ya!—"Enough!". Their twin goals were to end poverty and sickness in Latin
neighborhoods and to gain independence for Puerto Rico.

our way to the opulence of the Abyssinian Baptist Church, the old men would
tip their hats and old women in mink stoles and smart black suits would stop to
say hello."

Harlem was also the home to a kind of multiculturalism not often
explored—the mixing of brown people, sharing lives, sharing cultures, outside of
the eyes of the white world. African Americans, Puerto Ricans, people from the
rest of the Caribbean, and South Asians met, mixed, and formed families. When
South Asian men married African Americans or Puerto Ricans, the clerks in city
hall could not decide what to call them. As the historian Vivek Bald recounts,
the clerks alternated between "white, colored, Negro, Indian, and East Indian."
No matter what they were called, the newcomers added their voice to Harlem.
Indian Muslim men ran the hot dog stands along the avenues of Italian and
Puerto Rican East Harlem. The African American trumpet genius Miles Davis

liked to eat at Bombay India on 125th Street, picking up new musical ideas from the Indian music playing in the background.

More than any previous white politician in the city, Lindsay wanted to make a personal, one-to-one bond with the people of Harlem. To address problems, yes, but also to look in their eyes. In 1968, the entire United States faced a storm of passion and rage after the assassination of Dr. King, the King of Peace. Lindsay rushed up to Harlem, not to enforce order but to meet people, to be present. When rioting broke out on 125th Street, he told the police to let the windows be shattered and the stores looted. Rage needed its outlet and clashes between police and Harlemites would only enflame the city. New York survived the summer more peacefully than anyone could have expected. The next summer, while the world's media focused on the Woodstock music festival, Lindsay was one of the handful of white people who instead attended the Harlem Cultural Festival—

In Washington Square, groups from the Left viewed Lindsay's administration as far too moderate.

The Fifth Dimension • Abbey Lincoln •
The Edwin Hawkins Singers • George Kirby •
Olatunji • Max Roach / **June 29**
Mahalia Jackson • The Staple Singers •
Herman Stevens & The Voices of Faith •
Reverend Jesse Jackson & the Operation
Breadbasket Band / **July 13**
Stevie Wonder • David Ruffin • Chuck Jackson •
Gladys Knight & the Pips •
Lou Parks Dancers / **July 20**
Mongo Santamaria • Ray Barretto •
Cal Tjader • Herbie Mann • Harlem Festival
Calypso Band / **July 27**
Nina Simone • B. B. King • Hugh Masakela •
Harlem Festival Jazz Band / **Aug. 17**
Miss Harlem Pageant • La Rocque Bey & Co. •
Listen My Brothers & Co. / **Aug. 24**

TONY LAWRENCE HOST,

Harlem
Cultural
Festival
1969

SUNDAYS 3 P.M. MT. MORRIS PARK • ADMISSION FREE
SPONSORED BY THE PARKS, RECREATION AND CULTURAL AFFAIRS ADMINISTRATION
OF THE CITY OF NEW YORK AND MAXWELL HOUSE COFFEE

As the title of the documentary *Summer of Soul (. . . Or When the Revolution Could Not Be Televised)* indicates the festival should be much better known. You can hear and see a clip of Nina Simone at the event through the media link.

the so-called Black Woodstock—which remains almost unknown and unreported to this day. But even as Lindsay walked the streets of Harlem, the other side of New York's long struggle with race emerged. If he was too liberal and white for Black nationalists, he was far too friendly with African Americans for a whole swath of white New Yorkers who were just beginning to show their voice and political power.

Lindsay won the election in 1965 against two opponents, a Democrat and, on the Conservative ticket, the witty, combative columnist William F. Buckley. Buckley shared a birth date (four years earlier) and alma mater with Lindsay, and little else. Committed to civil rights, Lindsay saw the problem of race as central to the nation's future. When the Selma, Alabama, police clubbed John Lewis and his fellow marchers, Buckley blamed the press for not giving equal coverage to what he saw as provoca-tions from the demonstrators—as if both sides were equally to blame. Lindsay was a liberal Protestant; Buckley was an observant Catholic. Lindsay intended to create a review board to examine police brutality. Buckley's campaign said that the city's problem was "*too much crime,* not too much police brutality" (italics in the original). Though Buckley came in last, he drew strong support in some parts of the city, such as Irish sections of Brooklyn and among the police.

Quill was a former Communist union leader, Buckley a wealthy conservative media personality. But both saw in Lindsay a version of that old trap that had led to such brutal clashes in nineteenth-century New York: an elite liberal who was beloved by fellow Manhattan intellectuals for his attention to African Americans while he ignored, insulted, and diminished the lives of working-class whites such as the descendants of the Irish famine. Quill and Buckley were not the only figures to recognize white working-class anger. By the 1970s, builders such as Fred Trump and his son Donald were being sued for preventing Black and Hispanic people from renting in their New York housing developments. Their determination to preserve white neighborhoods would prove to have national resonance in the twenty-first century—especially as even more New Yorkers began to demand to be recognized and heard.

A WOMAN'S PLACE

In the spring of 1963, a reporter who had graduated with honors from Smith College and worked for the *New York Times Magazine* applied for an unusual job—to be a "bunny" (a costumed cocktail waitress) at the Playboy Club in New York. She was not out to make extra cash, nor was she enticed by the club's promise that "when you become a bunny your world will be fun-filled, pleasant, and always exciting." Rather, Gloria Steinem was going undercover to investigate the working conditions and experiences of the women who took those jobs. She found that the women were constantly judged for every aspect of their appearance, had to undergo an internal examination from a gynecologist, and were instructed to be friendly and agreeable to men (to get them to order more drinks) but never agree to go out with a customer (unless he was a special customer, in which case to refuse him could cost you your job). In other words, they were "merchandized" as a product while earning far less than was promised. Steinem was showing how women were forced to wear clothes, mouth lines, and play roles to please men at the club. But the club was just a stark expression of patterns in all women's lives.

Steinem understood the role that the media played in setting the rules for women. In 1968, she shifted from being a reporter to being one of the creators of *New York* magazine, which would cover all aspects of city life. Two years later, she was one of a hundred women who took over the offices of *Ladies' Home Journal*. The magazine—with its recipes, home decorating tips, and advice columns that told women how to "save" their marriages by working harder to suppress their frustrations and to please their husbands—was read by more than fourteen million people a month. Yet one of the (male) editors had told Steinem that he pictured those readers as "mental defectives with curlers in their hair." A year later, Steinem was one of the founders of a new magazine that was the touchstone of a radically different understanding of women: *Ms.*

The term *Ms.* was just coming into usage to give women a way to define themselves that had nothing to do with whether they were single (*Miss*) or married (*Mrs.*). A Ms. might be single, single by choice, married with her own name, married with her husband's name—but none of that mattered. She was herself, defined by her own interests and accomplishments. To title a magazine *Ms.* was to announce that this would be a home for women to explore and define their own identities—much in the way that, today, the use of *they* as a singular pronoun is used by some to make clear that they are not defined by the binary categories of male or female. Since the early days of the twentieth century, Manhattan had provided space for women to carve out careers in areas such as fashion, theater, publishing, cosmetics, and retail. *Ms.* magazine was another example of New York at work—the entire nation was now invited to try out and even surpass the kind of independent living and professional goals women had achieved in Manhattan. "For women throughout the country," remembered Professor Carolyn Heilbrun, "it was mind-blowing. Here was, written down, what they had not yet admitted they felt, had always feared to say out loud, and could not believe was now before their eyes, in public, for all to read."

In 1970, the year Steinem and others confronted *Ladies' Home Journal*, Bella Abzug challenged another image of male and female roles. She ran for a congressional seat against two men by using the slogan "This woman's place is in the House . . . the House of Representatives!" Sporting her signature wide-brimmed hat (which she had chosen since it looked more like something a man would wear), she won, representing Manhattan's liberal Upper West Side. When Abzug came to Washington and was sworn into office, she then held a second ceremony hosted by Shirley Chisholm from Brooklyn—the first female African American congressperson. Abzug earned her law degree at Columbia University and had a record of working for those who had little or no power. She brought that willingness to challenge convention to Washington. "I spend all day," she wrote in her journal, "figuring out how to beat the machine and knock the crap out of the political power structure." That is not how women had been trained to speak—

or even think—which made "battling Bella" a hero to some and an expression of everything wrong with feminism and New York to others.

Whether by demanding changes in language, creating new magazines, running for office, or being ready to confront the most entrenched forces in the nation, women in New York were creating new models for how to live. But at every turn, challenges to existing images of being a man, a woman, or someone who did not neatly fit either category brought both change and extreme resistance.

On June 28, 1969, police raided the Stonewall Inn, a bar on Christopher Street midway between the old site of Café Society and the apartment Dylan and Rotolo had shared. The bar was a haven for gay men and transgender people, and nearby were bars catering to lesbian women. While

This woman's place is in the House... the House of Representatives!

Bella Abzug for Congress.

Battling Bella brought the voice of Manhattan's liberal Upper West Side to Washington.

the police were usually bribed to stay away, the force still had the mandate to close bars where homosexuals gathered. This time the patrons—who had seen African Americans, women, college students, and Vietnam War protesters fight for their rights—fought back. Crowds of gay and transgender people filled the streets near Stonewall taunting the phalanx of riot police sent to contain them. Surging voices announced that to be gay was a right, expressing in public what Countee Cullen had written nearly fifty years earlier: "I love myself." Throughout the entire country, loving someone of your own gender was both socially condemned and against the law. Once again, the Village, New York, was on the forefront of demanding change. But this time the fierce demands on all sides were so strong, the city was at war with itself.

May 8, 1970. What a day for celebration—and despair. On this date, New York's teams completed their sweep of the nation's three major sports championships. In January 1969, the New York Jets, led by their brash, outspoken quarterback Joe Namath, were the first American Football League team to win a Super Bowl. The AFL was the young league that had lost the first two Super Bowls to the Green Bay Packers—the essence of solid, old-line football. Joe Namath's Jets changed that. By October, the impossible New York Mets—the National League baseball team given to the city in 1962 to replace the Dodgers and Giants, the team that had set a record by losing 120 games its first year—won the World Series. And on the May 8, the New York Knicks—coached by Red Holzman, whose coaching roots went back to the beginning of basketball in the city, and led by the heroic Willis Reed, the Ivy League Bill Bradley, and Walt Frazier, whose sartorial style emblemized the fashionable city—won the National Basketball Association championship. All three teams spoke for a city that was alive, young, interracial, breaking old ways, and embodying the energy and passion of the age. And on this date, the city broke apart.

A few minutes before noon, a thousand college and even high school students gathered at Wall Street to speak out against the Vietnam War. Two hundred

This photo taken from the Federal Hall National Memorial on Wall Street shows the rioting construction workers attacking people who were protesting against the war in Vietnam.

The *Daily News* headline and accompanying photos celebrate the World Champion New York Knicks—the joyous opposite of the Hard Hat riot.

construction workers from nearby sites descended on them, smashing anyone they could with tools used as weapons. Many of the students were either children of the same kind of elite families who had supported abolition in the nineteenth century or the Jewish left-wing social critics of the twentieth century. Many of the construction workers were descended from the same kind of working-class white families who had despised the wealthy abolitionists and their causes.

Peter J. Brennan, the president of the Building and Construction Trades Council of Greater New York, sided with his men and supported the war and President Nixon. Lindsay's clash with Quill was now being fought on the streets. Rather than symbolizing a shared vision of working-class solidarity, union membership was split into camps: conservative, largely white groups who supported the war, and liberal, increasingly Black and Hispanic unions who opposed it.

SHATTERED

The final blow to the longstanding New York ideal of integration took place on 128th Street and Madison Avenue. Everyone could see that there was only one pathway to a better future for the city's poor: education. New York was proud of how its public schools and City University had taught generations of the children of immigrants and given them pathways to success. The city, though, had never served African American or Puerto Rican children well. A gleaming new middle school, the most expensive ever built, now stood in Harlem, near both under-served communities. The city promised that it would be integrated, half white people and half Black people. Yet by 1966, not one white family had sent their child to attend it. The city claimed the school was integrated since it consisted of half Black students and half Puerto Rican students, but no one fell for that excuse.

Harlem parents had had enough. If the city could not integrate its schools, they wanted to take control for themselves. They insisted that local parents and officials should select the teachers, choose the curriculum, control their own budget. The powerful teachers' union, many of whose members were Jewish, saw the demands as the opposite of everything they had spent their lives fighting for: teaching as a profession with shared standards and protected jobs where no local voice could overrule a citywide contract. The fight over local control of schools split New York City's Left, liberal, and even former-Communist Jews from the spokespeople of local control and Black nationalism. New York, the home of mixture, was also the seedbed of ethnic separation, whether in Black Harlem or white Queens.

In the mid-1970s, seemingly all the forces in the city that had built Manhattan were at odds, and the city stood on the brink of collapse.

"FORD TO CITY: DROP DEAD"
October 30, 1975

The *New York Daily News* headline spelled the death of the city. New York was out of money, and the president was not willing to bail it out. Lenders were no longer willing to trust the city to make good on the billions of dollars it owed. On the edge of bankruptcy, New York might default on its obligations at any moment. Who could trust New York?

New York was just different from the rest of the country. The city behaved as if FDR were still president and its partner in New Deal spending. The actual president was Gerald Ford, a Republican football hero from Michigan who had pardoned Richard Nixon even after the former president was shown to have broken the law. As the city's critics saw it, New York was like an angry teenager: it spent with a free hand, expecting to be bailed out while flaunting its distinct set of values. Was the rest of the state, the nation, ready to help out this city that was so determined to set its own rules? Did America really need New York City?

No. "The people of this country will not be stampeded," said the president. "They will not panic when a few desperate New York officials and bankers try to scare New York's mortgage payments out of them." The country would rather let New York's finances crumble than give it financial life support. While Ford later changed his mind, his initial reaction—and the great newspaper headline—galvanized both the city's friends and those who stood to lose if it collapsed. New York State, for one, would be dragged down if the city went under. Governor Hugh Carey appointed a group of fiscal wise men, headed by Felix Rohatyn, an astute Wall Street investment banker, to save the city. Rohatyn's group put together a plan: they did get money from Ford, but they also forced all the actors in the city to the negotiating table. Unions agreed to scale back contracts and key unions agreed to use their own pension funds to support the city. The city began charging tuition at its public university, diminishing its welfare payments, and holding back on its public housing projects. A diminished, chastened city rose from the dead and had new stories to tell the world. But the pathway to the city's future had actually been laid out ten years earlier.

THE MESSAGE
October 3, 1965

President Lyndon Johnson was seated at a table in the open air beneath the Statue of Liberty. He was there to sign a bill that Congressman Emanuel Celler of Brooklyn had been working to pass for forty-three years. Celler was first elected to Congress in 1922, just in time to see the nation close its doors to immigrants like his Jewish grandparents. Now, with Johnson's signature, those restrictive quotas established in 1924 would be adjusted. The framers of the bill wanted to make a nod to more open immigration while still controlling entry. The golden door swung wider than they expected, and New York City would come alive as the receptive home to a new wave of immigration. Between 1970 and 2011, the percentage of New Yorkers born in other lands more than doubled, from 18 to 37 percent. There are now more immigrants in New York than people in Chicago. Not only was the city being revived by new immigrants, but the newcomers hailed from a vast array of new lands. The 1965 act invited East and South Asians, Central and South Americans, Caribbeans, and, for the first time, Africans to come to America, to New York, by choice. New New Yorkers gave the city new life.

Fidel Castro's revolutionary ideas gained some traction in New York, but the main effect of his government was to block direct connections between Cuba and America—except for refugees who managed to escape. Cubans who fled the island brought their musical ideas to Puerto Rico, and from there new versions of Cuban music reached New York, where African American and jazz influences were added and a fresh musical style was born. By the mid-1960s, and led by the Fania record label, bandleaders such as Tito Puente, Eddie Palmieri, and Willie Colón and the singer Celia Cruz created a new term and new kind of music: salsa. New York as the birthplace of salsa was just one way in which the city increasingly became a center of pan-Hispanic creativity. The rumble of the city's streets might bother accountants, but it inspired artists.

We can name the date and place where the city gave birth to another new kind of music—which allowed more and more young people to tell their stories in sound and words. New York's new open door once again brought people from

President Johnson signed the new immigration act against the apt, and dramatic, backdrop of New York Harbor.

the Caribbean to the city, including Clive Campbell, who arrived from Jamaica with his family in 1967. Six years later on August 11, at a party at 1520 Sedgewick Avenue in the Bronx that he was hosting to help his sister earn money for back-to-school clothes, Campbell (who would later be known as DJ Kool Herc) began the scratching and mixing of records that came to be called hip-hop. Life in the city was like this new music—one sound mixing with another, a track starting, going backward, being interrupted, joined by another. The mixmaster, the DJ, was the creator.

Beginning in 1972, the Nuyorican Poets Café (now located at 236 East Third Street) gave a home to poets ready to declaim their words and compete in poetry "slams" that have become internationally popular. Poets like Gil Scott-Heron and those at the Nuyorican Café were drawing on the traditions of African griots via the insult contests called "the dozens" and telling stories to beats—rapping about what they saw all around them. Grandmaster Flash and the Furious Five gave voice to their city—dangerous, crumbling, but exploding with power and the determination to survive—in "The Message." Smashed, abandoned, burning, the city's streets were, nonetheless, alive. Young people used every tool at hand—plastic tubs turned into drums, old records scratched, break dancing, rhymes—to recount headlines and portray love affairs. Armed with spray cans, graffiti artists "tagged" walls, storefronts, schoolyards, and subway cars. All faced arrest and worse if they were caught. But as artists such as Keith Haring and Jean-Michel Basquiat blurred boundaries between forbidden crime and the most highly praised (and valued) painting, yet another form of expression arose from the streets. New York's young creators used the cheapest tools—words, spray paint, whatever objects they could find—to tell their stories. As neighborhoods struggled, rap and graffiti gave a platform and a voice to the new city—and the nation. Destruction breeding creation: New York.

UNION SQUARE

The perfect example of New York City's decay was Union Square in the 1970s. Labor Day was no longer celebrated in the city with a parade—not enough people cared to come. The old union headquarters still ringed the square, but the city's fiscal crisis and a shift in national mood eroded their power. Since 1906, the commercial heart of the neighborhood had been the giant department store S. Klein's, which faced the east side of the square. In 1975, the store closed and the building remained locked and empty. No one wanted the space. The park was given over to those desperate enough to use it: the homeless—an expanding group as the city cut back on welfare—drug addicts, dealers, and thieves. Union Square was becoming a kind of ghost town, the relic of a left-wing New York that no longer thrived.

Perhaps it was the decline of the tattered neighborhood or its appropriately low rents that drew his attention; in 1968, Andy Warhol decided to move his silver-lined art space, the Factory, to 33 Union Square. Warhol was the precise opposite of the Abstract Expressionists who had recently filled the nearby Cedar Tavern. His art was about echoing the flatness of advertisements, not expressing inner feelings. Warhol's circle at the Factory included its own dealers, addicts, and cross-dressers. But his world overlapped with fashion, wealth, and advertising, and his crew were seen as stars. The Factory was the Deuce, "The Message," all over again—life born out of ashes. Across Union Square from the Factory stood the restaurant favored by Warhol, Max's Kansas City. Upstairs at Max's, glam rock began. And then in 1976, the park was reborn.

A small group of farmers decided to follow up on an idea that had first been tried on Fifty-Ninth Street: selling their upstate produce to city dwellers. The farmers weren't making enough money selling locally, and Manhattan seemed like it could use some fresh, homegrown produce. The Union Square Greenmarket became a spectacular success, not only in drawing ever-larger crowds but in inspiring chefs to build entire menus around its offerings. Restaurants such as the Union Square Cafe (owned by the creator of Shake Shack) began to fill in the streets around the square. Instead of a location to avoid, Union Square was becoming, once again, a destination. And New York was becoming, once again, a world city.

CHAPTER **29**

Windows on the World

WALL STREET

Felix Rohatyn and his fellow fiscal wizards stabilized the city and got it on its feet just in time for dramatic shifts in the global economy. In the late 1970s, more and more large companies became multinational corporations that would outsource their office work and send their manufacturing jobs anywhere in the world that offered good, cheap labor. In a modern, expanded, and international version of the piecework that had brought ready-made clothes to Stewart's department store in the nineteenth century, products were now made in factories scattered across continents, then assembled and shipped to key markets. Call centers in India handled problems in Des Moines. These global webs of interconnected commerce—as well as the equally intricate pools of wealth they created—were managed from headquarters in just a few world cities: New York, London, Tokyo. The city was about to fulfill banker Frank Vanderlip's promise and become the "wellspring of capital for the world."

The shining representative of the new city was the twin towers of the World Trade Center. At 110 stories, they hosted five hundred businesses employing fifty thousand people and eclipsed the Empire State Building. The North Tower was topped by a restaurant on the 106th and 107th floors called Windows on the World. Staffed by people speaking sixty languages and graced with the most spectacular views, the restaurant was "a symbol of the beginning of the turn-around of New York."

Being a major hub of global investment brought money back to New York and fundamentally changed the city. In 1977, top earners in the city earned ten times more than the lowest-paid New Yorkers. Nine years later, that gap doubled. By 2012, the top 5 percent in the city earned eighty-eight times as much as the entire bottom 20 percent—the largest gap in the entire country. New York, which had gone broke trying to provide for all, now catered to those who were global, educated, and rich.

Young professionals working on Wall Street needed places to live—in their single lives and then with their growing families. One by one, neighborhoods that had been decaying, abandoned by manufacturers, wholesalers, and factories, filled in with new restaurants, new art galleries, new trendy shops, new lofts, and refurbished housing. When the city had emptied during the crisis years of the early '70s, laws limiting or controlling rents were weakened, which meant

money could change a neighborhood. But the New Yorkers who were gentrifying the city did not want to rent at all. A city of renters paying low rates designed to protect those with limited incomes was changing into a city of buyers paying high, higher, and still higher market rates to own apartments and townhouses. High prices then sent young people, artists, and those without corporate incomes to Brooklyn, Queens, and beyond to find affordable spots. As the new New Yorkers arrived from Asia and the Caribbean, they, too, revived working-class neighborhoods in the same outer boroughs.

In 1987, S. Klein's was developed into a large complex of apartments that were sold, not rented, and was soon joined by dorms for New York University students across the park. Union Square was now abuzz with people day and night. Robert Moses had wanted to knock

The twin towers of the World Trade Center under construction in January 1971

down stretches of the Village to link his highways. Residents fought and defeated him—and managed to preserve many of their buildings. As the city grew wealthier, small buildings with interesting histories made Village real estate valuable. Artists, actors, and musicians still lived in the Village—if they were successful enough to be able to live next door to their neighbors, the top models, lawyers, and financiers.

Because of the city's longstanding commitment to integration and unionization, the new wealth created a new middle class. Since 1957, New York had forbidden discrimination in all housing, public and private. By 1965, the city's Commission on Human Rights began actively working to open jobs to all applicants regardless of race, religion, color, or national origin. Once there was something resembling a level playing field, especially in government jobs, African Americans began to experience an economic rise. Between 1977 and 1989, the Black middle class—located primarily in sections of Queens—grew faster than the white middle class. Clerical and hospital workers, many of whom were Hispanic or African American, joined unions that helped to defend and enhance their wages and benefits. To this day, 21 percent of the city's workforce is unionized, which is more than double the national average. By 1984, Luis Miranda, who had emigrated from Puerto Rico at age seventeen, became the director of the Office of Hispanic Affairs. When not working, he enjoyed sharing his love of Broadway musicals with his family. Yet even as the city recovered financially, it faced a health emergency on an unimaginable scale, one that seemed to challenge everything the city stood for.

SILENCE = DEATH

In the early 1980s, John Blair owned a bodybuilding gym on Sixth Avenue near Union Square that was frequented by gay men. In 1981, one of the particularly handsome, fit trainers suddenly became ill and left the city to return home to his family in Pennsylvania. Four months later, the young man, now looking skeletal and ancient, was dead. The *New York Times* announced in an ominous headline, "Rare Cancer Seen in 41 Homosexuals." By the end of the year, 162 cases of the strange disease had been reported in the city, and seventy-four people had died.

After the Stonewall protests, many New Yorkers had changed their attitudes toward homosexuality, but there were Americans whose views had not changed. Those people were sure they knew the source of the disease. Just as the moralists of the 1800s had blamed residents of the Five Points for contracting cholera and tuberculosis, some highly visible evangelical Christians saw the deaths as a form of divine judgment. Even for those outside of the city who understood that disease is a result of biology not theology, the growing epidemic in New York was a sign of how different the city was from the nation. Acquired immunodeficiency syndrome (AIDS) was identified and given a name in 1982, the same year that an activist group called the Gay Men's Health Crisis formed in the city. But President Ronald Reagan refused to use the acronym AIDS until 1985, three years later. By then, Ryan White, a thirteen-year-old boy from Indiana, had contracted the disease through a blood transfusion. Scientists already knew that the human immunodeficiency virus (HIV) could be passed through sexual activity, through the blood supply, through the needles shared by drug users, and from pregnant mothers to their unborn children. But Ryan's story—and his and his mother's fight to allow him to continue to attend school, which had initially banned him even though HIV cannot be passed through casual contact—began to change public perception of the issue. The disease was indeed a terrible killer that could only be combated by intense medical research, safe-sex practices, the spreading of awareness and knowledge, and caring treatment. It was not a divine judgment; it was an immense human tragedy—and challenge.

New York—and especially the communities in which gay men and trans people had flourished, such as dance, fashion, and theater—was devastated by AIDS. There were 1,960 AIDS-related deaths in the city by 1984, which nearly doubled to 3,766 the following year, and doubled again to 6,458 in 1986, reaching 24,835 in 1990. In 1995, AIDS was the largest cause of death for men aged twenty-five to forty-four nationwide. Yet some progress had been made in developing medications to combat the disease and, for the first time, deaths declined the following year. This good news also came with bad news: the majority of new cases in America were now African American men. The more people were informed about how to prevent infection, where and how to be tested, and what medications and treatments were available, and the more affordable those drugs were, the slower the rates of transmission and infection. Still, AIDS spread rapidly through the most vulnerable and least protected parts of the population.

The gay community in New York recognized that combating AIDS would require being all the more active and visible—not retreating into the shadows. If Stonewall was an assertion of individual pride and belonging, the AIDS crisis now helped shape gay men into a self-conscious, mature community. In 1987, the AIDS Coalition to Unleash Power (ACT UP) began demonstrating to demand more money for research and to speed up clinical trials of medications. Their slogan, "Silence = Death," was the essential truth of the epidemic. The problem was not whom a person loved; it was what a person knew about protecting themselves against the virus that causes AIDS and what treatments a suffering individual could afford. One drug, AZT, had been shown to slow the progress of AIDS, but it was impossibly expensive and had its own toxic effects. ACT UP, the Gay Men's Health Crisis, and the press around high-profile celebrities living with the disease, such as the basketball star Earvin "Magic" Johnson, began to spread understanding of how to avoid, treat, and combat AIDS.

St. Vincent's Hospital was located in the heart of the Village and had treated men beaten at Stonewall. It created a ward entirely devoted to AIDS, only the second hospital in the entire country to do so (the first was in San Francisco). While some administrators, doctors, nuns, and nurses shared biases against gay people, there were also extremely dedicated people of all professions and faiths who gave everything to patients in that ward. Nurse Maureen Satriano recalled, "It was the hardest I ever worked, but it was the best job I ever had.

This poster was the stark and urgent message of activists fighting the spread of AIDS.

You were making a difference to someone every single minute of your shift." Noel George, another nurse, added, "Once you came into the ward, it was like you stepped into another place. There was warmth and love and compassion. The nun who ran the unit—Sister Patricia—was full of love." This was another form of the city at its best—in the heart of an epidemic, people who would otherwise never meet were bonded in love.

As ever, New York's artists used their talents to tell the many devastating stories of the new plague. In 1993, Tony Kushner's epic play *Angels in America* opened on Broadway and explored the many layers of the epidemic. *Angels in America* is eloquent, passionate, nightmarish, and beautiful in the same way that *The Iceman Cometh* had been for an earlier generation. Whether in political demonstrations or onstage, the city found a voice to speak, even in the face of unspeakable tragedy. New York was not the problem; it was, as the play shows, the prophet. And the city was ready to tell new stories on Broadway.

BEAUTY AND THE BEAST SAVES FORTY-SECOND STREET
March 1993

One crucial part of the city seemed to resist all efforts at improvement: the Deuce. Or did it need fixing? The theaters showing porn films and the stores offering peep shows were making good money. Hustlers, sex workers, addicts, and those buying their services owned the street. If you came there, you walked fast, or knew what to expect. That made Forty-Second Street a fine backdrop for intense movies such as *Taxi Driver* and *Midnight Cowboy* (and, later, in homage to those films and that moment in the city's life, *Joker*) but a disaster for a reviving city. Plans to build gleaming office buildings sputtered. And Rebecca Robertson, a state official in charge of redeveloping the area, realized that much of the street "was in ruins, but there's something more powerful about ruins than any reality." Then, in 1991, the Walt Disney Company released the crowd-pleasing animated film *Beauty and the Beast*. Michael Eisner, head of Disney, saw an opportunity: If the film was so popular, could Disney create a live theatrical version? And if so, where would it, and other Disney musicals, play?

One fine March day in 1993, Eisner, his wife, and their two teenage

The New Amsterdam Theatre in 1905, two years after it first opened

sons, accompanied by colleagues of Robertson's and the architect Robert Stern, cracked open the doors of the relic that had once been Forty-Second Street's New Amsterdam Theatre. "We could see water leaking from the roof," Eisner recalled, "birds nesting in the ceiling, puddles mingled with rubble on the floor." The theater was a ghost of itself—with hints of its "lavish grandeur" still visible through the grime. Eisner liked it.

Disney—the very symbol of the suburban, California life that rejected Manhattan—was going to come to Forty-Second Street, but how? One idea was to seal off the street and turn it into a theme park—a Main Street New York the way Main Street in Disneyland is meant to echo small-town USA. But could you really do that on a public street in the biggest city in the nation? Disney realized it couldn't control every inch of the Deuce. Instead, it agreed to refurbish the theater so long as others followed. Madame Tussauds wax museum and the AMC movie theater chain were happy to agree. Forty-Second Street would come alive, not as bland office towers, nor as a spanking-clean Disney park. As the porn shops were swept away, a new generation's lights, sounds, ads, and attractions would take over. First, the New Amsterdam was lovingly revived and *Beauty and the Beast* set new records for musical success. In 1996, the New Victory, designed to feature attractions for children, opened next door. When *The Lion King* opened at the New Amsterdam the next year, it was the first new show to use the space in forty-one years and went on to surpass even *Beauty and the Beast*. Since then, *The Phantom of the Opera* quadrupled *Fiddler*'s run and is still playing. Theater was back on Forty-Second Street.

In its bones, Forty-Second Street is meant for spectacle, crowds, and light. If the new street would no longer be Hammerstein's turn-of-the-century operas and roof gardens, or the tea dances and jazz clubs of the '20s, or the palm readings and Runyonesque slang of the '30s and '40s, or the porn and peep shows of the '60s and '70s, it would be big, loud, and alive. As Robertson said when the new theaters began to open, "When we're done, we'll have sixty different tenants on Forty-Second Street, arguing, fighting for product and advertising space." And that is precisely what it is today. Some New Yorkers hate what came to be called the "Disneyfication" of Times Square. They find it too safe, too tame, too family-friendly. They miss the raw edge of the Deuce. But the Forty-Second Street of today is both a reasonable descendant of its prior incarnations and suited to the safer, richer city of SUVs, farmers markets, and strollers that surrounds it.

A TUESDAY IN SEPTEMBER 2001

The morning of the eleventh was one of the city's joys: clear blue skies with wisps of high clouds, just the right balance of ebbing summer's warmth and a hint of arriving fall chill. Michael Lomonaco, the chef at Windows on the World, was downstairs between the towers on an errand. Offices in both towers were filled, the streets buzzing with employees rushing to get to work, guests about to enter the buildings for early appointments.

At 8:46 a.m., a jet filled with twenty thousand gallons of fuel crashed into the North Tower. Reporters rushed to the scene, some aware that a small plane, lost in the fog, had banged into the Empire State Building in 1945. This was different. The hit was on the eightieth floor of the building—a gash, a wound, that did not look like an accident. Terrified workers in the floors above and below the flames desperately searched for the endless stairways down to safety. At 9:03 a.m., a second jet turned sharply and sliced into the South Tower. This was no accident; it was an orchestrated attack on the city and its shining symbol of international wealth and power. As firefighters rushed into the collapsing towers and people began leaping from the high windows, the steel and glass crumbled into rubble.

Reports came in of a plane crashing into the Pentagon near Washington, DC, and another down in a Pennsylvania field, and the scale of the assault became

September 11, 2001

The attack on the World Trade Center left a gouged skyline: a giant wound reminding every-one of the thousands of lives lost.

Smoke billowing from the twin towers announced the unfolding tragedy.

Above: Inhaling air turned gray with falling ash, firefighters searched for survivors and remains.

Right and below: The terrorists' attack reduced the proud towers to mountains of twisted steel and broken concrete. Workers searched the debris for any sign of the thousands of people who had been in the buildings.

clear. Were there more to come? Who was behind this? Was the city safe? And what of those in the burning, collapsing towers? Stores were filled with people hurrying to stock up on supplies. New Yorkers shared scraps of information and advice—what they'd heard, what they knew, where to go, how to get around in a city on high alert. Strangers became instant friends. While there were scattered assaults on Muslims and police surveillance of Muslim communities, much of the city rejected those expressions of prejudice and blame. For many New Yorkers, the assault made them value the multiracial city all the more.

The radio announced that first responders could use blood, cell phone chargers, bottled water for the many injured people they expected would require care. Yet as volunteers arrived at central spots to bring whatever they could carry, word started to filter through. The medical staff wouldn't need first-aid supplies. There weren't enough injured survivors. Most of the victims weren't hurt—they were dead.

Night after night, military planes flew over the city; New York was at war, alert for the next raid. Everyone was on edge, scared. And then, slowly, the city began to gather itself and to heal. Marchers holding candles wove their way to Riverside Park next to the Hudson, five miles up from where the towers had stood. They sang Irving Berlin's hymn to America and Woody Guthrie's "This Land Is Your Land," as well as "We Shall Overcome" and "America the Beautiful." When the crowd reached the lyric "and crown thy good with brotherhood," the phrase was a kind of anthem for a city that had been attacked, was under assault by some group who hated that vision, that version of how to live.

The terrorists who guided the planes into the towers aimed to destroy everything the World Trade Center and New York stood for: Wall Street, the global economy, American power, but also the city where people of every faith and from throughout the world had come to survive and prosper. The terrorists did indeed murder thousands, but they failed.

A total of 2,753 people are known to have died when the towers crumbled (and in its aftermath), the worst terrorist assault in our nation's history, including 343 firemen and -women, 71 from the police, and 79 employees of Windows on the World. Twelve percent of the victims, some 372 individuals, were citizens of foreign lands. To this day, we do not know how many undocumented immigrants lost their lives. Many of those victims did not have identifying information on them, and some families still need to stay silent about their absence for fear of attracting the attention of the authorities.

The 9/11 attacks changed the country, the world. The United States has been at war somewhere in the Middle East ever since then. We line up to take out laptops and pass through metal detectors at airports. The fear we felt in those September days is echoed anywhere in the world when there is a new attack. And yet each time, people rally and remind themselves of what they share, of what they stand for. For many, though not all, New Yorkers, 9/11 strengthened their commitment to our heritage of being open to the world.

A HARVARD GRADUATE ANNOUNCES THE ASIAN CITY

On December 27, 2011, the New York Knicks made an entirely forgettable announcement. While Iman Shumpert, one of their key players, recovered from an injury, they were going to give a young man who had done well in college but hadn't been drafted a chance to play. He'd fill in for the next week or so and then be released. But on February 4, Jeremy Lin surprised everyone by scoring twenty-five points against the New Jersey Nets. Six days later, just when everyone expected him to be dropped from the team, he hit a new high of thirty-eight points. "Linsanity" had officially begun. Lin, who was born in California to parents from Taiwan and China, became the first player of Chinese American background to play professional basketball. His electrifying play brought a new audience to watch the Knicks in person and on every available television screen. Basketball, which had linked white and Black New York via subways and playgrounds in the 1960s and '70s, now served as an announcement and embodiment of the increasingly Asian city. Ever since 1965, Chinese, Koreans, Filipinos, Japanese, and South Asians from India, Bangladesh, and Pakistan had been making New York their home, spreading from the old Chinatown in Manhattan along the number 7 subway line through Queens and to Sunset Park in Brooklyn. There are now more than one million Asians in New York—by far the most in any American city, and indeed the most in any city outside of Asia.

Chinatown and the Asian City Today

East and South Asian communities can now be found throughout New York City. While Manhattan's Chinatown is still a tourist attraction, it is also a vibrant community that serves the needs of its own residents.

Winding, narrow Pell Street has been at the heart of Chinatown since the earliest days of the neighborhood.

Signs and advertisements in Chinese are as welcoming for current immigrants as Yiddish signs were for arriving Jews in the early 1900s.

Fresh greens selected for local tastes spill out from markets onto street-side stands.

Right: Chinatown Rockits basketball club members cheering on their team at PS 1 Alfred E. Smith Elementary School

Left: Opening tip-off of the youth basketball league at PS 1 Alfred E. Smith Elementary School

Championship Day at the We Run As One youth basketball league hosted by the Dynasty Project and Apex for Youth in Chinatown

LA CAPITAL

New York, a Puerto Rican commentator named Luis Rafael Sánchez has written, would be the second capital of his island if it were not already "the capital of all of Spanish America." The shifts in population that came with the Immigration and Nationality Act of 1965 made New York not only a national leader in Spanish-speaking life and culture, but one of five world centers of Spanish-influenced culture (along with Barcelona, Madrid, Mexico City, and Buenos Aires). Los Angeles has more Spanish speakers, but they are predominantly from Mexico, as the Spanish-speaking population of Miami was historically and still is significantly Cuban. New York brings together Puerto Ricans, Dominicans, Mexicans, Ecuadorans, Colombians, and people from every Spanish-speaking land to be—once again—mixed together, and then to find ways to speak their stories to the world.

Luis Miranda's son, Lin-Manuel, always knew he wanted to tell stories. As a child he made flip-books, in college he joined a hip-hop comedy group, and then he found his voice in musicals. He began working on a show about his own neighborhood while in college, and *In the Heights* reached Broadway in 2008. That same year, after reading a biography of Alexander Hamilton while he was in Puerto Rico, Miranda began working on "My Shot," a song that was about his father and all of the city's hungry immigrants. The song was the seed of *Hamilton*, the rap musical he finally brought to Broadway in 2015. Lin-Manuel had grown up endlessly listening to Broadway musicals on vinyl records. He knew the format inside and out, even supplying new lyrics in Spanish for a revival of *West Side Story* in 2009 and quoting "You've Got to Be Carefully Taught" from *South Pacific* in "My Shot," but he used the musical language of his city. What *Fiddler* had done for the story of Jews and all of the city's early twentieth-century immigrants, *Hamilton*—using the rhythms, beats, and aggressive assertion of rap—did for twenty-first-century strivers.

Hamilton, the musical, brings us back to Alexander Hamilton, the man, and the long arcs of possibility and division in New York City.

Latin Manhattan

New York City is home to a great many distinct communities that are linked by heritage, language, or birth to Spanish-speaking countries. In Manhattan, the two largest groups are the long-established Puerto Ricans and the newer Dominican center at the tip of the island in Washington Heights. Both groups have faced challenges from poverty, racism, and gentrification, and both have deep resources of culture, activism, and self-expression.

Residents of East Harlem (El Barrio) welcoming the Northeast Contingent of the Poor People's Campaign (led by Dr. King) as they march to a rally in Central Park on their way to Washington DC to join Resurrection City on May 11, 1968.

Frank Espada photographed the Puerto Rican diaspora throughout the United States, capturing these musicians in Manhattan.

After the killing of Jose "Kiko" Garcia, an undocumented immigrant from the Dominican Republic, by an undercover police officer in 1992, protests swept across upper Manhattan and down to Tompkins Square in the Lower East Side.

Fifteen-year-old Lesandro Guzman-Feliz was killed by a gang in a case of mistaken identity. The community gathered to honor him, and a street corner has been given his name.

The Dominican Day Parade expresses the community's pride and presence in the city.

Led Black, who shares news, art, and culture through the Uptown Collective site, speaking with Carolina "Miss Rizos" Contreras at the opening of the Juan Pablo Duarte Community Space. Portraits of Duarte, one of the founders of the Dominican Republic, frame the event.

This mural in the Heights honors the many frontline workers in the community who have taken care of others during the COVID-19 pandemic.

CHAPTER 30

New York and the Nation, Two Versions

You could see this entire pageant of New York City history as a set of dialogues between pairs of streets: Wall Street versus Union Square—the grandees versus the people. Forty-Second Street versus West Fourth Street—commercial popular culture versus the experimental, critical artist. The rest of the city versus 125th Street—the segregation and prejudice that confined African Americans versus the nurturance African Americans found in their own community. And one more pairing: Hamilton, the man of principle and law, who wanted to keep power in the hands of the established, wealthy, educated class, versus Burr, the opportunist, who organized and gave voice to the white working class.

New York and the rest of the country are now more linked than ever before. Some still see New York as too immigrant, Black, Jewish, gay or lesbian, feminist, politically liberal. Yet after 9/11, the city seemed to stand for something essentially American. The gouged-out space where the towers stood is now a haunting black stone pool ever filling, ever emptying, its waters surrounded by the victims' names. Next to the pool, a proud tower stands 1,776 feet tall. Every day, thousands of visitors come to pay their respects. New York was ahead of much of the country in fighting racism, in embracing intermarriage, in advocating for the rights of gays, lesbians, the disabled, documented and undocumented immigrants. Slowly, in marches, protests, elections, media coverage, and Supreme Court decisions, a large swath of the rest of America has come to agree with the best of New York, while another large swath of the country has found its voice in the side of New York that has fought against that ideal.

Two ever-refilling pools now mark the footprints of what had been the North and South towers of the World Trade Center.

From blackface minstrelsy to jazz radio broadcasts, from Broadway musicals to *Ms.* magazine, from salsa to hip-hop, the media capital of New York has found local voices and given them a national audience, capturing and changing how the nation sees itself. New York did this for one of its own, the real estate developer, media star, and then president Donald Trump. New York gossip and celebrity columns focused on him when he was known for his partying and sequence of wives and girlfriends. New York book publishers eagerly promoted his (ghostwritten) books on making business deals. Fox News, based in New York, gives him a supportive media outlet. Key Wall Street leaders joined his cabinet and served his administration. And the white working-class New Yorkers that William F. Buckley courted were the seed of the national base Trump reached in the 2016 election. Those New Yorkers who saw African Americans as demanding, immigrants as threatening to steal jobs, intellectuals as snobbish and out of touch, feminists as harsh, the global economy that gave careers to MBAs as sucking jobs from the working class—they found their voice in Trump, as did their peers nationwide. Loud, opinionated, astute at using social networks and mass media, supported by the money his father made developing sites in the city, Trump is a New Yorker—even his move to Florida follows the path of his generation of older New Yorkers. Indeed, to his critics he epitomizes precisely what Hamilton said of his nemesis and fellow New Yorker Aaron Burr: he's an ambitious man who uses popular acclaim to be an "embryo-Caesar."

Trump represents a certain side of New York, and a challenge to the essence of the New York idea explored in this book—the creativity that comes from welcoming the world.

HARLEM

At 100 West 125th Street, just past the corner of Malcolm X Boulevard (Lenox Avenue) and Dr. Martin Luther King Jr. Boulevard (125th Street), stands a large Whole Foods. There has long been an interest in eating naturally among some in Harlem. But the stores that sold those products were tiny, local, and struggling—the opposite of a national chain owned by Amazon and found in every upscale zip code. Moving west along 125th, there are outlets for typical mall stores such as Banana Republic, T.J. Maxx, Burlington Coat Factory, the Gap. On the corner of Adam Clayton Powell Jr. Boulevard (Seventh Avenue), the large state office building houses an office of the William J. Clinton Foundation, though the former president's main office is near Wall Street. The Apollo with its Amateur Nights is still there, with its own foundation support. The Studio Museum in Harlem gives space to artists whose subject is Harlem or who live there. Along Malcolm X Boulevard are clusters of lively restaurants that nod to Harlem's soul food past (as exemplified by Sylvia's at 328) but with all sorts of new global spins. Harlem's central street honors Dr. King but exemplifies gentrification.

Central Harlem is getting whiter. Between 2000 and 2015, Central Harlem became 10 percent less Black. Mixture, as this book has argued all along, is what New York brings, but there is also danger and loss as communities change.

Stretches of Harlem are still poor, neglected, as removed as possible from the wealthy city of multimillion-dollar apartments. Harlem endured a century of prejudice and neglect, the ravages of which are still being felt. Is it really right for anyone with the cash to sweep in, refurbish a brownstone, and call the new Harlem home? Yet the newcomers do bring in money; shops and restaurants follow. Across 125th, many Harlems overlap. Market women in traditional African clothes sell from carts, young boys and elderly men hawk bottled water, groups of friends cluster to chat. The chain stores make Harlem less distinct than it once was. Yet considering how long it took the stores in white neighborhoods to open branches in Harlem, the chains are a sign of progress. Harlem is being knit back into the larger city—which is both an opportunity and a threat for its longtime residents.

MANHATTAN PRICES

There are consequences to being a wealthy world city. Manhattan is increasingly owned and populated by grandees. The ultra-rich who live in potentially unstable countries elsewhere park their money in America by buying Manhattan apartments and buildings for unthinkable tens and even hundreds of millions. Builders are using every available inch to construct ever-taller apartment buildings filled with upscale perks such as gyms, pools, and restaurants. The old railroad tracks in the West Thirties have been turned into Hudson Yards: a mini-city of gleaming towers that looks like the set of a science fiction film. New money and new buildings leave the island safe and comfortable—but in danger of losing its soul.

The high price of living in New York has had extreme consequences for children and education. Some studies have shown that the city has the most racially segregated public schools in the country, and the poorest neighborhoods remain disproportionately populated with Black and Latino people. This is a legacy of the city's long failure to create schools that fully blend families from different neighborhoods, backgrounds, and income levels. The clashes over integration in the 1960s were never resolved and are echoed again today. This is a disaster for the city of mixture, and several plans are being tried to address it. These kinds of splits have caused some to want to reject the entire direction of the city's economy.

On September 17, 2011, ten years after 9/11, activists began to occupy Zuccotti Park, steps away from the stock exchange, as a protest against Wall Street and the multinational corporations it finances. The Occupy movement rapidly spread throughout the country and beyond. It was more powerful as an expression of rage, and as an intense shared experience, than as a program. When the police removed the occupiers from the park in November, the movement faded. Yet the force of the protests showed a real unease at the race for wealth that is creating ever-steeper inequalities in the city, the nation, and indeed the world.

THE PANDEMIC

I had planned to end this book by glancing away from too-rich, too-expensive Manhattan to the wider city. But instead I am writing as the city, the nation, and the world face the unprecedented crisis of the COVID-19 pandemic; just at this moment, New York City is the global hotspot of infection and death. Medical studies show that the virus was spread to much of the nation by people who had contracted it in the city.

The pandemic challenges everything about New York City: global finance is frozen; all theaters, museums, galleries, restaurants are closed. Forty-Second Street is silent. The collective buzz of face-to-face conversation and creativity that is the very essence of the city cannot, must not, take place. Physical isolation is our only tool to slow the spread of the disease. Those of us who can, study, work, and communicate on screens, not streets.

Can Manhattan survive and revive after this blast of illness and death, after the shock to our economy that may well be as severe as the Great Depression? Is the globalism that is so central to the city now the most devastating danger?

Friends in Manhattan report that they hear only three sounds all day: no honking horns, no booming car radios, no planes—just silence, birds, and the wail of ambulances. But at 7 p.m. every evening, the silence ends. Throughout Manhattan, everyone from Broadway stars such as Brian Stokes Mitchell to the most scratchy-voiced neighbor leans out the windows, steps to the balconies, and claps, bangs pots, sings—to honor the health-care workers entering or leaving hospitals, risking their lives to care for the sick. Apartment dwellers clap, and bang, and sing in praise, in honor, in love. The pandemic workers are the modern version of African Americans who were caregivers in the 1822 pandemic or AIDS nurses at St. Vincent's, fighting death every day. The Manhattanites are also singing for themselves, to show that they, too, are alive, that they, too, must be visible and heard and seen; for those moments, they must join together.

Even as the pandemic forces us to isolate and shelter with our families, we experience how much we crave connection—and we use digital tools to see and speak with friends and relatives any- and everywhere. The physical separation that we must adhere to only confirms how much we need the kind of contact that is the heart of New York. That affirmation of determination to stick together, to share together, is how the city responded to 9/11, and it is how all of us are responding now. As much as it challenges Manhattan's future, the pandemic confirms its essence: the need for human contact.

The pandemic is also the sternest of warnings. Just as AIDS death rates revealed the most vulnerable in our society, the pandemic is an indictment. African Americans and Hispanics are dying at a much higher rate than others in many parts of the country, including New York. The race for wealth that one aspect of the city exemplified came at a devastating cost. We built a city and a nation without a true safety net for the jobs, lives, work, and health of all our citizens. That is what New York City aimed to do from the 1930s through the 1950s—though even that effort never fully embraced African Americans, or any people of color. One study argues that New York has done better than other large cities precisely because health care is more available for more people in the city, and the social safety net is stronger. But that is the point. Once the worst has passed—and I hope that is so by the time you read this—our task must be to rebuild from the bottom up. We can use the pandemic as a light to show us what we must fix—together. New York will always have finance, art, and culture, but the pandemic is reminding us what the city must also have: a soul. This is our chance to complete what the union city began—but this time with full inclusion of all people, all races, all ethnicities, all immigrants from any- and everywhere. The pandemic tells us we must be true to the city at its best, or we will face the worst.

As I write this, there is much discussion of the future for New York, for Manhattan. Has the pandemic accomplished what the suburban flight of the '60s, the economic crises of the '70s, the terrorist attack of 2001, and the global market crashes of 2002 and 2008 could not—sending the city into a death spiral? Will companies so rely on digital connection that they will not need expensive offices in the city? Without the tax revenue from those businesses (and all of the restaurants, taxis, clothing stores, theater and entertainment venues, and luxury markets that serve their employees), will the city shrink, grow dirtier, less appealing, more dangerous—sending more people scampering to welcoming leafy towns? That could happen. Indeed, many of the large retailers and restaurant chains—the kinds of companies that flocked to Manhattan in the wealthy 2000s and made it resemble malls everywhere—have left already. And yet the very threat to the city may point in another direction.

Expensive apartments are becoming cheaper. As of the summer of 2020, there was a higher percentage of unoccupied apartments in Manhattan than in any other area of the city, and rental prices had dropped an average of 10 percent. If this pattern continues, it will allow younger people, artists, immigrants, people who have recently been excluded to move in. As national brands and restaurants owned by corporations leave, space opens up for local businesses that reflect this population, this neighborhood, this moment. More and more streets in Manhattan are now only for walking and biking—no cars allowed. Outdoor restaurants and markets now fill what used to be car lanes. That is easier to do during a pandemic, but might Manhattan evolve into a giant walking, biking mall of creativity and culture? Imagine an island that would be similar to the national mall in Washington, DC, not devoted to politics or presidents but to theater, music, dance, and every possible sort of physical and digital mixture.

Pickup games and pickup bands, formal concerts and choreographed dances, voices from the entire city, the entire planet, exchanging rhythms and ideas and dreams in a space devoted to creativity and invention. That is what the best of Manhattan has always been—and, I hope, will be again.

When I began this book, I quoted my father as calling New York "the magic city"—constantly creating and re-creating itself out of the clash and confluence of its self-renewing resource: its people. New immigrants—Irish, Jews, Italians, African Americans, Hispanics, Asians—stream in and revitalize the city until others fight back in riots, politics, discriminatory laws, Americanization campaigns, restrictive quotas, plans for walls. Yet that clash of old and new yields art—musicals, anthems, raps that sweep across the nation. All the while, at the edges, old and new are actually blending in romance and families, in new forms of style and language and art. Clashes release energy, combination creates new energy, the city glows with life and is reborn—attracting new waves of people.

Looked at from the outside, the city should not make sense. Throughout history, people have sought comfort and security in sameness—living near people of similar beliefs, or wealth, or heritage, or hue. That's why the famous outsider phrase about the city is that it is a "great place to visit but I wouldn't want to live there." Guests want the products of the city without coming home to its polyglot streets. New Yorkers have tried separation as well. But then they are pressed back together by disease, or fire, or the mad dash to make money—or plain curiosity. We are close enough that even living separately makes us want to know what is going on over there, in that neighborhood. And then the cycle of friction, clash, creation, combination starts all over again. At any given moment, the city may be more at odds with itself or more pleased with itself; both are necessary. Conflict and creativity are what happen when people of every sort are crushed together and we lurch toward the future. Look at the skyline: the skyscrapers are the people's energy captured, crystallized, as we reach out, reach up for more wealth, more life, more. That's the magic of this city.

The organic city grows, splits, splinters, dies, and is reborn. New York is alive. When it is safe again, come walk its streets and bridges. Come see for yourself.

Manhattan Reaches for the Sky

Viewing Manhattan's evolving skyline is like watching a stop-motion film of a coral reef growing—adding crenelations, layers, and new shapes as it evolves, ever higher.

In 1908, the Woolworth building towered over the skyline.

By 1921, lower Manhattan had filled in with more high buildings.

A decade later, the Chrysler and Empire State Buildings created a new skyward tier.

By the 1940s, thin rectangles stretched upward amid the older pyramids of steel and concrete.

The 1960s and '70s saw anonymous window-filled cubes fill the sky and light up the night.

In 1972, when the World Trade Center was completed, the North Tower was the tallest building in the world.

Following Pages: Lower Manhattan as seen from Brooklyn Bridge Park. The towers compete to declare the wealth and ambition of the city.

TERMINOLOGY

There is much discussion today about language, the power of words, the right—even necessity—for people to define themselves. I recognize the importance of these conversations. However, outside of quotations or titles, where I follow the original author's usage, I have chosen to use the terms *African American* and *Black* even though in many of the periods I discuss, other words such as *Negro* or *colored* were more common. Similarly, the language of sex, sexual preference, and gender I use—*he/she, gay/lesbian*—was not always common and is being questioned and refined today. Several people have suggested that I use *people* rather than *men* and *women*, since the range of identities is not now and has never been captured by those two choices. I respect the concept, but in the times and places covered by this book, *man* and *woman* were so defining, both as social constructs and personal identities, that I think avoiding their use would be more confusing than helpful. But I do agree that in all times and places, individuals have found that those categories did not serve how they understood themselves. I use various terms for the original Americans, including *Indian,* both because that is one of the favored terms named in Roxanne Dunbar-Ortiz's *An Indigenous Peoples' History of the United States* (xiii) and because in speaking with members of various nations I have heard from those who prefer it—or, best, no collective term but just their own nation's name—to more recent and political formulations such as *Native American.* In most cases, I chose to use *Hispanic* for people culturally linked to Spanish-speaking lands and cultures even though some prefer versions of *Latinx. Hispanic* is the term used in the census documents I used to track the city's changing population, and echoing that makes it easier for others to make the connection between my narrative and those sources. I write in the language that is, I believe, clearest to the widest range of readers today. As usage changes, and if this book endures, I will consider adjusting the terminology.

AUTHOR'S NOTE
How I Researched and Wrote *Four Streets and a Square,* and Help I Was Given Along the Way

The initial idea that led to this book came to me some years ago when my wife and sometime coauthor, Marina Budhos, our two sons, and I were staying in my parents' house and I needed something to read. On their shelves of theater books, I found *The Merry Partners* by E. J. Kahn, a book from the 1950s about Harrigan and Hart—a nineteenth-century vaudeville duo I vaguely recognized. In *Yankee Doodle Dandy*, the movie about George M. Cohan that I list in multimedia link 14, there is a song, "Harrigan," that honors Cohan's predecessor. I heard it in the film as a child and I still find myself singing it at odd moments. The book talked about how their act made fun of, annoyed, engaged with, and portrayed the many ethnic groups in the city. As an 1886 essay said, Harrigan "shows us the street-cleaners and contractors, the grocery men, the shysters, the politicians, the washerwomen, the servant girls, the truckmen, the policemen, the risen Irishman and Irishwoman of contemporary New York." I began thinking about performance and New York's immigrant communities. What was the intersection of life, art, prejudice, role reversal, and affirmation—for the audience, for the performers, for the city, for the nation? That was the seed, and then there was the soil: the great historians of New York City I was fortunate to know or intersect with over the years.

When I entered the PhD program at New York University, Dr. Thomas Bender became my advisor. Now retired, Dr. Bender is a noted urban historian and expert, especially, on New York City's civic and cultural history. He published his important book, *New York Intellect: A History of Intellectual Life in New York City, from 1750 to the Beginnings of Our Own Time*, while I was his student. I was trained as a historian through his wide-ranging interests, his endless curiosity, and his astonishing ability to make the person he is speaking with feel intelligent even as it is Dr. Bender who is recognizing the nugget of fresh thought hidden in his correspondent's ramblings. We have remained in touch and, once again, in working on this book he offered a crucial insight. I mentioned that a famous book on Times Square we'd read in his class defined it as the first time the center of a city was not city hall, or a market, or a cathedral. No, he replied, that was Union Square—and sent me to his book *The Unfinished City: New York and the Metropolitan Idea*, in which he makes precisely that point. I had already decided on focusing on four streets, and now I had a square—which became all the more interesting as I followed his lead and explored its history.

Which streets? Wall Street, Forty-Second Street, and 125th Street were obvious choices, but what should I use for the Village? MacDougal Street certainly had a claim, as did Eighth Street, which would have made room for St. Mark's Place and the East Village. Bob Dylan suggested West Fourth Street—from his song "Positively 4th Street" to the folk music scene near there that was his launching pad. But there was another reason: there are excellent books on the history of the Village—the radicals and pretenders, their ideas, creations, foibles, egos, affairs, and influence.

But while the studies are engaging and thorough, none gave what I thought of as proper weight to the basketball court, treating it as if it were decoration, not a central part of the Village story. Picking West Fourth gave me a chance to right that wrong.

While studying at NYU, I was an editor at the book publishing company Henry Holt, and though I was working in the children's and YA department, I was given the wonderful chance to serve as the editor of the revised paperback edition of Eric Homberger's popular *Historical Atlas of New York City*. Eric and I became friends and had many enjoyable conversations in New York and in England, where he lived and taught. Working on his book—and Christine Stansell's *American Moderns* (about the Village radicals)—deepened my knowledge of the city's history. When Professor Ken Jackson sent out word that he was looking for contributors to *The Encyclopedia of New York City*, I got to write about aspects of book publishing in the city. While Dr. Jackson and I have not met, I found another avenue to his New York City work when Marina's editor Wendy Lamb introduced me to David Dunbar, who, along with Dr. Jackson, edited *Empire City*, a rich collection of writings about the city. Finally, also at Holt, I edited Steven Jaffe's book *Who Were the Founding Fathers?* Steven is a neighbor and friend; I got to read his *New York at War* in manuscript and in print, and received many useful suggestions from him in his time both at the South Street Seaport Museum and then at the Museum of the City of New York. The heart of the Snapshot timelines is research he and Charles Sachs did at South Street. Beyond all of those contributions, he gave me the thorough, thoughtful, and helpful reading of this book's manuscript in its final form. I owe so much to his knowledge and generosity. Steve also put me in touch with Dr. Robert Snyder, who was a student of Dr. Bender's just before I was. Dr. Snyder is now the official historian of the borough of Manhattan and gave my manuscript a crucial, detailed, close read that grounded my research at an important juncture.

The most exciting research journey I took in writing *Four Streets and a Square* also came through the prior work and generosity of historians. George Chauncey's *Gay New York* is one of those rare books that changed my understanding of a subject I thought I knew. It was through his work that I learned about the original meaning of "to come out," about the same-sex side of the immigration of single Italian men, and about LaGuardia's role in closing gay bars, and it was his book that led me to the astonishing letter that Countee Cullen wrote to Alain Locke in March 1923. I knew that the letter came a year before the event at the Civic Club that is often considered the official beginning of the Harlem Renaissance, but were they connected? I wrote to Dr. Chauncey, who was gracious and directed me to his source, an article by Alden Reimonenq in the *Journal of Homosexuality*. That article was primarily a rejoinder to other scholars who sought to question or downplay the homosexuality of key figures in the Renaissance. Interesting, but no use in answering my question. Just then, Jeffrey Stewart's monumental biography of Locke came out. I rushed to read it, learned so much, and then began an email exchange (continued in person when he gave a talk in New York) with Dr. Stewart. You get a sense in the book of how his restless intelligence keeps examining issues from new angles, and the same was true in our correspondence. He pressed me to think more carefully about visibility and invisibility, and about to what degree Black people—if not well known—were actually accepted in the Village. Even this refinement, though, helped me to look more deeply at that astonishing link I had first seen in Chauncey's book between the "soul windows" that opened up from accepting desire for other men to the affirmation of the power and beauty of "the New Negro."

Teachers, historians, friends—I had many avenues into the city, and one great stroke of good fortune. *Gotham*, the masterful multivolume modern history of the city, was begun by Ed Burroughs and Mike Wallace and is being continued by Dr. Wallace. Having first volume one and then, just in time, volume two by my side as I wrote was a godsend. Anyone who knows those books—and Edward Robb Ellis's *The Epic of New York City*—will be able to predict where a great many of my facts and quotations come from without even looking at the citations. My book would be impossible without theirs. The one problem with *Gotham* and another book I also made extensive use of, Jonathan Gill's *Harlem*, is that the publishers, for understandable but deeply regrettable reasons, did not provide space for the standard page-by-page citations. It is nearly impossible to link specific quotations or facts in the books with their sources. I did not doubt *Gotham*'s scholarship, but I could not follow a trail from the books in order to learn more. For *Harlem*, the citations were apparently at one time on a website that is no longer active.

Researching *Four Streets and a Square*, I kept running into the remarkable Johnsons—James Weldon and Grace Nail are in the text; James's brother J. Rosamond, who wrote the music to James's lyrics for "Lift Every Voice and Sing," could well be. I'd love to know more about all of them. James indirectly helped me in another way: one undergraduate summer, I was working in East Harlem on a cultural festival. I got a call to come to the James Weldon Johnson Houses, a public housing project. There, I had the remarkable opportunity to see and hear ragtime and jazz composer and pianist Eubie Blake play.

These contacts and books got me started. Then as I researched each beat of my story, I dove further into specialized studies. The open stacks of the Alexander Library at Rutgers University–New Brunswick were my second home. I could pluck one book after another, moving from an academic's analysis to works originally published as early as the nineteenth century. I could live in those aisles. Perhaps Marina wishes I did—I used my faculty borrowing privilege to bring sixty or more of the books home, where they fill my office like some ever-expanding fungus (to be killed off when I finally return them).

Even as I gathered information, I knew I was only starting—the next step was writing. Marina read the book in a number of different forms and drafts, always pushing me to turn summaries into stories, to cut out familiar wording and find fresh language, and to emphasize human drama over discrete facts. My ever-engaged, ever-patient editor, Hilary Van Dusen, also read several drafts, urging me to move past what I found easy to say to what would really fulfill the book's promise. Her insights shaped a much better book. She let me dash off to write another book under extreme deadline pressure and understood when my teaching took over my time. Sherry Fatla at Candlewick worked tirelessly, making use of every bit of her skill and experience, in shaping the book. Sherry, Hilary, and I have been true partners working on each line, paragraph, image, and page of the design together. Susan VanHecke and Jackie Houton currycombed the manuscript as copyeditors and nudged me to make sure I had each word right. My agent, Erin Cox, appeared often like the Good Fairy to keep me on task. Dr. Steven Ellman's insight and good humor deepened every aspect of my work. And then I sent the book out to a new set of readers. Dr. Mary Ann Cappiello gave me a detailed, thoughtful, and very helpful set of comments. Jim Murphy, who was an editor before he became an award-winning author, read a draft and offered his trained sense of how to reach readers, as did Paul Fleischman, who read a section. Sasha, my college-student son, had a long plane flight and loyally read the manuscript. He landed so filled with insight that Marina and I (and maybe even Sasha) realized that he is just a spectacular editor. Edwin Schloss—my schoolmate from seventh through twelfth grade and a former Broadway producer and Tony Awards judge—read the manuscript and gave me insightful notes on all of it, while assuring me that my history of the musical theater passed muster. I received encouraging words from Dr. April Bedford, dean of the School of Education at Brooklyn College, and the most wonderful help from David Brent Johnson. David is a jazz expert at WFIU radio in Indiana and creates his own deep dives into jazz history on the *Night Lights* show for the station. We met at a performance of Duke Ellington's *Black, Brown, and Beige* at Lincoln Center and remained in touch. David gave me some of the best multimedia links, including his own great program on Café Society. I am grateful to Vicky Smith's summer 2020 class on nonfiction at Simmons, which read a late draft. Their comments and suggestions led me to add the section on 1960s feminism. Thanks to my Rutgers colleagues Dr. Emil Lawrence for reading the whole manuscript with an eye to my use of gendered language and pronouns and Dr. Juan Gonzalez for suggesting several of the key photographers of Puerto Rican Manhattan whose images I used. Our friend and neighbor Dorothy Kelly did the impossible in combing through my endless drafts and books to piece together all the places I had stored my citations. I owe many people thanks for their assistance with image research, grouped here by the items they helped me to find:(Djuna Barnes) Amber Kohl, Special Collections and Archives the University of Maryland, Isabel Howe, Authors League Fund; (Led Black) Led Black, Rob Snyder; (Zach Buchner) Zach Buchner, Led Black; (Café Society) Elizabeth Surles, Institute of Jazz Studies, Rutgers University, Benjamin Knysak RIPM-Jazz; (Center for Puerto Rican Studies) Pedro Hernandez, Anibal Arocho, Eve Levy; (Maximo Colon) Maximo Colon, Steven Jaffe; (Ricky Flores) Ricky Flores; (Don Freeman) Roy Freeman; (Leo Goldstein) Naomi Goldstein, Regina Montfort; (Beverley Grant) Bev Grant; (Hamilton Lodge Ball) Melissa Jacobs, NYC Department of Education, Shauntee Burns, Kaitlyn Rotella New York Public Library; (Syd Hoff) Carol Edmonston; (Ren Hseih) Ren Hseih, Lilly Tuttle; (Walter Rosenblum) Naomi and Nina Rosenblum; (Feliks Topolski) Teresa Topolski, Daniel Warneke.

While all the people named here, and others, have been helpful to me, I am solely responsible for everything in this book—right or wrong.

SOURCE NOTES

INTRODUCTION

This opening is how I wanted to begin the book, but it is also an homage to one of the great New York memoirs, Alfred Kazin's *A Walker in the City*. Beautifully written, thoughtful, compelling, this is one city book everyone should read. I also wanted to use the opening to introduce some voices of the city, great writers who have described it. The citations take you to excerpts I used, but each author is worth exploring. I did not find a way to weave it into this introduction, but suited to this entry into the city and the island, and most readable, is E. B. White (yes, the author of *Charlotte's Web*), *Here Is New York* (New York: Harper & Brothers, 1949).

p. 4: "this magic city": Boris Aronson, "1976 Tony Awards ~ COMPLETE," YouTube, posted August 25, 2013, https://youtu.be/pGRw1qOr8Qg. Boris Aronson in the thirtieth annual Tony Awards ceremony, 1976, accepting the award for the sets for *Company*, a musical about New York.

p. 5: "Others will enter . . . the ebb-tide": Walt Whitman, "Crossing Brooklyn Ferry," in Jackson and Dunbar, 248. This is one of two compilations of writings on the city I used, and it was most helpful to have at hand. The other was Still's *Mirror for Gotham*.

p. 5: "power of the . . . its fortune": Henry James, *The American Scene*, quoted in Jackson and Dunbar, 478.

p. 5: "lamp beside the golden door": Emma Lazarus, "The New Colossus," quoted in Jackson and Dunbar, 315.

p. 6: "throbbing force . . . her a part": James Weldon Johnson, "My City," in his *Saint Peter Relates an Incident* (New York: Viking, 1935), 37.

p. 6: "the one permanent . . . change itself": Thomas Wolfe, *The Web and the Rock*, quoted in Jackson and Dunbar, 567.

CREATING THE CITY

I knew the basic outline of the city's history in this period before I began, so my research involved finding sources that took me more deeply into key events and added color to how I described events. My constant guide and companion was Edwin G. Burrows and Mike Wallace's *Gotham: A History of New York City to 1898*. This and its companion, *Greater Gotham: A History of New York City from 1898 to 1919*, are essential resources for anyone who wants to explore the city's history through 1919 in depth. They supplant any prior city histories. I found Frederick Trevor Hill's 1908 *The Story of a Street* in the Alexander Library at Rutgers; its focus on the actual Wall Street over time helped to frame my concept of this section.

Chapter 1: Manna-hata

p. 12: "people from Minisink": Grumet, 5–6. Grumet is an anthropologist whose academic research has concentrated on the Munsee and the Lenape. His decision to focus on the Munsee rather than the Lenape for Manhattan is not universally shared, but I was impressed with his scholarship.

p. 13: *nenapa*: ibid., 15. The reconstruction of the landscape comes from the Welikia Project (https://welikia.org); the description of a hypothetical Munsee is from Grumet.

p. 15: "Then we can . . . at a distance": Singleton, 14. Books like this written near the turn of the twentieth century sometimes contain gems, details from primary sources not easily available elsewhere, though Singleton's book itself is now a kind of primary source of early twentieth-century views and interests.

p. 16: "that looked of . . . wind and raine": Juet and Lunny, 36.

p. 17: Juet was looking for mines: Jaffe, *New York at War*, 1–5. Dr. Jaffe's book is well worth exploring for anyone interested in both battles in the city and the preparations the city made for battles that never took place.

Chapter 2: Wall

p. 18: Irving's story: Irving, 66–67. An entertaining document of a completely different era—more interesting now as literature than as history.

p. 19: An early letter: "Peter Schagen Letter," New Netherland Institute, https://www.newnetherlandinstitute.org/history-and-heritage/additional-resources/dutch-treats/peter-schagen-letter/.

p. 19: closer to one thousand dollars: Matt Soniak, "Was Manhattan Really Bought for $24?" *Mental Floss*, October 2, 2012, https://www.mentalfloss.com/article/12657/was-manhattan-really-bought-24.

p. 19: "The Indians were . . . who met them": Shorto, 51. Shorto's book is based on extensive Dutch-era records and helped reshape views of the city in that period. It is well written and accessible.

p. 19: The land was now just dirt. Grumet, 67

p. 20: The low brick . . . display: Singleton, 29–30.

p. 20: "rubbish, filth, ashes, oyster-shells, dead animals": ibid., 25.

p. 22: On Kieft: Grumet, 36.

p. 22: We do know . . . the Hudson River: Burrows and Wallace, *Gotham*, 64.

p. 22: "the Negroes's Farms": ibid., 33.

p. 24: "Jews, Turks, and Egyptians": "350th Anniversary of the Flushing Remonstrance: A Celebration of a Document and the Principles It Embodies," New York Newspaper Publishers Association, 2007, https://nynpa.com/docs/nie/niematerials/Flushing_Remonstrance.pdf.

p. 25: The trade made . . . around the world: Burrows and Wallace, *Gotham*, 82.

Chapter 3: British New York

p. 29: "Popish dogs and devils": Burrows and Wallace, *Gotham*, 98

p. 29: "poor ignorant and senseless people": ibid., 98–99.

p. 29: "You must be . . . makes the man": McCormick, 18. Leisler's rebellion has a great many ins and outs, but if a reader wants to dive in and learn more, this is a useful academic treatment.

p. 30: "Here bee not . . . none at all": Still, 23. Still was an important historian of the city based at New York University, before I came there. He provides rich context for the excerpts he selected, and this older book makes a nice pair with Jackson and Dunbar.

p. 31: "a very large . . . I ever saw": ibid., 17.

p. 34: City hall housed . . . pay their debts: Lepore, *New York Burning*, 64–66. Professor Lepore has written several highly readable books on the city. This is a clear, thoughtful effort to parse the meaning of the 1741 fires and trials, written for general readers. A good starting point for anyone interested in learning more

p. 35: Coffee shops soon . . . go out alone: William H. Ukers, *All About Coffee* (New York: Tea and Coffee Trade Journal Company, 1922), 125, http://www.cluesheet.com/All-About-Coffee-XIII.htm. This book has been digitized at Cluesheet.com, a fun site and an example of the byways of Manhattan's history that others have explored and you can find.

p. 35: "all sorts of sugar and sugar candy": Burrows and Wallace, *Gotham*, 123–125. Francis Spufford's *Golden Hill: A Novel of Old New York* is an engaging novel written for adults that explores the city in the eighteenth century and in particular the question of how to trust someone arriving with questionable credit. For those who enjoy historical fiction, it is another way to immerse yourself in the period through the Stamp Act protests and the Battle of Golden Hill.

p. 36: In 1711 . . . and hired out: Burrows and Wallace, *Gotham*, 128.

p. 36: "all negro and . . . Wall Street Slip": Janvier, 33. Another book that has useful primary-source gems but that has itself become an artifact of an earlier time. I love exploring these neglected volumes, with pages that threaten to crumble as you touch them. Their point of view is not ours, but you never know what you will find, like discovering a shelf of old books and a diary in a neglected summer house. Everything is dated—and a reading adventure.

p. 38: By 1721 . . . homes: Burrows and Wallace, *Gotham*, 127.

p. 38: Apparently the plan worked . . . city took revenge: ibid., 148.

Chapter 4: Two City Hall Trials
p. 39: "a monkey of the larger sort": Alexander, 11. The Zenger trial should be a staple for any history of colonial America. This is an academic edited edition of a primary source.

p. 39: "spaniel of about five feet five inches": ibid.

pp. 39–40: "If such an . . . all honest minds": ibid.

p. 40: New York's local . . . speech, and rights: Ellis, 123–124. Ellis famously began a daily diary as a teenager and kept it going continuously for more than seventy years. The skill he developed as a writer (he was also a journalist) is reflected in this readable, entertaining one-volume history of the city. It is dated in what it covers and how it interprets events. I would use it for a fun reading experience but would check it against Burroughs and Wallace for any specifics.

p. 42: "you . . . and lawful men": Alexander, 75.

p. 42: "false, scandalous and seditious": ibid.

p. 42: "how must a . . . taken a libeler?": ibid., 95.

p. 42: "wise men . . . against lawless power": ibid., 98.

p. 42: "The jury . . . crowded with people": ibid., 101.

p. 43: But in Hamilton's . . . law or custom: ibid., 24.

p. 43: The bigger the . . . he would be: Lepore, *New York Burning*, 49–50. The Salem witch trials are a staple of middle-grade education; I think pairing Salem in 1692 with New York in 1741 would be a better approach, especially since the connection was made at the time. Focusing on Salem alone makes the trials about New England and its Puritans, but pairing Salem with New York highlights the role of pack behavior that can happen anywhere.

p. 44: "Fire, Fire, Scorch, Scorch": ibid., 49.

p. 44: "burn the houses . . . kill them all": Burrows and Wallace, *Gotham*, 160.

p. 45: "I am a stranger to you": Lepore, *New York Burning*, 203.

p. 45: "horrible executions . . . the year 1692": ibid., 203–204.

p. 47: "It makes me . . . turn out alike": ibid., 204.

p. 47: "any body . . . to be burnt": ibid.

p. 47: "some people in ruffles": ibid., 202.

p. 47: "hostility to the Catholic religion": Hardie, 51. I found this in a used bookstore. It is like Janvier, a treat to explore—a periscope that allows you to see the city with an ancestor's eyes.

p. 47: "very unfriendly to the fair development of truth": ibid.

p. 47: New York City . . . people were burned: Lepore, *New York Burning*, xvii.

p. 47: "them that have the most money": Burrows and Wallace, *Gotham*, 160.

Chapter 5: Revolution
p. 49: On New York profiting from war: Burrows and Wallace, *Gotham*, 168–169.

p. 50: On the Stamp Act protests: I used Edmund S. Morgan and Helen M. Morgan's *The Stamp Act Crisis: Prologue to Revolution*, a classic still valuable on this era, and Gary B. Nash's *The Urban Crucible: The Northern Seaports and the Origins of the American Revolution*, which placed new emphasis on working-class issues and conflicts at the time.

p. 51: "The first man . . . We dare": Burrows and Wallace, *Gotham*, 199.

p. 52: "It is better to . . . lose our liberty": Ellis, 146. For more on nonimportation as a strategy and what that meant for women's roles in protesting, see T. H. Breen's *The Marketplace of Revolution: How Consumer Politics Shaped American Independence*.

p. 52: "cram the Stamps down their throats": Burrows and Wallace, *Gotham*, 199.

p. 55: "for the safety . . . and your persons": "Are There Instances of Raids Similar to the Boston Tea Party?" TeachingHistory.org, http://teachinghistory.org/history-content/ask-a-historian /20657.

p. 55: "a kind of key to the whole continent": Jaffe, *New York at War*, 78.

p. 56: "flying in every . . . the greatest confusion": Burrows and Wallace, *Gotham*, 240.

p. 56: "Good God . . . troops as those?": ibid., 240.

p. 58: "You can hardly . . . had quite lost": Jaffe, *New York at War*, 96.

p. 58: "Ethiopian Balls": Burrows and Wallace, *Gotham*, 249.

p. 58: As enslaved people slipped . . . African American city: Jaffe, *New York at War*, 102.

p. 59: "a vast pyramid of fire": ibid., 97.

Chapter 6: Capital

p. 62: "In this place . . . our deliverer": Burrows and Wallace, *Gotham*, 260.

p. 62: As a returning . . . an "unearthly aspect": ibid., 265.

p. 62: "as if they . . . or wild beasts": ibid.

p. 63: "I am totally ruined": ibid.

p. 63: As the Loyalists . . . "trade and commerce": ibid., 267.

p. 64: a stream called . . . to the Hudson: Nevius and Nevius, *Inside the Apple*, 5. This is a well-researched walking guide to the city.

p. 67: The presidential boat . . . in the afternoon: Silverman, 605–606. This deeply researched academic history is your one-stop resource for viewing the period of the revolution through the eyes of culture—not battles or laws.

p. 67: a table covered with red velvet: Brown, *Valentine's Manual of the City of New York: 1917–1918*, 133. Published to offer reading amusement to city history buffs a century or more ago, these manuals are fun to explore. I found this and others in the open stacks of Alexander Library at Rutgers.

p. 67: "I will faithfully . . . the United States": Ellis, 184–187.

p. 67: The crowd roared . . . it was done: Brown, *Valentine's Manual of the City of New York: 1917–1918*, 133.

Chapter 7: Money

p. 68: "if there is . . . it is New York": Burrows and Wallace, *Gotham*, 301.

p. 68: "shot": This is a reference to Lin-Manuel Miranda's musical *Hamilton* and the song "My Shot."

p. 69: One old dollar . . . made that offer: Chernow, *Alexander Hamilton*, 201. This is the book that inspired Lin-Manuel Miranda to write *Hamilton*, and though detailed and long, it is readable and engaging.

p. 70: "Who talk most . . . in the other?": ibid., 307.

p. 70: "Hamiltonopolis": ibid., 325.

p. 71: "an eternal buzz with gamblers": Burrows and Wallace, *Gotham*, 308.

p. 71: "scriptomania": ibid.

p. 71: "The merchant . . . accumulate large fortunes": ibid., 309.

p. 72: "almost every . . . the little shopkeepers": ibid.

p. 74: "malignant fevers": ibid., 125.

p. 74: "deep damp cellars . . . wholesome water": Janvier, 47.

p. 76: When another fever . . . island in Harlem: Burrows and Wallace, *Gotham*, 356–358.

p. 76: "Very few are . . . and the negroes" and "of great service in this dreadful crisis": Goodwin et al., 289. One more antique that yielded unexpected insights.

p. 77: "It's like a . . . dead dogs, cats": Burrows and Wallace, *Gotham*, 359.

p. 78: Equally notorious for . . . on Wall Street: Fleming, 81. Several books explore these paired men and their destiny. This is well written.

p. 78: "a grave, silent, strange sort of animal": Parton, 234. The first biography of Burr, originally published in the nineteenth century.

p. 78: "has not principle, public, or private": Isenberg, 118. A more recent take on Burr that seeks to counter myths and revive his reputation. It makes an excellent pair with Chernow for those who want to compare and contrast historical "takes."

p. 79: "In politics . . . half the battle": Chernow, *Alexander Hamilton*, 274.

p. 81: "superior *Management*": Fleming, 69.

p. 82: "it will not do to be overscrupulous": Chernow, *Alexander Hamilton*, 609. An example of Chernow's fair-minded approach. His book changed Hamilton's image, but he scrupulously discussed his failings.

p. 82: "As a public . . . 'tis Burr": Sedgwick, 209. Similar to Fleming above.

BUILDING THE CITY
This section takes us through much of the nineteenth century and deals with working-class New York and thus the Five Points; middle-class and wealthy New York and thus Union Square; Black and white New York and thus both clash and creation. There are clusters of books that I explored on each of these themes alongside *Gotham*.

Chapter 8: Redrawing the Map
p. 89: "the whole country . . . protruding mountains": Singleton, 10.

p. 93: "The ideal of . . . Washington Square" and "has a kind . . . long, shrill city": Henry James, *Washington Square*, 16. An early James novel, this features his unique insight and use of language without the later layers of complexity. For a lavishly photo-illustrated history of Union Square, see James Isaiah Gabbe's *The Universe of Union Square: At the Heart of New York's Progressive Soul*.

Chapter 9: Private Homes and Public Shopping
p. 98: Trailing the *Seneca* . . . the city's future: Peter L. Bernstein, 310–311.

p. 99: "the greatest commercial emporium in the world": Jackson and Dunbar, 228.

p. 99: "one vast city": quoted in Finch, 4.

p. 99: "covered with inhabitants": ibid.

p. 99: they were splintering . . . four Native nations: "Dispossession and Disruption," Erie Canalway National Heritage Corridor, https://eriecanalway.org/learn/history-culture/native-americans.

p. 99: "Its distance from . . . of the time": Homberger, *Mrs. Astor's New York*, 57. Dr. Homberger was working on this when I got to know him. The book is a kind of anthropology of a strange world of the wealthy, filled with fascinating details, written by a well-informed and critical historian.

p. 99: As they strolled . . . and such: ibid., 5.

p. 100: Mose was a . . . to his gang: Freeman, *City of Workers*, 67. Created to accompany an exhibit at the Museum of the City of New York, this is a collection of essays but filled with illustrations and written for a general readership. A central book on working-class New York in this period is Sean Wilentz's *Chants Democratic: New York City and the Rise of the American Working Class*. I used it for general background on the period.

p. 101: "irregular, narrow, crooked . . . of the inhabitants": Hardie, 146.

p. 102: In 1835 alone . . . America's wealthiest person: Burrows and Wallace, *Gotham*, 601.

p. 103: "When Uncle Dan'l says . . . bobs both ways": Geisst, 65. A useful guide to the history of stock trading in this country.

p. 104: "how the poor . . . for his family": Burrows and Wallace, *Gotham*, 617.

p. 104: "from distrust of . . . or bargain-makers": ibid., 667.

pp. 104–105: Stewart ran frequent sales . . . the latest offering: ibid.

p. 105: "everything depended . . . over and about": Toll, 19. An older but still useful account of blackface minstrelsy. Barnum gives context for popular attractions in the city.

p. 105: "Standing beneath . . . by the sight": "Stewart's New Store," *Philadelphia Evening Telegraph*, November 2, 1868, 2.

p. 105: "restless, ever-changing . . . activity and industry": quoted in Kirstin Purtich, "Palaces of Consumption: A. T. Stewart and the Dry Goods Emporium," Visualizing 19th-Century New York, http://visualizingnyc.org/essays/palaces-of-consumption-a-t-stewart-and-the-dry-goods -emporium.

p. 106: "There is no reason . . . material and labor": Stern, Mellins, and Fishman, 709.

p. 106: "extend[ed] for miles . . . attractive way possible": King, 843.

p. 106: "their lives in . . . and being seen": quoted in Burrows and Wallace, *Gotham*, 668.

p. 107: "Union Square or . . . were different cities": Bender, *New York Intellect*, 198. A richly detailed and crucial exploration of the layers and centers of creativity and thought in the city.

p. 107: After New York . . . sweep, sailor, barber: Anbinder, *Five Points*, 19. Readable and thorough, this is a modern view of the neighborhood, freed from earlier mythologies.

p. 107: Landlords found they . . . smaller apartments: ibid., 18. An important book that I consulted but did not quote from, and which explores the experiences of the women doing the piecework sewing, is Christine Stansell's *City of Women: Sex and Class in New York, 1789–1860*. This is a crucial resource for anyone who wants to explore the social history of working-class women in the city in this period.

p. 108: "race of beings . . . of the city": Anbinder, *Five Points*, 23.

p. 108: "wretchedness and want": quoted in Burrows and Wallace, *Gotham*, 593.

p. 109: "How shall I . . . in every direction": Auchincloss, 51. The diaries of Philip Hone and George Templeton Strong are key primary sources for aspects of nineteenth-century New York City history. This lavish edition has selections from both, along with period illustrations—so it's more of an enjoyable browsing resource than the full diaries. Auchincloss himself was from a famous New York family and was a highly respected twentieth-century author.

Chapter 10: The Wickedest House on the Wickedest Street

p. 110: "the most ignorant . . . in the world": Auchincloss, 54.

p. 111: "the Liberties of the United States": Wallace, 545.

p. 111: "Catholic superstition": Golway, 32. This is a relatively newer view of Tammany that does not demonize it and sees it in the context of Irish New York.

p. 111: Harper Brothers . . . supposed former nun: Burrows and Wallace, *Gotham*, 545–546.

p. 111: For people like . . . the Five Points: Golway, 2, 32.

p. 111: Of those emigrants . . . New York City: Anbinder, *Five Points*, 42–43.

p. 111: "This is the . . . in drunken frays": quoted in Jackson and Dunbar, 190.

p. 111: "the wickedest . . . in New York": Anbinder, *Five Points*, 67.

pp. 111–112: The Old Brewery was . . . "wailing children": ibid., 68.

p. 112: "doorless apartment . . . sickening to endure": quoted in ibid., 69.

p. 113: "Every house . . . was a filthy brothel": quoted in ibid, 207.

p. 113: "Every house was . . . brothel a hell": ibid., 208.

p. 113: "white women, and . . . virtue and humanity": ibid., 23.

p. 113: But in the . . . dumped their garbage: Fitts, 123. This is one of the actual documentary papers that records the evidence found in the garbage pits and what we can learn from it.

p. 113: Households in the . . . middle-class households: Brighton, 16.

p. 117: "a lively young . . . greatest dancer known": Jackson and Dunbar, 192.

p. 117: "Single shuffle . . . this to him?": ibid.

p. 117: "wolf's den": ibid., 191.

p. 117: On the birth of tap dancing: Anbinder, *Five Points*, 172–175.

p. 117: "suppleness": Lhamon, 12. The author is quoting from a book about the city's markets published in 1862. Lhamon's book is a brilliant exploration of blackface. The writing style is not academic but is experimental in ways that can take some decoding. This is an important book for a deep dive into the history of blackface minstrelsy. I also consulted but do not quote from *Inside the Minstrel Mask: Readings in Nineteenth-Century Blackface Minstrelsy*, edited by Annemarie Bean et al., which had several important contributions.

pp. 119–120: "Mr. T. D. Rice . . . by the tarantula": quoted in Lott, 3. This book added a rich dimension to the understanding of blackface minstrelsy by exploring what it meant to working-class white men.

p. 120: "longest-running form of American popular music": Wynton Marsalis, "History of Jazz—Minstrel Groups," *Jazz with Wynton Marsalis*, video, 0:56, http://www.joy2learn.org/jazz /history-of-jazz/origins-of-jazz/minstrel-groups/.

p. 120: "For almost a . . . most despised minority": Geoffrey C. Ward and Ken Burns, *Jazz: A History of America's Music* (New York: Alfred A. Knopf, 2001), 8.

p. 120: "the filthy scum . . . white fellow citizens": quoted in Lott, 15.

p. 120: "plantation darky": ibid.

p. 121: Onstage, Blacks . . . for the night: Toll, 31.

pp. 121–124: The original lyrics . . . Black people's eyes: Lott, 23–24.

p. 124: "repeatedly saw . . . fashion in Broadway": quoted in Shane White, 54. This book gives examples of African American life in New York that show training, talent, and ambition.

p. 124: "given up to . . . of the other": ibid., 55.

pp. 124–125: "the last thing . . . that environment": Marsalis.

p. 125: "It is something . . . a white audience": Lott, 37.

Chapter 11: Can the City Hold Together?

p. 126: This new electorate . . . governing the state: Golway, 7.

p. 127: "England is right . . . base, cruel, cowards": Jackson and Dunbar, 205.

p. 127: "We are natives . . . well as foreigners": Joshua Gottheimer, *Ripples of Hope: Great American Civil Rights Speeches* (New York: Basic Books, 2003), 12.

p. 127: "Irishmen have no . . . American Abolitionists": quoted in Anbinder, *Five Points*, 306.

p. 127: "Dark, sullen, ferocious . . . Ireland and Catholicity": ibid.

p. 128: From then on . . . Village and beyond: Burrows and Wallace, *Gotham*, 557–558.

p. 129: Every fifth horse-drawn . . . in this car": Brown, *Valentine's Manual of Old New York—No. 7, New Series 1923*, 210.

p. 130: "I'm a respectable . . . of this car": quoted in Burrows and Wallace, *Gotham*, 856–857.

p. 131: "melting pot for all humanity": Freeman, *City of Workers*, 40.

p. 131: "such white laborers . . . upon the premises": quoted in Burrows and Wallace, *Gotham*, 854.

p. 131: "The influx of . . . branches of labor": quoted in ibid., 85.

p. 131: Cynical politicians and . . . lower their wages: Anbinder, *Five Points*, 306–307.

p. 133: The park would . . . and Eighth Avenues: Burrows and Wallace, *Gotham*, 792.

p. 133: "attractive as to . . . and the rowdy": quoted in ibid., 793. For additional background on the park, see https://www.centralpark.com/visitor-info/park-history/overview/.

p. 133: For the understanding that Central Park was designed to be a place of transformation for the working class, see Catherine McNeur's *Taming Manhattan: Environmental Battles in the Antebellum City*, 199–200.

p. 134: "most park users . . . least entertaining, purpose": quoted in Christopher Gray, "Whinny If You Miss Central Park's Horses," *New York Times*, July 5, 2013, https://www.nytimes.com/2013/07/07/realestate/whinny-if-you-miss-central-parks-horses.html.

Chapter 12: New York's Civil War

p. 138: "With our aggrieved . . . a common sympathy": quoted in Pleasants, 114. This is an academic study that is useful for finding quotations not easily available elsewhere, though it requires a prior familiarity with the parties and factions of New York City and state politics of the period.

p. 138: "this hellish traffic . . . for twenty years": Whitman, 108.

p. 138: "What would become . . . metropolis, New York": Strausbaugh, *City of Sedition*, 137. Written for a general readership, this brings together some of the more academic scholarship to paint a clear picture of New York before and during the Civil War.

p. 139: "The ships would . . . Street and Broadway": ibid.

p. 139: "Change in public . . . a United North": quoted in Auchincloss, 203.

p. 139: "there can be . . . or its enemies": quoted in Ernest A. McKay, 58. A more academic dive into the same territory as Strausbaugh.

p. 139: "Now we don't . . . getting gloriously mended": ibid., 64.

p. 141: The Irish workers . . . to free Blacks: Iver Bernstein, 10. This is an older but still useful detailed study of the draft riots. A solid reference that can be used to check or confirm details found elsewhere.

p. 142: "Down with the rich men": Burrows and Wallace, *Gotham*, 890.

p. 142: Other rioters . . . sofas, chairs, clocks": Iver Bernstein, 21.

p. 142: "If there's a . . . these poor children": quoted in Jaffe, *New York at War*, 163.

p. 142: "the colored people . . . shall be driven": quoted in Iver Bernstein, 27.

pp. 142–144: "The laboring classes . . . for a draft": ibid., 36.

p. 145: "anxiously watch your . . . benedictions and tears": ibid., 67.

Chapter 13: Across the Square

p. 146: "the removal of . . . of the country": quoted in "Tammany Hall Hosts the City's First Democratic Convention: Susan B. Anthony, the KKK, and a Reluctant Nominee," The Bowery Boys New York City History, September 6, 2012, https://www.boweryboyshistory.com/2012/09 /tammany-hall-hosts-citys-first.html.

p. 147: Banners blaring the . . . decorated lively rallies: Burrows and Wallace, *Gotham*, 926.

p. 147: "our position must . . . *in the states*": Mushkat, *The Reconstruction of the New York Democracy, 1861–1874*, 130. Like the Pleasants book on Mayor Wood, this is rich in details but requires having a mental scorecard of the city's factions. I found the chapter on "The Politics of Race" riveting—the parallels between the appeals to white voters' racism in the elections of 1868 and 2016 were striking.

p. 147: Tammany came through . . . the party line: ibid., 140.

p. 148: Tweed was similar . . . and 320 pounds: Ellis, 327.

p. 148: Tweed played so . . . lucrative morning: ibid., 345.

p. 149: "New York politics . . . before my time": ibid., 328.

p. 149: "bribery or patronage or corruption": ibid.

p. 151: "I don't care . . . can see pictures": ibid., 350. I spent some time reading about the tangled, fascinating story of battles over the Erie Railroad, corruption, and the stock market and trying to fit them into this book. I couldn't, but those curious to learn more can start with John

Steele Gordon's *The Scarlet Woman of Wall Street: Jay Gould, Jim Fisk, Cornelius Vanderbilt, the Erie Railway Wars, and the Birth of Wall Street*. If you enjoy brazen financial skullduggery, you will love reading it.

p. 151: There it was . . . Tweed and company: Ellis, 348–349.

p. 151: "the Anglo-Saxon race": Golway, 101.

p. 152: "The public . . . be damned": Chernow, *The House of Morgan*, 22. Whether to see Morgan's actions as merely selfish and greedy or actually illegal is debated among historians. This book won the National Book Award and established Chernow's reputation as a biographer. For a more complete account of Morgan's actions that refines and further explicates Chernow's version but is no less skeptical of Morgan's role, see pages 93–95 of Jean Strouse's *Morgan: American Financier*, a very well-written biography drawn from original sources.

pp. 152–153: "no experience of . . . it is bewildering": Hood, 54. An accessible narrative of how the subway came to be with plenty of details for fans of its history.

p. 153: "We are coming . . . that's poor": quoted in Snyder, 15. An accessible journey into the origins of vaudeville in the context of the city's history. I was so pleased to learn about Pastor here and to get to read his lyrics.

p. 153: "The Upper Ten . . . huddled like sheep": ibid., 16.

pp. 153–154: "determined that if . . . materially extended": ibid., 17.

p. 154: "initial break in . . . a society sensation": ibid., 24.

p. 155: Drawing on the . . . across the land: Bianco, 13.

Chapter 14: "The Streets Belonged to Us"

p. 157: Mounted on a . . . power and authority: Burrows and Wallace, *Gotham*, 1091. For further background, see Epstein, 118; Howe with Libo, 120 (the central, canonical book on the Jewish Lower East Side—well researched, well written, packed with stories); and Diner, 114 (a work by a more recent scholar who pays more attention to women's experiences).

p. 157: LABOR BUILT THIS . . . NO MONEY MONOPOLY: Burrows and Wallace, *Gotham*, 1091.

p. 158: The rally led . . . lot in life: Anbinder, *City of Dreams*, 366. The same author who gave us a modern view of the Five Points here tackles the entire immigrant history of the city. Readable and wide-ranging, a good resource to use.

p. 158: In the next twenty-eight years . . . New York Harbor: ibid, 327.

p. 159: By 1900, the . . . of Eastern Europe: Howe with Libo, 120; Diner, 131.

p. 160: "is as unknown . . . as Central Africa": quoted in Anbinder, *City of Dreams*, 356.

p. 160: "Broadway beneath Tenth . . . overhang the sidewalks": quoted in Marc Aronson, "Democratic Standards: William Crary Brownell and the Literary Marketplace" (PhD diss., New York University, 1995), 145.

p. 160: "something fantastic . . . no known language": ibid.

p. 161: In 1895 . . . on earth: Anbinder, *City of Dreams*, 358–359.

p. 161: One survey in . . . five or more: Howe with Libo, 148.

p. 161: Until an 1892 . . . the entire family: ibid., 157.

p. 161: "Privacy in the . . . was practically unknown": Howe with Libo, 171; for further background, see Burrows and Wallace, *Gotham*, 1114.

p. 164: "Hester Street roared . . . of bargain hunting": Diner, 135.

p. 164: "The streets were . . . belonged to us": Howe with Libo, 256.

p. 164: "spoke of freedom": ibid., 258.

p. 164: "Choked for ages . . . in my prison": Diner, 21.

p. 164: "I am a Russian Jewess . . . suppressed desires": quoted in Howe with Libo, 269.

p. 165: "It was work . . . out to be": Anbinder, *City of Dreams*, 315.

p. 165: Indeed, in 1890 . . . in New York: ibid., 317.

p. 166: "On my first . . . some wild vision": D'Angelo, 74.

pp. 166–167: "how lovely and . . . enchanted city was": ibid., 80.

p. 167: "there are many . . . with baskets and carts": Still, 248.

p. 167: "We were becoming . . . of our parents": quoted in Laurino, 86. Not limited to New York but, of course, has a lot to say about life there.

THE CITY ELECTRIC

This section was great fun as it allowed me to explore music, song, dance, and theater within the context of the changing city. I knew nothing about Oscar Hammerstein before finding him in the cluster of books I read on Forty-Second Street. In an early draft of Four Streets and a Square, I tried to write his story as a treatment for an opera embedded within the narrative. I enjoyed myself, but it did not quite work for this book.

Chapter 15: Greater New York

p. 175: "With the sky . . . came into existence": "The New City Ushered In," *New York Times*, January 1, 1898, https://timesmachine.nytimes.com/timesmachine/1898/01/01/102085686 .html.

p. 176: On the Crystal Palace and the Latting Observatory: Burrows and Wallace, *Gotham*, 670; Daniel Russell, "Minerals at 1853 the New York City Crystal Palace Exhibition," Mindat.org, February 3, 2008, www.mindat.org/article.php/196/Minerals+at+the+1853+New+York+City +Crystal+Palace+Exhibition.

p. 177: "Skyscrapers . . . of clipper ships: Lewis Mumford, "The Metropolitan Milieu," in Klein, 25. This is an anthology similar to Jackson and Dunbar or Still, but as it is older, it features voices and approaches not found in the others.

p. 177: "space and light and sun": ibid.

p. 178: "paper city, buried . . . the glib automatons": ibid., 23–24.

p. 178: And yet even . . . to change society: ibid., 29–30.

p. 181: "in the name of the people": Ellis, 466.

p. 181: "the subway open": ibid.

p. 181: "would get up . . . metal lunch box": quoted in "Italian Laborers & the Big Apple's Underground City," *L'Italo Americano*, September 26, 2014, https://italoamericano.org /italian-laborers/.

p. 182: Others, such as . . . the new immigrants: Hood, 23–24.

Chapter 16: The Immortal

p. 183: Family stories about Hammerstein: Hammerstein, 149.

p. 183: "think, talk, listen, or sing": Anbinder, *City of Dreams*, 180.

p. 185: On Hammerstein in Harlem: Bianco, 12. Bianco's book is one of several on Forty-Second Street I read, all of which were written for general readers and are packed with engaging stories. See below for Traub and the immensely useful though more academic Taylor. I also consulted Marc Eliot's *Down 42nd Street: Sex, Money, Culture, and Politics at the Crossroads of the World*.

p. 186: On Hammerstein's real estate investments: Bianco, 12.

p. 187: On Thieves Lair: ibid., 16.

p. 187: "The sound of . . . city street lamp": S. Rosenbaum, "When the Gay White Way Was Dark," in Brown, *Valentine's Manual of Old New York—No. 7, New Series 1923*, 117.

p. 187: On the east side . . . to that corner: Traub, 44. Nice paired with Bianco above for a dive into Forty-Second Street aimed at the general reader.

p. 188: HAMMERSTEIN'S ROOF GARDEN: Bianco, 19,

pp. 188–189: "We wear the . . . wear the mask!": quoted in Carter, 81–82. While an academic study, this fills in the important life of Will Marion Cook and is accessible to the general reader, especially one with an interest in music.

p. 190: "lift your heads up high": ibid., 84.

p. 190: "white folks jealous . . . two by two": ibid.

p. 190: On vaudeville bookers trying to limit Black acts: Sotiropoulos, 44–45. An important book for understanding performance and race in a crucial period.

p. 191: on challenges to segregated seating: ibid., 70–74.

p. 191: On New Year's . . . counted down the seconds: Traub, 21–22.

Chapter 17: "Come On and Hear"

p. 192: "At Forty-second . . . Such is Broadway": Theodore Dreiser, "The Color of a Great City," in Klein, 413–414.

p. 192: On Diamond Jim Brady and lobster palaces: Traub, 28–29.

p. 193: "hodge-podge of people . . . of the town": ibid., 39.

p. 193: "The spirit of . . . Forty-second street": quoted in Erenberg, 82. An academic study, but easy to read and filled with eye-opening details about cultural crossing in dance.

p. 193: "If I didn't go . . . mother was right": ibid., 78.

p. 194: "there has been . . . has been here": Sotiropoulos, 88. The Library of Congress has both articles on ragtime and musical examples well worth exploring: https://www.loc.gov /collections/ragtime/.

p. 194: "hearing a negro . . . to the rhythm": Edward Berlin, 6.

p. 194: "When the band . . . band plays ragtime": Bob Cole, "When the Band Plays Ragtime," words by J. W. Johnson (New York: J. W. Stern, ca. 1902), Beinecke Rare Book and Manuscript Library, Yale University, https://brbl-dl.library.yale.edu/vufind/Record/3566002.

p. 195: "The most popular . . . is the rage": quoted in Edward Berlin, 8

p. 196: Yet experts debate . . . an African American: Hamm, 104. This book covers each song from this period in terms of text and music and also engages with larger issues such as Berlin's relationship to blackface minstrelsy.

p. 196: Berlin began as . . . hit-making machine: Philip Furia, "Irving Berlin: Troubadour of Tin Pan Alley," in Taylor, *Inventing Times Square*, 193. Taylor was a brilliant cultural historian, and this edited volume brings together many key experts on the area. Well worth exploring.

p. 196: On Chinese immigration and the first Chinese in the Five Points: Lee, 79; Anbinder, *City of Dreams*, 522.

p. 197: The Russian owner . . . which he did: Furia, 194.

p. 199: "immense blaze of . . . them in motion": Still, 260.

p. 199: "zig-zag lightnings . . . acre of signboard": ibid.

p. 199: The sign showed . . . off her petticoat: Berman, 7–8. Berman was an urban cultural historian who captured the flavor of an earlier Times Square. For anyone interested in the story of electric advertising, Tama Starr and Edward Hayman's *Signs and Wonders: The Spectacular Marketing of America* has a detailed description of the Heatherbloom sign on page 64.

p. 199: The Sarnoff story can be found in Wallace, 105–114. Lighter than the academic books, this is a quick read built around interesting individuals.

p. 201: "He was the . . . and the saddest": Jonathan Gill, 190. A fine one-volume history of Harlem for general readers, hampered only by the absence of any notes and citations. I also used Cheryl A. Wall's *The Harlem Renaissance: A Very Short Introduction*, an excellent introduction that was filled with surprises.

p. 201: "He has done more . . . fight my way": Jonathan Gill, 190.

p. 202: "honey of a . . . singable tunes": Langston Hughes, "When the Negro Was in Vogue," in Klein, 264.

pp. 202–203: "We did that . . . just natural talent": Kimball and Bolcom, 116. This is a scrapbook that captures the world of Sissle and Blake in images from many of their shows, a real treat to explore.

p. 203: "gave just the proper push . . . sculpture, music, and dancing": Hughes in Klein, 264. Also see Ann Douglass's *Terrible Honesty: Mongrel Manhattan in the 1920s*, which is like taking a class with a brilliant professor who goes everywhere—at times arriving at spectacular insights, at times rambling. It is a real exploration of the many meanings and crossings of Black and white, light and dark, in the Manhattan of the '20s. Read it for the intellectual thrill ride.

p. 203: "Negro capital of the world": Claude McKay, quoted in Daniel Matlin, "Harlem: The

Making of a Ghetto Discourse," in *Race Capital? Harlem as Setting and Symbol*, edited by Daniel Matlin and Andrew M. Fearnley (New York: Columbia University Press, 2019), 83.

DIFFERENCE

I knew the basic story of the Village and Harlem before I researched this section, but George Chauncey's book changed everything. I had also read some of the varying interpretations of the Harlem Renaissance but learned more from Gill. I spent delicious afternoons at the New York Public Library for the Performing Arts at Lincoln Center reading biographies of Duke Ellington and histories of jazz.

Chapter 18: "Our Whole Big Human Selves"

p. 211: "When I speak . . . no art": quoted in Beard and Berlowitz, ix. This is an edited book with contributions from key scholars, but written and illustrated with many archival images for a general audience.

p. 212: "winding streets": Federal Writers' Project of the Works Progress Administration, 141.

p. 212: "houses with steep . . . over huge fireplaces": ibid.

p. 212: A census of . . . to Gay Street: McFarland, 16. While an academic study, this is so rich in well-researched detail, it was a treasure for me to find.

p. 213: The Austin clan . . . and six grandchildren: ibid., 210.

p. 213: "so full of . . . no vacant place": ibid., 159.

p. 213: "at once alive and deadly": Wetzsteon, 115. Written by a veteran reporter who had lived in and covered the Village for a lifetime, this is a full, unsparing history filled with stories and yet animated by an appreciation for the Village; it pairs well with John Strausbaugh's *The Village, 400 Years of Beats and Bohemians, Radicals and Rogues, a History of Greenwich Village*, a more recent similar survey.

p. 213: "air of a ruler": Dowling, 119.

p. 215: Immigrant women worked . . . many bathroom breaks: McFarland, 141.

p. 215: "I want to . . . a general strike": quoted in Annelise Orleck, "The Needle Trades and the Uprising of Women Workers: 1905–1919," in Freeman, 90.

p. 215: "They're burning . . . can't stop them": McFarland, 164.

p. 216: "We refuse to . . . they be radical": Wetzsteon, 48–49.

p. 216: "Yet we are free . . . such as we!": ibid., 4.

p. 217: "bourgeois pigs": Kayton, 22. Well researched and a nice companion if you want to explore the Village with an eye to a key aspect of its history.

p. 217: "If two people . . . that love exists": Goldman, 154.

p. 218: "meeting place for . . . in new ideas": Terry Miller, 219.

p. 218: Rodman, supported by . . . and won: McFarland, 200.

p. 219: "We're sick of . . . human selves": quoted in Wetzsteon, 177.

p. 221: "both men and . . . and talk together": Crunden, 387. Luhan's salon is described here as one example of a larger and interesting phenomenon.

p. 221: "Socialists, Trade-Unionists . . . speech called Free": McFarland, 194.

Chapter 19: War

p. 222: "Many people . . . of the world": Burrows and Wallace, *Greater Gotham*, 921. The second volume of this magnificent chronicle.

p. 223: "We have an . . . for the world": ibid., 923.

p. 223: "act as Americans . . . Native Americans": ibid., 914.

p. 223: "cling to the speech . . . they have left": ibid.

p. 223: "an asylum for the oppressed": ibid., 953.

p. 223: "We cannot . . . of the earth": ibid., 954.

p. 225: "The nation that . . . and adventurous qualities": Theodore Roosevelt, "The Strenuous Life" (speech, April 10, 1899), Voices of Democracy: The U.S. Oratory Project, https://voicesof democracy.umd.edu/roosevelt-strenuous-life-1899-speech-text/.

p. 225: "an indispensable factor . . . strength and vitality": Hofstadter, 197. Hofstadter was one of the great American historians, and while this is an older book, it is still relevant and sparkles with important insights. Anything of his is key reading as you dig into our past.

p. 226: "intolerable pretensions to equality": Burrows and Wallace, *Greater Gotham*, 966.

p. 226: "The country is . . . the national wealth": Wetzsteon, 76.

p. 232: "transnational America": Stansell, *American Moderns*, 216. While sexual freedom and liberated relationships were watchwords in the Village, they had unequal outcomes for women and for men, as Stansell shows.

p. 232: "the home of 'pansies' and 'Lesbians'": quoted in Chauncey, 235. Another essential book for understanding the city's history, filled with new insights.

p. 232: "wear expensive gowns . . . a young lady": ibid., 236.

p. 233: "admitted but not welcome": ibid., 240.

p. 233: "'gay capital' of the nation": ibid., 28.

p. 233: "I read it . . . myself in it": ibid., 284. See my discussion of this letter in my author's note on page 380.

Chapter 20: "The Pulse of the Negro World"

p. 234: "Debut of the Younger School of Negro Writers": quoted in Stewart, 416. A dense, brilliant, pathbreaking biography.

pp. 234–235: "For generations . . . or 'helped up'": Locke, "Enter the New Negro," 631.

p. 235: "His shadow . . . than his personality": ibid.

p. 235: "the pulse . . . beat in Harlem": ibid., 633.

p. 235: "self-respect": ibid., 632.

p. 235: "race pride": ibid.

p. 235: "one of the . . . Negro ever published": Johnson, 277.

p. 236: "Within the past . . . the Harlem group": ibid., 275.

p. 236: In 1908, the . . . fortunately failed: Gill, 182.

p. 237: "the father of colored Harlem": ibid., 175.

p. 240: "The whole movement . . . precipitate a flight": Johnson, 150.

p. 240: By 1918 . . . in the world: Gill, 184.

p. 240: "Harlem is a state of mind": Harris, 22.

p. 240: "This is a . . . be held guilty": Marcus Garvey (speech, July 8, 1917), Initiative for Urban Research, Southern Illinois University Edwardsville, https://www.siue.edu/artsandsciences /political-science/about/iur/projects/illinoistown/marcus-garvey.shtml.

p. 241: "This deep feeling . . . of Negro life": Locke, "Enter the New Negro," 632–633.

p. 242: "the proudest band . . . a marching melody": Gill, 220.

p. 242: "The Hellfighters marched . . . whooped things up": Anderson, 118. One of several anthologies that offer many avenues into understanding Harlem. I also enjoyed *The Harlem Reader*, edited by Herb Boyd.

pp. 242–243: "If we must . . . but fighting back!": Claude McKay, "If We Must Die," https://www.poetryfoundation.org/poems/44694/if-we-must-die.

p. 244: Smith played at . . . to attend: Gill, 195.

p. 246: "unfailing sense of . . . and graceful": Chauncey, 247.

p. 246: "an all-white . . . to the blacks": Claude McKay, *A Long Way from Home*, 106.

p. 247: "fancy clothes . . . a diamond stick-pin": Wall, 48.

p. 247: "one really didn't . . . one knew Gumby": "The Unwritten History": Alexander Gumby's African America, Columbia University Libraries, https://exhibitions.library.columbia.edu /exhibits/show/gumby.

p. 247: "the first unpremeditated interracial movement in Harlem": ibid.

p. 249: "These magic words . . . all night long": Nicholson, 31–32.

p. 249: "malnourished": Gill, 285.

p. 250: "dancing, love-making . . . and advertisement": Chauncey, 257.

p. 250: "All the men . . . of every kind": ibid., 258.

p. 250: "The ball was . . . but acceptable": ibid., 259.

p. 250: The singer Gladys . . . at the ball: Haleema Shah, "The Great Blues Singer Gladys Bentley Broke All the Rules," *Smithsonian*, March 14, 2019, https://www.smithsonianmag.com /smithsonian-institution/great-blues-singer-gladys-bentley-broke-rules-180971708/.

p. 250: "best feminine figure . . . best looking gown": Abram Hill, "The Hamilton Lodge Ball," August 13, 1939, Schomburg Center for Research in Black Culture, Manuscripts, Archives, and Rare Books Division, New York Public Library, https://digitalcollections.nypl.org/items /16910cf0-7cf4-0133-46b1-00505686d14e#/?uuid=16acce70-7cf4-0133-d749-00505686d14e.

p. 250: "decidedly brown skin . . . manners and carriage": ibid.

p. 250: "an original creation . . . Broadway designer": ibid.

p. 250: "Even here . . . the annual affair": ibid.

p. 251: "Harlem was wide open": Chauncey, 244.

THE CITY SUFFERS

The authors of *Gotham* stopped at 1919, so I was on my own in researching the rest of this book. The Geisst book on Wall Street helped me to understand the stock market part of this section, while the Freeman-edited book on the working-class city explained the radicalization of the unions.

Chapter 21: "The Splendid Mirage"

p. 255: "We were somewhere . . . of the desert": F. Scott Fitzgerald, "My Lost City," in Jackson and Dunbar, 609. The essay contains a gorgeous line I could not find a place to use. Describing arriving in the city in 1919 with little money, Fitzgerald wrote, "New York had all the iridescence of the beginning of the world" (604). That's how it can often feel when you arrive there after a gap of time.

p. 255: At midday on . . . and Nassau Streets: Ellis, 515.

p. 256: Wall Street had . . . total by 1901: Taylor, 17.

p. 257: In 1917 . . . bonds later matured: Geisst, 44.

p. 257: "a large, new army of investors": ibid., 151.

p. 259: "sunburst centre at Times Square": Taylor, 111.

p. 260: When she sings . . . give herself away: Knapp, 187. Knapp offers musical suggestions to go with his text. I used it with John Bush Jones's *Our Musicals, Ourselves: A Social History of the American Musical Theatre* to ground my understanding of the Broadway musical.

p. 260: But when Robeson . . . keep on fighting: Knapp, 190.

p. 260: "New York . . . approached hysteria": Fitzgerald in Jackson and Dunbar, 608.

p. 260: a hysteria of . . . in New York: Traub, 55.

p. 261: "New York dominates . . . to be modern": quoted in Still, 298.

p. 261: I found the Elsie de Wolfe story in Wallace, 203–216.

p. 262: "splendid mirage": Fitzgerald in Jackson and Dunbar, 610.

Chapter 22: Depression New York

p. 263: "overthrow of capitalism . . . and farmers' government": Ellis, 539.

p. 264: Even as New . . . problem of race: Freeman, *City of Workers*, 110–113.

p. 265: "One Hundred and Twenty-fifth . . . quick as lightning": McKay, "Harlem Runs Wild," in Huggins, 381.

p. 265: The buildings from . . . in the city: Gill, 284.

p. 266: Once white New . . . could ignore it: ibid., 285.

p. 266: Blumstein's eventually became . . . African American features: ibid, 301.

p. 268: That night, Harlem . . . were injured: ibid, 303.

p. 268: "this dark Harlem . . . and seething unrest": Locke, "Harlem: Dark Weather-Vane," 457.

Chapter 23: "Sing, Sing, Sing"—Experiments in Integration

pp. 269–270: "discrimination in the . . . and musicians' unions": Denning, 336. An extremely detailed but readable academic study, filled with nuggets for anyone interested in the arts and the Left in this period.

p. 270: One day in . . . named Eleanora Fagan: Prial, 45. Hammond deserves to be better known, though he has important critics and is ripe for a more recent evaluation.

p. 270: This was one . . . a white band: ibid., 61.

p. 270: "I wanted . . . together out front": Denning, 325.

p. 270: "a night club to . . . of stuffed shirts": ibid., 326.

pp. 270–271: "One thing that . . . even get in": John S. Wilson, "Barney Josephson, Owner of Café Society Jazz Club, Is Dead at 86," *New York Times*, September 30, 1988, http://www .nytimes.com/1988/09/30/obituaries/barney-josephson-owner-of-cafe-society-jazz-club-is -dead-at-86.html?pagewanted=all.

pp. 273–274: "Lights out, just . . . burned with it": Denning, 327.

p. 274: George Gershwin . . . not an opera: Rimler, 62. This book helped me to understand Gershwin better.

p. 274: The Metropolitan Opera . . . on its stage: Knapp, 195.

p. 274: And they were . . . and musical accomplishment: For African American response to *Porgy and Bess*, see Allen and Cunningham.

p. 274: "With a libretto . . . power and importance": Tommasini, 20. Tommasini is a skilled writer and music critic, and this lengthy biography will be useful to anyone interested in American classical music in the twentieth century.

p. 274: "It was not . . . kind of Negroes": Ross, 163. Another one of the great books I got to read. This is about music, not the city, but it engages brilliantly with classical music and jazz. It's well worth reading, as is his rich website: https://www.therestisnoise.com.

p. 275: "Gershwin the greatest": Rimler, 171.

p. 275: "*Porgy* loomed high . . . ever been produced": Johnson, 211.

p. 276: "Negro Ballet: South and North": Vaill, 88. A close look at Robbins's personal and creative life that offers many avenues to pursue for anyone interested in twentieth-century dance, theater, and creative New York.

p. 276: On Gershwin's skill with polyrhythms: Rimler, 85–86. The connection often made between traditional Jewish and African American music has to do with the use of the pentatonic scale, a topic well worth exploring for anyone interested in music and cultural history. For an excellent article that offers links to music from the opera as well as an introduction to debates about it, see Michael Cooper, "The Complex History and Uneasy Present of *Porgy and Bess*," *New York Times*, September 19, 2019, https://www.nytimes.com/2019/09/19/arts/music /porgy-bess-gershwin-metropolitan-opera.html.

p. 277: The feel-good . . . audiences craving distraction: Bianco, 102–105.

p. 278: "It was offering . . . of the moon": Brooks McNamara, "The Entertainment District at the End of the 1930s," in Taylor, 181–182.

pp. 278–279: "the first transnational Hispanic-American pop celebrity": Remeseira, 11. This is an edited volume with contributions from a variety of scholars. I learned so much in its pages. I'd love to see a popular version that covers some similar territory and introduces people like Gardel to a wider readership.

p. 279: "the slang capital of the world": Taylor, *Inventing Times Square*, 214.

p. 280: Luisetti used a one-handed jump shot: "Stanford Great Credited with Revolutionizing Sport," ESPN Classic, December 21, 2002, http://www.espn.com/classic/obit/s/2002/1221/1480886.html. For more on the interwoven histories of the city and basketball, see *City/Game: Basketball in New York*, edited by William Rhoden. My son, Sasha, and I contributed to the book and to the exhibit of the same name at the Museum of the City of New York that I suggested and helped to create.

p. 280: His tales of . . . some twenty movies: Taylor, *Inventing Times Square*, 225. I owe the insight of the oral quality of Runyon to Taylor's wonderful essay "Broadway" in this book.

Chapter 24: "Tear Down the Old"

p. 282: "by far the largest manufacturing center in the country": Freeman, *City of Workers,* 107.

p. 282: "Tear down the . . . a new America": Richard Price, "The Rise and Fall of Public Housing in NYC: A Subjective Overview," *Guernica*, October 1, 2014, https://www.guernicamag.com/the-rise-and-fall-of-public-housing-in-nyc.

pp. 282–283: Legend has it . . . on bigger plans: Ellis, 551.

pp. 282–283: On Robert Moses: Anthony Flint, *Wrestling with Moses: How Jane Jacobs Took on New York's Master Builder and Transformed the American City*, 114. Robert A. Caro's *The Power Broker: Robert Moses and the Fall of New York* is the classic study of Moses and stands as a magnificent historical accomplishment. Caro appreciates but also severely criticizes Moses—and was the one to make the case about the low overpasses. More recently, Hilary Ballon and Ken Jackson created the edited volume *Robert Moses and the Modern City: The Transformation of New York*, which shifts the image of Moses. Their argument is that, seen in a national context, Moses was responsible for creating the modern city for cars and planes, and what he could and couldn't accomplish was constrained by external forces. In particular, the book disputes the overpass claim, pointing out that there were other forms of public transportation to the beach in question (161). However, Martha Biondi's essay shows the key role Moses's segregationist views played in New York public housing (116–121).

p. 283: "When you create . . . making democracy function": Ballon and Jackson, *Robert Moses and the Modern City: The Transformation of New York*.

p. 286: For more on New York basketball history, pick-up basketball, and tournaments such as the Rucker, see Rhoden's *City/Game*. The classic book that brought readers (as opposed to spectators) to learn about the legendary players and games was Pete Axthelm's *The City Game: Basketball from the Garden to the Playgrounds*.

p. 286: General Motors' World of Tomorrow: Flint, 51.

p. 288: For the next . . . on their terms: Chauncey, 342.

p. 288: "infected": Baldwin, 82.

p. 288: "violently still": ibid.

p. 289: "In America . . . We know": quoted in Gill, 326.

p. 290: "the mob fanned . . . across 125th Street": Baldwin, 92.

p. 290: "bars, stores, pawnshops, restaurants": ibid.

p. 290: "white power": ibid.

p. 290: "needed something to smash": ibid, 93.

p. 290: By the time . . . by the police: Gill, 330–331.

p. 290: "was actually a . . . in the community": quoted in "Jacob Lawrence: Exploring Stories" (online exhibition), Whitney Museum of American Art, https://whitney.org/www /jacoblawrence/meet/harlem_community.html.

pp. 290–291: "I thought about . . . and even beauty": Jacob Lawrence, *The Great Migration: An American Story* (New York: HarperCollins, 1992), introduction.

p. 291: "Strolling in Harlem . . . makes new acquaintances": Johnson, 162. I learned about George Starling from Isabel Wilkerson's *The Warmth of Other Suns: The Epic Story of America's Great Migration*, a central, prize-winning book for understanding twentieth-century American history.

WORLD CITY, FRACTURED CITY, WORLD CITY

I used Freeman on working-class New York and more focused sources on art, theater, the Lindsay years, Harlem, and gender issues for this section. Freeman was especially useful as it reminded me of the Robert Wagner years of union New York and the rise of liberal Democrats, which I had experienced but had not studied.

Chapter 25: "Somewhere"

p. 295: But at night . . . dimmed its lights: Jaffe, 252–253.

p. 298: "New York is . . . the United Nations": Homberger, *The Historical Atlas of New York City*, 158. A deeply researched yet highly readable and visually informative history of the city through newly created (and historical) maps. A real treat.

p. 299: "the superficiality of racial barriers": Jones, 152.

p. 299: "a special American . . . like ballplayers": Vaill, 96.

p. 299: "my beautiful city": ibid., 108.

p. 300: "I got no . . . any of them": Appel, 307.

Chapter 26: New York Center, Left, Far Left

p. 303: A growing country . . . market higher and higher: Geisst, 266–273.

p. 304: Lee Krasner . . . male-oriented environment: Mary Gabriel's *Ninth Street Women* has deepened and in many ways changed how the Abstract Expressionist moment is understood—and would be a good starting point for anyone interested in exploring the subject.

p. 305: On this date . . . fill the square: Freeman, *Working-Class New York*, 56.

p. 306: "on the basis of race, creed, color, or national origin": ibid., 68.

p. 306: in 1952, nearly half the city was Catholic: ibid., 25.

p. 308: Before America entered . . . passports if necessary: Josephson and Trilling-Josephson, 234. Gathered by Josephson's wife, this memoir is a fine way to get a sense of Café Society.

p. 308: Leon was called . . . answer their questions: ibid., 233–237.

p. 308: New York's gossip . . . downtown and uptown: ibid., 238.

p. 308: *Life* magazine . . . of Russian spies: ibid., 239–241.

p. 309: Then, on March 2, 1949 . . . closed its doors: ibid., 255.

p. 309: "as an organization . . . advancing their causes": Vaill, 117.

p. 310: In 1953, though . . . work and more: ibid., 243–244.

p. 310: "The special task . . . the class struggle": Petrus and Cohen, 39. Created to accompany an exhibit at the Museum of the City of New York, this photo-filled book is an excellent way to visit the folk revival in the Village of the 1950s and '60s.

p. 311: Folk musicians could . . . New York radio programs: ibid., 70–71.

p. 312: In 1957, just . . . the Folklore Center: ibid.

p. 314: On *West Side Story*: The best guide to the play as both theater and social history is Julia Foulkes's *A Place for Us: "West Side Story" and New York.*

Chapter 27: Generations

p. 316: "I cannot impress . . . race or color": Freeman, *Working-Class New York*, 34–35.

p. 317: In the early . . . in *The Honeymooners*: ibid., 175.

p. 319: "The place looked . . . which they stumbled": Traub, 113–114.

pp. 319–320: All along West . . . stories in song: Petrus and Cohen, 151.

pp. 320–321: At her rehearsal . . . his own songs: Hammond with Townsend, 351. Shaped surely by how he wanted to be seen, this is still an engaging story of a man who had a deep influence on jazz, folk, and rock and roll.

p. 321: Dylan and his . . . *Freewheelin' Bob Dylan*: Rotolo, 216. An engaging autobiography by his former partner that gives a great you-are-there sense of being in the Village with Dylan.

p. 321: His eyes were . . . change the world: Hammond with Townsend, 352.

p. 322: "a glory for . . . & for him": Vaill, 365. Alisa Solomon's *Wonder of Wonders: A Cultural History of "Fiddler on the Roof"* is a rich, readable, and thoughtful exploration of the show and, through it, our society.

pp. 322–323: The show struck . . . the city's history: Knapp, 215.

Chapter 28: City on the Brink

p. 326: "a juvenile . . . respect the city": Cannato, 84. Cannato is more critical of Lindsay than many were before his book came out—at least in liberal Manhattan. For a wider range of views, see *America's Mayor: John V. Lindsay and the Reinvention of New York*, edited by Sam Roberts. Another book attached to a Museum of the City of New York exhibit, it is also filled with images and offers an accessible introduction to the issues of the time.

p. 326: As the columnist . . . the city's past: Cannato, 82.

p. 327: When the strike . . . from the first: ibid., 90.

p. 328: from 631 in 1964 . . . a decade later: Roberts, 224

p. 328: "the greatest manufacturing town on earth": Freeman, *Working-Class New York*, 8.

p. 329: The vicious cycle . . . grappled with race: Cannato, 60.

p. 330: "It was not . . . an acceptable apology": Freeman, *Working-Class New York*, 192.

pp. 331–332: "On crisp Sunday . . . to say hello": Boyd, 245.

p. 332: Harlem was also . . . the white world: Bald, 163. Bald has recovered a missing history that I enjoyed getting to know.

p. 332: "white, colored, Negro, Indian, and East Indian": ibid., 170.

pp. 332–333: The African American . . . in the background: ibid., 175.

p. 334: When the Selma . . . equally to blame: Cannato, 37.

p. 334: "*too much crime* . . . much police brutality": ibid., 40.

p. 334: Though Buckley came . . . among the police: ibid., 53.

p. 335: "when you become . . . and always exciting": Gloria Steinem, "A Bunny's Tale: **Show's** First Expose for Intelligent People," *Show: The Magazine of the Arts*, May 1963, 91; for further background, see Debra Michals, "Gloria Steinem," National Women's History Museum, 2017, www.womenshistory.org/education-resources/biographies/gloria-steinem.

p. 335: "mental defectives with curlers in their hair" and the *Ladies' Home Journal* takeover: Erin Blakemore, "When Angry Women Staged a Sit-In at the Ladies Home Journal," History, August 27, 2018, https://www.history.com/news/women-feminist-protest-ladies-home-journal.

p. 336: "For women throughout . . . all to read": Rosen, 210. This is an excellent introduction to the women's movement and a good starting place for further research.

p. 336: "This woman's place . . . House of Representatives!": Yanker Poster Collection, Library of Congress Prints and Photographs Division, 1971, https://www.loc.gov/item/2016648584/.

p. 336: "I spend all . . . political power structure": Abzug, 209.

p. 340: The fight over . . . and Black nationalism: Michael R. Glass, "'A Series of Blunders and Broken Promises': IS 201 as a Turning Point," Gotham Center for New York City History, August 1, 2016, https://www.gothamcenter.org/blog/a-series-of-blunders-and-broken-promises -is-201-as-a-turning-point. I found this to be a most useful corrective to previous accounts that were more critical of the IS 201 parents.

p. 341: "The people of . . . out of them": For Ford's statement and the *Daily News* headline of October 30, 1975, see "New York Saved from Bankruptcy," History Central, https://www .historycentral.com/Today/NYSaved.html.

Chapter 29: Windows on the World

p. 346: "wellspring of capital for the world": Burrows and Wallace, *Greater Gotham*, 923.

p. 346: "a symbol of . . . turnaround of New York": Greg Morabito, "Windows on the World, New York's Sky-High Restaurant," Eater New York, September 11, 2013, https://ny.eater.com /2013/9/11/6547477/windows-on-the-world-new-yorks-sky-high-restaurant.

p. 347: In 1977, top . . . paid New Yorkers: Freeman, *Working-Class New York*, 294.

p. 347: By 2012, the . . . the entire country: Sam Roberts, "Gap Between Manhattan's Rich and Poor Is Greatest in U.S., Census Finds," *New York Times*, September 17, 2014, https://www.nytimes.com/2014/09/18/nyregion/gap-between-manhattans-rich-and-poor-is-greatest-in-us-census-finds.html?mcubz=3.

p. 348: Between 1977 and . . . white middle class: Freeman, *Working-Class New York*, 295.

p. 348: In the early 1980s . . . by gay men: Tim Murphy, "7 New Yorkers Remember the Early Days of the AIDS Epidemic," *New York*, May 29, 2014, http://nymag.com/intelligencer/2014/05/memories-aids-new-york.html.

p. 350: On St. Vincent's Hospital: "St. Vincent's Remembered," *Out*, August 17, 2010, https://www.out.com/news-commentary/2010/08/17/st-vincents-remembered.

p. 350–351: "It was the . . . of your shift": ibid.

p. 351: "Once you came . . . full of love": ibid.

p. 351: "was in ruins . . . than any reality": Traub, 162.

p. 352: "We could see . . . on the floor": quoted in Bianco, 279

p. 352: "lavish grandeur": ibid.

p. 353: "When we're done . . . and advertising space": Berman, 198.

p. 360: "the capital of all of Spanish America": Remeseira, 21.

Chapter 30: New York and the Nation, Two Versions

p. 367: Mixture, as this . . . as communities change: Andrew Small, "The Gentrification of Gotham," *Bloomberg CityLab*, April 28, 2017, https://www.citylab.com/life/2017/04/the-gentrification-of-gotham/524694/.

p. 368: These kinds of . . . the city's economy: John Kucsera and Gary Orfield, "New York State's Extreme School Segregation: Inequality, Inaction and a Damaged Future," The Civil Rights Project, University of California, Los Angeles, March 26, 2014, https://www.civilrightsproject.ucla.edu/research/k-12-education/integration-and-diversity/ny-norflet-report-placeholder.

p. 369: African Americans and . . . including New York: Editorial Board, "How to Save Black and Hispanic Lives During a Pandemic," *New York Times*, April 11, 2020, https://www.nytimes.com/2020/04/11/opinion/coronavirus-poor-black-latino.html.

p. 370: dropped an average of 10 percent: Matthew Haag, "Manhattan Vacancy Rate Climbs, and Rents Drop 10%," *New York Times*, August 18, 2020, https://www.nytimes.com/2020/08/18/nyregion/nyc-vacant-apartments.html.

BIBLIOGRAPHY

Abzug, Bella S. *Bella! Ms. Abzug Goes to Washington*. New York: Saturday Review Press, 1972.

Alexander, James. *A Brief Narrative of the Case and Trial of John Peter Zenger, Printer of the New York Weekly Journal*. Edited by Stanley Nider Katz. Cambridge, MA: Belknap Press, 1972.

Allen, Ray, and George P. Cunningham. "Cultural Uplift and Double-Consciousness: African American Responses to the 1935 Opera *Porgy and Bess*." *Musical Quarterly* 88, no. 3 (Autumn 2005): 342–369.

Anbinder, Tyler. *City of Dreams: The 400-Year Epic History of Immigrant New York*. New York: Houghton Mifflin Harcourt, 2016.

———. *Five Points: The 19th-Century New York City Neighborhood That Invented Tap Dance, Stole Elections, and Became the World's Most Notorious Slum*. New York: Free Press, 2001.

Anderson, Jervis. *This Was Harlem: A Cultural Portrait, 1900–1950*. New York: Farrar, Straus and Giroux, 1982.

Appel, Marty. *Pinstripe Empire: The New York Yankees from Before the Babe to After the Boss*. New York: Bloomsbury, 2012.

Auchincloss, Louis, ed. *The Hone & Strong Diaries of Old Manhattan*. New York: Abbeville Press, 1989.

Axthelm, Pete. *The City Game: Basketball from the Garden to the Playgrounds*. New York: Harper's Magazine Press, 1970.

Baker, Paul R. *Stanny: The Gilded Life of Stanford White*. New York: Free Press, 1989.

Bald, Vivek. *Bengali Harlem and the Lost Histories of South Asian America*. Cambridge, MA: Harvard University Press, 2013.

Baldwin, James. *Notes of a Native Son*. New York: Bantam Books, 1955.

Ballon, Hilary, and Kenneth T. Jackson. *Robert Moses and the Modern City: The Transformation of New York*. New York: Norton, 2007.

Barton, Melissa. *Gather Out of Star-Dust: A Harlem Renaissance Album*. New Haven, CT: Yale University Press, 2000.

Bean, Annemarie, James V. Hatch, and Brooks McNamara, eds. *Inside the Minstrel Mask: Readings in Nineteenth-Century Blackface Minstrelsy*. Middletown, CT: Wesleyan University Press, 1996.

Beard, Rick, and Leslie Cohen Berlowitz, eds. *Greenwich Village: Culture and Counterculture*. New Brunswick, NJ: Rutgers University Press, 1993.

Bender, Thomas. *New York Intellect: A History of Intellectual Life in New York City, from 1750 to the Beginnings of Our Own Time*. New York: Alfred A. Knopf, 1987.

———. *The Unfinished City: New York and the Metropolitan Idea*. New York: New York University Press, 2002.

Berlin, Edward. *Ragtime: A Musical and Cultural History.* Lincoln, NE: iUniverse, 2002.

Berlin, Ira. *Generations of Captivity: A History of African-American Slaves.* Cambridge, MA: Belknap Press, 2003.

Berman, Marshall. *On the Town: One Hundred Years of Spectacle in Times Square.* Brooklyn: Verso, 2009.

Bernstein, Iver. *The New York City Draft Riots: Their Significance for American Society and Politics in the Age of the Civil War.* New York: Oxford University Press, 1990.

Bernstein, Peter L. *Wedding of the Waters: The Erie Canal and the Making of a Great Nation.* New York: W. W. Norton, 2010.

Bianco, Anthony. *Ghosts of 42nd Street: A History of America's Most Infamous Block.* New York: William Morrow, 2004.

Blake, Casey Nelson. *Beloved Community: The Cultural Criticism of Randolph Bourne, Van Wyck Brooks, Waldo Frank, & Lewis Mumford.* Chapel Hill: University of North Carolina Press, 1990.

Blake, E. Vale. *History of the Tammany Society or Columbian Order from Its Organization to the Present Time.* New York: Souvenir Publishing Company, 1901.

Boyd, Herb, ed. *The Harlem Reader: A Celebration of New York's Most Famous Neighborhood, from the Renaissance Years to the Twenty-First Century.* New York: Three Rivers Press, 2003.

Breen, T. H. *The Marketplace of Revolution: How Consumer Politics Shaped American Independence.* New York: Oxford University Press, 2004.

Brighton, Stephen A. "Prices That Suit the Times: Shopping for Ceramics at the Five Points." *Historical Archaeology* 35, no. 3 (2001): 16–30.

Brown, Henry Collins, ed. *Valentine's Manual of the City of New York: 1917–1918.* New York: Old Colony Press, 1917.

———. *Valentine's Manual of Old New York—No. 7, New Series 1923.* New York: Valentine's Manual, 1922.

Burrows, Edwin G., and Mike Wallace. *Gotham: A History of New York City to 1898.* New York: Oxford University Press, 1999.

———. *Greater Gotham: A History of New York City from 1898 to 1919.* New York: Oxford University Press, 2017.

Cannato, Vincent. *The Ungovernable City: John Lindsay and His Struggle to Save New York.* New York: Basic Books, 2001.

Caro, Robert A. *The Power Broker: Robert Moses and the Fall of New York.* New York: Knopf, 1974.

Carter, Marva Griffin. *Swing Along: The Musical Life of Will Marion Cook.* New York: Oxford University Press, 2008.

Chauncey, George. *Gay New York: Gender, Urban Culture, and the Making of the Gay Male World, 1890–1940.* New York: Basic Books, 1994.

Chernow, Ron. *Alexander Hamilton.* New York: Penguin Books, 2004.

———. *The House of Morgan: An American Banking Dynasty and the Rise of Modern Finance.* New York: Grove Press, 1990.

Clarke, Norman. *The Mighty Hippodrome.* New York: A. S. Barnes, 1968.

Commager, Henry Steele, and Richard B. Morris, eds. *The Spirit of Seventy-Six: The Story of the American Revolution as Told by Its Participants.* Edison, NJ: Castle Books, 2002.

Cornog, Evan. *The Birth of Empire: DeWitt Clinton and the American Experience, 1769–1828.* New York: Oxford University Press, 1998.

Crunden, Robert M. *American Salons: Encounters with European Modernism, 1885–1917.* New York: Oxford University Press, 1993.

D'Angelo, Pascal. *Son of Italy.* Montreal: Guernica Editions, 2003.

Decker, Malcolm. *Brink of Revolution: New York in Crisis, 1765–1776.* New York: Argosy Antiquarian, 1964.

Delaney, Edmund T. *New York's Greenwich Village.* Barre, MA: Barre Publishers, 1968.

Denning, Michael. *The Cultural Front: The Laboring of American Culture in the Twentieth Century.* New York: Verso, 1996.

Diner, Hasia R. *Lower East Side Memories: A Jewish Place in America.* Princeton, NJ: Princeton University Press, 2000.

Douglas, Ann. *Terrible Honesty: Mongrel Manhattan in the 1920s.* New York: Farrar, Straus and Giroux, 1996.

Dowling, Robert. *Eugene O'Neill: A Life in Four Acts.* New Haven, CT: Yale University Press, 2014.

Dunshee, Kenneth Holcomb. *As You Pass By.* New York: Hastings House, 1952.

Eliot, Marc. *Down 42nd Street: Sex, Money, Culture, and Politics at the Crossroads of the World.* New York: Warner Books, 2001.

Ellis, Edward Robb. *The Epic of New York City: A Narrative History.* New York: Basic Books, 2001.

Ellison, Ralph. *Invisible Man.* New York: Vintage Books, 1972.

Epstein, Melech. *Profiles of Eleven: Profiles of Eleven Men Who Guided the Destiny of an Immigrant Society and Stimulated Social Consciousness Among the American People.* Detroit: Wayne State University Press, 1965.

Erenberg, Lewis A. *Steppin' Out: New York Nightlife and the Transformation of American Culture, 1890–1930.* Chicago: University of Chicago Press, 1981.

Federal Writers' Project of the Works Progress Administration. *New York City Guide.* New York: Random House, 1939.

Finch, Roy G. *The Story of the New York State Canals.* State of New York, 1925. http://www .canals.ny.gov/history/finch_history.pdf.

Fitts, Robert. "The Rhetoric of Reform: The Five Points Missions and the Cult of Domesticity." *Historical Archaeology* 35, no. 3 (2001): 115–132.

Fleming, Thomas. *Duel: Alexander Hamilton, Aaron Burr and the Future of America.* New York: Basic Books, 1999.

Flint, Anthony. *Wrestling with Moses: How Jane Jacobs Took on New York's Master Builder and Transformed the American City*. New York: Random House, 2011.

Foulkes, Julia. *A Place for Us: "West Side Story" and New York*. Chicago: University of Chicago Press, 2016.

Freeman, Joshua B., ed. *City of Workers, City of Struggle: How Labor Movements Changed New York*. New York: Columbia University Press, 2019.

———. *Working-Class New York: Life and Labor Since World War II*. New York: The New Press, 2000.

Gabbe, James Isaiah. *The Universe of Union Square: At the Heart of New York's Progressive Soul*. New York: Raconteur, 2010.

Gabriel, Mary. *Ninth Street Women: Lee Krasner, Elaine de Kooning, Grace Hartigan, Joan Mitchell, and Helen Frankenthaler: Five Painters and the Movement That Changed Modern Art*. New York: Little, Brown, 2018.

Geisst, Charles R. *Wall Street: A History*. Updated edition. New York: Oxford University Press, 1997.

Gill, Brendan. Introduction to *The Portable Dorothy Parker*. New York: Penguin Books, 1978.

Gill, Jonathan. *Harlem: The Four Hundred Year History from Dutch Village to Capital of Black America*. New York: Grove Press, 2011.

Goldman, Emma. *Emma Goldman: A Documentary History of the American Years, Vol 1: Made for America, 1890–1901*. Edited by Candace Falk, Barry Pateman, and Jessica Moran. Urbana: University of Illinois Press, 2008.

Goldstein, Leo. *East Harlem: The Postwar Years*. New York: Powerhouse Books, 2019)

Goldstein, Richard. *Helluva Town: The Story of New York City During World War II*. New York: Free Press, 2010.

Golway, Terry. *Machine Made: Tammany Hall and the Creation of Modern American Politics*. New York: Liveright/W. W. Norton, 2014.

Goodwin, Maud Wilder, Alice Carrington Royce, Ruth Putnam, and Eva Palmer Brownell, eds. *Historic New York*. 2 vols. New York: G. P. Putnam's Sons, 1898.

Gordon, John Steele. *The Scarlet Woman of Wall Street: Jay Gould, Jim Fisk, Cornelius Vanderbilt, the Erie Railway Wars, and the Birth of Wall Street*. New York: Weidenfeld & Nicolson, 1988.

Gordon, Lorraine, and Barry Singer. *Alive at the Village Vanguard: My Life in and out of Jazz Time*. Milwaukee: Hal Leonard, 2006.

Grumet, Robert S. *First Manhattans: A History of the Indians of Greater New York*. Norman: University of Oklahoma Press, 2011.

Haas, Britt. *Fighting Authoritarianism: American Youth Activism in the 1930s*. New York: Fordham University Press, 2018.

Hamm, Charles. *Irving Berlin: Songs from the Melting Pot: The Formative Years, 1907–1914*. New York: Oxford University Press, 1997.

Hammerstein, Oscar Andrew. *The Hammersteins: A Musical Theatre Family*. New York: Black Dog & Leventhal, 2010.

Hammond, John, with Irving Townsend. *John Hammond on Record: An Autobiography*. New York: Penguin Books, 1977.

Hardie, James. *The Description of the City of New York; Containing Its Population, Institutions, Commerce, Manufactures, Public Buildings, Courts of Justice, Places of Amusement, Etc.* New York: Samuel Marks, 1827.

Harris, Eddy L. *Still Life in Harlem: A Memoir*. New York: Henry Holt, 1996.

Headley, Joel Tyler. *The Great Riots of New York, 1712–1873*. New York: Thunder's Mouth Press, 2004.

Hemstreet, Charles. *Nooks & Corners of Old New York*. New York: Charles Scribner's Sons, 1899.

Henderson, Mary C., and Alexis Greene. *The Story of 42nd Street: The Theatres, Shows, Characters, and Scandals of the World's Most Notorious Street*. New York: Back Stage Books, 2008.

Hill, Frederick Trevor. *The Story of a Street: A Narrative History of Wall Street from 1644 to 1908*. New York: Harper & Brothers, 1908.

Hindus, Milton, ed. *The Jewish East Side: 1881–1924*. New Brunswick, NJ: Transaction Publishers, 1996.

Hofstadter, Richard. *Social Darwinism in American Thought*. Boston: Beacon Press, 1944.

Homberger, Eric. *The Historical Atlas of New York City: A Visual Celebration of 400 Years of New York City's History*. New York: Henry Holt, 2005.

———. *Mrs. Astor's New York: Money and Social Power in a Gilded Age*. New Haven, CT: Yale University Press, 2002.

Hood, Clifton. *722 Miles: The Building of the Subways and How They Transformed New York*. Baltimore: John Hopkins University Press, 2004.

Howe, Irving, and Kenneth Libo. *How We Lived: A Documentary History of Immigrant Jews in America, 1880–1930*. New York: Richard Marek Publishers, 1979.

Howe, Irving, with Kenneth Libo. *World of Our Fathers*. New York: Harcourt Brace Jovanovich, 1976.

Huneker, James. *New Cosmopolis: A Book of Images*. New York: Charles Scribner's Sons, 1925.

Irving, Washington. *A History of New York*. Edited by Michael L. Black and Nancy B. Black. Boston: Twayne Publishers, 1984.

Isenberg, Nancy. *Fallen Founder: The Life of Aaron Burr*. New York: Viking, 2007.

Jablonski, Edward. *Irving Berlin: American Troubadour*. New York: Henry Holt, 1999.

Jackson, Kenneth T., and David S. Dunbar, eds. *Empire City: New York Through the Centuries*. New York: Columbia University Press, 2002.

Jackson, Kenneth T., ed. *The Encyclopedia of New York City*. New Haven, CT: Yale University Press, 1995.

Jaffe, Steven H. *Activist New York: A History of People, Protest, and Politics*. New York: New York University Press, 2018.

———. *New York at War: Four Centuries of Combat, Fear, and Intrigue in Gotham*. New York: Basic Books, 2012.

James, Henry. *Washington Square*. New York: New American Library, 1964.

Janvier, Thomas A. *In Old New York*. New York: Harper & Brothers, 1894.

Johnson, James Weldon. *Black Manhattan*. New York: A. A. Knopf, 1930.

Jones, John Bush. *Our Musicals, Ourselves: A Social History of the American Musical Theatre*. Waltham, MA: Brandeis University Press, 2003.

Josephson, Barney, and Terry Trilling-Josephson. *Café Society: The Wrong Place for the Right People*. Urbana: University of Illinois Press, 2009.

Juet, Robert, and Robert M. Lunny. *Juet's Journal: The Voyage of the* Half Moon *from 4 April to 7 November 1609*. Newark: New Jersey Historical Society, 1959.

Kahn, E. J., Jr. *The Merry Partners: The Age and Stage of Harrigan & Hart*. New York: Random House, 1955.

Kaplan, Carla. *Miss Anne in Harlem: The White Women of the Black Renaissance*. New York: Harper Perennial, 2013.

Kayton, Bruce. *Radical Walking Tours of New York City*. 3rd ed. New York: Seven Stories Press, 2016.

Kazin, Alfred. *A Walker in the City*. New York: Harcourt, Brace, and World, 1951.

Kimball, Robert, and William Bolcom. *Reminiscing with Noble Sissle and Eubie Blake*. New York: Cooper Square Press, 1973.

King, Moses. *King's Photographic Views of New York*. Boston: Moses King, 1895.

Klein, Alexander, ed. *The Empire City: A Treasury of New York*. Freeport, NY: Books for Libraries Press, 1971.

Knapp, Raymond. *The American Musical and the Formation of National Identity*. Princeton, NJ: Princeton University Press, 2005.

Koeppel, Gerard. *City on a Grid: How New York Became New York*. Boston: Da Capo Press, 2015.

Kouwenhoven, John A. *The Columbia Historical Portrait of New York: An Essay in Graphic History*. New York: Harper & Row, 1972.

Laurino, Maria. *The Italian Americans: A History*. New York: W. W. Norton, 2015.

Lause, Mark A. *The Antebellum Crisis and America's First Bohemians*. Kent, OH: Kent State University Press, 2009.

Leach, William. *Land of Desire: Merchants, Power and the Rise of a New American Culture*. New York: Pantheon Books, 1993.

Lee, Erika. *The Making of Asian America: A History*. New York: Simon & Schuster, 2015.

Lepore, Jill. *Joe Gould's Teeth*. New York: Alfred A. Knopf, 2016.

———. *New York Burning: Liberty, Slavery, and Conspiracy in Eighteenth-Century Manhattan*. New York: Alfred A. Knopf, 2005.

Levine, Lawrence W. *Black Culture and Black Consciousness: Afro-American Folk Thought from Slavery to Freedom*. New York: Oxford University Press, 1977.

Lhamon, W. T., Jr. *Raising Cain: Blackface Performance from Jim Crow to Hip Hop*. Cambridge, MA: Harvard University Press, 1998.

Limmer, Ruth. *Six Heritage Tours of the Lower East Side: A Walking Guide*. New York: New York University Press, 1997.

Locke, Alain. "Enter the New Negro." *Survey Graphic* 53, no. 11 (March 1925): 631–634.

———. "Harlem: Dark Weather-Vane." *Survey Graphic* 25, no. 8 (August 1936): 457–462, 493–495. https://socialwelfare.library.vcu.edu/eras/great-depression/harlem-dark-weather-vane/.

Lott, Eric. *Love and Theft: Blackface Minstrelsy and the American Working Class*. New York: Oxford University Press, 2013.

Luhan, Mabel Dodge. *Movers and Shakers. Intimate Memories Volume 3*. New York: Harcourt, Brace and Company, 1936.

Maier, Pauline. *From Resistance to Revolution: Colonial Radicals and the Development of American Opposition to Britain, 1765–1776*. New York: W. W. Norton, 1991.

Marcus, Leonard S. *Storied City: A Children's Book Walking-Tour Guide to New York City*. New York: Dutton Children's Books, 2003.

McCabe, James D. Jr. *Lights and Shadows of New York Life; or, the Sights and Sensations of the Great City*. New York: Farrar, Straus and Giroux, 1970.

McCague, James. *The Second Rebellion: The Story of the New York City Draft Riots of 1863*. New York: Dial Press, 1968.

McCormick, Charles Howard. *Leisler's Rebellion*. New York: Garland, 1989.

McFarland, Gerald W. *Inside Greenwich Village: A New York City Neighborhood, 1898–1918*. Amherst: University of Massachusetts, 2001.

McGinley, Paige A. *Staging the Blues: From Tent Shows to Tourism*. Durham, NC: Duke University Press, 2014.

McKay, Claude. "Harlem Runs Wild." In *Voices from the Harlem Renaissance*, edited by Nathan Irvin Huggins. New York: Oxford University Press, 1995.

———. *A Long Way from Home*. Edited by Gene Andrew Jarrett. New Brunswick, NJ: Rutgers University Press, 2007.

McKay, Ernest A. *The Civil War and New York City*. Syracuse, NY: Syracuse University Press, 1990.

McNeur, Catherine. *Taming Manhattan: Environmental Battles in the Antebellum City*. Cambridge, MA: Harvard University Press, 2014.

Mendelsohn, Joyce. *The Lower East Side Remembered and Revisited: A History and Guide to a Legendary New York Neighborhood*. New York: Columbia University Press, 2009.

Miller, Donald L. *Supreme City: How Jazz Age Manhattan Gave Birth to Modern America*. New York: Simon & Schuster, 2014.

Miller, Terry. *Greenwich Village and How It Got That Way*. New York: Crown, 1990.

Mollenkopf, John Hull, ed. *Power, Culture and Place: Essays on New York City*. New York: Russell Sage Foundation, 1988.

Morgan, Edmund S., and Helen M. Morgan. *The Stamp Act Crisis: Prologue to Revolution*. Chapel Hill: University of North Carolina Press, 1995.

Morris, Willie. *New York Days*. New York: Little, Brown, 1993.

Mushkat, Jerome. *The Reconstruction of the New York Democracy, 1861–1874*. East Brunswick, NJ: Associated University Presses, 1981.

———. *Tammany: The Evolution of a Political Machine, 1789–1865*. Syracuse, NY: Syracuse University Press, 1971.

Nash, Gary B. *The Urban Crucible: The Northern Seaports and the Origins of the American Revolution*. Cambridge, MA: Harvard University Press, 1986.

Nevius, James, and Michelle Nevius. *Frommer's 24 Great Walks in New York*. Hoboken, NJ: Wiley, 2010.

Nevius, Michelle, and James Nevius. *Inside the Apple: A Streetwise History of New York City*. New York: Free Press, 2009.

New York in MCMXXIII. New York: New York Edison Company, 1923.

Nicholson, Stuart. *Reminiscing in Tempo: A Portrait of Duke Ellington*. Boston: Northeastern University Press, 1999.

Parmet, Herbert S., and Marie B. Hecht. *Aaron Burr. Portrait of an Ambitious Man*. New York: Macmillan, 1967.

Parton, James. *The Life and Times of Aaron Burr*. 2 vols. New York: Mason Brothers, 1964.

Petrus, Stephen, and Ronald D. Cohen. *Folk City: New York and the American Folk Music Revival*. New York: Oxford University Press, 2015.

Pleasants, Samuel Augustus. *Fernando Wood of New York*. New York: AMS Press, 1966.

Prial, Dunstan. *The Producer: John Hammond and the Soul of American Music*. New York: Farrar, Straus and Giroux, 2006.

Quigley, David. *Second Founding: New York City, Reconstruction and the Making of American Democracy*. New York: Hill and Wang, 2004.

Reaven, Marci, and Steve Zeitlin. *Hidden New York: A Guide to Places That Matter*. New Brunswick, NJ: Rutgers University Press, 2007.

Reich, Jerome R. *Leisler's Rebellion: A Study of Democracy in New York, 1664–1720*. Chicago: University of Chicago Press, 1953.

Remeseira, Claudio Iván, ed. *Hispanic New York: A Sourcebook*. New York: Columbia University Press, 2010.

Rhoden, William, ed. *City/Game: Basketball in New York*. New York: Rizzoli, 2020.

Rimler, Walter. *George Gershwin: An Intimate Portrait*. Chicago: Chicago University Press, 2009.

Roberts, Sam, ed. *America's Mayor: John V. Lindsay and the Reinvention of New York*. New York: Museum of the City of New York, 2010.

Rose, Al. *Eubie Blake*. New York: Schirmer Books, 1979.

Rosen, Ruth. *The World Split Open: How the Modern Women's Movement Changed America*. New York: Penguin Books, 2000.

Ross, Alex. *The Rest Is Noise: Listening to the Twentieth Century*. New York: Farrar, Straus and Giroux, 2007.

Rotolo, Suze. *A Freewheelin' Time: A Memoir of Greenwich Village in the Sixties*. New York: Broadway Books, 2009.

Scheiner, Seth. *Negro Mecca: A History of the Negro in New York City, 1865–1920*. New York: New York University Press, 1965.

Sedgwick, John. *War of Two: Alexander Hamilton, Aaron Burr, and the Duel That Stunned the Nation*. New York: Berkeley Books, 2015.

Shorto, Russell. *The Island at the Center of the World: The Epic Story of Dutch Manhattan and the Forgotten Colony That Shaped America*. New York: Doubleday, 2004.

Silverman, Kenneth. *A Cultural History of the American Revolution*. New York: Columbia University Press, 1987.

Singleton, Esther. *Dutch New York*. New York: Dodd, Mead, 1909.

———. *Social New York Under the Georges, 1714–1776*. New York: D. Appleton, 1902.

Snyder, Robert W. *The Voice of the City: Vaudeville and Popular Culture in New York*. New York: Oxford University Press, 1989.

Solomon, Alisa. *Wonder of Wonders: A Cultural History of "Fiddler on the Roof."* New York: Metropolitan Books, 2013.

Sotiropoulos, Karen. *Staging Race: Black Performers in Turn of the Century America*. Cambridge, MA: Harvard University Press, 2006.

Spufford, Francis. *Golden Hill*. London: Faber & Faber, 2016.

Stansell, Christine. *American Moderns: Bohemian New York and the Creation of a New Century*. New York: Metropolitan Books, 2000.

———. *City of Women: Sex and Class in New York, 1789–1860*. Urbana: University of Illinois Press, 1987.

Starr, Tama, and Edward Hayman. *Signs and Wonders: The Spectacular Marketing of America*. New York: Currency/Doubleday, 1998.

Stein, Charles W., ed. *American Vaudeville as Seen by Its Contemporaries*. New York: Da Capo Press, 1984.

Stern, Robert A. M., Gregory Gilmartin, and John Massengale. *New York 1900: Metropolitan Architecture and Urbanism, 1890–1915*. New York: Rizzoli, 1995.

Stern, Robert A. M., Gregory Gilmartin, and Thomas Mellins. *New York 1930: Architecture and Urbanism Between the Two World Wars*. New York: Rizzoli, 1994.

Stern, Robert A. M., Thomas Mellins, and David Fishman. *New York 1880: Architecture and Urbanism in the Gilded Age*. New York: Rizzoli, 1999.

Stewart, Jeffrey C. *The New Negro: The Life of Alain Locke*. New York: Oxford University Press, 2018.

Still, Bayrd. *Mirror for Gotham: New York as Seen by Contemporaries from Dutch Days to the Present*. New York: New York University Press, 1956.

Stokes, I. N. Phelps. *New York Past and Present: Its History and Landmarks 1524–1939*. New York: Plantin Press, 1939.

Strausbaugh, John. *City of Sedition: The History of New York City During the Civil War*. New York: Twelve, 2016.

———. *The Village: 400 Years of Beats and Bohemians, Radicals and Rogues, a History of Greenwich Village*. New York: Harper Collins, 2013.

Strouse, Jean. *Morgan: American Financier*. New York: Random House, 2014.

Taylor, William R. *In Pursuit of Gotham: Culture and Commerce in New York*. New York: Oxford University Press, 1992.

Taylor, William R., ed. *Inventing Times Square: Commerce and Culture at the Crossroads of the World*. New York: Russell Sage Foundation, 1991.

Toll, Robert C. *Blacking Up: The Minstrel Show in Nineteenth-Century America*. New York: Oxford University Press, 1974.

Tommasini, Anthony. *Virgil Thomson: Composer on the Aisle*. New York: W. W. Norton, 1997.

Traub, James. *The Devil's Playground: A Century of Pleasure and Profit in Times Square*. New York: Random House, 2004.

Vaill, Amanda. *Somewhere: The Life of Jerome Robbins*. New York: Broadway Books, 2006.

Wakefield, Dan. *New York in the Fifties*. New York: Houghton Mifflin, 1992.

Wall, Cheryl A. *The Harlem Renaissance: A Very Short Introduction*. New York: Oxford University Press, 2016.

Wallace, David. *Capital of the World: A Portrait of New York City in the Roaring Twenties*. Guilford, CT: Lyons Press, 2011.

Wetzsteon, Ross. *Republic of Dreams: Greenwich Village: The American Bohemia, 1910–1960*. New York: Simon & Schuster, 2002.

White, Norval, and Elliot Willensky with Fran Leadon. *AIA Guide to New York City*. 5th ed. New York: Oxford University Press, 2010.

White, Shane. *Stories of Freedom in Black New York*. Cambridge, MA: Harvard University Press, 2002.

Whitman, Walt. *New York Dissected. A Sheaf of Recently Discovered Newspaper Articles by the Author of Leaves of Grass*. New York: Rufus Rockwell Wilson, 1936.

Wilentz, Sean. *Chants Democratic: New York City and the Rise of the American Working Class, 1788-1850*. New York: Oxford University Press, 1984.

Wilkerson, Isabel. *The Warmth of Other Suns: The Epic Story of America's Great Migration*. New York: Vintage, 2011.

Wilson, James Grant, ed. *The Memorial History of the City of New-York: From Its First Settlement to the Year 1892*. Vol. 2. New York: New-York History Company, 1892.

Yamin, Rebecca, ed. "Becoming New York: The Five Points Neighborhood." *Historical Archaeology* 35, no. 3 (2001): 1–5.

Yochelson, Bonnie. *Berenice Abbott: Changing New York*. New York: The Museum of the City of New York, 1997.

Zabin, Serena R. "Places of Exchange: New York City, 1700–1763." PhD diss., Rutgers University, 2000.

IMAGE CREDITS

Paul Robeson, June 1, 1933; p. 248, Carl Van Vechten, *Portrait of Zora Neale Hurston*, April 3, 1938; p. 256, *Anarchist bombings, New York City*, 1914–1920, Bain Collection; p. 257, Joseph Pennell, *That liberty shall not perish from the earth - Buy liberty bonds Fourth Liberty Loan / / Joseph Pennell del. Ketterlinus Phila. imp.*, 1918; p. 259, *Chrysler Building, New York, N.Y.*, 1930, Detroit Publishing Company photograph collection; p. 259, *Empire State Building*, April 22, 1931; p. 262, *Crowd of people gather outside the New York Stock Exchange following the Crash of 1929*, 1929, New York World-Telegram and the Sun Newspaper Photograph Collection; p. 273, William P. Gottlieb, *Portrait of Billie Holiday, Downbeat, New York, N.Y.*, February 1947, William P. Gottlieb Collection; p. 275, *Scene from "Porgy and Bess,"* 1935-1936. *Theater Guild production*, 1935–1936, Farm Security Administration - Office of War Information photograph collection; p. 287, Gottscho-Schleisner, Inc., *World's Fair views. Constitution Mall, four statues and trylon and perisphere*, Sept. 29, 1940, Gottscho-Schleisner Collection; p. 296, Marjory Collins, *New York, New York. Times Square during the wartime dimout at night*, September 1942, Farm Security Administration - Office of War Information photograph collection; p. 296, *New York, New York: Times Square and vicinity on D-Day*, June 6, 1944, Farm Security Administration - Office of War Information photograph collection; p. 297, Fred Palumbo, *Sailors and civilians watching electronic sign in Times Square for news of D-Day invasion*, June 6, 1944; p. 297, Dick DeMarsico, *Crowd of people, many waving, in Times Square on V-J Day at time of announcement of the Japanese surrender in 1945*, August 14, 1945; p. 303, Angelo Rizzuto, *Wall St. looking toward Broadway from Hanover St. - Below center is Bank of N.Y. (48 Wall St.) founded 1784*, October 1952; p. 307, Roger Higgins, *Julius and Ethel Rosenberg, separated by heavy wire screen as they leave U.S. Court House after being found guilty by jury / World Telegram photo by Roger Higgins*, 1951. New York World-Telegram and the Sun Newspaper Photograph Collection; p. 311, Al Aumuller, *Woody Guthrie, half-length portrait, seated, facing front, playing a guitar that has a sticker attached reading: This Machine Kills Fascists*, March 8, 1943, New York World-Telegram and the Sun Newspaper Photograph Collection; p. 311, Joseph A. Horne, *Washington, D.C. Pete Seeger, noted folk singer entertaining at the opening of the Washington labor canteen, sponsored by the United Federal Labor Canteen, sponsored by the Federal Workers of American, Congress of Industrial Organizations (CIO)*, February 1944, Farm Security Administration - Office of War Information photograph collection; p. 312, Bernard Gotfryd, *Thelonious Monk at the Village Gate, New York City*, October 1968; p. 317, *Front cover of Jackie Robinson comic book*, 1951; p. 319, Marjory Collins, *New York, New York. North Side of 42nd Street, Between Seventh and Eighth Avenues*, September 1942; p. 327, Orlando Fernandez, *Mayor Lindsay carries in his budget / World Telegram & Sun photo by O. Fernandez*, April 15, 1966, New York World-Telegram and the Sun Newspaper Photograph Collection; p. 337, *This woman's place is in the house -- the House of Representatives!: Bella Abzug for Congress*, 1971–1976, Yanker poster collection; p. 347, Thomas J. O'Halloran, *View of the New World Trade Center [New York City]*, January 12, 1971, U.S. News and World Report Photograph Collection; p. 352, *New Amsterdam Theatre, New York*, 1905, Detroit Publishing Company photograph collection; p. 354, *Skyline of Manhattan with smoke billowing from the Twin Towers following September 11th terrorist attack on World Trade Center, New York City*, September 11, 2001; p. 355 (top left), *Two fire fighters looking into car while another New York City firefighter pulls water hose from fire truck amid smoke and debris following September 11th terrorist attack on World Trade Center, New York City*, September 11, 2001; p. 358, Carol M. Highsmith, *A messenger delivers food to a restaurant in the Chinatown district of New York, New York*, 1980–2006; p. 358, Carol M. Highsmith, *Scene in Lower Manhattan's Chinatown neighborhood in New York City*, July 10, 2018; p. 358, Carol M. Highsmith, *Produce stand in Lower Manhattan's Chinatown neighborhood in New York City*, July 10, 2018; p. 365, Carol M. Highsmith, *Display inside the National September 11 Memorial & Museum (more frequently known simply, as the 9/11 Memorial) in the Manhattan borough of New York, New York*, January 27, 2018.

Courtesy of the New-York Historical Society: p. 68 (detail) and p. 73, Francis Guy, *Tontine Coffee House, New York City*, c. 1797, the Louis Durr Fund, 1907.32; p. 76, Manhattan Water Company, *Section of water pipe*, 1800–1840, gift of J.W. Rutherford, 1907, X47; p. 97, George P. Hall & Son, *Tammany Society Building (Tammany Hall) and Tony Pastor's Theater*, undated photograph, nyhs_PR024_b-11_f-95_003—1; p. 98 (detail) and p. 104, *Interior of Stewart's Astor Place Store*, c. 1880s, Bella C. Landauer Collection of Business and Advertising Ephemera, 70132; p. 116, "*Backgrounds of Civilization – Ball-Room of Mr. Pete Williams, Deceased, at Present Conducted by Mr. Pritties,*" *New York Illustrated News*, February 18, 1860, 79294d; p.

140, *Great Union Meeting, Union Square, April 20, 1861*, E. & H.T. Anthony, publishers, PR 065-791-5, 37363; p. 163, *Hester Street, west from and including southwest corner of Norfolk Street*, 1898, PR 020, 37363; p. 192 (detail) and p. 200, George P. Hall & Son, *Hammerstein's Roof Garden (Victoria Theater), Seventh Avenue and 42nd Street*, 1908, PR024, 67588; p. 211 and p. 217, Jessie Tarbox Beals, *Washington Square North*, 1920s, PR 004, 66658; p. 219, Jessie Tarbox Beals, *Getting ready for a village revel at Liberal Club*, 1904–1940, PR 004, 65436; p. 227, Jessie Tarbox Beals, *Patchin Place, leading off from 10th Street*, 1916, PR 004, 61201; p. 228, Jessie Tarbox Beals, *Jessie Tarbox Beals, self-portrait with camera*, 1918–1920, PR 004, 63649; p. 228, Jessie Tarbox Beals, *A Busy Corner in Greenwich Village, Will o' the Wisp Tea Room, Idee Chic [?], Aladdin Tea Room*, 1905–1940, PR 004, 8381d; p. 228, Jessie Tarbox Beals, *Romany Marie's in Greenwich Village—as vivid as a scarlet bird against a mountain pine!*, 1916–1920, PR 004, 75239; p. 229, Jessie Tarbox Beals, *Grace Godwin's garret*, 1917–1918, PR 004, 58128; p. 229, Robert L. Bracklow and Alexander Alland, *Bruno's Garret, Washington Square, New York City, 1914*, 1914, Bracklow photograph collection. nyhs_pr-008_66000_450.

Courtesy of the Museum of the City of New York: p. 75, H. M. Hale, *Map of Collect Pond and its Vicinity in the City of New York in 1793*, 1939, 39.541; p. 115, John M. August Will, *Old Brewery in Five Points*, 1855, 29.100.1718; p. 115, McSpedon & Baker, *Five Points, 1827*, c. 1850, 97.227.3; p. 162, Jacob A. Riis, *Hester Street. The Street, the school children's only playground*, 1890, 90.13.4.259; p. 168, Lewis Wickes Hine, *Immigrants on Ellis Island*, 1905, X2010.11.9996; p. 218, Jessie Tarbox Beals, *Interior view of Polly's Restaurant, with waiters and customers*, 1910s–1920s, 95.127.21; p. 282, Harold Rhodenbaugh, *Mayor La Guardia for Look Magazine*, 1940, *Look* magazine, X2011.4.11638.81; p. 283, *Robert Moses in front of a map of New York City*, 1925–1940, F2012.58.960.

Courtesy of the Billy Rose Theatre Division of the New York Public Library: p. 97, *Theatres -- U.S. -- N.Y. -- Acme (Union Square)*; p. 154, *Two playbills advertising Tony Pastor's Vaudeville acts*, 1878; p. 261, *Paul Robeson in costume for Show Boat*.

Courtesy of the Jerome Robbins Dance Division of the New York Public Library: p. 300, *Jerome Robbins in Fancy Free*, 1944; p. 300, *Lobby card for 1959 production of On the Town at the Carnegie Hall Playhouse*, 1959; p. 315, *David Winters, Harvey Hohnecker, Tony Mordente, Burt Michaels, Eliot Feld, others as members of the Jets, no. 2*, 1960.

Courtesy of the Lionel Pincus and Princess Firyal Map Division of the New York Public Library Digital Collections: pp. 8–9 and p. 23, John Wolcott Adams, *Redraft of the Castello Plan, New Amsterdam in 1660*, 1916; p. 11, *A Description of the Towne of Mannados or New Amsterdam as it was in September 1661, lying in latitude 40 de: and 40m: anno Domini 1664*; pp. 134–135, George Hayward, *Plan of The Central Park, City of New York, 1860*.

Courtesy of the Manuscripts and Archives Division of the New York Public Library: p. 287, *Theme Center - Trylon and Perisphere - View across lot*, 1935–1945; p. 287, *Theme Center - Trylon and Perisphere - Close-up of Helicline*, 1935–1945; p. 287, *Theme Center - Trylon and Perisphere - Aerial view of Fair site*, 1935–1945; p. 350, *Silence = Death*, 1969–1997, ACT UP New York records.

Courtesy of the Miriam and Ira D. Wallach Division of Art, Prints and Photographs: Print Collection, New York Public Library Digital Collections: p. 29, *No. 1. the residence of Jacob Leisler on "the Strand" (now Whitehall Street, N.Y.)*, 1801–1900, Eno Collection of New York City Views; p. 46, *A plan of the city of New-York, reduced from actual survey*, 1763, engraving, I.N. Phelps Stokes Collection of American Historical Prints; p. 53, Elkanah Tisdale, *Judgment day of Tories*, 1790–1799, engraving, Wallach Division Picture Collection; p. 59, Franz Xaver Habermann, *Representation du Feu terrible a Nouvelle Yorck*, 1776, Eno Collection of New York City Views; p. 62 (detail) and p. 66, Peter Lacour, *Federal Hall the seat of Congress*, 1790, engraving, I.N. Phelps Stokes Collection of American Historical Prints; p. 94 (top), *Junction of Broadway & the Bowery*, 1801–1886, Emmet Collection of Manuscripts Etc. Relating to American History; p. 94 (bottom), Charles Spangenberg, *Proposed Plan Improvements Of Union Park*, 1871; p. 100–101, *Grand Canal Celebration. View of the fleet preparing to form in line*, 1825; p. 115, *A Five Points Rum Shop*, 1872; p. 115, Van Ingen & Snyder, *The sights and sensations of New York*, 1872; p. 128, E. W. Clay, *An amalgamation polka*, 1845; p. 132, *South St. from Maiden Lane*, 1834, I.N. Phelps Stokes Collection of American Historical Prints; p. 143 (top), *The riots in New York: destruction of the coloured orphan asylum*, 1863; p. 147, *Grand demonstration of the Democracy in New York City*,

p. 231: Djuna Barnes, "How the Villagers Amuse Themselves," *New York Morning Telegraph Sunday Magazine*, November 26, 1916. Digital Collections. Special Collections & University Archives, University of Maryland, College Park. Used with permission from the Authors League Fund and St. Bride's Church, joint literary executors of the Estate of Djuna Barnes.

p. 251: "The Artist Pictures the 'Girls,'" March 7, 1936, and "And, Girls, How They Carried On!" March 1, 1932, *New York Amsterdam News*.

p. 267: Carlos Ortiz, *Apollo Theater marquee for Machito and his band*, 1951. Carlos Ortiz Papers, 1940s–2006: CaOr_b20_f12_0001. Center for Puerto Rican Studies Library & Archives, Hunter College, CUNY.

p. 272: *Boogie Woogie Kings from Café Society* and *Teddy Wilson at Café Society in 1939*. RIPM-Jazz and the Institute of Jazz Studies at Rutgers University.

p. 284: *Manhattan: 6th Avenue - 40th Street*, 1934. Irma and Paul Milstein Division of United States History, Local History and Genealogy, The New York Public Library. New York Public Library Digital Collections.

p. 289: Beauford Delaney, *Portrait of James Baldwin*, 1944. Pastel on paper, 24 x 18¾ inches. Knoxville Museum of Art, 2017 purchase with funds provided by the Rachael Patterson Young Art Acquisition Reserve.

p. 305: Syd Hoff, *Untitled Mural for Café Society*, 1930. Courtesy of Carol Edmonston.

p. 309: Walter Rosenblum, *Three Children on Swings, Pitt Street, New York*. Copyright © Estate of Walter Rosenblum.

p. 313: Photo by Leo Goldstein copyright © Leo Goldstein Photography Collection LLC.

p. 315: (top) Photo by Leo Goldstein copyright © Leo Goldstein Photography Collection LLC.

p. 320: Feliks Topolski, *Sketch of Bob Dylan*. Courtesy of Teresa Topolski.

p. 322: *Sketch of Tevye's House in Fiddler on the Roof*. Aronson-Budhos Collection.

p. 327: To Hell with Quill button. Aronson-Budhos Collection.

p. 330: Justo A. Martí, *Robert Wagner, Susan Wagner, and Fidel Castro*, 1960. Justo A. Martí Photographic Collection, 1948–1985. JAMa_b10_f03_0002. Center for Puerto Rican Studies Library & Archives, Hunter College, CUNY.

p. 331: Sketch by Feliks Topolski courtesy of Teresa Topolski.

p. 332: Bev Grant/Getty Images.

p. 333: Bev Grant/Getty Images.

p. 334: Gind2005/Creative Commons.

p. 338: *Construction workers raising American flag on the steps of Federal Hall, May 8, 1970*. NYPD Intelligence Records, Photograph Files, NYC Municipal Archives.

p. 339: *New York Daily News Archive. Courtesy of Getty Images*.

p. 343: Yoichi Okamoto, *President Lyndon B. Johnson Signing Immigration Bill*, October 1965. Lyndon B. Johnson Presidential Library. A1421-30a.

p. 355: (top) Michael Rieger/FEMA News Photo; (bottom) Andrea Booher/FEMA News Photo.

p. 359: Photos courtesy of Chinatown Rockits Basketball.

p. 361: (top) Bev Grant/Getty Images.

p. 361: (bottom) Photo by Frank Espada.

p. 362: Photos by Ricky Flores.

p. 363: Photos courtesy of Led Black | Uptown Collective.

p. 363: (bottom) Photo by Zach Buchner.

INDEX

Page numbers in italics indicate images or captions.

Index TK